THE CALLING

A life rocked by mountains

Advanced Reading Copy

BARRY BLANCHARD

THE CALLING

A life rocked by mountains

patagonia®

Ventura, California

THE CALLING

A life rocked by mountains

Patagonia publishes a select number of titles on wilderness, wildlife, and outdoor sports that inspire and restore a connection to the natural world.

First Edition
Editor: John Dutton
Photo Editor: Jane Sievert
Book Design and Production: Haruna Madono
Cover Design: Jeremy Dean

Printed in ?? on ??% recycled paper

ISBN XXX-X-XXXXXX-XX-X
E-Book ISBN XXX-X-XXXXXX-XX-X
Library of Congress Control Number xxxxxxxxxx

cover This info is TK

back cover This info is TK

colophon All attitude and ability, Mark Twight, I, Ward Robinson, and Kevin Doyle below the Rupal Face of Nanga Parbat before we made our first attempt. Pakistan. Photo: Hank Van Weelden

For my mother, born Paulette Francis Ann Pelletier,
forever a pillar in my life.

THE CALLING PLAYLIST

Ch 2 Skinny Puppy
Assimilate

Trisomie 21
The Last Song

Joy Division
Shadowplay

SNFU
Strip Search

The Clash
Rock the Casbah

The Sex Pistols
Anarchy in the UK

The Rolling Stones
Paint it Black

Led Zeppelin
Whole Lotta Love

The Pogues
If I Should Fall from Grace with God
Dirty Old Town

U2
With or Without You

Dead Kennedys
Holiday in Cambodia

Sisters of Mercy
Gimme Shelter

Ch 3 Joy Division
Love Will Tear Us Apart

Ch 6 The Rolling Stones
Sympathy For the Devil

Jerry Jeff Walker
L.A. Freeway

Roger Miller
King of the Road

Ch 7 AC/DC
Highway to Hell

Johnny Cash
A Boy Named Sue

Vivaldi
Spring

Louis Armstrong
Zip A Dee Do Dah

Ch 8 Star Wars
Cantina Song

Ch 9 Jimi Hendrix
All Along the Watchtower

Jerry Jeff Walker
Up Against the Wall Redneck Mother

TABLE OF CONTENTS

Chapter 1

THE **AVALANCHE**

I SAW THE AVALANCHE COMING. It charged over the step of dirty brown ice above like a breaking wave of black water. It hammered back down into the gulley, driving into us like the fist of god, and I screamed.

The avalanche slapped my crampons out from under me, and I was folded in half. I was going to die. The animal in me fought to force my hand into the torrent, to grab something solid. My crampons raked over the ice as I stumbled, thrusting my knees into the pressure of the onslaught, trying to get my feet under me. I shouted and I thrashed and the surging snow pushed my arms down at the same time that it swept my feet out to flap like rope-anchored logs in a strong current. My anchor leash was as tight as cable; it hummed with a high-frequency vibration that was transmitted into my bowels along the waist-belt of my harness. My senses where overcome; I didn't know which way was up. I was terrified.

The avalanche surged onto any surface that opposed it, and I felt the power and the weight of it. It felt like hundreds of tons of sand pouring through the hourglass of the mountain, piling onto us, burying us. Desperate and profane objections were torn from my lips, then muffled and swept off down the mountain. I thought that I would never see my wife again. I knew that I could lose love and life here. I started to plead, to pray, "No. Please, no."

The Rupal Face of Nanga Parbat, the highest mountain wall on earth, seen from below Shigri Peak. Photo: Barry Blanchard

The avalanche began to pulsate. My right hand found my locking carabiner. My fingers wrapped into it and the muscles of my hand bulged into a firm hard fist. My left crampon scratched into the ice. I slammed its metal spikes in four times and forced myself upright into the flow. I sensed Ward to my left, had felt the knocking of his body against me and heard the rip of his screams like the tearing of air from an open window when trains pass. I looked up and saw the hazy warmth of his yellow jacket like the flash of a fast moving hull from deep under-water. There was no air. Because I'd leveled my face to the avalanche's flow, an ice-cold seal of moving snow pressed over my face until I panicked and thrust my head down to create a channel in which to breathe.

The avalanche continued, for minutes, and the rushing snow drummed like a waterfall onto the taut fabric of my hood, stretched tight over my helmet. There were surges and with each surge I quivered and prayed that there would be no chunks of solidly bonded snow. I knew the impact of any firm mass would snap the single nine-sixteenths-inch loop of webbing that the three of us were anchored to. I did not want to die. I wanted my life. Ward was still beside me, and left of him I assumed, and prayed, was Kevin. Mark had been on rappel, last man down, when the avalanche hit. I did not know about Mark.

"Please, please let Mark be alive, please."

The pressure was so cold. Millions of ice fragments—the snow—poured over my head and neck and back, each one stealing a small measure of my body heat. After fifteen minutes I was trembling from hypothermia. The avalanche continued. At twenty minutes my mind allowed the macabre irony of dying from the cold, instead of the physical violence of the avalanche, to enter.

The avalanche had become an opponent by then, an enemy. I hated it, swore into it, challenged it. "Alright, you fucker. Give us a break, you fuck! Enough already, you rotten cocksucker!" The raging snow carried my curses into the vortex that it had created: a foot long funnel below my down-turned face. I shook violently, my body jackhammering to pro-duce heat. Then the avalanche hissed away down the polished glare of the ice like the retreating edge of an ocean wave over wet sand. Snowfall turbined around us, and the air felt like cold metal on my teeth. The atmosphere quivered and I could hear the tension of the storm's electrical charge—white noise crackling in my ears. The midday sky was as dark as dusk. I scraped hard-packed snow from the face of the watch that was threaded through my harness. It was 3:47 p.m., July 13, 1988. The avalanche had ended twenty-seven minutes after it had begun.

Ward's face looked old. Deep lines dragged down the corners of his mouth; I had never seen those lines in his face before. His eyes had the improperly focused look of shock, with too much black in his pupils. Streams of snot and compacted snow ran from his nose and snow had been rammed into his collar and hood because he hadn't had the wherewithal to lower his face from the flow, to protect himself. He was sick from the altitude—cerebral edema. The swelling inside his head was killing him.

"I was just going to unclip and get it over with," he said in a flat emotionless tone.

"Where's Mark?" I gasped, my jaw in spasm.

"I'm here." I saw him left of Kevin and I sighed, "Thank God."

Between us Kevin began shaking the snow off like a wet angry dog.

"Alright, that's enough of this fucking shit!" he snarled, looking very much like he intended to slug someone. "We are getting the fuck out of this fucked up place!"

Comically, half-meter-high dunce caps of snow had accumulated on our heads and shoulders. Mark reached across and pushed mine off.

"We have to get the hell out of here," he said.

I saw fear, and resolve, in his eyes. The four of us stood anchored to one tubular drive-in ice screw. It was hitched with a purple bar-tacked sling the width of my ring finger, which, if it were loaded with 1,000 pounds, would sever. When the four of us had snapped tight to it we must have hit it with over eight hundred pounds. We stood at 25,300 feet on the Rupal Face of Nanga Parbat, the ninth-highest mountain in the world. We were 1,300 feet below the summit and we had nearly 14,000 feet of the face to descend. I twisted in another screw.

The summit of Nanga Parbat reaches 26,661 feet (8,126 meters). The Himalaya Range proper ends at the Indus River in Northern Pakistan and Nanga Parbat, the last 8,000-meter peak in that chain, stands guard over its western terminus. In Urdu, Nanga Parbat is the "Naked Mountain"; its barren foothills slope down to the serpentine gorge of the Indus, north of the great river lies the Karakoram. A hulking massif, Nanga Parbat holds three wide and incredibly tall flanks: the glacially tortured Rakiot to the North; the snowy Diamir on the west; and to the south the immense and soaring Rupal which falls for over three linear miles. From its base, in the meadows of Tap Alp, at II,500 feet, the Rupal rises I5,000 feet. It is the tallest escarpment on the planet; no other mountain wall presents more relief. For mountain climbers it is the biggest face in the world. Our base camp of five small mountain tents sat I4,000 feet below us in the cropped grass, cow shit, and blossoming flowers of Tap Alp.

We were cocky. Mark was twenty-seven, I was twenty-nine, Kevin thirty, and Ward thirty-three. The four of us had come to the Rupal holding the conviction that we could climb its Central Spur using two ropes nine millimeters in diameter. The ropes were 200 feet long and we planned to tie two of us to a rope when the climbing got hard; the rest of the time we would climb together carrying the ropes in our packs. Our ascent and decent would have to be accomplished in five to seven days, stopping only to bivouac.

The Central Spur had been climbed once, in 1970, by a large German expedition led by Dr. Karl Herrligkoffer. Twenty climbers, aided by a dozen high altitude porters, spent three months anchoring over I0,000 feet of rope to the mountain. They established five permanent camps and on the twenty-seventh of June the brothers Gunther and Reinhold Messner stood on the summit. A storm of controversy surrounded the brothers' decision to descend via the Diamir Flank, the opposite side of the mountain. A dozen court cases have played out between Reinhold and other members of the team as to what actually happened, but the 2005 discovery of Gunther's body seems to confirm what Reinhold has always said, that his brother was swept away in an avalanche at the base of the Diamir.

Reinhold had been a hero to the four of us. We all subscribed to his powerful alpine manifesto, *The Seventh Grade*. Like Messner, Mark, Ward, and I believed in training hard, while Kevin preferred to live hard. Yet we all believed in climbing mountains as quickly and as boldly as possible. We'd come to climb the Central Spur in five days using 9,600 feet less rope than the 1970 ascent. Nor would we establish any camps: We'd carry our tents, sleeping bags, and stoves in our backpacks and camp nightly where the mountain, and our wits, would allow. We called it "pure alpine style" and our unwavering belief in it defined us as "alpinists." Alpinism was the most important aspect to our lives, our fountainhead. We believed in it, and the mountain, unconditionally.

Rawalpindi, Pakistan, had changed since my first time there four years earlier, in 1984. Mrs. Davies Guest house, were we'd eaten breakfast next to the mystical Polish alpinist, Voytek Kurtyka, and his cast-iron-hard partner, Jerzy Kukuczka, had been demolished. At the time I didn't know that the tall sinewy guy with the haunted eyes was Voytek, or that his cannonball sidekick was equally legendary. Like us, they ate the complimentary cornflakes with coarse gray sugar and warmed milk, using cutlery and china left over from the Raj. We were all trying to save money. They always came to breakfast wearing the embarrassingly too-short cheap nylon running shorts of the day and you could see the long, chiseled strength in Voytek's legs as opposed to the squat, thick power of Jerzy's.

We had pleasant chats with Voytek, who spoke better English, and they told us their plans to traverse Broad Peak North. I didn't know exactly where that was, or what it meant at the time, but over the next few years, as I learned more about the culture of alpinism, I came to appreciate Voytek as one of the most visionary alpinists in history. I am now one of the many who consider his 1985 climb of the west face of Gasherbrum IV—the Shining Wall—with the Austrian Robert Schauer, to be the greatest ascent of the twentieth century.

This time our group stayed at Flashman's, and although much had changed the heat and the dust and the smell of diesel were the same. One hundred and sixteen degrees Fahrenheit: My T-shirt felt like it had been dipped in hot water and pasted onto my back as soon as I stepped from my room. The heat made concrete look overexposed, a blurry white, and asphalt melted then clung to my trainers like gum; I left footprints in it. We hid from the heat watching CNN (another change) in our air-conditioned rooms.

Late afternoons we'd walk into the Intercontinental Hotel to sit by their pool to read, swim, and drink lassis. No one questioned us, thanks to the color of our skin. There was a small door at the back of Flashman's where we could each buy six Murree beers a day, since we had a stamp in our passports that identified us as Christians (infidels). When India was partitioned, Rawalpindi became part of Pakistan. The new country continued the profitable brewing of beer and exportation of it to India.

By day four in Pindi we started drinking some beer. We needed to drive up the Karakorum Highway (KKH) to the town of Gilgit, one of the hubs of Northern Pakistan. Fighting had broken out between the Shia and Sunni in the Gilgit area. The mountain track that would take us up the Astor River to the remote village of Tarshing, the road head for our one-day trek into base camp, had been closed. We had no choice but to enter into a frustrating waiting pattern, with all our plans at the mercy of ancient religious divisions. Rumors from the KKH became hard currency. We heard that the Burgess twins, Aid (Adrian) and Al, had their bus turned back to Gilgit at gunpoint. The twins were two buccaneerish mountaineers and streetwise Yorkshire men, and when I heard this, and recalled Adrian's voice telling me tale after tale of he and his brother's rowdy excesses, I laughed, because I couldn't think of "two nicer fellows." Almost all of Aid's stories ended with "...and so I hit 'em."

Mountaineering expeditions to Pakistan can be made or broken by the qualities of the liaison officer, the government appointee, usually an army officer in Pakistan, whose job is to see that you get through the country experiencing a minimum of strife, and that we "infidels" create the least amount of cultural impact. The expedition underwrites the salary and expenses of the appointee.

Liaison officer Captain Chanzeb was a gem. Thirty-five years old, medium height and build, hair shaved down to a quarter inch on his light-bulb head, maintaining a neat beard and mustache, he strode into the Flashman's compound carrying a black briefcase, and I immediately wondered what was in it. A handgun? Top-secret documents? Chanzeb looked on the world through gold-wired aviator glasses that changed shade with the sun. For half of the day I could always see into his brown eyes. In an unguarded moment I glimpsed into his briefcase and saw spare underwear, a toiletry kit, and a collection of Urdu books and magazines. It was his suitcase.

I don't know that we really ever figured out what he did in the Pakistani Army. When we pushed him he'd reply, "Lots of reconnaissance. You can never have too much reconnaissance." But he didn't go into further detail. I do know that he would have done almost anything for us. We were poor guys in North America but in Pakistan we were rich and being with us offered Chanzeb a chance to relax and enjoy life a bit. His principle concern on the days when we worked on our expedition logistics and prep in Pindi was, "Where will we make the lunch?"

Late one afternoon, after another fine lunch, Mark and I walked away from a meeting at the Ministry of Tourism (MOT), where we'd arranged for our porter insurance. The MOT occupied a building in the capitol city of Islamabad. The modern city had been built in the 1960s and was a fifteen-minute cab ride from the traditional center of Rawalpindi. Chanzeb told us that the incredibly wide main street had been designed for use as an airstrip in times of "emergency." One pass down the middle with a bulldozer, to flatten the street lights, and it would be good to go.

Songbirds chirped from the trees outside the MOT, routinely being drowned out by the whines of motorcycle rickshaws, or the heavy growls of diesel trucks. Dozens of men sat on stools along the sidewalks with old ribbon typewriters in front of them. They were in the business of preparing the reams of paperwork destined for the various ministries. Mark and I wandered to the railroad tracks, snapping pictures. A gothic scene presented itself. We saw men, powdered black from head shawl to sandal, shoveling coal into open freight cars in 116-degree heat, the coal dust hanging on them like an aura. They looked like the damned.

Further on, we came upon a man stripped to the waist hacking into a clay bank with a spade-sized mattock. "Holy shit," blurted Mark, "look at this fucker."

He scrambled down the embankment and went to greet the guy, gesturing with his camera until he understood and agreed to have his picture taken. I played photographer, something relatively new to me as I had rarely been able to afford a camera. I squatted, then got overhead, trying to frame and compose a good shot. Mark was better at this than I was; he'd actually made money at it.

Mark borrowed the mattock and went at the clay bank himself for five minutes. He hacked until I could see striations in his deltoids under his sweat-saturated shirt. The man looked on standing with his arms folded behind his back and the serene unreadable mask of Asia on his face. I suspected he was happy to have a break, even at the hands of two long-haired white boys dressed like hooligans from a B-grade Hindi film. Breathing heavily, Mark handed the man back his mattock. He respected this man because he was strong; Mark has always favored the strong.

After being stuck in Pindi for six days our communal strength, and patience, was being taxed. We had planned to spend three days there but the road up the Astor River was still closed because of the Shia-Sunni conflict. Someone's nephew had been installed as a deputy-deputy-deputy minister of tourism. He was younger than us, had been to school in London, and was far more into talking about the London disco scene than laboring through stacks of expedition paper-work. Stern Muslim men, many years his senior, yet farther down the social ladder by birth, pushed the appropriate reams of tawny legal-sized paper in front of him as I sat opposite his desk. To have a chance to climb, we needed to get to higher altitudes and start our acclimatization. Nanga Parbat felt very far away.

Day seven, back at the Ministry. The men were still busily typing.

"The road is still closed, unfortunately we cannot let you leave until it is safe," stated the deputy-deputy-deputy disco minister.

"What if we go up to Gilgit, then on to Karimabad? The road up that way isn't closed, is it?" I asked.

One of the older men standing beside him cupped his hand to his mouth and whispered in his ear. "Yes, the Karakorum Highway is open to travel as far as Karimabad."

The next day we loaded all of our equipment into a Bedford bus that had been so finely detailed in floral cut plastic, hand-pounded tin, and chain pendants that it looked like a gargantuan jewelry box on wheels. Every bus and truck that we saw was as ornately decorated, including murals; we took to calling them "Silver Bullets" because they reminded us of gaudy beer cans. We drove out of Pindi in the dark hours of the morning to traverse the Punjabi plains before they started to swelter.

Kevin's girlfriend, Yolande Leduc, was trekking into base camp with us, as were Hank Van Weelden and Darryl Wierstra. I'd met Hank and Darryl in the fall of the previous year, 1987, when I'd done a semester at the University of Alberta, in Edmonton. I'd dislocated my shoulder leading on a rock climb late that summer and couldn't climb or guide, so I went to Edmonton to be with my wife while she studied physiotherapy. I studied and trained and worked on organizing our expeditions to Nanga Parbat and Everest for the next year.

"We must stop at my parent's house for tea," Chanzeb had said during our planning. Our Silver Bullet bus jingled to a stop in a small roadside town in the Punjab. The inside of Chanzeb's white cement house was spartan, the furniture worn. Like so much of Asia his birth house seemed to have been arrested in midconstruction and had been falling behind since then. But the hospitality was warm and we sat sipping water with slices of orange followed by strong black tea, eating freshly peeled and salted cucumber. Chanzeb's younger brother and uncle sat opposite us, his father absent working, and his mother and sister flitted in and out bringing fresh tea and water.

As Chanzeb translated, we talked about our families, confirming that none of us had any children, but that Ward and his wife, Jan, were expecting a baby in August. All three men offered their blessings on the child. We told of our homes in Canada, and yes they were relatively close to Vancouver, a mere 1,000 kilometers away, not that far by Canadian standards. Mark ended up placing his home, Chamonix, France, into context for them by saying that is was close to Switzerland. Kevin and I described our 1984 ascent of Rakaposhi, a 25,551-foot-high mountain close to Nanga Parbat. All that we said was acknowledged with sighs and

Orange slices, salted cucumber, and strong black tea: Ward, Mark, and Kevin in Captain Chanzeb's home. Photo: Barry Blanchard nods. I loved the heirloom pictures on the mantel of Chanzeb and his brother with long 1970s haircuts, full mustaches, and high-collared shirts open to the third button, both men looking like tanned versions of Ringo Starr. Several relaxed hours passed and we got back on the bus.

Twenty-four hours later we all stood by the side of the Karakorum Highway and gazed at the wide bulk of Nanga Parbat. It looked like a massive cloud anchored to the rugged brown backs of the hills. So big, so white, so distant. Kevin and I had seen this view four years earlier, but it was not our mountain then. I quivered a bit staring across the miles from where I stood in the warmth to where the summit glowed twenty thousand feet above me. The last light of the day was leaving it. The temperature would already be far below freezing, within the hour it would feel like the absolute cold of space had descended onto it.

"Man, it's a big mountain," Ward smiled. "I hope I'm ready for it."

"You'll do fine, Ward," said Kevin.

"But I haven't been as high as you guys, the highest I've been is Peru."

"Ya, and you did fine there," Kevin replied, "this won't be that different."

We all got back on the bus and continued on to Gilgit.

On the third day of sitting in Gilgit and waiting for the road to open, an American guy strode into our hotel. He had gone native, almost. He wore the long-tailed shirt and baggy pants, the *shalwar kameez,* which all Pakistani men wear, but he'd topped it off with a straw cowboy hat that had seen better days. He was hanging out in the Hunza, climbing peaks, and he'd been doing that for a year.

"What happened is, someone broke the fast of Ramadan," he stated in a slow Californian drawl, "I can't remember if the offender was Shiite or Sunni, but really it was just an excuse for all the tribesmen, who've been locked up in their villages all winter and bored out of their skulls, to grab their shotguns, descend on Gilgit and have an adventure."

"How long will it last?" I asked.

"Good question," he replied.

We arranged to drive one hour farther up the Karakorum Highway to Karimabad and hike up into the high meadows of the Batura Group, to spend five days acclimatizing. We pitched our tents next to some stone shepherds' huts. The grass around us had been chewed down to

Kevin, Ward, Hank, I, and Darryl looking
stylish in our embroidered skullcaps
in the high meadows of the Batura Group.
Photo: Mark Twight

lawn by goats and sheep. Four bummed-out British climbers were camped close by, waiting for the weather to let them get on the perfect granite spire of Bublimotin—Ladyfinger Peak. We joked with them that the Lady was indeed giving them the finger, as rain spit down from a concrete-colored sky.

To acclimatize, we climbed daily up the couloirs and ridgelines that rose from the meadows. The shepherds warned us of the dangers of falling down the long snow gullies, and on our fifth day they followed us in their rubber gum-boots and cut a line of kitchen-chair-sized steps across a gulley for us, with hand spades. They were genuinely worried that we'd plummet to our death; they'd obviously seen this happen in the past.

By then, the Shiites and Sunnis had put away their shotguns and gone home. We heard that somewhere between one and a thousand men had been killed. We opted for the smaller number, which seemed like reasonable odds to us. So the next day we descended to Karimabad and drove back to Gilgit where the road to Tarshing, and the Rupal Face, started.

PLAYLIST

Skinny Puppy	*Assimilate*
Trisomie 21	*The Last Song*
Joy Division	*Shadowplay*
SNFU	*Strip Search*
The Clash	*Rock the Casbah*
The Sex Pistols	*Anarchy in the UK*
The Rolling Stones	*Paint it Black*
Led Zeppelin	*Whole Lotta Love*
The Pogues	*If I Should Fall from Grace with God*
	Dirty Old Town
U2	*With or Without You*
Dead Kennedys	*Holiday in Cambodia*
Sisters of Mercy	*Gimme Shelter*

Chapter 2

THE JOURNEY TO NANGA PARBAT

TWO WEEKS AFTER LANDING in the country we finally loaded all of our stuff into four long-box jeeps and drove away. The ribald and irreverent lyrics of the Pogues pounded in my ears. We all had Walkmans and Ward and I were expanding our punk tastes beyond the Clash and the Sex Pistols via Mark's bulging black box of tapes. Mark was a dark prophet of all that was antiestablishment and vanguard. He told me that his gods talked to him through the music and a lot of what they had to say was loud and dark and contentious: the Sisters of Mercy, Skinny Puppy, Trisomie 21 (a French band named for the gene that causes Down Syndrome), and most importantly for me Joy Division. Hank added **SNFU** (Society is No Fucking Use, or Sausages Never Fry Unevenly—the lead singer, Mr Chi Pig, refused to commit to one version) to the mix. Hank knew every lyric and had climbed on stage to accept the microphone from Chi at several gigs. Kevin dabbled in some of it but tended to stick to the Stones and Led Zeppelin.

Hank's taste was lighter. I'd watch him and Mark play "Hey listen to this" with their Walkmans and speakers until they found a song to which they could air guitar themselves into a whirling slam dance. Mark and I concentrated on the hard-edged and the dark. We discussed Hemingway: the courage of Santiago "in the face of no

Mark climbing the razor's edge unroped.
The Welzenbach Couloir and its horrid sérac
threaten just above. Photo: Barry Blanchard

chance at all" (to quote Charles Bukowski) in the *Old Man and the Sea*, the nobility of El Sordo's last stand in *For Whom the Bell Tolls*. I ripped through *The Sea Wolf*, Jack London's novelization of Nietzschean philosophy, and passed it to Mark like a hard-thrown football. He devoured it and we tried to live its strength. But as far as Mark and I pushed into the black, Kevin had lived it further. Something that I knew about Kevin, and Mark was learning.

Shane MacGowan's whiskey-ravaged voice growled "If I Should Fall From Grace With God" a fitting accompaniment to the 300-foot plummet below us straight down into the raging, dirt-colored waves of the Astor River. I could have dropped a rock into it from my corner of the jeep. To call the cut that had been blasted out of the cliffs above the Astor River a road would be like dubbing Niagara Falls a fine watercourse for punting. Traveling in Northern Pakistan is like living in an Indiana Jones movie. Active landslides are common. At several points we had to unload everything, carry it across three hundred feet of rockslide that had buried the road, hire other jeeps on the far side, and continue. Some of the slides were still spitting rocks and boulders, but were drivable. We'd post a watchman whose job was to scream "Run!" if he saw a rockslide coming. The rest of us would cross, one jeep at a time. Late in the day, we bogged down to the axels in a mud hole. An hour of pushing, pulling with chains, and prying with logs got us out and on our way to Tarshing.

The next day, loads were divided and carried on the backs of ten porters and half a dozen donkeys. Kevin and I told the story of how our porters staged two sit-down strikes on our one-day approach to Rakaposhi, four years before. The second strike stranded us 1,200 feet below our base camp and we'd spent the next five days ferrying up over sixty loads. Now Chanzeb stood up and shouldered his hand-made shotgun. He looked up the trail, already stepping toward it and stated, "There will be no porter strikes here." We seven westerners walked from the stone and thatched huts of Tarshing following a foot-wide trail pounded into the resilient, close-cropped grass, everywhere sprinkled with sheep shit. We were all plugged into our morning music, U2 for me, the Dead Kennedys for Mark.

The Rupal Valley is flat bottomed and narrow, just a little more than a mile from mountain slope to mountain slope at its widest. Rupal Peak rose on our left looking pyramidal, snowy, and low. We'd heard that the few trekking groups that visited the valley sometimes climbed it. It would be our first acclimatization outing. On our right the Rupal Flank of Nanga Parbat grew, and grew, and grew.

Midday we stumbled over chalky granite on the Chhungphar Glacier. The rock was broken, angular, and dusty, so freshly ground from the flank of the mountain that it glowed white in the hot sun. Where there was more than twenty degrees of slope, the rock glided on the underlying ice—I felt like I was roller-skating on one foot with a shoe on the other.

I shuffled down the last steps of loose gravel and walked away from the Bazhin Glacier's lateral moraine; it was the second glacier we'd traversed that day. The meadow of Tap Alp rolled gently up valley. I was 500 meters from the site of our base camp and I stopped and looked to the mountain. The Rupal Face soared into the sky like it was a corner of the planet that had broken through the skin. I looked at it dead on and realized that if I held my gaze midline, without shifting my eyes, it filled my field of vision from periphery to periphery. "Holy fuck," I whispered. A powerful intimidation entered my mind. It felt like a shadow had opened a door and stepped in. It was a deeper feeling than I'd felt standing beneath a mountain face in a long time, and I felt a trace of dread. Two beats passed, I found my breath and followed it to the rise and fall of my chest. "You're going to be living beneath this mountain for the next six weeks," I said to myself, and I turned and stepped toward base camp.

Mark was sitting cross-legged on a rock. His broad shoulders were curved in, and he was wearing a Rothmans T-shirt that he'd found somewhere, then cut the sleeves off of. We'd been offered some tobacco money but had voted it down (something that my philosophy professor had congratulated me on), so Mark wore the tobacco company's shirt to goad us ("I've got no problem with cigarettes."). His stand-up, black punk hair was headbanded with one of the colorful woven scarves that we'd bought in Pindi. His earphones were out and his eyes were glassy with the sheen of a tear.

"It is so fucking beautiful," he said.

Base camp, a half a dozen tents, geodesic splashes of color like massive flowers sprouting amongst the stunted evergreens and cow-grazed pasture. Mark didn't own a tent so he made do in one of our two tiny mountain tents, a small hard place to be when it rained. Kevin and Yolande named their tent "the pleasure dome"—at least until Yolande left, when it reverted to bachelorville just like the rest of ours.

Our kitchen was a lean-to that Kevin, the carpenter, erected by lashing up a roof from fallen branches and logs supported by two large boulders. We stretched the leaky canvas army tarps that we'd bought in Pindi over it then sealed the drips with garbage bags and yards of our precious duct tape. We made benches out of stones and branches. A blue Coleman cooler was our table. It looked like something out of Gilligan's Island, but it fit into our meager budget.

I'd sold Nanga Parbat as a training climb in preparation for the main event: an attempt on an unclimbed line on the northwest flank of Mount Everest, post-monsoon, that same year. The training climb was actually more of a main event than the main event, but Everest's name kept the communication company that I was working with happy and it did help land us what little corporate money we'd gotten. The eight-man support group who planned to accompany us into Tibet and on to Everest Base Camp that fall was providing much of the budget for both expeditions.

When I'd stacked the last of our tinned milk in beside the biggest boulder, our pantry, Mark said, "There, once we turn all of this into shit we can go home."

We all laughed, then stepped outside to look around for acclimatization possibilities and to feel out Chanzeb on what would be politically permissible for us to climb. He swept his hand across the whole valley and said, "Climb anything that you want." I loved that guy.

Kevin, Ward, Yolande, and I chose to spend five nights on Rupal Peak, a moderate summit directly across the valley from the Rupal Face, but dwarfed by it like a dinghy bobbing next to an aircraft carrier. Hank and Darryl continued to try and hurt themselves on their mountain bikes, and Mark went off climbing by himself.

Four days later Ward and I were crossing a broad, forty-five-degree snow gulley on the northwest side of Rupal Peak. We were on our way to the summit. The sun had just broken the skyline somewhere to the east, I could see blades of light cutting out from the ridgeline a thousand feet above, and I twisted off my headlamp. The snow had frozen as firm as hard-packed mud overnight and ahead of me Ward kicked the edge of his boot three times across the slope to carve a half-inch-deep step. He'd then ease onto the step and kick three times again for his next foot.

I balanced onto each edge precisely. Below me the slope fell away 5,000 feet to a glacier in the valley floor. I must have over-rotated on my uphill foot, my left foot, because suddenly it swished out from under me, I hit my left side, and immediately began to accelerate. My clothing hissed. I could feel the rasping vibration of speed through my left hip, then the hundred days that I'd spent teaching self-arrest came to my rescue and I was rolling onto the pick of my ax, my arms clamped powerfully to my sides and the pick levering into the hard snow, spraying a rooster tail of white pellets. I came to a stop, then carefully stood, and swore.

"Are you OK?" yelled Ward, "Do you need me to come down there?"

"I'm OK. I'm a fucking idiot, but I am OK." I breathed out the acidic taste of my fear, then carefully, and ever-so-attentively, I climbed back up to Ward.

An hour later we were standing on the summit gawking to the southeast, smitten. A perfect alpine wall, the top opening like a Japanese fan, fluted snow ridge paralleling fluted snow ridge and all running to the summit skyline. Emerald strips of water ice etched gleaming lines up the vertical black rockwalls guarding the bottom of the face. An apron of snow angled gently from the rock down to the flats of the Shigri Glacier.

"We have to climb that," I said.

"Oh yes we do," replied Ward.

Base camp: Sahjad, our cook, served up hot chapatis with fresh eggs and tinned cheese, black tea with milk and lots of coarse-grained sugar, then more chapatis—only deep fried this time—which we smeared with peanut butter, let it melt, then added jam. Yolande, Darryl, and Hank were sharing a last meal with us. After breakfast they would be walking down valley to travel home. Two donkeys had already trotted away carrying their packs and duffels.

Our Pakistani Army map didn't name the peak that we'd set our sights on, but it did place its summit at 18,000 feet. We knew that was bullshit because Mark had seen that it was higher than he was on the summit of Laila, over 19,500 feet. I asked one of the shepherds who occasionally passed through if he knew the name of the peak. He told me that it was Ali Peak, Then I asked him what his name was. "Ali" he said. We decided to instead call it Shigri Peak for the glacier that flowed from its feet.

Our two small mountain tents, one blue, one yellow, sat on the glacial moraine like a couple of origami pieces set at the center of a clean white banquet table. The late afternoon sun was warm and we stayed outside the tents, layering up on clothes as the temperature dropped. We joked and laughed while we prepared to climb. The face looked to be about 3,000 feet high and we reasoned that we could be up and down it in one day. Knowing that we would run out of water and need to rehydrate, we packed a stove and an ensolite pad in addition to our climbing hardware and ropes. We were four men in the prime of their lives who'd all pursued their love of alpine climbing as if it were an art form. We believed that we painted lines on these magnificent mountain walls. Shigri was beautiful, seductive, and virgin.

The alarm screeched, 2:30 a.m. When I stepped from the tent one hour later the snow was frozen firm underfoot and it crunched as I walked to take a piss. Swinging my headlamp onto the other tent I saw that Mark was not packing. I walked over.

"What's up man?" His eyes looked heavier than usual, like they'd sunk in a bit.

"I have a bad feeling about this one."

"You're kidding." It was like an elbow to the ribs. I was excited to have all four of us climbing together. "What kind of bad feeling?"

"It just doesn't feel right to me man. I'm not going."

Kevin, Ward, and I agreed that we still had a good feeling about the climb so we all agreed that Mark would stay behind and come up to meet us on the descent.

Kevin, I, and Ward outside our origami tents when we thought that the face of Shigri Peak was 3,000 feet. Over the next day and a half we would learn that it was 5,000 feet.
Photo: Mark Twight

"Take care man, we'll see you later tonight," I said as we left.

"You guys take care, be careful up there."

"We will."

Kevin, Ward, and I climbed onto the lower snow slopes by head-lamp. When the slope angled up from the glacier we stepped over the threshold and entered our sacred space. The Himalayan dawn heated the eastern horizon with an orange-blue light that soon simmered to yellow. Row on row of jagged peaks looked like a northern forest backlit by headlights. We took off our headlamps and climbed one after the other onto the glassy, fragile ice. Crystal shards skated down the chrome surface with each swing of our axes and kick of our crampons. I felt so optimistic, positive, alive. We were climbing a new route on a virgin Himalayan peak, and I really felt good.

The sun ascended. Radiant energy pounded into the face heating the dark rock, pieces of ice and rock melted off and fell toward us. We'd climbed 1,000 feet by the time we stopped and decided to tie-in to the rope. From there we moved together with the rope clipped into the mountain via whatever gear placements we could find. The rhythm of the climb played out to the cadence of our breath. We skirted below the black rock anchored into the ice with our technol-ogy. Ward took a sobering chunk of ice on the helmet and swore.

A narrow, green gulley cleaved the last rockband and we swung our way up it as the Asian sun beat down. A little later Kevin was hit in the right shoulder and he bellowed in rage, his vocabulary far more profane than Ward's, and he put much more energy into it. Black Irish. Midday we were 3,000 feet up what the map had told us was a 3,000-foot wall and we'd just passed the change of angle that sepa-rated the steep lower face from the shallower upper—it was much bigger than we'd thought. The heat was oppressive, I felt like I was climbing in a sauna. We'd climbed over 20,000 feet above sea level for the first time on the trip and it felt like the altitude had draped a shawl of chain mail onto my shoulders.

The yellow rope scraped slowly up the crusty gray ice, the black and red spiral of its braid jumping forward eleven inches at a time when Ward stepped up, then settling back three inches when he weighted his foot. One half ropelength above me, he methodically swung his axes, kicked his crampons. Below me, tied-in to the end of the rope, Kevin did the same: ax, ax, crampon, crampon; ax, ax, crampon, crampon. Two ice screws were clipped onto the running rope and at that point in time they were all that anchored us to the mountain. Our pace had withered to a funeral march. Too-thin air bellowed in and out of my straining lungs and my throat felt like I'd swallowed a shot glass of talcum powder. We had to stop.

Two thirty in the afternoon, June 19, 1988, we were 4,000 feet up the wall when we lashed ourselves onto a small rock ledge. I sat facing out with Shigri Peak at my back, my scarred black front points reached out over the drop. Glowing slopes of snow and ice surrounded us, they fell away to the glacier like a vast bridal train sweeping the fresh white waves of avalanches out onto the mottled gray surface. Our stove was balanced, and tied-in, to my right and for two hours it hummed along melting liter after liter of snow and ice.

The sun had swung off the face when we started climbing again. Immediately the snow thickened from sloppy mush to a firm spongy plastic. The rocks, and the ice chunks, quit falling. We barged through hip-high flutings of snow and teetered over small granite overlaps, our front points finding enough to set on. Ward led a rising traverse arcing to the right, to where we trusted we could get off of the face. Five hundred feet above, the sharp edge of a sérac bore down on us like a guillotine. Looking to it I felt a hot coal of anxiety smoldering in my stomach, yet the sérac marked the summit ridge-line. We were getting closer, and we'd be out from under it in one more ropelength.

I pressed up onto a platform that Ward had stamped into the largest of the flutings. The rope hadn't moved in five minutes, I'd gathered several yards of it in my hand. I hadn't been able to see Ward for the fluting. Now I saw that he was in trouble. His limbs were locked and I could see tension in his core. He stood crucified facing into a seventy-degree patchwork of ice, snow, and downsloping rock. His blue eyes locked on to mine.

"I'm going to fall," he stated calmly.

A bucket of cold water to the face. "OK!" I replied as I greedily ripped in the slack rope between us throwing a loop behind my back to get him on a body belay. I hammered my crampons in, braced my shoulder to the mountain and prayed that the piton he'd placed between us would hold. And then he scratched off and rasped down the face and I felt his 165 pounds choke hard into my waist and my body shifted a few anxious inches...and then I stopped. Everything stopped. The eighteen-inch sling attaching the piton to the rope quivered like a guitar string. Breath burst through my clenched lips and I hauled in long lungfuls of the thin air.

"What the fuck is going on, man? Why aren't we moving?" Kevin was pounding up the steps below me, a huge loop of rope—and risk— lying limp from his harness. He was pissed, angry at being stalled under the sérac.

"Ward just fell." I said, enjoying a heartbeat of understatement.

"Oh fuck! You're kidding. Is he OK?"

"Yes, he's OK. He's climbing back up. Take in the slack."

"Ya, ya. I'm sorry man, I didn't know."

Night fell and we dug out our headlamps. Everything became quiet save for the deep draws of our breath and the crunching of our foot placements. We climbed ropelength by ropelength now and our pace had slowed to pathetic. It hurt to force every step, yet I had to chuckle when I glanced down and saw the syllogism that both Mark and I had embroidered over our chest pockets: "I hurt, therefore I am."

The cold stole my body heat and I began to tremble. In the dangerous clear cold of that Himalayan night I impressed myself by fighting into my overpants while I stood waiting at a belay stance with the world dropping away to black all around me; with quivering hands I wrapped the pants over my crampons and under my harness. A risky act of balance that I had performed well. I'd saved some of my life-sustaining heat.

Around midnight we stopped. I engineered an anchor while Ward and Kevin stamped a ledge the size of a desktop into the snow and ice. We sat on our ensolite pad and melted snow on the stove, then we hunkered down to shiver and to suffer. I felt the night fear. It always comes. Despite dozens of nights passed in this situation on many mountains, I can never fully convince myself that I will see the dawn. I've always feared losing control in the dark. If a storm broke we could have been trapped there, if it were violent enough we may not have been able to retreat, if it went on long enough we could perish...

One mile lower we saw Mark's headlamp bobbing up the glacier. We shouted and heard faint yells in reply. It felt so good knowing that someone cared about us; we flashed our headlamps at him. Eventually his headlamp turned down the glacier and we watched it descend. He understood that we wouldn't be making it down that night. It was so sad to see him go.

"Mark is an alright guy you know," said Kevin, having stood to beat his arms around his chest in an effort to stay warm. "Don't get me wrong. He's dark, but he's searching. I like that in a man."

Kevin and I were soon spooning and rubbing each other like lovers.

"My back is cold man, rub my back," I asked. Ward sat at the other end of the ledge quaking from the cold.

"You guys are weird," he chattered.

Too cold to sit any longer, we were on the move before dawn. When the warm sun finally hit us, it felt like salvation. By l:00 p.m. we'd climbed another thousand feet. Since he hadn't been doing much alpine climbing before the trip, Kevin was coming up last. Alpinism was pretty much all that Ward and I had been doing, so it made sense for us to do the leading. Now Kevin asked for the lead and he confidently bridged up the last pitch like it was what he'd always done. At 2:00 p.m. Ward, the last man, pulled through to stand on the summit ridgeline, then he hobbled toward us, sat on his pack, and levered his boots off.

"I can't climb up anymore," he stated, pain pinching down the corners of his eyes. He drew in a breath over clenched teeth. His feet were an ugly mess. Inch-wide burns started midfoot and wrapped back around his anklebones on the inside and outside of both feet. The skin was gone and the underlying flesh oozed plasma. Before the trip he'd had a friend make him a pair of liners out of yellow ensolite pad. They were warm and light, but ended up being snug. He'd decided to go without socks, just as Mark had done on Nuptse the year before—the difference being that Mark's liners had a fabric on the inside while Ward's were the rough grippy surface of the yellow ensolite.

"The summit is just over there, less than an hour. We'll be able to descend the way we planned," I urged.

"I just can't go up anymore. My feet can't take it."

"Ward's telling the truth man. I think that we should drop off of the back side here," Kevin added.

"We don't know what's down there. We don't even know if it's the same drainage. It may lead out to the ocean for all we know," I said.

I was outvoted. Ward slopped his feet back into his boots and we started down the far side of the mountain. Our adventure continued. At one point we traversed under a Mediterranean-blue sérac roughly the size and shape of a hotel. It was no place that any of us wanted to linger. We made it off the mountain and late that night we bedded down in the moraines of a glacier that filled the valley floor. We'd had nothing to eat since yesterday. A cool katabatic wind soon had me shivering, yet I did manage to sleep some. Kevin stayed awake all night walking around. In the morning he told Ward and I that he liked this glacier, had gotten to explore and know some of it in the night. It's always interesting being with Kevin.

When we stepped from the glacier, Ward removed the plastic shells from his boots and began fast hobbling in his liners. We walked twenty-three miles that day. I have no idea how he endured the pain. We walked around the Rupal Ridge, then passed back through Tarshing where we bought crackers and cookies on credit, then walked on to repeat our former approach to base camp.

Late in the day we traversed the Bazhin Glacier. I saw Mark running toward us.

"I thought that you fuckers were dead," he blurted, then he wrapped me in a bear hug and picked me up off the ground. He was crying, I was crying; but most importantly he had sweet black tea and fresh chapattis. I'd lost fifteen pounds in the last three days.

"I don't know where these guys get off changing the Stones," Kevin challenged as he lifted the tarp and stepped into the kitchen, yanking out his earphones. "It's rape, murder; not murder, rape." Mark had given Kevin a Sisters of Mercy cover of "Gimme Shelter" to listen to. The Sisters of Mercy were, by far, Mark, Ward, and my favorite punk band.

Kevin was not amused. "You can't change the Stones man, you just can't change the Stones. The Stones wrote it as an escalation—murder is worse than rape."

"I'd say that depends on who's getting raped," countered Mark, "and do you really think that Jagger and Richards thought about it that much?"

An hour later Kevin and Mark had tired of arguing about lyrics, and Ward's and my stomach muscles ached from laughing. We needed to continue with our acclimatization, but the problem was Ward couldn't bear anything but flip-flops on his butchered feet.

Two pots of tea later we'd concluded that Ward would hobble up to Mazeno Pass, 17,715 feet above sea level, and camp there while Kevin, Mark, and I climbed as high as we could on the Schell Route on the side of the Rupal Face. Outside of the acclimatization, we needed to know if we could use the Schell as a descent after climbing the Central Spur.

On August 11, 1976, the Austrians: Siegfried Gimpel, Robert Schauer, Hilmar Strum, and their leader, Hanns Schell, left an open bivouac at 26,350 feet and climbed to the summit of Nanga Parbat. It was their second night, without a tent, above their 24,500-feet high camp. The four men had put up a new route to the left of the Rupal Face, the Southwest Ridge. They'd established four camps and fixed half of the route with rope. The two nights in the open high on the mountain gifted Schauer some of the chops that would allow him to survive the west face of Gasherbrum IV, with Voytek Kurtyka, nine years later.

I got to know Robert Schauer in 1992, when I was thirty-three. We sat together on the jury at the Banff Mountain Film Festival and several years later Robert invited me to be on the jury at his mountain film festival in Graz, Austria. We talked about Nanga Parbat and he told me that Hanns Schell had, years after the ascent, reflected on how Himalayan alpinism had developed and concluded that the four of them had done something special and significant, but how that conclusion had come to him too much after the fact to do anything with it.

The summer of their success had been my last summer of high school. While Robert had been climbing hard on Nanga Parbat, I was leading my first rock pitches and learning about the joys of sex and challenges of beer (it is true, rock-climbing was dangerous back then, and sex was safe). I'd learned about Nanga Parbat through reading Reinhold Messner's *The Seventh Grade*, a book that had been so overdue my high school librarian paged me over the intercom. *The Naked Mountain* existed in my consciousness like a cloud; I had to look up Pakistan in an atlas.

———————

Ward limped off with our blue tent while Kevin, Mark, and I climbed away with our yellow one.

The route felt moderate. We scrambled and climbed unroped past fixed lines aged by the sun, twisted from avalanches, and knotted by the hands of climbers past. The three of us prided ourselves on not touching the fixed ropes—fixing was cheating. Kevin and I gleefully wasted a half hour busting our guts to lever easy-chair-sized boulders loose and trundle them down the massive scree and grass slopes that flanked the ridge.

"Man, you Canadians are kind of primitive," observed Mark.

"We just love getting down to some righteous destruction," I beamed. "It makes us feel bigger than we are." The acrid smell of exploded rock lay dense in the thin air.

The next morning Kevin swung his axes into the steepest passage yet. A shoulder width funnel of crisp, frost-locked snow and dirty gray ice contained between bulges of fractured granite. The sun was an hour off and the night-chilled air dragged harsh and raw over the end of my tongue.

"How is it, Kev?" I asked from under the protection of a rock roof.

"It's OK. You can c'mon up. I'll hang out here until you get close to me." It would be safer the closer I stayed to him as any ice he knocked off wouldn't hit me with as much force.

Mark had moved to Chamonix, the mecca of alpine climbing, the year before and he was into whatever the best French alpinists were into (even changed his name from Mark to Marc, to be more French-like). Kevin and I had decided to follow Mark's lead and go with headbands instead of helmets (a decision we reneged on after the Schell).

I front pointed in underneath Kevin, the racks of his ten points five feet above my head. Ice and snow fanned out below like a colossal inclined hockey rink. A fall would be fatal. With my right ax drawn back to swing, and only my left secured in the ice, a fusillade of ice fragments drummed into the top of my skull. I felt a thud, like a dropped fist, hit my left shoulder.

"Fuck! Take it easy up there!" I wailed.

"Sorry. I'm doing the best that I can!"

Climbing up was my best option. I swung hard and kicked quickly, I needed to be up this fast. I needed to be safe.

"Ice! Shit man, ice!" Kevin shouted.

The hit slammed my jaw shut and I saw white pinpoint pops of light shot into the black of my clenched eyelids. And then I lost it.

"Doyle! You fucking asshole! That nearly took me off, you fuck! Stop moving right fucking now, you fucking prick!"

"The ice is fucking brittle up here, man! I'm doing the best I can!"

We shouted until I could feel the veins in my temples pulsing against the inside of my headband and my throat felt like a splintered piece of wood, then Kevin was able to climb away left and out from above me. I continued up to where he'd kicked out a step.

We apologized, as we always had over our decade of climbing together. It seemed that we occasionally had to lose our tempers to communicate under stress.

Two nights later our small yellow tent was pitched at 22,000 feet. Broad glacial snowfields swept up above us to meld into the summit pinnacles of Nanga Parbat. The weather was perfect. We discussed climbing to the summit, but in the same instant we knew that doing so would be like injecting a virus into the body of our motivation. It would be too easy, back in base camp, to tell ourselves, "Hey, we climbed the peak, maybe we should be happy with that and go home." But we'd come to climb the Central Spur of the Rupal Face in pure alpine style and we were willing to fight for that commitment, even if it meant fighting ourselves.

We breathed the air up there for three days, venturing to 23,000 feet, then we descended to base camp. Our acclimatization was done, we were ready for the Rupal.

"I think that I've come up with a viable plan for myself," Ward said.

The four of us were sitting around the blue cooler-cum-table sipping mugs of milky black tea sweet with sugar. Ward was able to wear his boots again. He'd decided that he would try to solo the south face of Rakiot Peak while Kevin, Mark, and I made our attempt on the Central Spur. For two years I'd been envisioning four men high on the Rupal. I wanted my dream, badly, and the thought of not having Ward there, the man that I'd done the finest, and hardest, climbing of my life with...it felt like a cornerstone had shifted. I forced a dry swallow.

"Man, you've come all this way to climb the Rupal. I don't think that you'll be happy if you go home without even trying," I said.

"I'm not as acclimatized as you guys. I think I've come up with a good option."

"Ward, we came here to climb the Rupal Face," Kevin said. "Either you want to do it, or you don't."

"You guys should lay off and let me go climbing."

"I don't think you should quit," said Mark, pointing to his base-ball cap and the words, Never Quit, that he'd written on it with a black felt marker.

Later that day Ward came to my tent and said, "OK, I'll go with you."

July 9, 1988, I knelt and sunk my lips into the cold clear water. The spring bubbled from a crease in the landscape that delineated pasture from slope, the foot of the Rupal Face. We'd been drawing our water from here for the last month and today it tasted cool and good. For the first time I noticed the movement of a half dozen underwater beetles, black bodied with flecks of gold, the length of the end of my little finger. They melded into the coarse golden grains of granite perfectly. Verdant mounds of moss bulged from the edges of the pool, pale yellow flowers...so much life. I rose and swung my pack onto my shoulder and it settled heavily. We'd whittled our packs down to thirty pounds each, but that would be after we put on most of our clothes and had the ropes and hardware out.

The morning sun bore down. I could feel the heat of it like hot towels laid onto the black bands of my tiger-striped Lycra underwear. Mark had pointed out to me that "black is the sun's favorite color." I stepped onto the slope—crossed the threshold—ski poles in my hands, my pack the weightiest it would be.

Decades of cow's hooves had embossed dry steps of dirt into the lower slopes of the mountain. I wove my gray boots through rough stalks of brown grass that rose between the dirt steps like small picket fences and acted like trip wires. It felt good to be moving uphill, yet my spirit quivered some knowing that the four of us were going to try to climb the largest mountain wall on earth with two ropes and what we were carrying on our backs. I was living the boldest expression of alpinism that I could imagine. I felt strong. I felt ready. But the mountain was massive; it would be so easy to get lost.

By 6:00 p.m. the four of us had pitched our yellow and blue tents on platforms that we'd leveled into a skirting of snow blown onto the lee of the ridge. We sat outside on our ensolite pads and brewed tea and joked and laughed as night, and the temperature, fell. A relaxed joy encompassed the four of us. We were excited and committed, and we were safe. Above us loomed 11,000 feet of the mountain, the true tests would be up there, yet for the moment we could sit and enjoy the Himalayan sunset, and our friendship.

"...I told him, 'I'm heading back to the tent.'" Mark was telling us a story about climbing in the Tetons with his buddy Colm. "I wanted to climb and he wanted to stay and party around the campfire. So I'm back in his Bibler, and you know that they are as small as our tents here, and I'm asleep when I hear two voices outside the tent. Colm and this gal. And then I can't believe it, they come into the tent! Into the sleeping bag that I'd loaned him! And I've just gotta pretend like I'm asleep. And then salamander sounds started—*sluuu, slewww, slew*." Mark pinched his cheek and was pumping it in and out to replicate the sounds.

Sweet milk tea exploded from Kevin's cheeks and he howled, "Did you actually just say 'salamander sounds'?"

"Ya I did. And then my face was being banged into the wall of the tent and I just had to lie there and take it! Thump, thump, thump."

This time tea came through Kevin's nostrils. Laugh lines crumpled the corners of his eyes and he chortled so deeply that tears welled and ran in glittering streaks down his sun-bronzed cheeks. We all bent over choking on laughter, our arms pressed hard over our stomachs trying to stop.

Mark straightened his back and wiped tears from his eyes and continued. "In the morning she left. 'Colm, you fuck! I can't believe you fucking did that! And in my sleeping bag too, you asshole. 'No, man, don't worry, we had it zipped open. The Therm-a-rest took all the action...see.'"

My stomach muscles ached, and our trash talk rippled off into the Himalayan night.

The cold predawn air penetrated my fingertips with a thousand pin-pricks of ice and I stuffed my hands back into my gloves. Exhaled breath hung as a sparkling cloud arrested in the tunnel beam of my headlamp. My heart beat five times before my fingertips tingled back to life. With a closed fist I rammed my down jacket into the top of my pack then cinched the drawstring down and tied it off. I wanted to do all of this well. For ten years I'd strived to be the best alpinist I could be, fifteen hundred days in the mountains had built to this day.

I was the first to climb away over the frost-shattered rock. The backbone of the ridge bulged dark against a black sky shot through with a thousand points of starlight, my gloved hands reached to grab the rock that led to it. In time, the three headlamps of my part-ners fell in behind me and I made myself stick to the more solid rock, even if the scrambling was harder, I'd be less likely to drop anything on anyone below.

A narrow couloir of snow reached down into the rock from the upper mountain—a frozen finger from the realm of ice and permanent snow, there was no life up there. We snapped into our crampons and strapped them tight, then stepped onto the snow.

An hour later the four of us stood on a rounded hump of Styrofoam-hard snow that sat against the mountain like a small flat island in a sea of incline and precipice. We could put our packs down without worrying that they'd slide away. Golden fingers of the sun's first rays beamed across us like a touch of benevolence. Kevin's smile was lit from within and once again I was awed by how he could live a moment with such totality, truthfully becoming whatever he was feeling without restraint or artifice. In moments like these he simply was, and that could be anything from pure rage to true joy.

"This is so beautiful," he said. "Thanks so much for bringing us here, Blanch."

"My pleasure, Wally." (I'd called Kevin 'Wally' or 'Walter' since seeing a home renovation show in the late seventies that featured a carpenter, like Kevin, of that name.) "My pleasure."

"How are you doing, Ward?" Kevin asked.

"I'm diggin' this. This is awesome. I want to thank you too, Barry, thanks for bringing us here man. I'm loving this."

Kevin and Mark talk trash in hopes of getting the other to snort milk tea out of his nostrils.
Photo: Barry Blanchard

Mark circled around us taking pictures.

Snow led to glacier, glacier led to ice face. We began a long, rising traverse to the left under tombstone black rock that had been named for Ulrich Wieland, a climber who had died fifty-four years before.

By midday the firm face of ice and snow had softened to fields of mush and the sun pressed heat into any body surface offered to it. When I turned my face to the sun I felt a smoldering heat, like I'd inched my face too close to the fire. Hours of swinging and kicking amassed to cloak my mind in the ether of routine, and complacency. The heat cooked the edge off of my senses.

"Rock! Rock! Rock!" screamed Ward.

My gaze snapped to the Wieland Rocks. A cinder-block-sized hunk of brown rock was bounding down the ice, gaining bounce and rotational energy every time it chunked into the ice face. I groped to the right forcing my limbs to move through the hot, heavy air. Five meters to my left the rock ripped the air with a baritone *whiirrrr*! I was safe, but I wished that I'd been able to move faster. The sun beat down. We pounded on for thousands of feet.

Finally there was a break in the Wieland Rocks. A gully of rock, snow, and ice broke the bulwark of granite and we climbed to it as if it were a ladder lowered from a ship's gunwales into the sea. Ward and Mark climbed into the gully as I kicked up to Kevin, slammed in my ice tools and clipped myself to them. Thirty feet higher Mark and Ward were dancing around trying to force a mixed section.

"Why are we doing this?" I shouted up. It seemed too dangerous. It pissed me off. Why not just use the rope?

"You guys are being too pushy!" shouted Kevin.

Silence, and then they climbed from view. Kevin and I waited, blobs and sloughs of moist snow plopped down from above, the detritus of their climbing, then the ends of our orange and yellow ropes arced down through the air like an apology and we tied-in and climbed up.

Five hundred feet higher we gained a beautiful snow-and-ice arête, the prominent feature of the route for the next 1,500 feet, but the snow on it had been baked to total slop. We had to kick and swing through a foot and a half of saturated snow to reach the security of the ice. Wet snow washed away from every foot placement and fanned out downslope like waves of water. The angle had backed off and we'd untied from the ropes. Thirty feet below us a sun-bleached tent lay in ruin. Crushed by snow load it looked like crumpled wrapping paper that had been left out in the rain, washed into the gutter, then dried to parchment by the sun. A few streamers of threadbare fabric hung limp in the calm air and looked like banners of permanent defeat.

On May 28, 1984, Fuji Tsunoda, Shigoeh Hida, Nobuyuki Imakyurei, and Takashi Kogure had arrived in Tap Alp to attempt a siege ascent of the Central Spur. They established four in situ camps over the next month, the highest being at 24,125 feet. After a rest in base camp they began their summit attempt. On July 6 they made an evening radio call with their liaison officer. The four Japanese men were never heard from again. We heard, and wanted to believe, that they had climbed into the Merkl Gully, the summit feature of the route, and that a storm broke and they'd been lost. Kevin climbed down to the abandoned tent to check. It was empty.

Out front I continued breaking trail, yet every time I looked back down the line of steps I saw Mark falling farther behind. Something was wrong. I couldn't believe it was the altitude, he'd been far too strong. Ward huddled with him, then yelled up for my baseball cap. I left it in the snow, it had a Clash button on it and a quote from one of their songs written on it in black felt marker, "Know your rights."

An hour later Ward caught me up.

"How's Mark?" I asked.

"I think he has heatstroke. He was staggering, told me that he felt like he might fall off and that's when I saw that his scalp was scalded pink in the part of his hair. I gave him some water. I think the baseball cap has helped."

"Is he doing OK now?"

"Ya, he got it together, I think. He's still coming."

We had climbed 5,000 feet to 19,400 feet above sea level, the same relief as the north face of Mount Temple back home in the Canadian Rockies. In front of us the arête merged onto an office-building-sized, crescent-moon-shaped glacier. We tied-in and Ward led a short vertical step to gain the rounded slope topping the glacier. On top of that pocket glacier the snow lay like warm oatmeal two feet thick. It took me a half hour to slosh up the last 150 feet to a bergschrund. It was time to stop, we were all knackered. I screwed the shovel blade onto my ax handle and went at hacking tent platforms into the dune-like drift on the lower lip of the 'schrund like a man possessed. I pushed myself hard, taking the lion's share of the shoveling, thinking on how wild our position was, how much we'd accomplished that day, and how I loved these guys and I didn't mind hurting for them. Mark sat on his pack and started both of our stoves. We all needed to drink, especially Mark. I worried about his ability to continue the next day, a day that we all agreed had to start earlier.

One in the morning and my watch's alarm shrieked like a ravenous baby bird. Everything was black and my mind strived to anchor to something. Was I still within the vibrant dream of climbing in the sun with my wife, or was I in my tent in base camp—my mind's default for home, and security, for the last month. Then my consciousness snapped and righted itself and a jolt ricocheted down my central nervous system jerking my limbs and popping my eyes open.

A guttural "*Hnnhhh!*" escaped through my chilled lips. More black, but now I knew that I was on the Rupal and that I needed to start the stove. I'd placed my watch inside my toque to keep it warm, and to make sure that I heard it. It felt like it was a tiny bird pecking at the top of my skull. I'd snugged the portal of my sleeping bag down tight and in the dark it felt claustrophobic, like it wasn't allowing me enough air and I rushed to wriggle a hand free and open it. I needed to breathe, and I needed to see, and I needed to strangle the baby bird.

Two hours later I watched Mark's headlamp bob away in disbelief. I was trying to match his pace, but couldn't. His recovery was amazing and I knew that he was pushing hard to prove that to himself.

Above him the pale arc of the arête cut a scythe into the black wall of the Rupal. I felt a band of muscle contract over my lower abdomen pulling the wings of my pelvis together. The line of the ice was so linear and perfect that it could have been carved out of white marble—the razor's edge. In my mind I saw Mark and I gazing at Kurt Diemberger's iconic photo of the Peuterey Ridge on Mont Blanc. In it a lone figure was tacked to an edge of ice so much like what we were climbing on. In the picture, clouds clung and swelled from the arête. Far below the black towers of the Aiguilles Blanche and Noire were being lost to a darkening sky. There was malice, and magic, and Mark had asked me, "Doesn't that make your balls suck up?"

Snow as hard as plaster coated the ice, and I had to swing hard to reach through it and embed the tip of my right pick into ice, my left I just stabbed into the snow like a dagger. It was an aid to my balance but provided little security. For a thousand feet the four of us crunched along, each lost in the rhythmic synchronization of his limbs to the clouds of his exhaled breath.

Dawn dialed our world from gray to white. Already the rounded heads of cumulous cells had risen to form a thick quilt over the valley floor. Soon the cloud would swell and engulf us, there would be little heat today. And with the cloud would come the worry of a storm, and the anxiety of being lost in a whiteout.

We grouped up at the first rock step all agreeing that we would continue unroped. Ward was amazing. He moved over the mixed rock and snow with a feline grace, no hesitation, an intuitive surety that his three points of contact were good, that his balance and body tension would spot-weld him to the mountain. My most cherished book on alpinism is *Conquistadors of the Useless.* In it Lionel Terray describes how he and his partner, Louis Lachenal, had attained, at times, a state where they were able to "dance in the vertical" seemingly immune to gravity. I saw that in Ward now.

One hundred feet higher the ground opened up and we four individuals made our own choices. Kevin was to my left swinging hard to reach through the snow and get at the ice. Mark and Ward worked their way up the mixed rock and snow on the right. I had made a mistake. I'd thought that the middle ground would cede the easiest passage, require the least force, be less exposed to falling. But I ended up on snow that had no ice under it, then I felt the sickening vibration of my crampon points grating over the featureless rock that was under the snow. I was slowly slipping. If I fell off here, I would die.

A surge of panic locked all of the muscles in my legs, trunk, and left arm. My right hand shot out at a hank of brittle old fixed rope, and mauled it. Immediately I was terrified of the rope snapping and in one vaulting stride I stiffened my left leg like a rifle barrel and bayoneted my crampon into one of Kevin's steps. Feeling my front points bite into ice was miraculous and I hauled off and swung my left hammer with an energy that Thor would have been proud of. Secure again, I breathed my heart rate, and my mind, back down. On some level I was choking on my hubris, but really I was simply grateful to be alive.

After several minutes I climbed on in Kevin's footprints, swinging harder than I had too and kicking with a force that I would not be able to maintain.

His steps swung up in a rising traverse to the left under steep brown rock and toward the Welzenbach Couloir. For the next half hour I allowed the rhythm of my climbing to settle back into step with the mountain. The heads of the cumulous clouds had billowed up and caught us, an Arthurian mist framed Mark and Kevin. They stood anchored to ice screws silently uncoiling our two ropes. Ward and I clipped in and began threading figure-eight knots into our harnesses. It was time to add the security of the rope; the Welzenbach was threatened by an unstable ice cliff the size and shape of an oil tanker's bow. Kevin wrapped my yellow rope around his waist in a traditional hip belay. It was the fastest belay but demanded a lot of skill and attention. I knew that Kevin would hold me if I fell.

We all agreed where the safest line lay, that it would involve harder climbing, and that we could still be crushed by a collapsing wall of sea blue ice.

"We need to dodge to the right as soon as we can," I stated, my heart rate elevating despite the fact that I hadn't moved yet.

"Hail be to that, brother Bubba," joked Mark. Kevin chuckled and Ward locked his blue eyes onto me and smiled.

I pounded into the chute, nervous sweat glazing the small of my back. We barked commands to each other as fear pushed me to move faster while the lack of oxygen compromised my ability to do so. Kevin's constant inquisition didn't help.

"How's it look?"

"Fucking horrible!" I twisted in an ice screw and clipped the rope through it and pounded on.

"How's it going?"

"Slowly!" and I had to sacrifice a full breath to reply, a breath that I could have dedicated to moving.

"Is it safe?"

"No!"

A piton, then the final sprint to a protected belay below a subsidiary couloir where we'd be shielded from the sérac by a fin of rock.

My chest was heaving and my pulse banged away at my temples. I hauled in the rope, threw on a belay and began to bring over the boys.

Ward and Kevin led through and Mark and I followed at the end of one rope each. We climbed up with ice fragments and debris showering down constantly. And then the ropes stopped and frustration built with each direct hit that we took. Mark didn't have a helmet so he suffered more.

"Fuck this noise," he snarled, and with that we both started punching up the ice, long loops of slack grew below us until they were jerked in from above. A sword blade of stone rose from the mist on our right and looked so incredible, mythical.

The couloir ended on a snow mushroom the size of a VW Beetle that was parked against a vertical rockwall. We had to go down and traverse back into the Welzenbach, back under the sérac. I tensioned down to a traverse ledge and back into the line of fire.

"Hey, B! I think that you should anchor where you can and belay us while we lower!" Kevin stated.

I couldn't believe the arrogance of the request and I protested, "Are you all fucking high?" I did not want to hang out under the crusher. Surely they could figure out a way of getting down there. Communication was bad and Kevin was adamant, so I wired up a hasty anchor and belayed Ward over. In a huff I climbed away without a belay. I'd done my bit and I wanted to get out from under that big blue frozen wave. Two more ropelengths and we were level with it, out of harm's way.

It was late afternoon, the cumulous cells had settled with the sun's rotation to the west. Oblique shadows cut across the face and hazed out into the atmosphere like dusty shafts of light slanting down from cathedral windows. Frost descended and we all added layer on top of layer of clothing. I led the steep exit to the Welzenbach climbing well, my axes sunk securely, front points set onto rock edges, my full pack on my back. I'd regained my confidence. Kevin led through onto shallower ground, Ward followed. Mark and I untied from the ropes so that Ward and Kevin could drag them.

The fighting Irish Doyle waded up through thigh-deep snow that was as faceted as the coarse grains of sugar we mixed into our tea.

Laborious work, torturous. Mark, Ward, and I drafted along in Kevin's wake—a trench two feet wide and two and a half feet deep. The three of us wanted to help with the trail breaking...but we couldn't catch up. Kevin kept going. I pushed, floundered, lost ground, while up front I could see him sprinting and stopping, panting, ignoring all of the dictums of altitude and pace, fighting on. Before coming on the trip, Mark, Ward, and I had dedicated hours each day to training for the Rupal. Kevin had gone running twice.

"How can he keep pushing so hard?" Mark panted.

"He can push through pain that stops the rest of us," I replied.

"Kevin's the fastest guy I've ever been in the mountains with," Ward stated.

"I think that he's willing to hurt himself permanently to get what he wants," Mark concluded. And the three of us slogged on trying to catch Kevin.

One hundred and sixty-five feet higher we climbed by a weathered orange duffel that was anchored to the rockwall on our right. A relic from the siege ascents of the past, probably the Japanese in '84. We would have had to traverse fifty feet to get to the bag so we all cataloged it in our minds and continued to try and catch up with Kevin.

We caught up to Kevin one ropelength higher. He'd stopped on a relatively flat roll of snow against the rockwall and dug out his headlamp. He was raking out a flat spot with his crampons.

"I think that we should stop here," he said. "What do you think, Bubba?"

"I think that I need to rest some. That was some fucking amazing trail breaking, that there, Wally."

"Ya, I was feeling good so I thought that I'd give 'er for a bit." He and I both knew that he'd just pushed as hard as only he could.

"Well you managed that, my friend." I had to lean to my axes and pant for a couple of beats. "We couldn't catch you, man." Breathe, breathe. "We couldn't catch you."

Blocks of solidly bonded snow tumbled off into the night. I was doing it again, hacking the shovel blade into the snow like a man possessed, working hard to get good tent platforms. We were at 22,000 feet and had climbed 2,600 feet that day; it would be good to rest.

Forty-five minutes later Mark and Kevin climbed into one tent, and Ward and I the other.

The hanging stove hissed away melting liter after liter of snow. I sat cross-legged at the front of the tent manning the stove and occasionally reaching out into the cold black night to scoop up more snow. At the back of the tent Ward rocked back and forth with his arms clasped tight and his gloved hands holding fast to opposite elbows. His eyes were clamped shut and he moaned to the cadence of his rocking, "*ahhhhh, ahhhhh.*" Pain had begun simmering between his temples as soon as we'd crawled into the tent and settled into our sleeping bags. He'd downed several liters of fluid and I'd given him some Diamox and Tylenol, despite this the pain had amped up.

"Ahhh! Fuck! This hurts!" he blurted.

Eventually he was able to sleep. I set my alarm for 4:00 a.m., less than six hours away. Ward woke to a headache, but stated, "I'm going for it." He took more Tylenol and Diamox. After an hour of brewing up, he started to pack.

The dawn was slow in coming, and with it long skeletal fingers of cirrus reached into the summit pinnacles of the Rupal. An obscuring mist pulsated in and out of our world. "Oh fuck, no, not now," I said to myself. A storm would stop us, it could also challenge our survival in getting down. Thirty-six hours was all that we needed to summit and get back to here. "Please, not a storm now." Clouds rose and engulfed us and I felt a brick stack onto my heart.

Kevin and I busted a trench up onto the arête, there the snow firmed up and allowed us to kick steps. The cloudbank sank and my heart rose with the warmth, and sight, of the sun. Perhaps it would all clear off. A sérac straddled the spur above us and looked, to me, like a ghost version of the Great Wall of China. Left of us it was shattered in the chaotic angular remnants of a recent collapse.

"That looks like death," Mark said, stepping up to Kevin and me. The right flank was steep with a short overhanging section that would be difficult to climb. It glowed. Sculpted edges of glassy ice jutted from alabaster. The face was unbroken and secure looking.

My lead. As it steepened, the straps of my pack pressed down on my shoulders like an opponent's hands and I knew that I wouldn't be able to climb with it. I pounded in an ice screw, shucked the pack off, and left it hanging. Brittle, chrome-colored ice reared past vertical and my pulse began to hammer. Thin air charged in and out and in and out of my bellowing lungs. I breathed three times before moving any one limb. A black-and-white checker pattern oscillated at the edge of my peripheral vision. It felt like I was climbing into a tunnel. I calculated one more stick with my right tool, two vaulting steps, and I gambled that I would be able to stand in balance. The moves stole the last of my endurance and I teetered into balance astride the razor's edge of falling. Fine lines of failure radiated from the tube of the ice screw as I levered on it with my ice ax. A rifle shot cracked from the screw and shot off deep into the ice and for several anxious seconds I stood in shock, still feeling for a shattering that never came, then I continued to twist the screw home. The fractures were symmetrical and beautiful like fine cut glass and I fixed my mind on them as my body breathed itself back to equilibrium.

Higher, I ran out of rope and anchored.

A dismal fog immersed us, from it I saw Mark's pink-and-black suit swimming toward me. He had clipped my pack to the crotch strap of his harness and he was ascending with both his pack and mine. It was a phenomenal effort. I could see it in his heaving chest and agonized face. His lips were peeled back and air ripped across the grate of his teeth.

"Holy shit, Doom!" I yelled, "Let me lower you a loop and I'll haul my pack!"

Unable to speak he pushed my suggestion aside with his hand and labored up. I knew that he was living his philosophy: That which does not kill you will make you stronger.

The snow sucked at my boots and the cloud felt hot, like steam. We wilted and 1,000 feet higher ground to a stop under the shelter of a small triangular sérac. It was one of a pair, the sole interruptions to the massive white cloak of the Merkl Icefield.

It was our fourth day on the Rupal. We were at 23,000 feet above sea level and had climbed 11,500 feet above our base camp. I could feel the shrinkage in my muscles. Each morning I synched the harness tighter. Lactic acid ground against all my motion like coarse sandpaper biting into wood. My eyeballs felt loose in their sockets. We pitched our two small tents at midday and crawled in to bloat ourselves on liquid and gain back what we could on sleep.

It felt strange to rest. I knew that my body needed it, but there was no escaping the knowledge of how exposed we were. If a storm broke we had more than two vertical miles to descend. Our meadow was so far below us. But our spirits rose with each liter we drank, every minute we dozed. In the hour of optimism, before we bed down, we agreed to gun for the summit the next day.

"Twenty-four hours is all we need," said Kevin. "We'll be able to make it to the summit and backtrack to a bivy at the top of the Merkl Gully. I think that it's flat there."

"I don't know Kevin. My head is fucking killing me," Ward replied, and then he groaned. In the awkward moments that followed I worried that Ward could die in the night. He had some degree of altitude sickness, we all knew that. So much of what I'd read and studied on the malady ended in tragedy.

"Look, Ward, either you want to climb this mountain, or you don't," stated Kevin.

More silence.

"I'm going for it," Ward said, and in the tent that I was sharing with him he went back to rocking and groaning. An hour and a half later Ward was still groaning.

"Hey, Ward! Shut the fuck up, man!" shouted Kevin.

"But it makes me feel better," Ward replied.

"Yeah? Well it doesn't make us feel any better. And there's three of us!" countered Kevin. And with that Ward took to suffering in silence.

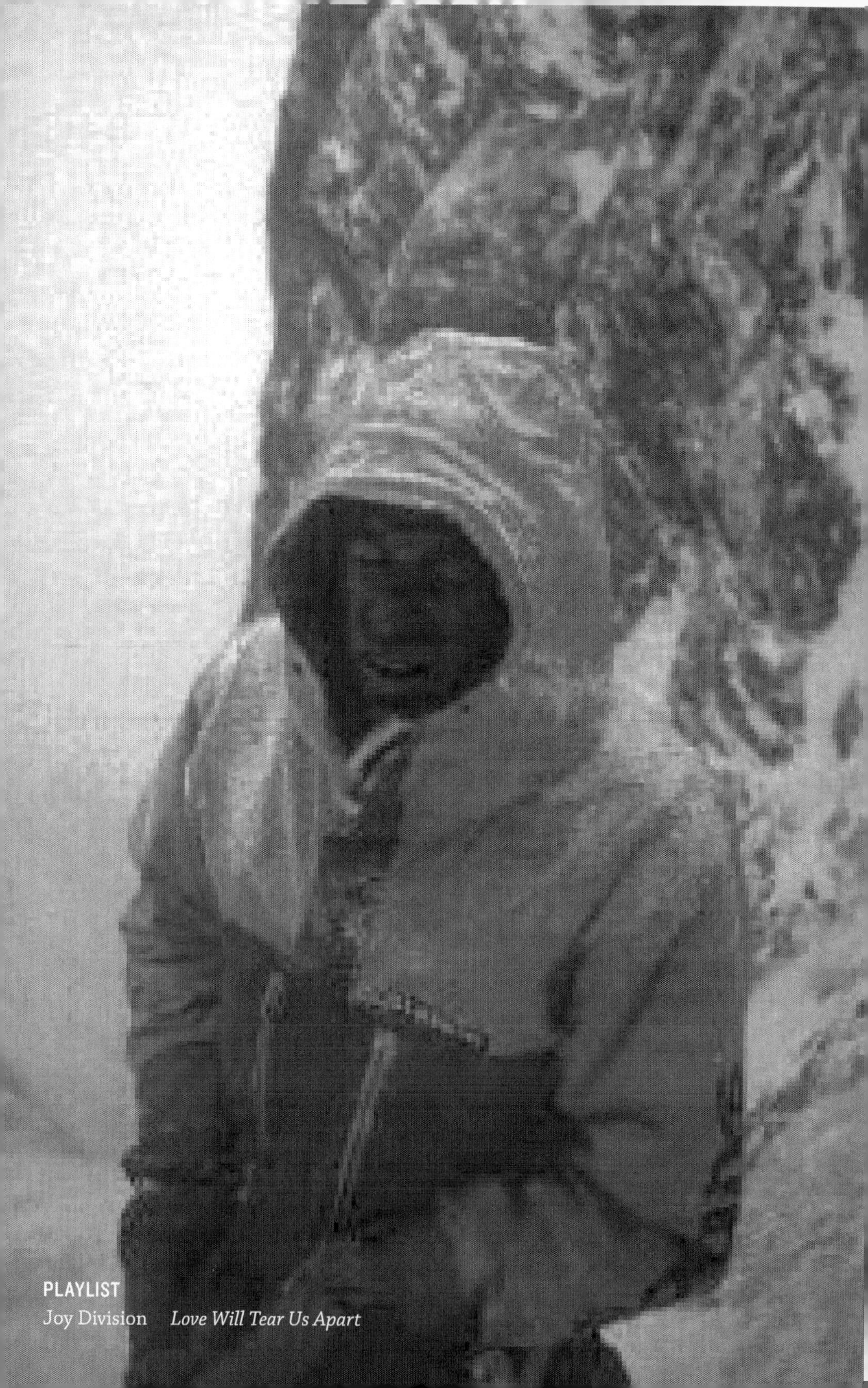

PLAYLIST
Joy Division *Love Will Tear Us Apart*

Chapter 3

THE **STORM**

HALF-INCH-LONG FEATHERS OF FROST grew from the inside walls of the tent—the moisture of our exhaled breath condensed to ice crystals. It sprinkled down with any movement so I eased myself to a sitting position and choked the portal of my sleeping bag down tight to my waist. I needed to keep the hoarfrost out of my bag. I kept a lighter in the breast pocket of my second layer so that it was warm and would work. The cold aluminum of the hanging stove bit through my liner gloves and my numb fingers fumbled to flick the lighter. After five tries, the stove *popped*! to life with a fist-sized blue fireball that lit up the tent like a camera flash and singed my glove liners instantaneously. The acrid smell of burned nylon hung in the tent.

A cold black sky scattershot through by hundreds of stars, light from another world shining through. The Merkl Icefield held the pallor of pewter in the moonlight. It swept up to, and was lost into, the flat black of the Rupal's shadow. Kevin's headlamp slashed left, then right, gaining ground at a foot and a half per step, raging. This night held no fear for him. He devoured the fifteen-hundred-foot Merkl Icefield in an hour and a half. Ate it for breakfast. None of us could catch him. Every hundred steps I stopped to swing blood back into hands gone numb from the cold and, occasionally, feet; Mark was the only one of us who didn't need to do that. Ward fell behind.

Mark later described this picture as "Ward with his soul about to leave his body." Ward subsequently passed out and smacked his head against the ice of the Merkl Gully. Photo: Mark Twight

55

The dawn was clear and icy. Mark, Kevin, and I flaked out the ropes below the entrance to the Merkl Gully. We talked about what we would do if Ward couldn't make it: One of us could stay in a tent with him at the top of the gully while the other two went to the top, we could split the gear and one of us could start descending from here with Ward, or maybe we'd all have to go down. So much ambition, so little empathy.

"I'm doing OK. I can keep going," Ward stated when he arrived.

Mark traversed sixty feet to the left then climbed up toward the Merkl Gully. The sun swept onto him there and from where the three of us stood anchored in the shade, in the last awnings of the night, it looked like the light was shining on him from inside the mountain. Like the castle door had slowly eased open spilling a radiant benediction onto him. Mark was crossing the threshold and only he could see what lay ahead. The three of us wanted to be where he was.

"How does it look?" Kevin bellowed.

"Hard!"

My heart pounded like a war drum inside my chest, my back straightened and my shoulders locked. I felt ready to slay dragons.

Mark led for four ropelengths. Vast plates and knuckles of compact black rock soared into the sky. The left wall bulged to overhanging. Our blunt axes bounced against ice that looked like medieval armor, rounded crampon points rasped jagged white lines of failure.

"We should have brought a file," I said to Kevin. "We could have sharpened our shit in the tent yesterday."

The gully was deep. The rockwalls that contained it were a hundred feet high. In places it necked down to five feet wide.

"You're going to have to lead, Bubba," Mark gasped when I arrived at his high anchor. "My mind is toast."

I shouldered the rack and pounded on. Clouds, all cold now, ebbed in and out of that dark fissure in the mountain.

At 25,300 feet above sea level a ten-foot-high by ten-foot-wide wall of dirty brown ice barricaded the upper gulley. I'd never dreamed that we would find climbing this hard so high on the mountain. Kevin took the lead and fought his way up, his lungs red-lining, his prize-fighter's heart charging. I went next.

The vertical, mud-colored ice demanded more oxygen than my lungs could deliver and my peripheral vision was blacking in as I pulled over the top. I stood for minutes as my lungs heaved thin air in and out at their full capacity. I felt the muscles in my upper back and neck pulling to inflate the last cubic inches from my chest. My head drifted with each inhalation. It felt like I was standing on a wobble board and I fought to keep my balance. One hundred breaths later the gases in my bloodstream had compromised on some sort of equilibrium and I started up to Kevin. Mark came up next, and then Ward.

Two ropelengths higher a spindrift avalanche forced Mark back to the belay; then all hell was unleashed on Nanga Parbat.

A storm smashed into the Rupal and everything went dark. It was like the sun had been totally eclipsed. The rate of the snowfall was hard to believe. Dense white sheets of it slapped into us, plastering everything. It was difficult to see. The first seventy mile per hour windblast shrieked down the gully brushing us to the side like dry grass, then a white-hot explosion of lightning lit our world like a starburst. Everything quivered. The thunderclap was immediate and deafening and I felt a pressure wave pass through my lungs. My chest compressed, and rebounded, then the lightning struck again and in that flash of white light I saw a cornered animal in Kevin's eyes. The thunder sounded like an aircraft fuselage tearing.

The storm raged. I felt the anxiety of the hunted claw its way up inside me. It would be so easy to be overwhelmed, flushed down the sewer like rats. We couldn't climb up through the storm.

"We might be able to dig a cave up against that rockwall!" I screamed through the maelstrom. Ward had retreated inside his hood, his eyes looked blank and dumb and I couldn't tell if he'd understood what I'd said. The hum of building electricity was constant. I waded up and right through surging spindrifts and staggering downdrafts. Kevin followed in my steps.

All of my shovel strikes hit black stone. If we couldn't get inside the relative security of affixed snow, we couldn't stay. It was too steep to pitch our tents—fifty-five degrees—and even if the snow were deep enough to get a platform the spindrift would pile onto the tents like sand, in time it would crush them and shove us off. We wouldn't survive an open bivouac.

"There isn't enough snow!" I shouted at Kevin, "I think we have to go down!"

"Ya, Blanch, you're right," and I saw his jaw strengthen and jut, ready for a fight. "We have to get out of here!"

Kevin and I reversed our steps to Mark and Ward and we began to fight our way down, rappelling through heavier and heavier spin-drift sloughs. I descended first to set anchors, Kevin came next to chop out stances, and Ward came third contained and protected within the sequence. He was hurting. He spoke short words now and we all knew that we had to get him down. Mark was the lightest, he came down last after pulling any backup anchors. The avalanche hit us at the bottom of our third rappel.

After the avalanche: six hours for six rappels. The storm settled to steady snowfall driven by wind. Spindrifting snow flowed constantly over the black rock. It looked like the roiling water of a creek tumbling over bedrock. Every half hour avalanches thundered down the gully. Their physical fronts were terrifying, walls of charging snow that would crash by us like big ocean waves. The Merkl had become an inhuman place, but we four were not hammered again, we always managed to scurry to the sides when we heard the roar of the onslaught, seconds before it came.

"Here comes another one!" Kevin bellowed as he leaned onto the ropes and drove to the edge of the gulley. I'd chosen another protected place to anchor and I grabbed at my leash as everything went black. My body vibrated against the rush and the pressure of the charging snow, my left shoulder was pressed against the cold hard rock and only the rock felt solid, unmoving, everything else seemed to be flowing down. Slowly black sifted to gray and the roar subsided back to the steady tearing of the wind. None of these subsequent slides lasted as long as the first—the one that had almost killed us.

We were fighting to survive, and we fought hard and we fought well. All of my experience and energy was focused on getting the four of us down. In my heart I knew that the storm could rage for days.

The anxiety of being swept off was constant. Always there was the possibility of the next slide being big enough to rip us off; yet as the hours, and the avalanches, passed, we locked into the routine of the descent: rappel, anchor, chop a stance, get all of us down—repeat. Our job was to get out of hell.

At dusk we rappelled through the gates to the Merkl. This time Kevin went down first. Next was Ward. I could see ten extra years in his face. Deep creases fell from eyes that had shrunk and no longer filled out their sockets. Jaundiced skin sagged.

Twenty-five feet into the rappel Ward looked back up to Mark and me. "I can't breathe," he said, and his eyes sank from us as his body slumped forward and his head bounced against the metal-hard ice.

"Oh fuck," I said. I did not know what to do. Beside me I heard Mark stacking up deep draws of breath, then he began shouting commands, "C'mon, Ward!...Get up, man!...Get on your feet, Robinson!...You are not going to fucking die here!" I pulled and jerked on the ropes.

A few beats passed. Breathless from shouting, Mark heaved in lungfuls of thin air. I hauled hard on the taut lines that connected us to Ward. More anxious heartbeats, then the yellow fabric of his hood quivered and snow fell away and the force of his will pushed him upright. He pressed a gloved fist against the pewter-colored ice and wordlessly stepped back into his rappel.

"That was too fucking close," Mark panted.

Kevin and I fighting to dig a snow cave at our highpoint in the Merkl Gully. Photo: Mark Twight

"I thought Ward was dead," my voice cracking with sorrow, and regret. Later, after the Rupal, Mark and I would joke about how we had watched Ward's soul leave his body when he'd looked up to us. Perhaps only Ward knows if that is a joke or not. Ultimately alpinism is a measure of the human heart. Simply put, Ward is the toughest man I've ever climbed with. He will always fight.

"We have to take care of him," I said.

"I'm on it," Mark replied.

Kevin and I stood at the next anchor, our last before hitting the Merkl Icefield.

"The ropes are not going to pull through that," I said pointing to a sheaf of rock plates. Already the ropes were clamped tight into two separate vices. "I'll throw them off and down climb."

"Alright," said Kevin, "I'll rap down and help Mark with Ward."

Ward has quaking with hypothermia when he landed at the lower anchor. Mark carved out a ledge for him in the snow. He got Ward into his sleeping bag and fired up a stove. Ward got the first hot liquid—soup—that we'd seen in eighteen hours.

"Off rappel!" Kevin's command came from the dark. I twisted my headlamp on. Snow swirled with the twisting tension of a blizzard trapped in the high beams. I unclipped the ropes and heaved them off. They whipped through the frame of my headlamp then sliced into the night. I removed the anchor—we'd need all the gear we had to get down—then stepped down and planted my front points. Carefully I climbed down onto the icefield.

Ward had come halfway back to life with the soup and the heat of his sleeping bag. The warrior within him had risen to his feet and Mark was stuffing his sleeping bag when I arrived.

"I can lower Ward on both ropes tied together," I said. "That'll get him down 400 feet."

"No!" Ward barked, "I can get down this myself." And as I hauled at the ropes to stack them Ward stepped down and began following Mark down the Merkl Icefield.

"Hey!" I shouted. "Let us at least take your pack, man. Kevin and I can get that down for you."

"Ya, Ward, that's a good idea. Give us your pack."

Ward shucked it into Kevin's sure grip, then turned back to kick down Mark's steps.

Kevin tied the pack into one end of our ropes and I ran the ropes through a friction hitch at the anchor as Kevin jockeyed the pack sideways down the Merkl. The rope spiraled through the hitch six inches at a time.

Finally I held the end in my hands. Kevin stood 400 feet below me. I could no longer see his headlamp. The rope came tight, then stopped. I held the end out from the wall.

"I'm letting go of the ropes!" I bellowed.

Two ropelengths lower, Kevin heard: "Let...go of the ropes."

"OK!" He shouted, untying his end from Ward's pack. I let go of my end. Kevin felt a powerful tug when the ropes whipped past him far off to his left.

"OK! OK! If you want them that bad, you can have them," he muttered to himself. Our yellow and red ropes, the 400 feet of braided and hawser-laid Perlon that tacked us onto the mountain—kept us safe—tumbled off into the night. I assumed that Kevin had them, he assumed I did. Neither of us realized then that the ropes were gone.

White snow spiraled into black night. It took several hours to down climb the Merkl. Each of us largely locked in the cells of our own movement. Mark arrived first at the tent platforms we'd left twenty-two hours earlier. He had the new snow cleared from one of the platforms and was pushing a pole into a tent when I showed up. Somewhere above us Kevin was helping Ward down.

"Fuck!" Mark spat it out. I twisted to see the yellow tent slither off down the face, its fabric rasping. The flexed pole had sprung the tent from Mark's gloved hand. A mistake, one that Mark was already beating himself up about. He stared after the tent, dumbfounded, then he echoed a joke that Ward and I had told him from a similar situation earlier that year, "Well, we don't have to carry that anymore." He drew his arm back and threw the poles off after the tent.

"I'll start digging a snow cave," he said.

We finished it just as Ward and Kevin arrived. Kevin and Mark crawled into the cave. Ward's face was back to a normal color and he was aware again. He helped me to anchor the tent then he and I crawled in. The four of us did not fall asleep so much as we collapsed into comas.

Morning, the one cup of piss in my pee bottle looked like thirty-weight motor oil. My anus burned with a clear caustic fluid that my body was excreting. Mark had long ago, after other hard days, named it "butt vinegar." I smelled like matted sweat and fear.

The world was gray. Snow had stopped falling and the wind was gone, we were immersed in charcoal-colored cloud. Twelve inches of wind-bonded snow rested on every surface that was less than vertical. My mind ran a horror show clip: A black crack shot across the Merkl Icefield, the wind slab below failed, then checker boarded into chunks before churning into chaos. None of us said much as we packed up. Then I asked Ward, "Have you got the yellow rope?"

"I haven't seen the yellow rope...or the red."

A long solemn moment passed as the four of us realized that no one had seen the ropes since yesterday.

"They have to be here," I stated, a narrow uneasiness teetering my voice. Then I ripped into my pack.

"No! No!" I bleated as each pack emptied and no ropes appeared. We searched the ledges and the snow cave. Kevin and I relived our exchange of the night before.

"I said, 'I'm letting go of the ropes.'"

"I heard, 'Let go of the ropes,'" Kevin replied, then added, "Aw, fuck!"

It was like we were witnessing the hull split, seeing the rush of green water sluicing in and all of us knowing that we were going to the bottom. Four pairs of gaping eyes met and for four heartbeats no one breathed.

"They have to be here!" Panic was rising in my voice. "They have to fucking be here!" And then I lost it, snapped like a dry twig, the closest I've ever come to having a nervous breakdown. I grabbed my axes and charged into the slope ripping into the fresh and lethal windslab, trying to fish out the ropes. Frantic desperation floundering toward defeat.

"Bubba, come back man," Mark said sternly. "You're going to kick off a slab out there dude."

"Ya, Blanche, it's not good out there. The ropes are gone, Bubba, they're gone," Kevin added.

My arms and legs quaked with each thrust as I traversed back to the ledge. I trembled with adrenalin, and then it left and I crashed. The panic left. My throat felt dusty, the sand-dry taste of exhaustion. I slumped over next to the ledge my head bowed and heaving. I was spent. Kevin reached down and pulled me up.

We sat on our packs and lowered our heads. Then Kevin looked up and said, "We can down climb to the old fixed rope and cut some of it out to rappel on."

"You mean that yellow waterskiing stuff?" Mark asked.

"What else can we do?" Kevin replied. "We'll get down this."

"There might be something we can use in that bag that's back on the last rockwall," Ward added.

We tacked our way down on the edge of the slab. One thousand feet lower Ward put his knife to the crackling orange fabric of the bag and cut into a miracle: thirty pitons, fifteen screws, two dozen carabiners, ten four-year-old Fruit and Nut chocolate bars, and, perfectly preserved and encased in ice in the bottom, two brand new ropes! We chipped them out with the tenderness of archeologists then ran them through a friction hitch to clear them of ice.

"Oh my fucking lord!" chortled Mark. "They're Beals! The same brand as our sponsorship!" We laughed until the tears ran. Kevin gagged on one of the briquette-like chocolate bars and we laughed more. When the laughter subsided he said, "Now we have a chance."

"We owe each of those Japanese guys one," Mark added.

I set anchors. We rappelled all day, slid down thousands of feet. I made myself do everything right and none of the raps jammed.

The cloud stayed. Some of the time we glimpsed snippets of the mountain, most of the time our world went to gray within a radius of fifty feet. Sometimes it snowed, sometimes it didn't.

Toward dusk we down climbed the ice arête and regained our camp on top of the crescent glacier, 19,520 feet. Kevin was adamant on melting water while the rest of us fell into sleep. A couple hours later he woke to silence, the stove having long since ran out of gas. The water had boiled off and the aluminum pot had been fired to the point of flaking.

The next day we opted not to down climb diagonally below the Wieland Rocks—the way we'd come up—but instead rappel to, and descend, the broken glacier below. We could walk there, while the ice face skirting the Wieland Rocks would demand front pointing.

Midday I descended to my three partners standing stymied by a large and overhanging crevasse. We looked down from the topside of a twenty-foot drop.

"There's nothing to rap off of," Ward stated, "and there's no way around it."

I came as close as I dared to the edge and began stamping out a platform. The snow I displaced rushed away like a waterfall splattering onto the lower lip far below.

"Here's hoping that it's soft down there," I said.

"You're not going to..." Mark asked, his chin in retreat.

"Hell yes I am." Then I squared off, held my breath, and launched. A charging rush of air, my arms and axes windmilled forward for several full revolutions, then the hammering crunch of compression, and blackness, a starburst of white light inside my eyelids. But no pain. I opened my eyes. I had augured in chest deep.

"It's OK!" I shouted as I thrashed to free myself from the snow.

"Oh! Fuuuuck!" wailed Mark as he leapt, likewise Ward, and then Kevin. It was a comical bit of lightness in an otherwise dark and malevolent space. Like we had returned to boyhood for the moments that it took to take the dare and jump. Then it was back to the march through storm and avalanche, back to war.

The glacier gave way to snow, the snow led to shattered rock. Snowfall morphed to sleet and, finally, heart-crushingly, it became rain. We got soaked to the bone and looked like drowned rats, but with each meter we descended the threats retreated. For the first time in four days, since the storm started, we began to lower our guard.

The reek of ammonia hung constant in my nostrils. We'd run out of food and I knew that my body had been digesting muscle. I'd felt that change when we'd climbed into the Merkl Gully. There was always a period of low energy while my body abandoned food and switched to burning stored fat. When it ran out of that it started in on muscle. Now it felt like I was burning brain tissue. I had to stop often and rest. When I'd get up I felt weak and lightheaded, like I might faint. Before the rain I could feel the bagginess of my clothes, daily I'd seen the wasting when I snugged up my harness tighter and tighter. Now everything hung heavy and wet on me like I'd just stepped, fully clothed, from five minutes in the shower.

The four of us were sitting and regrouping on a flat spot on the ridge when Kevin lost it. The zipper on his salopettes had, once again, jammed on the stupid flaps of fabric that supposedly made them windproof.

"That's fucking *it*!" he cursed, bolting upright and shearing the legs apart with his powerful hands. *Rrripppp*! "I've had it with these fucking-piece-of-shit pants!" He swung them through a mighty roundhouse, water arcing off of them, and slapped them onto the wet rock. *Smack*! Then he sat down triumphantly on his pack. Mark, Ward, and I waited. We'd already started talking about coming back up for a second attempt. Gradually the smug rage left Kevin's face.

"I guess that wasn't very smart, was it? I'll need those pieces-of-shit if we come back up here."

"Don't worry about it, Wally," I offered. "I've got another pair in base camp that will work. You're welcome to them, buddy."

At 6:00 p.m. we walked, wet and weary, into base camp. Chanzeb and Sahjad fried us up paratha and eggs, brewed sweet milky tea, but we ate halfheartedly. The feeding frenzy would begin in the morning. Sleep was the important thing now.

That night I dreamed of my wife, and sunshine, as the rain pounded down on the tent fly. The storm lasted nine more days. Thirteen days in total.

The next day we ate for hours and hours.

"We are going to need more food," Kevin observed, wiping his shirtsleeve across lips glistening with grease. All of the good stuff was gone and the storm was showing no sign of letting up. We decided to send Chanzeb and Kevin off to Astor to buy more food. Three days later they returned burdened with food, and stories, and we gathered around our blue picnic cooler table.

On July 24, 1988, the sun came out. Three days later we bivouacked at our high camp. We were at the bottom of the Merkl Icefield at 23,000 feet, and we'd climbed 11,500 feet in two and a half days. Knowing what we now knew about the Central Spur, we'd climbed all of that terrain ropeless. The face had lost much of its mystery.

Ward quietly endured a torturous headache that night. His will could not force his body to accept the altitude. We agreed that he would retreat with one of our ropes while Mark, Kevin, and I went for the top with the other.

At dawn on the twenty-eighth the three of us stood at the gates of the Merkl Gully. A lenticular cloud was drawn taut over the summit of Nanga Parbat. I realized that I was living in the dream that I'd visualized seven weeks earlier when Ward and I had sat on boulders on the Chhungphar Glacier and laughed, then gazed to the wave of cloud stretched tight over the top of the Rupal for the first time. The cloud was the harbinger of another storm.

"We do not need to get our asses handed to us again," Mark said.

We down climbed to Ward. Thirteen hours later we clomped wearily into base camp.

Porters and donkeys came in the morning. Midday, in Tarshing, we climbed onto the first of a series of jeeps that relayed us between rockslides and blasting sites, all of which blocked the road.

Darkness halted us. Chanzeb arranged for us to pitch our tents in a field next to one of the road-blasting camps. The guy in charge, who held the same rank as Chanzeb—army captain—invited us into his wall tent for tea and a video. A kerosene lamp lit the tent and the tea was made on a kerosene stove. Outside a small gas generator hummed. It was jury-rigged to an old TV and older VCR. Young Arabic women twirled across the screen competing in what looked like the

The Merkl Gully sits dead center below the summit of Nanga Parbat; our highpoint was one rope length below its end. Photo: Mark Twight dance of the seven veils without unveiling anything. Insects chirped on the other side of the canvas wall as the cool of the black night slid down the slopes of Nanga Parbat. Inside we sipped tea and gazed at the first source of light and sound, other than fire, that we had seen in over two months. We'd stepped back, the descent into civilization had begun.

Heat quivered over Islamabad like a mirage. The fans at the Ministry of Tourism squawked revolution on revolution. I'd been listening to Joy Division for thirty-six hours, and rereading Sam Shepard's *Motel Cronicles* for the third time, when the young deputy minister, who pined for London discos, asked how Nanga Parbat was, I wanted to shock him.

"It was like having sex with death." I said.

I always believed that I would return to the Rupal, for the next five years I even considered soloing the route. Now I know that I won't be going back there.

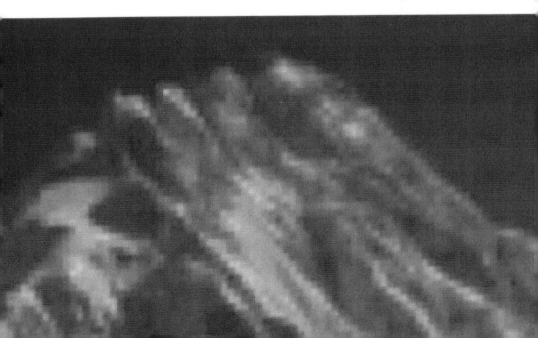

Chapter 4

GROWING UP

IN MY MIND the gunshot shatters the tranquility of the Southern night and I see my paternal great grandmother, Esther, charge to my grandmother, Irene, and clamp her hard in her arms, crush her to her chest, protect her. My great-grandfather Blanchard had murdered Irene's baby sister in her crib. Infanticide. The world falls apart.

My great-grandmother fled the southeastern United States to Canada. She and Irene landed in Medicine Hat, Alberta, in the 1920s. There she met and married widower Harry Edwards, a railroad man. Irene was melded in with the seven Edwards boys and raped by one of them when she was twenty. My father was born the bastard of a crime that no one could talk about. He was a Blanchard, as Irene had remained. Kenneth Norman Blanchard. The surname has come down to me.

By the age of twenty Stormin' Norman was an effective and accommodating bellboy on the local hospitality scene. He owned a convertible and was a master at piloting it "sidesaddle"—sitting at right angles to the steering wheel and controlling it lazily with his left hand, his right arm stretched over the bench seat invitingly, right knee jauntily hitched up onto the seat and the gas and brake worked by his left foot. His buddy assumed the same "come onto the couch" posture in the back seat as they cruised Main Street prowling for

Christmas, 1963, at my grandma's house. Medicine Hat, Alberta. Photo: Barry Blanchard Collection

69

girls in bobby socks and blue jeans. My mother, Paulette Frances Pelletier, had quit school in grade eleven and been accepted into the Air Force. But before joining, she and her cousin, Anne, bused to Medicine Hat from Indian Head, Saskatchewan, to vacation while staying with Anne's aunt. They were walking down the main street of "the Hat" on their second day in town when Norm's convertible purred up.

My mother was a knockout: A hauntingly beautiful and mysterious Métis princess. She could have acted Elizabeth Taylor's part in *National Velvet* if the story had taken place in an Indian Nation. We Métis are a distinct culture in Canada. Early Scottish, English, and French fur traders intermarried with native women. Their country-born sons and daughters became the Métis—the mixed-blood. For over two hundred years my maternal ancestors made their living hunting buffalo off of horseback, trapping for fur, and guiding across the great Canadian Northwest, an area that is now the provinces of Manitoba, Saskatchewan, and Alberta.

One of my forebears was Cuthbert Grant, son of a Scottish father and Métis mother. At a young age Cuthbert was sent away to be edu-cated at Grant's College in Scotland. When he returned he went to work in the fur trade and eventually rose to the position of captain of the buffalo hunt, the highest title within Métis culture in the early 1800s. In 1816, at the age of twenty-three, Cuthbert led the Métis to victory in a bloody confrontation at Frog Plain in modern day Winnipeg, Manitoba.

The Hudson's Bay Company had embargoed the trade of pemmican. Pemmican is dried buffalo meat and fat pounded together with prairie berries and was the staple for the voyageurs that paddled the fur trading canoes. Its sale was also the Métis' principal source of livelihood. The confrontation, in which the governor of the Red River Colony, Robert Semple, along with twenty other Hudson's Bay men and settlers were killed, is more widely known in Canada as the Battle of Seven Oaks. Later in life Grant was appointed warden of the plains.

Now I meditate on the sole surviving picture of Cuthbert and I easily see my eyes in his, my face the shape of his face. I close my eyes and I can feel the prairie quake under the thundering onslaught of hundreds of thousands of buffalo hooves, I can see the golden dust rise to black out the sun like a sandstorm in the Sahara. I was gifted adventure in my blood.

My mom and her sister, my Auntie Joanne, had an old black-and-white picture of my maternal grandfather, Paul, and his two brothers, Albert and John—'The Three Musketeers'—framed for me. It is from the spring of 1940 and they're stood against a barbwire fence in the Qu'Appelle Valley. Stalks of willow braid a backdrop that haunts of the low woven fences that I've touched within vacated sun-dance lodges, lodges that are in the process of going back to mother earth. The three brothers are dressed in their regimental khakis, and my granduncle Albert holds a hand-rolled cigarette between the trigger and middle finger of his right hand. Albert's arm hangs long and the wet end of the roll-up rests against his right thigh. All three are smiling into the camera. They look proud.

My grandfather is roughly the same age as I was when I attempted the Rupal Face of Nanga Parbat and incredible to me is that we were both sporting the same haircut—a wide over the top Mohawk with whitewalls, shaved sides—albeit I had a lot of "party-at-the-back" going on in Pakistan. I look like him.

'The Three Musketeers' shipped overseas. My grandfather was wounded at Dieppe in 1942. The raid on the German-held French beach on the English Channel was a bloody, bloody day for Canada. Of the 6,000-strong Allied Infantry, 5,000 were from Canada. The Canadians numbered 3,367 of those killed, wounded, or taken prisoner. Paul got plucked from the water, gunshot and bleeding.

My grandfather is the man that I most identify with in my family. I hold great pride in his wartime service, and in his endurance and dedication as a father and provider. I always imagined that I would grow up to be a carpenter like him. For many years I have prayed to him, offered tobacco to the sky, the earth, the four cardinal directions, and, lastly, toward my chest; recently I have done the same in the name of his firebrand partner, my grandmother, Josephine.

"I don't like being married," my mother quaked over the phone.

"You come home girl," Josephine replied.

I was three, my sister, Kimberly, one. Norman and Paulette were divorced soon after. My mother met Gerry Roy and entered into a common law marriage with him and we moved to Calgary, Alberta. My brother David was born in 1963, my sister Glenna in '65. I remember my mother holding my hand and walking me to my first day of grade one at Sunalta School that year, 1965. My youngest brother, Steven, came in '66.

The house at 1905 Tenth Avenue SW in Calgary was a "Victory" house, one of many built to accommodate Calgarians returning from the war in 1945. Gerry Roy, the father of my youngest sister and brother, Glenna and Steven, had found it and the rent was cheap because its owner had hung himself in the root cellar. We rented from the dead man's widow. One day in the late sixties Glenna and Steven pounded up the stairs wailing "bloody blue murder," as my mom is fond of saying. They had seen a man with horns, "a Viking," in the root cellar. From that day on they refused to set foot in it.

The heavy four-pointed glass ashtray thumped into the plaster wall like a large caliber bullet. Gerry Roy ducked; plaster shards rained down onto the back of his head and right arm wrapped over it for protection. The ashtray smacked onto the floor. It did not break. My mother had thrown it from the far side of the living room where she stood trembling with rage and confusion and heartbreak. Her tears ran down a face that clicked between crumpled sorrow and rock-hard rage as she hurled profanities and accusations—and objects—at Gerry. My four siblings and I stood in the doorways to our two shared rooms crying, shaking, and desperately protesting, "No! Mommy no! Please stop!"

I yearned to be bigger, to be a man and to be able to step in and put a stop to the violence. Gerry flipped a derogatory insult at my mother and she darted into the kitchen. I saw panic in his eyes as he fumbled with the front door knob, then vaulted down the snow-covered steps two at time going sideways in his slippery black dress shoes anxiously grabbing for the handrails. My mother hauled the door open and arched her back and put all she had into the butcher knife. It clattered into the fence close to where Gerry's hand was white-knuckling the gate, fear and shock sparked in his eyes. He clambered into the back of the Yellow Taxi and pulled away, soon to pull right out of our lives.

Alberta had long since baked out to brown. The parched prairie rolled on in endless fields of wheat, braised brown clear out to the horizon. My forehead was pressed to the cool glass of the window of the Greyhound Scenicruiser, where the Freon-smelling crisp air hissed up. Grandmother Irene had walked me onto the bus in Medicine Hat.

I'd held her hand as she asked the bus driver, "Would you look out for him, would ya? He's my grandson."

The driver was a big man and he wore the gray uniform and gray driver's cap and he pinched the bill between his right forefinger and thumb and said, "Yes mam, I will. Put the little fellow in the front seat there where I can see him."

My mother, Paulette (left), holding me, and one of her eighty-one first cousins, Bertha (pushing the stroller), and Bertha's daughter, Leanne, not amused at having their picture taken by a street photographer. Indian Head, Saskatchewan.
Photo: Barry Blanchard Collection

"Would you like to see some cool pictures?" I'll guess the woman speaking to me was about twenty-five and I remember her having slate-colored hair and gray eyes and a casualness in the way she sat with her legs wrapped under her like women were not supposed to sit in 1968. I was nine years old and for the next hundred miles she read to me from *The White Spider* and showed me photos of Heinrich Harrer, Fritz Kasparek, Anderl Heckmair, and Ludwig Vörg, the four men who made the first ascent of the north face of the Eiger.

Heroism murmured like clear creek water in the words she recited to me. I could see it in the black-and-white pictures of men tied to each other with a twisted braid of hemp and pitoned to the dark precipice, their heads hooded and bowed to an onslaught of spindrifted snow showering down on them from the hourglass of time. These men were living to a higher ideal then most of the men that I'd known in my life. As the bus edged on to Calgary I could see the blue bulk of the Rockies serrating the far horizon, something called to me.

It was the later part of August. My mother stood waiting for me at the bus station in Calgary. She held her black vinyl purse in front of her with both hands. She smiled beautifully to me as the driver walked behind me down the steps from the bus. He'd called me, 'little man.' "Be careful on these steps little man."

"Did you have fun at your grandmother's?"

"Yes mom, I did." We walked out and caught a city bus home.

"Let's get rid of this creepy crawler," my Aunt Marlene slurred drunkenly to my sister, Kim. Auntie, and the man that she had been drinking with, had just staggered into the little hole of an apartment that she was renting above a Chinese restaurant on Seventeenth Avenue SW in Calgary. It was 1972 and Kim was eleven and babysitting our infant cousin, Danielle, whom we all called 'Cookie,' and who was sound asleep in her crib. The guy was taking a piss and when he stumbled out of the bathroom Marlene told him that he had to leave. He didn't and Marlene was soon poking him in the chest and telling him to "get the fuck out!"

He came out swinging and threw Marlene onto the couch wrapping her long black hair into his left hand and slugging her in the face with his right—repeatedly. Kim was frozen into stone at the foot of the couch. Horror had short-circuited her being. She remembers that every time he bent over to hit his too tight jeans popped open and that he had to stand to re-snap them and then lean in to hit again.

Blood dripped from my auntie's face. He threw the case of beer they'd bought home against the wall and it exploded and showered Marlene in glass and froth. Kim remembers beer and blood and terror. Done, he staggered away. Marlene pulled herself together and swayed downstairs and the restaurateur called the police.

Tears, self-recrimination, and anger swirled around our kitchen table as my mother and her four sisters talked through the beating. Marlene wore dark sunglasses over black eyes. The whites of her eyes were patched and hazed with blood. I was thirteen years old and I burned to be full grown. I wanted to find her assailant and I wanted to kill him and I knew that I would do that without fear, and without mercy. That night, alone, in the room that I'd moved into in the basement, I lay awake for long hours and I swore an oath to myself, "I will never be a man who hits women."

By a fluke of geography I grew up in a poor, old, industrial part of Calgary called Sunalta (Sunny Alberta), yet one city block to the south a glacially sculpted rise of land ascended into one of the richest neighborhoods in town, Scarboro. I went to school with, and was raised beside, some of the wealthiest kids in Calgary, as well as some of the poorest, like me.

Somehow my mom squeezed enough out of our welfare check to buy me a Scout uniform and I was able to join the eighty-seventh troop. Jonathan Body, my declared "best friend" from grade one; Bobby Williams, three years older than me and my boyhood mentor from across the alley; Mark Wolfe, Bobby's best friend and two years older than me; and I would walk up to Scarboro United Church on Wednesday nights. It was a beautiful white chapel on the hill. One of our scoutmasters, Mr. Montgomery, had been a mountain climber, but he'd taken a fall and had to give it up. He cut a heroic figure of medium height with wide, powerful shoulders and blonde hair swept back, his Scouting uniform complemented and emphasized by a Peterson Aran pipe. In my mind I see Clint Eastwood in *The Eiger Sanction* when I think back to Mr. Montgomery.

I can still hear Mr. Montgomery's words: "The rock spike that I landed on got through my pack, through its wooden frame and canvas back pad, through all of my clothing, and still took a chunk out of my back." He cradled the bowl of the Peterson and withdrew it from between his lips and teeth. Blue smoke seeped out on his exhaled breath and it smelt sweet, like honey and pine. "I haven't been able to climb since."

He told it like a war story and it held all of us rapt, including the other three grown men who were his fellow leaders. My heart drummed inside my chest, something reverberated in my bloodstream.

"Mr. Montgomery is the real thing," Bobby stated on the way back down the hill. He had his hands stuffed deep into his pockets and his gaze fixed straight ahead. His posture challenged the rest of us to disagree. None of us did.

"He's a hero," Bobby concluded. There where no strong father figures among us and we hungered for strong, clear, and just masculine role models. Within our boys' tribe we etched out codes of being, strived to define right and wrong, emulate the heroic, and battle the bad.

"I want to be a mountain climber," I said. And the ambition may have as well been to be an astronaut as I'd been to the mountains maybe twice during my young life of poverty.

Later that year Bobby wrote a story that gained him some of the only accolades he would receive in the course of his education. Two men are ascending a mountain. One dies in a fall and his partner valiantly digs a grave for him in the ice with his ice ax. I felt like I was receiving something hallowed as Bobby read it to Mark and me. It resonated in my blood. The story came back to me in 1985 when I saw the same plotline in Theatre Calgary's production of the Broadway play, *K2*. Ironically I would perform as the climbing double for the character that dies—Harold—in Hollywood's 1991 version of *K2*.

A new house, a new life. Paulette moved us from the haunted Victory house in Sunalta to the southwestern edge of Calgary and a newly built four-bedroom townhouse in Gladstone Park, a complex that included a lot of government subsidized housing. She was thirty-one years old with five children between the ages of five and twelve. She'd thrown the last object at Gerry Roy earlier that year; she would never again live with a man.

Two months into grade seven was a hard time to be uprooted. I got challenged to a fight on my first day at A. E. Cross Junior High School. Phil Conway called down on me, but we never did fight, rather we went on to be good friends who have tried to figure out some of life together. Phil would be the first guy I ever went climbing with, but first I learned to rappel.

Grade eight, I was thirteen when I decided to join the 1292 Lord Strathcona's Horse Army Cadets (I'd left Scouting when we left Sunalta). One fall day I had jet-black hair down to my shoulders, and the next it was stubble shorn clean down to the white of my scalp. The ridicule was merciless. Many of the guys I knew chased me down the halls to rub my head and laugh. None of them had decided to join, to be a 'Herbie.' I found a secluded corner and cried, then sucked it up and put on a bold face. The six other cadets that I knew had all run the same gauntlet.

It was a warm spring day when our Department of Defense bus pulled into the camp north of Calgary. Alberta was greening up. Fields of verdant farmland rolled into foothills that, in turn, bordered the blue Rockies, their peaks thrust into the azure sky. We stepped off the bus and jostled into a standing formation.

The rappel tower was thirty feet high and had been built just after the Second World War. Our rappel master was a regular in the Canadian Forces and as soon as it was hot enough he stripped off his khaki field shirt. The man was barrel-chested and ginger colored. The fading tattoos on his squat forearms were fuzzed over with a rust-colored fleece of hair. He took charge and taught us how to tie a simple diaper harness from a length of one-inch tubular military spec webbing. A single steel carabiner was clipped into the focal knot of the harness with the hawser-laid rope spiraled up the spine of the 'biner for three revolutions.

The hardwired mammalian fear of falling backward to the earth seized my psyche when I backed into position and it felt like a strong hand was squeezing my throat.

Our weathered rappel master had seen it many times. "Relax lad. You can trust the rope. Look at me lad, breathe. You can do it."

My teetering and jolting first steps saw me clamping down on my brake hand with every move, and then the rope lay to the edge of the tower and I found stability and started walking backward down the boot worn, desiccated planks that had felt the tread of thousands of cadets and soldiers before me. The ribs of rope made the rappel jittery, it felt like I was bouncing down the stairs on my butt.

I loved it, did as many rappels as time allowed before we broke, and filed back onto the bus. Within me, deeper than the military applications, a wee flame flickered—rappelling was a mountain climbing skill. I sat at the rear of the bus and looked back to the Rockies as we pulled away.

"I'll smuggle the smokes in, and you sell them for twenty-five cents a piece. We'll split the profits." He was a civilian janitor who'd taken to talking to me.

"Sounds good to me, I'm in."

I got dismissed from the National Army Cadet Camp in Vernon, British Columbia. That summer, 1973, was the end of my military career. At least the cigarette money had been good, I didn't smoke.

My best friend, Jonathan Body, is a naturally gifted athlete. At full sprint he would toss his head side to side to draw air and his flaxen hair would stream and fan behind him like a horse's mane. He'd have pulled away from me at stride number three and none of the boys could catch him as he just kept getting smaller and smaller in the distance up ahead.

In the early 1900s a number of four- to six-story-high red brick warehouses went up along Eleventh Avenue SW in Calgary. The J. H. Ashdown Hardware Warehouse was built in 1910. In 1972 the building was bought by the Lewis Stationery Company and one year later, at two thirty in the morning, Jon and I were on the building's roof and crouched tight to its waist-high facade that fronted onto Eleventh Avenue. Sixty feet below a Calgary City Police cruiser had pulled up, and stopped, directly in front of the building. Our boy's world of fantasy, adventure, and fun instantaneously dissolved into fear and crime and punishment.

The climbing rope had had a glistening sheen where it sat on the shelf in the old Hostel Shop. It was 165 feet long and nine millimeters in diameter and it felt tight bound in the factory wrap.

"What do you think?" Jonathan had asked.

"This is the one," I replied, noting that we could afford it and that it was dark, like the night.

We bought it to further our ambitions as cat burglars (an ambition that we'd picked up from an episode of the TV series, *Banacek*). Friday night I'd bused down to Jon's and we'd organized a "sleep-out" in the pop-top trailer that his father had built. At 1:00 a.m. we switched on flashlights and pulled on dark clothing, then retrieved the rope and our one carabiner from their hiding place and stealthily started making our way up the back alleys of Eleventh Avenue.

An old iron emergency fire escape ladder was drawn up off of sidewalk level by a counterweighted cable and pulley. Jonathan could just catch the bottom rung with his maximal running jump. He caught it in his right hand and clung and the ladder banged down rung by rung clanging and resonating through all six stories of the fire escape's metal structure. It sounded like a freight train braking. I grabbed on to the rungs and Jon and I stood stock still listening for any sound or alarm along the deserted and dimly lit side street. We were poised to hightail it. I listened to my heart pound ten times and then we were on our way up.

"What's he doing?" Jon asked. Our blue climbing rope was tied off to the flagpole and thrown down the right side of the building. I'd tied the diaper harness that I'd learned in cadets around me with yellow water ski rope that we'd stolen from Jon's dad's boat. It bit into my inner right thigh as I slowly rose to a crouch and eased my gaze from our dark island in the sky to the lit front side of the building where light, the only light, streamed up like a diaphanous and planar flow of water. Small particles of black shingle the size of coarse sugar grains sprinkled down from any, and all, of my touching. I felt the building's seventy-three years of exposure to the elements, it felt like weathered barn board. I hoped that the flagpole was still firm and anchored. It had felt solid to the touch. I eased my eyes into the sheet of light.

"He's just sitting down there. I don't think they're here for us. Maybe they're eating doughnuts."

"No, we're fucked," Jon cursed under his breath. "My mother told me that she wouldn't even come to court again."

And then the cruiser's driver's-side door swung open and a cop stepped out and my heart rate spiked and I froze in some form of timid gargoyle.

It is amazing how, in the course of our day-to-day lives in the city, we seldom look up. The cop walked forward and shone a flashlight into a parked car, then he went back to the cruiser and sat in it for long minutes before he finally pulled away and Jon barked, "We are getting the fuck out of here!"

I wrapped the rope through the gate of the carabiner three times then screwed it shut. Jon would untie the rope from the flag-pole after I hit the ground and throw it down, he'd then retreat by the fire escape.

I slithered over the edge and began bounding into the rappel. My third kick was too big and I let too much rope zip into the 'biner. The red brick blurred as I accelerated into a free fall. My rappel was out of control and rope sliced through my gloved hand like line whipping off a marlin rod. The ground charged through the dark night, then the rope in my brake hand hardened and torqued and twisted into an iron hard tangle that jammed against the carabiner. The rope stretched like I'd landed on a trampoline and I gently tethered to a stop and then snapped five feet back up the brick wall.

Fear and relief were spliced into each other with the margin between them being the momentary rebound of the rope, it was like the firing squad had all fired and missed. I bobbed on the end of the rope wrenching the tight fist of tangles free, and then I slowly continued down the rappel. Jonathon and I hung up our burglar-ing ambitions and cleaned up our acts before we turned sixteen, the age when the court would be adult and the consequences real.

A dozen books on mountaineering sat on the beige metal shelves of the Viscount Bennett High School library; Heinrich Harrer's *The White Spider* was among them.

Next morning we discovered that Vörg had sat motionless, without a single movement of a muscle, so that Heckmair's sleep might be undisturbed.
          Heinrich Harrer, The White Spider

That sentence had clung to a corner of my mind for seven years since I had heard it on the Greyhound that day, on my way back from my Grandmother Irene's when I was nine. It was the image that spoke the strongest to me of care, compassion, and courage. Now I wanted to be like Vörg, to be a mountain climber like him, Heckmair, Kasparek, and Harrer. I combed through book after book, holding on to the good ones for weeks past their due date.

The school PA system came to life sounding like someone had dropped a cloth wrapped rock into an empty forty-five-gallon oil drum. "Barry Blanchard please report to the library over break. Thank you." A dong that sounded like a twelve-pin bowling ball hitting the floor in a submarine closed the announcement.

"Ah crap," I said softly as I pushed back into my seat and arched my back and grinned at all the smiling faces and arching eyebrows of my classmates as they pivoted to snicker at me.

"I pity you, Mr. Blanchard," my physics teacher, Mr. McGuire, stated from the front of the class. "Mrs. Graham is ruthless in her pursuit of the truant book borrower." And those of my classmates who understood what he had said giggled, and the rest giggled at the giggling.

"*Basic,* and *Advanced Rockcraft* are both overdue by forty-three days," Mrs. Graham said in a deadpan monotone statement of fact. She stared right into my eyes, her shoulders square to mine and her hands on her hips. She looked like a gunslinger.

"Sorry. I guess I'm a slow reader. I'll bring them back tomorrow."

"That would be splendid."

I pivoted through my façade of teenage angst, lowered my gaze to the floor, and slunk out past head-high rows of books.

To this day I am still in awe of the canon that mountaineering has amassed. Climbing writing was my first literary passion and I doubt that I would have read as much, or as widely, as I have were it not for the excited awakening that I felt through the words of Bonatti, Terray, Diemberger, Gervasutti, Rébuffat, Harrer, Patey, Herzog, Bonington, Maraini, Messner, Haston, Robbins, Harding, and Chouinard.

Royal Robbins diagramed the tying of étriers in *Advanced Rockcraft,* I bought webbing and knotted up a couple. Looping the next cross in the basement floor joists was difficult without a harness and cow's-tail to provide some stability and "thrash and dangle" became a real concept for me as did the pinch and bite of my two carabiners when my body weight hung on to them and the webbing would cinch and capture a fold of flesh from my hand.

"Just keep sitting on the bed, David," I admonished my younger brother. "Otherwise I'll fall to the ground. OK?"

"OK, Brother, but I think that you're crazy, man."

The medium-gauge dog chain was wrapped and tied to the bed with the other end lowered out of the second story bay window (our climbing rope was still in hiding at Jon's house). I scraped over the window frame like I was lowering back into a swimming pool. My twelve-year-old brother sat on the bed grinning, happy to be involved. The chain clunked and lumbered through the carabiner feeling like a car coughing on the edge of a stall while starting out in third gear. Two rattling rappels down the chain was even enough for me at the time.

Jamie sat naked on her bed, her elbows hitched on her knees, chestnut hair hung straight and heavy to her shoulder blades. A column of warm summer sunlight shone between her smooth, soft, and pale legs. The hair there was one shade deeper and damp and glistening and looking at it made me quiver. I was naked and rock hard and swirling in a whirlpool of anxiety, confusion, and doubt. Her parents had left and we'd headed to her bedroom to "do it," something that I'd told her and most of my buddies that I had done, but hadn't. Jamie had, and wanted to do it with me, as I was now her boyfriend.

Five minutes of clothes ripping and escalating heat and desire had ended in me frantically failing my insertion. I didn't know what I was doing. I never dreamed—from within my fantasy world, which was prodigious—that anything could go wrong. I wanted to scream, I wanted to apologize, I wanted to cry.

I lifted my gaze to her. She was beautiful, with playful gray-green eyes streaked with flares of hazel, an aquiline nose sat over pouty impish lips that had offered me everything, eagerly, and were now lifting into a mischievous smile. I parted her knees and lay onto her again, and she eased onto her back and smiled at me. She took me gently into her hand and firmly guided me into her. She sighed as I entered her and glinted at me. I kissed her, and then I exploded into manhood.

This was indeed worth giving up childhood for. Once I got the hang of it we addictively tried to wear each other raw, and succeeded. Jamie was sixteen and I was one year older. It is interesting to me that sex and rock-climbing came into my life at the same time, and at a time, as the T-shirt says, when rock-climbing was dangerous and sex was safe.

Chapter 5

STARTING
TO CLIMB

MY BUDDY PHIL CONWAY had taken an introductory rock-climbing weekend and inherited some equipment from his older brother. On a September night in 1977 Phil and I stood at the hot cutter in the old Hostel Shop on Kensington Road in Calgary. The Southern Alberta Hosteling Association had bought the bungalow that had been built just after the First World War and converted it into a store. It was one of the only places to buy climbing equipment in Calgary, and for Phil and I the Hostel Shop facilitated face-to-face interaction with real climbers. I felt the encompassment of culture there, like the front door was a threshold on the outside of which was normality, and inside was climbing. But I was masquerading, and very conscious of it. Reading had given me a good understanding of how climbing worked, but I had never climbed and I stood there feeling unjustified, a false participant.

Autumn, the southern Albertan days were shrinking by four minutes a day yet the sun was still in the sky for nearly thirteen hours. Phil picked me up early Saturday in the red 1970 Toyota Celica that his older brother had sold to him cheap. We motored west on the Trans-Canada Highway turning south into the Kananaskis Valley.

The Gonda Traverse, Tunnel Mountain, Banff, 1980. I'm wearing my prized Peter Storm sweater that my mother bought me and then quickly shrank in the dryer. Photo: Kevin Doyle

Wasootch Slabs rise in an angled row of clean gray limestone bedding planes one hundred feet high. A seasonally dry and braided creek bearing the same name has filled the valley with rounded, water-worn rocks save for within several yards of the cliffs where the rock underfoot is jagged and angular and deposited by gravity and rockfall. Up valley and across from the farthest slabs an individual tower of rock rises 2,000 feet above the creek bed and its solitude caused the Stoney Indians to name it Wasootch, "unique."

Frost had melted to dew and the dew was slapped onto our shins by silvery boughs and knee-high grass and it stained our blue jeans indigo and pasted them to us cool and damp; it felt like thick velvet.

"We'll climb here," Phil announced, unshouldering his rope and thumping his pack to the broken stone underfoot. He looked to a wide crack topped by a corner, a resolute conviction furrowed his brow and sold me on his choice. We unpacked our gear and I wrapped the borrowed Whillans sit harness around my waist then slid an orange Joe Brown helmet onto my head. Phil organized his rack onto a shoulder sling, frequently turning his hardman gaze to the route like he was surveying an approaching armada that was still well, well out of range.

He looked noble. Just over six feet, his shoulders were already broadening. He'd recently cut his copper curls into a side part and wave. Phil looked like, and possessed all the boyish charm of, Donnie Osmond, but a Donnie widening into manhood. I slung the rope around my waist to secure the hip belay that I'd learned in *Basic Rockcraft* (I'd practiced the belay in the basement with my brother suspended from the cross braces).

"On belay?" Phil asked, his hands already touching the steep gray stone.

"You're on belay."

"Climbing." And Phil stepped up onto the cliff and the battle began.

Other climber's had told Phil that the Canadian Army had painted the letters onto the rock in the fifties. Five steps to my left, a foot-and-a-half-high black letter B sat framed within a two-and-a-half-foot square of white paint slapped onto the cliff at eye level. Paint dripped like candle wax from all the lower horizontal lines and it looked like bad graffiti, a delinquent depiction of an alphabet block. I assumed that it kept the soldiers from getting lost.

Forty-five minutes later Phil was thirty feet up and he was scared, and had been so for the last twenty-five feet.

"Oh fuck, Blanch! This is fucking hard! I have to get some more protection in." Phil's hard-man gaze had clicked to wide-eyed and out-of-control thirty minutes ago. His left hand clung rigid to the vertical edge of the crack, the knuckles chalk white. They looked like plump parsnips. His left foot was pasted to the opposite wall—a clean sweep of gray limestone—and it jittered continuously and I could hear a repetitive fast four count stamped out by his heel. His right hand was frantically sweeping the rock overhead as he strived to find something to hold on to. There was nothing.

He clanged through the rack and unclipped an orange knifeblade piton and stabbed it at a crack. The pin rebounded from his grip and clattered down the face, pinging into free fall and a whirring rotation before hatcheting into the head of my right clavicle. My breath exploded in a wave of white pain.

"Fuck! Fuck! Fuck! Conway, that fucking hurt...Fuck!"

"I'm fucking sorry man, but it is serious up here. I think that I'm going to fall! I could die!"

"Arrrgh." I bent forward with my left hand clamped tight onto my throbbing right shoulder. I breathed deep to expel the pain and rocked back and forth moaning lower and lower, and then I looked back to Phil.

A large pine tree grew out from a cave-shaped bowl in the rock five feet of overhang above him.

"Oh f-f-fuck, man. I'm going for it." A resigned and remorseful sorrow hung on his voice and I was afraid for him, knew that there were tears.

"You'll be OK, Con, you can do it, buddy. I know you can." Anxiously I paid out rope. I'd read about lead falls but never thought that I'd experience one on my first day climbing. Jolting, unsure, nervous grabs and thrusts, ragged breathing and guttural grunts, sighs of shock, and then he slapped his hand onto a beautiful sap-hardened bough and his feet cut loose from the wall and he screamed in a pitch that I'd last heard from my eleven-year-old sister, Glenna. Phil surged onto the top side of the tree and stood there trembling. Spit trailed from his mouth and settled, to pool, in the bark's folds.

Phil breathed. Minutes passed.

"I'm fucking coming down." His voice was drained to the floor in an adrenalin hangover. "Can you take my weight?"

"I've got you," I said, reefing tight on the rope and bracing my right foot against the cliff.

"Are you sure that you've got me, Blanch?"

"Yes, Con, yes. Come on down."

He scraped himself over the far side of the tree and I felt the rope slice and pop over the rim of my hipbone and weight plunged onto my right foot and I pushed back against the cliff to maintain control of the belay. Phil's hands slammed onto the taut rope and he retreated the cliff in jerky Frankenstein steps.

His PA rock shoes settled into the broken rock at the base and I fed out more rope and he immediately sank into a cross-legged Indian sit, and then he blew out and his head settled to his chest and he said, "That was fucking intense, man."

"It looked it," I said, placing my hand on his shoulder. He breathed for a while, and then I said, "How about I give it a try?"

The limestone felt porous, like a wall of pumice. It accepted the flesh of my hands and finger pads and I could feel the pulling and bunching of my skin as I gripped and stepped up. There were so few proper holds and the holds that I did find took minutes to isolate and align my hand on to pull and not have my hand pop off. Many of the holds I found by touch.

I girth hitched Phil's tree trunk with two double-length slings of white military spec webbing threaded through each other and clipped with a Bonatti carabiner. Wrestling the rope into the 'biner took two hands because I had the opening end of the gate rotated into the sling and there just wasn't much room for the rope.

I pressed my back to the tree and my feet to the rock and chimneyed up. The rough troughs of tree bark made if feel like I was squirming under a car parked on a gravel road. Higher, I stepped onto a branch and combed the rock above for a hold to pull onto. The equinoctial sun pressed heat into my back and sweat dripped from my chin and dotted the cement-colored rock with dime-sized dots two shades darker. I loaded up twice to lift my left foot from the branch, but at the moment of commitment I balked and settled back roughly onto the branch and the breath that I'd held burst out in a pneumatic blast. And then I panted and listened to the pounding of my heart.

"How's it going?" Phil had repeated the question every five minutes; this was his sixth repetition. No matter what state my mind I was in I'd always reply curtly, "Fine, it's going fine."

I stepped up again and clamped on to the same slanted three-finger hold with my right hand. I pressed on it until the outer edge of my fingernails blanched and the nail beds blossomed red and my last finger joint inverted, and then I bore down. A gut-propelled gasp hissed through gritted teeth and my left foot leapt from the bough and smacked against the rock. Instantly my full weight torqued onto my hands and I went rigid. I started to pant, frantically scanning the rock overhead for holds.

I had to move so I slapped and clamped on to the best looking holds and clumsily wobbled into balance above the overlap. "Fuck!" I gasped to myself knowing that the moves had been out of control and that I was just going for it—risking a fall. It was all that I knew, all that I had. I couldn't see a way up and I knew that I couldn't climb down. What if I got stuck? My lungs bellowed air in and out. I could hear my pulse in my temples.

A strip of black vinyl lined the forehead band of the Joe Brown helmet and I could feel the lubrication of my sweat against it. The helmet clunked around gliding on my sweat-glazed skin and dripping hair. It felt like hot sauce had been sprayed into my eyes and I clamped them shut trying to squeeze out the burning and I dragged my brow onto the rolled-up sleeve above my left elbow and whipped it up and down there like a cat looking for attention. I did not let go of the rock.

"How is it going?"

"Fine, just fine," I lied.

Opening my eyes and looking down to my feet for one of the first times and I saw bigger holds than the ones that I'd staggered blindly onto. Incrementally, nervously overcompensating at each move, I shifted my hips out from the wall and stepped my feet, one at a time, to face up-valley. A hold the size of half a red brick pivoted outward under the weight of my right heel, and then it cracked off and fell away and my weight jerked onto my three remaining points of contact. The fear was reflexive and breathtaking for the two beats that it took me to haul myself back from the fall. The hold exploded into the talus ten feet from Phil.

I snapped, "Holy fucking shit! Fucking fuck!" My gut and lumbar spine trembled and I clung even harder to compensate and willed my shaking to stop! "Stop it man, stop shaking. For Christ's sake stop shaking. You are going to make yourself fall."

"Are you OK?" Phil asked.

"Ya. I'm fine, just fucking fine. How are you?"

"I'm OK, but that rock was close to me, Blanch. I think that you should come down."

"I don't think that I can, man. I'll be more careful."

I breathed myself down for four minutes, eventually getting stable enough in body and mind to lean my shoulder to the rock and let go and try to find some protection.

The end of the piton was flat black and the size of a postage stamp. I placed it in an inch-long straight section in a jagged fracture that looked like a crack in the sidewalk. I tapped the piton hammer onto the head of the pin. Minute grains of dirt sifted from the crack and tumbled down to settle on brown stalks of dead grass that reached like tarnished tinsel from the crack. The piton set and I let go of it and found my handhold and hammered. The pin sunk in a half inch of its four-inch length. An ascending ring and resistance assured me that it was good. Twice I felt the hammer slipping from my failing grip and I had to stop, breathe, and rest.

Finally it was sunk to the eye and I clipped it and my fear zoomed from macro to micro. For the next few bodylengths I climbed awkwardly, but quickly, feeling the confidence of protection. Ten feet above the piton the fear of falling rose inside me like a lava plume and I stepped back into the breach within my mind.

One hour later I was thrusting with both legs as the rope dragged the harness down off of my hips. For one hundred feet the rope scraped over coarse limestone at acute angles zigzagging up my poorly managed protection. But I could touch the first tree of the forest! I yarded up rope like I was pulling a full net from the sea and passed a bight around the trunk, knotted it, and clipped into my harness with a locking carabiner and shouted, "Off belay!"

"You did a great job on that pitch, Blanch. Better than me." Phil's words sounded incredibly clear, like the trickle of a mountain stream. Phil's car seemed to glide back to Calgary.

The leaves were just beginning to turn, yet when I looked out across the predominantly coniferous green foothills their splashes looked like van Gogh's brushstrokes in a *Wheatfield with Cypresses*— bold, vibrant, radiant. I felt good, at peace, and when I lay in my bed that night I thought that I might be able to be a climber.

Spring days are massive in southern Alberta. It's like they grow parallel to the harried rush of the newly sprouted grass. The solstitial sun lights the sky from four in the morning to eleven at night, it pounds heat into the province and everything comes to life and blossoms— bears, crocuses, grass, poplars, and aspens...and mosquitos.

My bad buddy, Tim Shatto, had dropped out of school and his mother had banished him to the basement. Tim maintained a milk crate full of girly magazines, slept until noon, and then rose to boil a pot of Uncle Ben's rice, slather it in a quarter pound of butter to slurp down while he watched soap operas and game shows.

He and his younger sister, Val, had been adopted, but their parents divorced shortly before they moved to Gladstone Park at about the same time that we had. His absent father's form of childcare was to occasionally buy Tim things and, to Tim and I, a brand new Kawasaki KZ400 was a beautiful thing. It didn't fill the hole inside of Tim, but it allowed us to speed away from it for a while.

"Fuck!" I blurted, and my math binder hit the hallway floor. I'd just spun the combination to my locker and pried open its squeaky door. Tim was folded up in there like a blond, spectacled, pimple-faced gremlin. Scared the shit out of me.

"Shatto" I hissed, "you know that you aren't suppose to be on school property. I was going to meet you on the street."

"Whatever."

"Have you got my pack?"

"It's on the bike."

"OK, head out there and wait for me man. I'll be out in a minute. I just can't be seen."

I skipped my last class and swung my leg over the passenger seat of the motorbike and one hour later we were crunching up the rounded river rocks of Wasootch Creek. I led, Tim belayed attentively, then mauled his way up the pitches by leveraging his natural brute strength. Climbing was not his calling (nor was crime, but he went on to investigate that much further).

The stars came out as we motorcycled back to Calgary through the warm night air. I sat on the back of the bike and felt good, felt as deeply as I did when Jamie and I made love, but different. Different when I touched the earth than when I touched her.

The dark blue KZ400, with Tim, my backpack—stuffed plump with Phil's rack, Jon and my cat-burglar rope, and my newly purchased Whillans harness and Joe Brown helmet—sat idling like a purring lion on a dozen afternoons of my twelfth-grade school year. I'd skip class and Tim and I would speed off climbing.

My mother was sitting in the vice principal's office when I was ushered in. Her brown eyes were pinched at the corners and the displeasure that she was feeling with her number-one son, me, was as palpable as a napalm strike. I recognized a stack of forged absentee notes on the VP's desk and I grinned a stupid grin. I'd nailed my mother's precise cursive small letters, but not her ornate capitols P or B; but after careful evaluation of many of my female classmates' handwriting I got Susan, the gal who sat in front of me in homeroom, to trace those for me.

The VP looked up from the accordioned IBM printout. A stern man in an ash-gray suit, he was pissed.

"Barry, you've missed one out of every five school days since Christmas. That's twenty percent of this semester."

I'd turned eighteen two months before, and by law, could write my own absentee notes. I was also free to sink or swim on my adult decisions, and that was what was concluded in the meeting. Some slack got cut for me when the VP scrolled down the printout and blurted, "Dwayne Stark has missed twenty-five percent of this semester! One out of every four days!" I knew that Dwayne wasn't out rock-climbing, in my mind I saw him on his basement sofa getting high and watching TV.

In spite of my absenteeism I matriculated high school and registered for the University of Calgary because it was what most of my peers, like Phil, were doing. I was the first person in my family's history to go to university and that presented challenges—I didn't know what a registrar was and no one in my family could tell me.

Phil's Toyota sputtered to a halt in the Muleshoe picnic area on the old Banff-to-Laggan (Lake Louise) coach road. Construction of the road began in 1911 and it had been largely built on the backs of Ukrainian internees who had been rounded up nationwide under the War Measures Act of WWI. The men were tented during the summer in a concentration camp below Castle Mountain thirty-two kilometers to the north.

Phil stepped from the driver's side wearing a green and brown plaid shirt, brown corduroy knickers, and green wool knee-length socks. He had a red bandana tied around his neck. It was important to Phil to look like a climber. I wore blue jean painter's pants and a white Santa Cruz Skateboards T-shirt. I dearly would have liked to look like a climber, but I couldn't afford it.

Phil, my girlfriend, Jamie, a number of my high school buddies, and I all had part-time jobs at Sport Chek; Calgary's first big-box sports retailer. Phil had worked there longer and helped me get my job in the tennis and fledgling skateboard departments. Hard to believe that part of my job was to rocket around the perimeter of the parking lot on Saturday afternoons on Calgary's sole motorized skateboard. All of my paychecks were being spent on basic climbing equipment and partying and I hadn't got to the point of considering climbing clothing.

"How many do you think there are?" I asked.

"Looks like at least a half dozen."

In a gravel flat in the Bow River far below us, and close to the truncated oxbow that looked like a mule shoe and gave the area its name, a cluster of black bears were milling about in the sun.

"Shit, you don't think that they'll come up here do you?" I asked.

"I don't know. I hope not. Let's go up there," Phil said, pointing to the southwest face of Mount Cory, high above the other side of the highway.

Plate upon plate of sedimentary limestone scraped upward looking like a massive deck of tarot cards that had been dragged backward so that half of the face of each of a half dozen cards was exposed and stacked onto the next card, the next fortune. The strata lay to the same incline as Wasootch Slabs, but for 1,000 feet—ten times the height of my previous climbs. A single crack split the left side of the face from bottom to top. The most obvious rock-climbing line in the valley, Cory Crack.

In 1960 Hans Gmoser was a hardworking Canadian mountain guide who had emigrated from Austria in 1951. His client that day was Jack Mackenzie, a successful Calgary businessman who would soon partner with Hans to create the new venture of heli-skiing. Hans went on to become the most financially accomplished mountain guide in the history of our profession. Of his and Jack Mackenzie's first ascent of Cory Crack Hans wrote: "It was one of the most enjoyable rock climbs that I have ever done. The rock was as solid as concrete and from the top it was an easy walk back to the highway."

Rain had weathered the limestone to gray and it was clean and pleated with inch-deep runnels that reminded me of the skin of a giant cactus, but not leathery or spiny. The edges of the crack felt as hard as marble. At the crux the crack necked down to eight inches and it was vertical and as compact as poured concrete that had been polished. A dead tree was locked into the crack above me, bone dry and ash gray like an elephant's femur baked in the sun of the savanna. Above it a basin of scree and talus was held in check. Getting by the bone tree felt like wrestling an opponent who was twice my size and immovable. I resorted to swarming and I was a wreck when I teetered into the pool of loose rock, a volley of which clattered off toward Phil.

"Fuck, Blanch! Take it easy up there man." His shouts wafted up to me on a cloud of gravel dust.

In a sitting hip belay, I brought up Phil then continued on to lead all of the pitches. I seemed to be able to figure things out better than Phil. To hang on through the long minutes of desperation and mounting panic as I groped for holds and committed to faith, jerking from point of balance to point of balance while mimicking the techniques I'd read about, working to make my protection placements look like what I'd seen in books.

We tromped back into the Muleshoe parking lot. In 2006 Hans Gmoser fell from his road bike here and became a quadriplegic. A man of iron-cast will, he chose to pull the plug two days later after nodding goodbye to his wife and two sons. Cory Crack bore witness to his crash. We now call it the Gmoser Crack.

Two months after Phil and my ascent I borrowed my Aunt Joanne's mustard-colored 1976 Toyota Corolla and drove off to the Muleshoe parking lot to sleep in the car. Any sound snapped me upright to wipe my condensed breath from the passenger's side window and peer out into the night.

I was sleeping nervously against the edge of two things that I wasn't supposed to be doing. The first was sleeping in the car, which must have been against some regulation. The second was that I was planning to solo Cory Crack the next day and I'd only been climbing for six months. Then I sank into a deeper sleep and didn't wake until I felt the humid heat of the morning sun cutting into the Toyota and steaming off the condensation and making it feel like a green house. I unzipped my Scouting sleeping bag, flannel grizzly bears and cowboys jumped into my consciousness like Looney Tunes.

I was up the route in an hour and a half. The climbing commanded all of my concentration and I felt in control. It felt good to correct the mistakes that Phil and I had made, and I felt a glow of competency and pride in the accomplishment. Interestingly I would not solo again for a couple of years and it would be a decade, and several thousand days of climbing down the road, before I really did a lot of it. On Cory Crack I was much more interested in trying to get better, to become a real climber. Climbing without a rope at lower grades didn't hold as much attraction as pushing my envelope on the sharp end of the rope.

A funnel of frost-shattered shale marks the top of the Calgary route on Mount Yamnuska. The mountain's name is a Stoney word that translates to "sheer cliff face" and that is apt because some of the routes are over 1,000 feet long, engirding bold 300-foot sweeps of overhangs that back into space for tens of feet. To see the copper tint of the early morning sun glow across the mile-wide south face is to see its climbing lines revealed and radiating like polished tigereye.

On top of the Calgary route hard-edged tawny fragments of shale the size of a deck of cards lie in file looking like they've been raked. Gravity funnels them to fall, in time, into the two-and-a-half-foot-wide, abysmally black crack that is the final squeeze of the route. Shoulders of water-washed Precambrian limestone jut out from the dark slot, precipitation and wind have swept the rock clean like an archeologist's brush revealing a chisel-cut corner of marble. In 2011, like most years, I passed the place a half dozen times walking down the gentle backside descent trail. I forever see myself huddled into the swale of the funnel hypothermic and hallucinating at two in the morning on a late October morning in 1977. I was eighteen and holding fast to a sit-anchored hip belay with my partner Gray's full body weight cutting the rope into me, deepening the dark ring of bruises that partially circled my waist like the lash marks of a whip.

Gray Dickson worked in the shoe department at Sport Chek. He was reserved and quiet compared to most of my friends, and he lived with his mother. Gray was her only child. The one time I met her, in her house, I could feel the legacy of Great Britain on the tea and crumpets.

Gray had done what I dreamed of doing: Climbed several routes on Mount Yamnuska. It was where the heroes from my hometown climbed—Brian Greenwood, Urs Kallen, Jim Elzinga, and foremost John Lauchlan. I'd seen several of John's slideshows about climbing in the Saint Elias range and even effused congratulatory ravings at him after he returned from the south face of Mount Logan. He was intense and gracious and fully aware of the fact that I didn't have a damn clue. I knew as much about the greater ranges as I did the headwaters of the Amazon—the river was wet, the mountains were snowy.

Gray and I decided to attempt the Calgary route. Hans Gmoser and his lifelong friend and climbing partner, Franz Dopf, put up the route in 1953. I borrowed the 1959 Plymouth Fury station wagon that had sat in a barn for a decade before my uncle Ken had bought it from the farmer for a hundred bucks. It had started first turn, had foot-high tail fins, and push-button Torqueflite gear shifts on the dash. Gray and I had just enough cash between us to fill it with gas. It rumbled into the old Yam parking lot low and heavy like a slow-moving tank.

The fallen leaves had aged from gold to mottled brown, and they crackled under my feet. Bark peeled in curls from the trunks of the aspens and it looked like papyrus but crumpled like the skin of a wasp's nest when I pulled on the tissue thin sheets. Skeletal branches reached into the cold morning air. The foothills had long since turned to brown and there had been a frost overnight. Once Gray got us onto the approach trail I charged, red-lined my pulse well over 200 beats per minute and marched on double time, head bobbing, until sweat was weeping from my chest and my lungs raged. The morning sun was touching the top of the wall and washing it copper. I was so excited.

The south face of Yamnuska, from the Stoney Lakota word, Iyamnathka, "the flat faced mountain."
Photo: Barry Blanchard

"Hurry up Gray," I chanted to myself and I bent at the waist shifting the weight of my pack off of my shoulders and onto my flattened back and I braced my hands to bent knees and breathed and waited for Gray.

I led everything and we were doing OK, and then we entered the squeeze chimney that forms the top four ropelengths of the route. I fought. Knees pressed to stone, elbows paddling backward over black rock and bracing the bones of my forearm, like a wooden truss in a mine shaft, against the flattened flesh of my palms, my fingers fanned out and pasted down the wall. I'd gain inches by squirming my shoulder blades and scraping my back up while torquing tension onto my elbows, palms, backs of my hips, splayed out knees and backward-and downward-thrusting soles of my feet. It was sick. My chest would get wedged and I'd panic and thrash to free it, to breathe. I'd start to slip and I'd push harder, stapling the imprint of the rock's surface into blanched skin. I felt like a bullfrog in bondage.

Every so often I would find an incut hold and brace a heel onto it and rest and breathe and try to rationalize the arc of the ropes hanging from my harness and disappearing into the darkness like lines dropping into a deep dark well. "How much farther until I find some pro?"

Gray couldn't climb the chimney. "Keep the rope tight!" he wailed.

A current of bewildered fear crackled on his words like radio static and then he fell. The rope ratcheted hard on my waist and my body went rigid and I was scraped six inches toward the coal chute of the crack. He fell five more times, and then just sat on the cable taut rope for ten minutes. The pressure parted the subcutaneous fat over my left hip and the rope burned down onto the bone.

"Gray! What the fuck are you doing?"

"I can't fucking do this!" His reserved manner was gone and he sounded like a grade school kid on the verge of tears, and that just made me madder.

"You fucking have to do it! We can't get down from here!" I'd never done a five-hundred-foot retreat and neither had he. The walls around me seemed to close in.

"Can your hold the green rope tight?" Gray shouted.

"Yes." And I wrapped it around my waist with my left hand while holding Gray's belay with my right.

"OK! The green rope is OK."

"Are you sure?" More fear.

"Yes! I'm fucking sure. Yes!"

The pressure shifted from Phil's brown rope onto the green. Two hours later Gray pulled onto my stance. He'd ascended the ropes by tying an overhand knot into one, stepping his weight into it, and then tying a higher overhand in the other and stepping up into it. Soon the chains of knots were jamming below him and he had to step down and untie them to clear them. He kept himself safeguarded by clipping slings from his harness into both of the overhands that he was working with. I sat braced against the walls holding his bodyweight, and then I would lead. Anxiety waxed on the waning sun.

"Can you see the top?" Gray pleaded.

"No, there's more."

Darkness. The absolute dark of night in the bowls of the crack, a surreal slice of starlight, and the night sky, cut and defined by the outer walls like a door cracked open to faint and distant candlelight. I led by feel and the faint match-flame-blue illumination from the sparkling of static electricity as my positively charged clothing scrapped over the grounded rock. A new form of fear within me— the real night-fear of the unknown, my honest doubt as to whether we would survive.

I ended the pitches where I could brace my body and hold Gray. He took three times as long to climb the pitches as I did. The rope bit deeper. I began to hate him for not being able to suck it up and fight for the chimneys, to deal. When I came onto the ammo box with the route register in it I signed my name in by starlight and feel and I didn't sign Gray in.

At 2:00 a.m. I slapped my cold and swollen hands onto the water-washed limestone shoulders at the top of the route. I pressed up and staggered into the funnel and swale of broken shale. I'd eaten the last of my food, a box of Smarties, at noon the day before, washed them down with the last of my water. I sat down and braced myself and shouted to Gray to start, and then I suffered.

A cold wind out of the west swirled into the funnel and bit. Spasms of violent shivering rattled my skeleton every four minutes. I'd clench my eyes and blather prayers. I made a number of promises to God that I would go on to break. My hallucinations were magnificent. The headlights of the sparse traffic and the lights from the houses on the Stoney Reservation became a massive space complex like something out of Star Wars. I watched a bear amble by me, could hear his breathing. A neon orange sign spun at me from the horizon like a zooming shot of a newspaper in a movie clip, VOTE ROSS ALGER in bold black capitol letters. A procession of bowed supplicants walking upward in a torchlit line, their heads hooded in burlap swaddle. I prayed in time to their murmured chanting. I prayed to survive.

Gray arrived. For hours we groped and stumbled down the descent trail, down the scree. I wore through my fingerless Miller gloves sitting on my ass and easing down the scree on locked arms and dug in heels. Toward tree line we began to catch glimpses of headlights darting up and down the road to the parking lot, and red and blue flashers.

"Climber on the mountain!" echoed from the cruiser's PA.

By 9:00 p.m., the night before, my mother had become frantic with worry. She called Gray's mother, then she called the Calgary City Police, the Royal Canadian Mounted Police (RCMP), the Fire Department, and the Banff Wardens. Basically anybody with a hat got a call. Soon the Calgary Mountain Rescue Group called her. John Lauchlan had to put down his beer and leave the party he was at.

Dawn came slowly. I finally found the road and fell from the forest into the ditch. I was totally fucked, shattered. I stood slowly and shouted back to Gray. He tumbled out of the forest just as the RCMP cruiser charged to us and ground to a stop wheels locked, dust swirling. I folded back onto my ass in the ditch.

"You two are in a whole lot of shit," the officer bellowed stepping from the driver's side. But then Don Forrest, the leader of the Mountain Rescue Group, was there and he barged in front of the Mountie and squatted down on his haunches and looked me in the eye and kindly asked, "How are you boys?"

"I'm thirsty. I'm really thirsty."

John Lauchlan thumped his pack down beside Don. Nothing dangled from the outside of the pack. John had on Galibier Super

Guide mountain boots, gray knickers, and a Peter Storm sweater. I felt like a fake in my battered blue jeans. He handed me a red aluminum water bottle with a wired stopper. I sprang the stopper and greedily guzzled half, then handed it to Gray who was talking with Don and the Mountie. John's intense blue eyes bore into me from behind his teardrop glasses. I shifted my gaze to the dirt between my feet and then raised it to meet John's.

"I'm sorry for making you be here man," I said. He smiled, and told me that he had done the exact same thing on the Grillmair Chimneys route once upon a time.

"No shit?" I asked.

"No shit."

Gray fell into a coma in the passenger's seat. At the Scott Lake Hill the Trans-Canada Highway gains about seven hundred feet of elevation. As I drove the road ramped up into the sky and the foothills fell away and cypress trees lined the shoulders. I blinked and shook my head side to side but the hallucination persisted. I kept the Fury between the cypress trees, and then the road rounded to horizontal and the cypress trees dissolved into evergreens and I could see the gas station at the top of Scott Lake Hill.

Gray's mother came down the sidewalk to meet him. She put her arm around his shoulder and shepherded him into the house. When I got home my mother made sure that I was OK and then she fed me. Delicious warm brown bread rolls completely enveloping ground beef and, after a half dozen of those, white ones stuffed with cherry pie filling. They were one of my favorite things that my mom made. She'd buy the dough premade and frozen and as I sat at our kitchen table in Gladstone Park that morning I remembered how she'd told me that she had gotten bored carrying me in her ninth month of pregnancy, when she was nineteen, and taken to bouncing down the stairs on her butt to get me out. I would be nineteen in five months. I climbed the stairs to my bedroom slowly. I slept for eighteen hours. When the next dawn woke me I was in the same position that I'd fallen asleep in, I hadn't moved.

The next day was Monday, and I skipped my university classes and spent a lot of the day on the couch. I drank a lot and ate as only a

Approaching the Cheeseburger, a huge discus of snow, on the north face of Mount Kitchener. Canadian Rockies, 1982.
Photo: Kevin Doyle

young man can eat—eight thousand calories, if it were one. A soft light infused my world. Everything looked like the scenes in *Star Trek* when a beautiful woman's face is zoomed into portrait and wreathed in a halo of glow that radiates to the four corners of the TV screen. I felt light, good, and slow. The Calgary Route had been, by far, the most intense experience of my life, but I'd promised God that if he just got me down from it I'd never go back up there again. Now I wanted to return, climbing was calling to me.

I never climbed with Gray again, I don't know if Gray even climbed again. Phil was not being called to it, but Ron Humble was. Ron graduated from Viscount Bennett High School two years ahead of me and was now at the University of Washington on a downhill skiing scholarship pursuing his chosen field of aeronautical engineering. He'd come home to Calgary for Christmas, spring break, and the summer, and we'd get out climbing as much as possible.

Ron got a lot of red at birth. Red hair, ruddy complexion, and a tinderbox temper much like my own. He was a bit clunky socially, didn't get invited to high school parties as much as Phil and I did. Intense and obsessive, he'd built his own hang glider in junior high school and actually got airborne in it, and then crashed. That didn't deter him though. While he was at grad school he bought a small aircraft and told me a story about flying it across Canada and having to follow the Trans-Canada Highway so low under storm clouds in Ontario that he had to pull a pine bough out of the landing gear when he got back to the ground.

Ron went on to finish a PhD. I dropped out in my second semester having started with physics, but finished with a study of beer, girls, and climbing. It was the summer of 1978 and I was working at Sport Chek full time. Jamie and I had broken up, as had Brenda and I, and now I just couldn't decide on any one girl, or, possibly, they weren't content with me? I'd bought my first car, a yellow 1974 Mazda 606, for four hundred bucks. It took me to the parties, and the mountains.

The German mountain guide Hans Wittich and his client Otto Stegmaier first climbed the east ridge of Mount Temple in August 1931. They didn't take crampons and somehow Ron Humble and I concluded that we would not need them either, or ice axes (Wittich and Stegmaier had carried one between them forty-seven years before). But we were nineteen and twenty-one, young and dumb and drunk on a cocktail of naiveté and enthusiasm. We agreed that we would be able to avoid the summit glacier.

Blue jeans and hiking boots, somehow I managed to lead 5.7 climbing on the Big Step. At the time Ron and I classified it as hard; we had little understanding of what the rock grade meant. On the next step, the little step, I battled my way up an outward slanting chimney. A shale band marked the little step's top and blades of wind-eroded shale stood in stacks like the cooling fins on a gargantuan motorcycle piston. The chimney had been physical, but not technically hard—lots of grunting and pushing. Finishing it, I traversed left pinching the fins and surfing the broken plates of rock underfoot.

I sat into an alcove and braced my left hip to the rock and shouted "On Belay!" Ron couldn't pull me out of there, and he wasn't going to fall anyway. I didn't need an anchor.

Twenty minutes later the rope snapped tight as a tow strap and I slapped my brake hand to my gut as my body was lifted and my left side got smacked into the shale fins. My heels gouged trenches into the broken rock as I fought for stability and to not be pulled off of the mountain. Tense minutes of stalemate in my lethal tug-o-war and then the tension on the rope relaxed and Ron started climbing again.

We spent the night three hundred feet higher huddled to each other, sitting on our packs, both of us within the cocoon of our down jackets. The hour of the wolf, just before dawn, when the cold hunted and bit, we both woke up shivering and drew our knees up into our jackets and prayed for the sun.

The dawn came slow, the sun slower. We made our way up to the "notch" in the Black Towers where we anchored and laid on our bellies and, side by side, looked over the edge, down the Sphinx Face. Immense sweeps of gray ice funneled from tombstone black cliffs a thousand feet high. Gargoyles of brindled snow clung high over aprons of pewter-colored ice that angled down all of the ledges. I could see no horizontal surfaces for the whole half-mile concave run of the face. The entirety of it spiraled down 3,000 feet to where the forest looked like a dimpled bath mat and the creeks like silver threads.

"Now I know what the north face of the Eiger looks like," I said.

"We have to get out of here," Ron replied.

And we retreated all the way back down the complexity of the east ridge, and that is something that impresses me to this day. We didn't get high enough to need ice axes or crampons, but of more significance, and vital importance to our development as climbers, was that we had bonded in partnership. I was getting to know Ron better than most of the guys that I had more in common with. Ron and I shared an essential and innate passion for climbing and we had now seen each other in the arena of the mountains. We'd lived through the other's rage and brilliance and compassion. The mountains were a prism that fanned out and projected the spectrum of our beings, we were tied to each other. I led the hard stuff and Ron made sure that we got out there.

"I'll pick you up at six tomorrow morning," Ron said over the phone.

"I'll be ready."

I staggered in from the party at 4:00 a.m., drunk, and I was still drunk, and snoring, when Ron knocked on the front door. Getting no answer he came in and up the stairs past my mother's room, past Kim and Glenna's room, past David and Steven's room and shook me awake.

"Blanchard! You're drunk."

"Yes, I know that."

"You said we're going climbing, and now you're going climbing."

He harassed me into dressing, grabbed my pack, and manhandled me down the stairs and into the passenger seat of his mustard-yellow 1972 Ford Pinto station wagon. It had fake mahogany panels and when I opened the door I thought about how hard it would be to clean vomit from the framing around the fake wood. I rolled down the window and laid the seat right back and slept all the way to the parking lot.

The trail was steep and it had been a chute of slick mud at some time in the last week and I knew that because I could see the rake lines of a Vibram boot sole where a climber had slipped sideways and locked up his legs and slid like a hockey player until his feet had mashed into the dense low juniper that bordered, and defined, the trail. The sun had baked the oily mud to a hard cobble that was studded with rock fragments and reminded me of broken glass winking dully from dusty stucco. Plump drops of my sweat plopped onto the brick-hard trail and it was water that could ill afford to lose—my head was floating in fuzz and my teeth felt like miniature fisherman's knit sweaters against my tongue and tasted like kerosene.

The approach stitches a zigzag of switchbacks up a thirty-degree slope intermittently treed with spruce, subalpine fir, and the occasional lodgepole pine. Eight-inch-high hedges of kinnikinnick and juniper checkerboarded the slope and when my dehydrated, free-range brain clunked up against the inside of my skull I'd stagger and have a vision of tumbling through it knowing that it would feel like wee rows of German razor wire. Coming onto the corners felt like stepping onto a wobble board and my arms would shoot out, palms down, fingers fanned.

"I am so hungover." And then I farted long, deep, and dry. It sounded like a horse.

"Oh fuck, Blanchard! There is something dead and rotting inside of you, man"

"Killed by alcohol, I think."

"Ahhh! It's fucking gross. That's it, I'm going in front." Ron reached forward and grabbed the coils of Phil's rope where it laid across my shoulder and pack and he pulled me to a stop and pushed past me.

Two Engelmann spruce trees have somehow managed to survive to a stately maturity at the base of the Red Shirt route. So many of the other trees that skirt the south face of Yamnuska get destroyed by rockfall or succumb to thirst, yet the bulging yellow walls that cradle these two, at the apex of a feature that climbers call "The Bowl," must shelter them. The cupped hand of the wall holds moisture, plus the twin spruce had profited from sixteen years of climbers' piss. I held on to a low bough of the biggest Engelmann, the one that stands right under Red Shirt, and it felt smooth in my hand, looked shiny, polished by hundreds of climber's hands and the gear they draped onto it.

I splattered the surface roots with apricot-colored piss, but my head felt clear, and when I looked up to the crack and the deep yellow slot of the route I tried to visualize myself on the rock, squinted to make out the line. Dick Lofthouse, Heinz Kahl, and Brian Greenwood had made the first ascent in 1962. For me, Greenwood was "the man"— the hardest climber in the Rockies. A friend of Ron's had once seen Greenwood climb. "He has fingers like pitons," Ron repeated. Red Shirt was a Greenwood route, named for a shirt that he had worn to tatters forging his legacy on the hardest routes in the range.

I'd bought a pair of Vasque Ascender II rock shoes from the Hostel Shop that week and I was proud of them because each piece of gear that I owned bought me closer to being a real climber. If I looked like a climber, I would be a climber. I thought that I could buy authenticity.

I wiped my damp palms on the thighs of my Levis and pulled up onto Yamnuska, but before my left foot touched the rock I knew that I couldn't hold myself on and I had to step back down onto the ground. "Shit, this is hard." And so many of the moves were, every three feet there would be something that would force me to think. The route was 885 feet long.

One hundred feet up a two-foot piece of two-by-four had been pounded into the crack. It was canted off of level and driven upward at an angle just below horizontal. Pica piss stained it and gave it an air of permanency, almost like it was petrified in place. I hadn't seen anything like it on a climb and when I thumped it with the heel of my hand it felt like it was embedded in concrete and when I smacked it with the broadside of Phil's rock hammer it resonated like I'd just hit a curb with a baseball bat. A belly of manila hawser-laid cord hung from it and I clipped a carabiner and sling to it, a second 'biner to my rope, and bridged wide with my feet and pulled hard. I had to cut loose and commit to climbing continuously, but I could see ahead to where, ten feet higher, I should be able to stand in balance.

That read imbued me with confidence and I climbed with a feeling of control, and that was an important incremental improvement from the year before when I would simply survive from hold to hold with little interpretation of what the rock was presenting, or where the route lie. My climbing was becoming calculated and that was encouraging and empowering.

And then Red Shirt threw the fourth pitch at me and it was beyond anything that I'd ever dreamed of seeing on a rock climb. I left the anchor and bridged up a wide chimney for several bodylengths. Ron was directly below me, and I could see in his wide, focused, and unwavering eyes the threat of me dropping anything, or falling, onto him. I tried to move out left and around an outside corner as Urs Kallen's *A Climbers Guide to Yamnuska* directed.

"Fuck, man. I'm too high. I've got to climb down. Shit! Take in the rope, Ron." My hands were wrapped on to good holds, but my down climbing was unrefined and my feet clunked down the rock like I was thumping down the open and unfinished wooden stairs to our basement.

"OK, OK. Take it easy man," Ron replied, following my every move and gently regaining the rope.

Leaving the encompassing walls of the chimney was like stepping out of a window to shinny along the outside ledge thirty floors up. I had to talk down the primal part of me that was panicking and wanting to be back inside the walls. I clipped a fixed piton that confirmed that I was on route, and made a fall less horrible. My will forced my feet to follow my intellect and advance onto the small gray footholds that edged out above air. My handholds felt rough and porous but they seemed no bigger than the side of a crayon and I eased myself across the ten-foot traverse feeling ethereal, light, and insecure—like I was hanging on to a cloud.

My left foot reached and settled onto the opposite wall of the groove like I was making a wide step from the deck to the dock. I braced my feet against the opposing walls and felt secure and then I breathed. Fifteen feet down the groove, then an equal amount of traversing to the left and I was teetering on an edge of rock and looking down onto a slab that looked to be the same size and smoothness as the hood on a black 1957 Cadillac Eldorado. I was supposed to step down onto it, but I couldn't believe it and I danced around looking for any other option.

"How in the wide world of fucking sports did Greenwood do this?"…"Fingers like pitons." The quote clanged around my brain as I talked myself down, "Calm down Blanchard, you can do this. Fingers like pitons! Breathe, Blanchard, breathe."

My mind told me that I would slip if I stepped down onto the slab, it wouldn't work. I steeled myself—"Fingers like pitons!"—and stepped my left foot down onto the slab. It vibrated and trembled and then I shifted my hips over it and my Vasque Ascender stuck and settled. I brought my right foot over and eased my hands to upright. They found poor holds above a two-foot-high overlap that arched across the slab. I stood and breathed for minutes, then padded to the left side of the slab balancing on the razor's edge of believability.

A curving crack defined the edge of the slab with the vertical rise of the overlap above. Two small slots opened in the crack at ten and eleven o'clock. Three feet lower and to the left I could see the "small but good ledge" that the guidebook marked as the belay. I inserted my fingers into the slots and they went as deep as the first digit, and then I pushed on them harder—"Fingers like pitons!"— and lowered my hips to the edge of the slab while twisting torsion onto my rigid hands.

The toe of my left boot reached for the ledge and I felt my center of mass, just above my pelvis, rotate out and I thought that I was going to fall. My eyes flared open and I held my breath and locked my core and my toe touched the ledge. My right foot snapped down to mate with my left. I eased my weight onto my heels and slid my hips and chest below the edge of the slab like I was doing the limbo under a running chainsaw. There was a cluster of fixed pitons there, I clipped into all of them.

"You've got to be fucking kidding me," Ron exclaimed after he'd rounded the outside corner and surveyed the down climb and traverse from the top of the groove. When he arrived at the hood-of-a-'57-Cadillac slab his eyes were clear, wide, and focused.

"How the fuck did you get over there, Blanchard?"

"It doesn't look like it will work, I know, but it does. I've got you man, just be delicate."

"Delicate, fuck delicate. I want some fucking handholds."

His PAs stuck as well as my Vasques, but he had much bigger thighs and glutes than me, amassed from his downhill skiing. When his hips came onto the edge of the slab his weight rotated out and he fell the last foot onto the ledge. Both feet slapped onto the ledge and Ron squawked, "Fuck!" but he didn't lose it. He caught himself on his hands.

"Fingers like pitons," I said.

"Fuck," Ron sighed, and then he slumped down onto the ledge. A minute passed.

"What do you think, Blanch?"

"I think that we should keep going."

"Ya, but there's four more pitches. Do you think that there's more climbing like that?"

"The AO section is right here, those three pitons," and I pointed to a yellow and gray wall that rose from the far side of our ledge, four feet away. It was plumb and the guidebook stated that the pitons could be used as handholds giving it an Aid Climbing Zero rating (AO), or it could be free climbed at 5.7 or 5.8, the rest of Red Shirt being graded 5.6.

"If it's too hard I think that we can rappel from here. We may have to leave some gear, but I think that we can get down." I commented.

The thought of leaving some of his expensive equipment piqued Ron's miserliness, and sparked his red, "Fuck that, man. Let's get up this thing."

As I racked up, Ron looked back to the Cadillac slab, "I have no fucking idea how Greenwood figured that out in mountain boots."

"Neither do I man...fingers like pitons, fingers like pitons."

I took my left foot from the security of the belay ledge and pasted it onto the left wall. My right foot rotated from the ball of my foot to the inside edge of the sole. I felt the hard edge of the limestone block bite and I knew that my foot would not slip. The block was the size of a steamer trunk and it sat on end at the left edge of the ledge. I lifted my right foot from it and stepped the inside of my big toe onto a half-inch-deep hold one foot higher and in line with my right hip. Then I reached and caught the slanting left edge of the crack with my right hand, thumb up, like I'd grabbed the edge of a metal fire escape and was leaning to the left to see something on the sidewalk.

My forearm burned as I rushed to lift a knotted sling over my head and clip one of its carabiners into the first fixed piton, then fumble to grab the other 'biner and bring it to the rope at my waist and clip it in—all done with one hand. My lungs were heaving and my right hand cramping; I had to climb down, or clip into the piton and aid climb, or go for it—whatever I was going to do I had to do it immediately. I pulled up, locked off sideways and reached, and the climbing just began to flow.

"You've got it, Blanch. Hang in there, man," Ron said. He paid out the precise amounts of rope necessary and never more: More would mean a longer fall. "You've got it, man."

I pulled into balance above the third piton and breathed and breathed. "That's it man! I freed it! Yeehaw!"

"Great, but you are going to have to keep me on a tight rope, I don't know if I can do what you just did. How does it look from there?" Ron asked.

"I don't know. I can't really see a lot, not as steep as that though. It looks easier." And it was until the very last pitch.

Hans Gmoser's confident gaze stared out to me from a half page black-and-white photo in the guidebook. He wore a guide's sweater, knickers, klettershoes, a canvas knapsack on his back, and no helmet on his head. The rope arced clean and unprotected from the left edge of the frame to Hans on the right edge. He'd knotted the end into a harness around his chest.

"He looks like Anderl Heckmair on the north face of the Eiger," I said, holding the guidebook, matching the picture to the terrain.

"Ya, except it's sunny here, and there aren't any avalanches."

"Well, yes, there is that."

I traversed out to where Hans had so calmly looked back from a decade and a half before, and then I traversed onto the outside, exposed corner. Eight hundred feet of air was framed between the quivering thighs of my Levis. The stately 150-foot-tall Engelmann spruce that sat at the base of the route looked like a blade of grass. It was a wholly unnatural position to be in. The animal within me was fully aware of that and feeling cornered and beginning to howl to escape, fast. My right hand frantically swept over the rock. I could not find a handhold. The lugs of my Vasque Ascenders quaked on small edges.

And then I lost it, screamed, "Alright guys, where are all of the fucking pitons!"

The rope tensed up; Ron, connected to me and concerned. "Take it easy man," he said from the belay. "You can't fall there."

I breathed in and out and reached and caught the hard edge of a flake and it felt like a half-inch sheet of plywood. Then I found a fixed piton and sixty feet later I balanced onto a ledge that was stacked with broken rock, the backside of Yamnuska sloped away gently. Fifteen feet back from the edge a stunted and wind-tortured pure Engelmann spruce stood three feet tall and a foot across at the butt; it was an old tree. I tied off to it, sat braced and strong, and wrapped the rope around my waist and bought up Ron.

"Ya!" he shouted, "Oh man, that was amazing!"

"Humblini," the nickname I'd given him, "we've cracked the 5.6 barrier!"

I wrestled the rope from the brittle scales of bark, desiccated branches bit like small racks of antlers. I've tied to that spruce another four dozen times over the last thirty-four years, the tree is five feet high now and its roots run deep in the rock of Yamnuska.

September 1978, my best friend from first grade—a guy who would go on to stand as best man at both of my weddings—Jon Body and I started digging ditches with Custom Trenching and Excavating. It was better money than Sport Chek so I quit the store. At least two mornings that fall Jon and I left an all-night party and drove to my mom's house to get my work clothes, then drove to his place to do the same, and then we'd drive straight to our jobsite.

"You talk a lot about being a mountain climber, but I don't see you doing it." Ross stated it plainly, his blue eyes looking into my brown ones, no malevolence or judgment. More of a reality check, creative

criticism. Ross was in his late twenties and ran a one-man outdoor merchandise outlet shop out of a defunct gas station. The Mountain Miser was strategically placed a couple of doors away from the Hostel Shop, and a competing outdoor retailer used the location to sell off their overstock cheap. Ross lived on an elevated plywood bed that he'd framed up above a hot plate and minifridge in the back of the store. I thought that he had it made and did some shifts for him and he came out climbing with me some. Ross always gave me honest mentoring.

He was right. I'd continued to read a lot about climbing, but I still wasn't a real climber. All that I knew about climbing I'd figured out from reading and then applying what I'd read while climbing with Ron, Phil, Tim, and Jon. Ron was away at university most of the time, Phil had largely hung it up, Jon only did it to appease me, and Tim was in jail.

Tim's dad had gotten Tim a janitor's job at McMahon Stadium in Calgary. One night, after a game, Tim and his partner, Les, robbed all the popcorn and soft drink money from the stadium, about $7,000 in one- and two-dollar bills. Tim sent Les to buy their tickets to Hawai'i the next day. When Les counted out hundreds and hundreds of ones and twos, the ticket agent got suspicious. The RCMP walked into the airport boarding lounge the next day and hauled Tim and Les off in their Hawaiian shirts, shorts, and flip-flops. The first thing that Tim did in the Calgary jail, Spy Hill, was to beat up Les and that got him an additional two months. I visited Tim in there— the authoritative hiss and clunk of the barred metal doors that seal the free from the detained is haunting. It was the door that closed on Tim's and my friendship. I wanted to climb, and I wanted to do more than dig ditches.

I had a buddy, Richard, who was doing well selling mailing machines and photocopiers with Pitney Bowes. He got me an interview with the sales manager in Calgary and I got a junior sales rep job and a half territory. The bank gave me a loan and I bought a snapdragon yellow 1974 MGB, a black Samsonite briefcase, and two business suits. I drove around making cold calls on businesses trying

Guiding on the Redshirt Route, Mount Yamnuska, in 2010, calm and collected in a position where my Vasque Ascender boots had quaked with fear thirty-two years earlier. Photo: Kai Larson to sell them mailing machines and visiting customers trying to get them to buy more machines. My partying became less high school and more business-like. One of the sales reps rented me a room in his house and I moved out of my mom's.

Ron and I started getting up things that summer. Rather than defeat and retreat, we went and we sent. Conrad Kain and Albert MacCarthy's 1916 route up the incredible Mount Louis—the mountain looks like an arrowhead aimed into the sky. Hans Gmoser, Leo Grillmair, and Heinz Kahl's 1957 Yamnuska test piece, Direttissima—where Ron and I shook hands on top and walked off down the descent trail feeling like we had really accomplished something. And then we went back into the big mountains.

"We'll be able to get up anything with these babies," Ron assured me, handing me the half dozen red ice screws that he'd found in the bottom of a cardboard box at the Army War Surplus Store and bought for a buck fifty a piece. The screws were heavy and tubular and about the same diameter and length as a fountain pen. A confusing singular oblong window of about half an inch in length had been cut longitudinally in the shaft just above the tip; I never did figure out what that window was for.

We had talked ourselves into attempting the Hourglass route on the north face of Mount Athabasca. We reasoned we had a better chance at getting up it rather than the North Face route because the Hourglass presented a crux of ice climbing, and we had done four hours of ice climbing, whereas the crux of the North Face was mixed climbing and we'd done none of that. Dave Giesler, a high school buddy and skier from Ron's class, two years older than me, wanted to come with us.

After work on a Friday I was at the University of Calgary's Outdoor Centre renting a seventy-centimeter ice ax and a pair of Salewa Everest crampons with inclined front points. Phil had bought me a copy of Yvon Chouinard's *Climbing Ice* for my twentieth birthday; it is by far one of the best that I've read in the instructional genre. I loved the anecdotes from Yvon's climbing life that end each chapter, the first of which is set in the Rockies—a fumbled attempt on what they thought was Mount Alberta in 1958:

At last we were real alpinists! On the summit snow ridge we
moved together, carrying coils just like Gaston Rebuffat does
in his books. We literally ran the last few hundred feet to the
summit. The tin-can register said: 'Mount Woolley, 11,170 feet.'
Over to the west, barely visible through the approaching
storm, we made out the enormous, evil-looking Alberta.
Yvon Chouinard, *Climbing Ice*

I was on fire to get on the ice, but my reading far outstripped
my experience—Ron and I had spent the good part of a day sur-
mounting a twenty-foot-high bulge of ice in a frozen creek the
previous Christmas with primitive rental crampons and handholds
chipped into the ice with our rock hammers. Four hours was the
extent of my ice climbing experience.

The one-quarter-inch military spec webbing tied into a wrist loop
through the rental ax's head came up short compared to the picture
in *Climbing Ice*, so I tied it into a slip knot that constricted onto my
wrist, but allowed me the length to swing the tool from the ferule and
spike as a Yvon instructed. In my other hand would be my prized new
purchase, a Forrest Mjöllnir hammer, the first piece of ice gear that I'd
bought, with three interchangeable picks it could function on rock,
waterfall ice and alpine ice. I felt proud and excited holding it in my
hand, it brought me one step closer to being a climber.

Ron picked me up in the Pinto and we picked up Dave in Banff
where he was working as a bartender and then we continued on to
the Columbia Icefields and bivied on the alluvial outwash of the creek
that drains the north Athabasca Glacier.

Yvon recommended getting an early start so we were up at 2:00
a.m. shuffling around by flashlight. The air was cool and crisp, it felt
like an icy mist on my tongue.

Somehow we found the north glacier and dawn played witness
to the three of us marching up a line of footsteps that looked like per-
forations in a sheet of white paper. We were unroped and Dave was
falling behind Ron and me.

"Wait, you guys! Wait!" came a plaintiff wailing from Geisler. When I looked back down the line of steps he looked small. Ron and I thumped our packs down onto the glacier and then sat on them.

Dave crunched up, "I can't do this. My thighs are burning, they're killing me. How are you guys' legs?"

"Mine are fine. No problem," Ron said.

"I'm doing OK," I added.

"I'm going to have to go back. I can hardly stand," Dave pleaded. "I'll give you guys the stuff I'm carrying and wait for you at the car."

"You're sure you don't just need a break?" I asked.

"No, my legs are fucked. Really fucked."

The cauldron of the North Face was austere and magnificently alpine, Ron and I meandered through a swath of sérac debris. Aquamarine sharp-edged chunks, several the size of cargo vans, sat on the glacier as an arctic equivalent of the boulder field that Ron and I had descended through after climbing the Belfry route on Mount Yamnuska. Deep gouges scarred the upslope of the bigger chunks like a metal hull had been hauled over sand, the sides and downslopes of the blue chunks encased in a matrix of plaster-hard snow and clear ice fragments that looked like glass held in mortar. It was mythically beautiful, a field of colossal emeralds, and as easy to walk on as concrete and blessedly Ron and I had little sentience on how recent the collapse had been, or its destructive power.

"This is cool." Ron exclaimed.

Fifteen hundred feet to our left gullies of ice the color of graying bone draped runnels between ribs of tawny rock that ran to join the backbone of the northeast ridge like a leviathan's emaciated rib cage. Melding onto the north face the ice became contiguous, a sweep of pewter l,500 feet wide and 900 feet tall. Ron and I stood below the bergschrund looking up to the route.

A ten-story-high sérac, the one that had calved not days ago, overlaid the ice face, its footing five hundred feet up to our right. It was the frontage of the Silverhorn Glacier, a pocket glacier blown into the lee of the long sculptured ice arête. The mountain bespoke power and everywhere I looked it seemed that it towered over me and I felt nervous and exposed, anxious to move. Three hundred feet above us a sole outcropping of rust-colored rock broke the surface of ice like a small island. It looked to be about the size of a Volkswagen Beetle. I racked up and aimed for it.

The red ice screw screamed with resistance when I slotted the pick of my hammer into it. Plates of gray ice fractured and cracked and lifted off in increasing concentric circles that looked like an ice blossom. One hundred feet lower my calf muscles had gone to a place that they had never been before. Now they quivered in a queer oscillation approaching simple harmonic motion. I cranked again and the rotten little screw bent like a nail in the claws of a hammer.

I couldn't stand on my front points any longer, my calves were failing and it was a long way down to Ron. My whole body trembled, I'd braced my knees against the ice for support and pushed on them to keep my shaking from popping my front points out. I spun a sling around the bent shaft of the screw and clipped it into my harness. With a couple of comic back pedals because my front points were popping at the ice, my eyes hubcapped and hands mauled the sling that wasn't holding me. Then it snapped tight, the ice screw held and I slumped onto the ice sideways and groaned from the searing pain in my calves.

Ron's calves were equally useless when he reached me, although mine had recovered some by then. Below us two other people were following our tracks through the field of sérac debris. We decided to try to get to the rock outcrop, and when I did it was my savior because my calves were cooked again, but there was one square yard of horizontal to stand on. I'd never guessed how tortuous sustained alpine ice could be if the only technique in your quiver was front pointing. Ron's calves buckled before he got to the outcrop and I held him on the rope until he could continue. He floundered onto the outcrop and we dangled three hundred feet up that oceanic expanse of ice like two men shipwrecked clinging to flotsam.

That's when Dick Mitten and Carl Austrom happened by and rescued us. They were real climbers from Squamish who knew what they were doing. Ten Chouinard tubular ice screws—technology so hallowed that it was a precious commodity, dealt around like contraband. Dick and Carl graciously offered to leave the Chouinards in for me to clip and Ron to clean. Ron and I were in so far over our heads that it was laughable, but we were still keen. We climbed on imitating Dick's graceful *pied troisiéme* and learning how to ration our calf endurance. I'd read about the technique in Yvon's book, it was French for putting a foot sideways into the three o'clock position, or the third position in ballet.

At one of the belays Dick palmed one of the little red screws and said, "You know, my dad gave me one of these that he'd climbed with in the sixties. I use it as a corkscrew to open wine bottles. It even sucks at that."

The Hourglass is named for a narrow gulley squeezed tight between the far right-hand edge of the north face rockband and the bulkhead of the Silverhorn sérac. It was a wild place to be in, I could touch the swirling tension in the azure ice with my right hand. It looked like twisted rock strata exposed in a road cut. Eight feet to my left black limestone buttressed the ice and rose shear and compact and dark into the slate-colored underside of low lying clouds. Vertical green water ice lay over the contorted glacial ice like candle wax dripped down brocade. Getting up it was an act of desperation for Ron and me and—there is no other word for it—Carl and Dick hauled us up. The slipknot that I'd tied to make a wrist loop on the rental ax bit like barbwire.

"Is that a slipknot?" Dick asked when I finally reached the belay.

"Ya, it's all of the sling that I had."

"Never do that again man, you could lose your hand."

Anchored in, and waiting for Ron, I gazed along the leading edge of the sérac that was so alien and breathtaking to me. That was the first time that I stood close to such glacial power, the line of it running away from me for hundreds of feet and so linear it looked like it had been sliced with a knife. Still and silent locked in a stalemate with gravity, thousands of tons of dense ice waiting for the crack of structural failure and the chaotic collapse and charge to the glacier below.

Two hours later we pulled over the top, four hungry young men. I had a bread bag with about a pound of pork slices from the roast that my mom had cooked that week. Carl and Dick were confessed vegetarians who'd eaten the last of their vegetables below the bergschrund six hours ago.

"Ya, I'll have some," Carl replied when I offered him some pork.

"This tastes good," Dick added. Ron and I followed them back to the car. We'd been on the mountain for twelve hours and Geisler was giddy on seeing us.

"You guys are alive!" he shouted.

"Yes," Dick smiled, "thank god they didn't die. Now they can go try something harder."

Later that summer Ron and I succeeded on something easier; Feuz and Hickson's 1926 route on Eisenhower Tower.

Laurie had hair the color of sunshine and I called her that, 'Sunshine.' She was a gifted artist and sketched a fine pencil drawing of me on the top of the tower and gave it to me for my birthday the next year.

"God, it's amazing. Thank you, Sunshine."

Ron went back to school and I continued in the life of a full commission salesman who dreamed of being a climber. One evening that fall my roommate introduced me to Maureen, a woman that he was seeing.

"I have a brother who climbs," she said. "You'll have to meet him."

Later that week I was introduced to her brother, Kevin Doyle.

PLAYLIST

The Rolling Stones	*Sympathy For the Devil*
Jerry Jeff Walker	*L.A. Freeway*
Roger Miller	*King of the Road*

Chapter 6

KEVIN

MY MG PURRED TO A STOP in front of Al Coleson's house
that I rented a room in and I flicked the headlights off, opened the
door, and pushed myself up to standing from the low seat. My black
briefcase was six inches wide and heavy with sales brochures. I
tugged it from behind the seat and walked the bone-white precast
patio stones that laid a sidewalk up the right side of the house to the
front door.

Al was still in his suit, although he'd relaxed the Windsor in his
wide, navy blue tie and he and Maureen were laughing, glasses of red
wine held by the stems in their hands. Sitting on the black flagstone
in front of the humming gas fireplace was a guy about my age. He was
looking up to them and laughing along, a glass of red wine cradled
like a cappuccino bowl between his palms. He wore a tight, tan T-shirt
and blue jeans. Bronze curls framed an adonic forehead and blue
eyes that sparkled because they had teared over from laughter.

"Barry, this is my brother, Kevin, the climber," Maureen said, smiling.

Kevin set his wine glass down and pulled the collar of his T-shirt
up and wiped away the tears with it and then he pushed himself up.
He strode four quick steps across the living room as I climbed the half
flight of stairs from the front door. We shook hands and I saw that his
forearms were as big, or bigger, than his biceps, blue veins surfaced
at his inner elbow and cabled his pale skin like girdling roots woven
over a tree trunk.

Kevin, aka Wally, in 1980, the most naturally
gifted climber I've ever tied-into a rope with.
Photo: Barry Blanchard

"Howdy," I said.

"Pleased to meet you. My sister here tells me that you're a climber." His blue eyes were locked on mine and his chest was out. Kevin stood to the same height as me, five nine and a half, but whereas I was barrel chested he had a compact chest set on stacks of abdominal muscles that were visible through his shirt.

"Ya, I like to climb. I'm a climber."

"So what have you climbed?" He pitched it out there as a challenge, one that I took hold of.

"Me and my buddy Ron climbed the Direttissima Route on Yamnuska this summer. It's graded 5.7."

"Ya, I know, I climbed it a couple of years ago with Ken Degner. It's a great route. The inside corner on the second pitch is one of my favorite pitches on Yam. Did you lead any of it?"

"I led all of it."

"Cool, that's cool. Do you know Degner?"

"No."

"What about Stewart Buroker? Do you know Stew Buroker?"

"I've never met him, but I know his younger brother, Craig. I've done some skiing with Craig."

The Burokers were related to the Shattos by blood, or religion, or both. Lena Shatto was the woman who had adopted my incarcerated buddy, Tim. Tim loved to downhill ski, as did Craig, who was a year or two younger than Tim and me. The three of us had skied together, once I started working and could afford to buy my own gear and pay for a lift ticket. Stewart was Craig's older brother and Stewart was legend in the Shatto/Buroker world for having traveled to the Asia to find god, yet returned home after concluding that the Baptist God of his upbringing was the God, a conclusion he soon abandoned in favor of secular hedonism. The second thing that he'd discovered in the Himalaya was mountaineering.

Stewart and Kevin were best friends and climbing partners. They called each other 'Zoltan' (Stewart) and 'Klugan' (Kevin), and they ascribed to *truckma*, as opposed to karma, truckma being the belief that your future lives determine the one that you are presently living. On a day yet to be Stewart would stand with his feet pressed together and his hands held in the yogic heart center position: "If you believe the universe to be circular and that time exists within the universe you'll have no problem with truckma," and then he bowed forward reverentially presenting me the gleam of his bald head and added, "Grasshopper," tilting his head sideways grinning and winking.

"You look kinda big to be a climber," Kevin challenged. And it was true, my salesman's lifestyle was adding a toll, I was up to 185 pounds, 20 pounds over my fighting weight. Kevin looked to be twenty-five pounds lighter than me.

"I can climb. Don't worry about that."

We made plans to head out to Okotoks Rock on Sunday, two days away. I was very aware of the fact that Kevin would be the first climbing partner of mine, besides Gray Dickson, who wasn't one of my school buddies.

Anna Christina opened the door to the basement suite.

"Hi! I'm AC. You must be here to go climbing with Kev, come on in." Playful as a pixie she batted her brown eyes and pirouetted and sauntered off to fetch Kevin. He'd told me that they were living together while he finished off his carpentry apprenticeship, one glance at their fledgling nest told me that they were playing house.

In front of the house Kevin's avocado green 1967 Mercedes 200 diesel sat at the curb. It had fins, a small acquiescence of German tradition to the American dream. The car suited Kevin, it was not a car that his father would buy. There was nothing light about the Mercedes and when the trunk bit a bloody avulsion into Kevin's right trigger finger he linked together an eleven-word chain of profanity the likes and volume of which I'd only previously heard from myself. I was impressed. We tramped back into the basement and AC got some white athletic tape. She pressed the flap into place and Kevin mummified his finger.

"There, that should work," AC smiled. And it had on his mood; he'd spun a one-eighty from livid rage to happy optimism largely via AC's tenderness and care. Kevin and I chugged south from the city.

Okotoks Rock looks like a gargantuan cinder block that has been karate chopped in two. It is the largest glacial erratic in the world and it has settled into the prairie like two Victorian houses lain on their sides and canted toward each other. The Blackfoot Indians believe that the rock was cleaved by a bat who flew into it at the behest of Napi—the Old Man trickster—whom the rock was chasing. The bat got his face pushed in, the rock was split, and Napi was safe.

A cordilleran glacier deposited the Big Rock—a piece of Cog quartzite—on the edge of the foothills 10,000 years ago. Cog is the hardest rock in the Rockies and the best to climb on. The climbing tribe found Okotoks in the fifties and since then it has evolved from a practice area into a prime bouldering venue.

The Big Rock sat as tawny as the wheat that stood shorn to stubble from the harvest and surrounded it like a sea of sand. I'd climbed here with Ron, Tim, and Jon. Kevin bridged and palmed past moves that I'd aid climbed. He climbed far better than me and I immediately wanted to climb as well as he did.

The only named line on the Big Rock was the Greenwood route and it was where Ron's friend had witnessed Brian Greenwood climb and seen that the man had "fingers like pitons."

It was going on dusk and Kevin and I had been climbing for hours, sometimes bouldering, sometimes top-roping. Golden autumnal light streamed onto the west boulder and the quartzite gained distinction in coppers and duns and from the pale pastel green blooms of map lichen the size of quarters, and dime-sized colonies of orange lichens that bled to rust at their perimeters and spotted the Okotoks like drops of rain.

"This is Greenwood's route," Kevin said, and he wiped his palms over his blue jeans. "It's hard."

He pulled onto the wall and statically and precisely climbed to a two-foot-wide roof that looked like it had been chiseled to right angles by stone cutters. He paused and wiped his palms over his outer thighs, then he breathed in and held it and flowed over the roof with a balletic grace that I'd never seen before.

I tried, but the holds felt too small and when I shifted my hips toward commitment the fear of falling backward onto the fractured blocks that ringed the bottom of Okotoks like wrecked cars stopped me. I climbed down finding one of the right handholds by a spot of Kevin's blood that had lost its brightness and dried to russet.

"Good try, Blanch, you were close. It took me awhile to figure that one out. I think that you'll get it next time."

The next weekend Kevin and I chose Chockstone Corner to be my first 5.8 on Yamnuska. Further, it would be a test of the practicality of our partnership. We both wanted to climb, but could we do that together?

The ninth pitch of Chockstone Corner was the crux and it started with a chimney that choked down to a wide crack in a corner that protected on softball-sized chockstones, the stones that gave the route its name. Body tension, core strength, I made moves that hardened my forearms until they bulged like constricting snakes, but I found control in the heat of it. The climbing made sense to me.

Kevin and I made plans for the coming ice season. "You've got to do some ice climbing, Blanch. Guy's gotta have those skills for the big mountains."

Okotoks Rock, with a climber on the Greenwood problem. Photo: Brad Wrobleski

"The double boots are two hundred and fifty dollars." The floor person at the Hostel Shop had an auburn beard and shoulder length hair. He looked like a mountain man and told me that he did some ice climbing.

"That's a lot of money," I said.

"I don't think of it as a lot for having warm toes."

"It's a quarter of a thousand dollars."

"That is another way of looking at it, I guess."

I bought a pair of Galibier Peuterey Ridge single boots for a hundred dollars less, and a pair of SMC rigid crampons, and a Forrest Sérac Sabre ice ax to pair with my Mjöllnir hammer. Back at Al Coleson's house I heated his oven to 150° F and placed my Galibiers in for five minutes and then took them out and slathered Sno-Seal into the hot leather and placed the boots back into the oven. I repeated the process three times, just as Kevin had instructed.

Kev took me down to the Army War Surplus Store, "These are the ones, Blanch." He pulled a pair of green wool pants from the shelf and handed them to me. The material was amazingly thick, sat like a heavy wool blanket in my hands.

"They're Army winter exercise pants. You need to buy them big, forty-inch waist. Wash them in super hot water and dry them on hot-hot, they'll shrink down and be super dense, keep you warm. Man-eating-clam pants, you'll need suspenders, but hey! They're only five bucks."

In November, Kevin coaxed the tired twelve-year-old Mercedes up the Big Bend on the Banff-Jasper highway. The highway had been started in 1931 during the Great Depression. Men in relief camps worked south from Jasper and north from Banff. Much of the work was done by hand and the two crews met at the Big Bend in 1939, just in time for the Second World War.

The grade of the Bend is incredibly steep. Kevin and I counted down from three and thrust our chests into the steering wheel and dash, respectively, in an effort to boost the Benz up the Bend.

"Three, two, one, thrust!" Kevin bellowed over top of Mick Jagger who was, himself, bellowing about having rode in a tank while holding a general's rank, "Pleased to meet you. Hope you guessed my name."

The Hilda Creek Hostel was a legacy from the work camps. It's three Pan-Abode buildings were gifted to the Southern Alberta Hosteling Association when the road was done and the men went off to war. Kevin knew Ben Gadd and his wife, Cia, who were acting as the houseparents at Hilda Creek that season, living there with their two young sons, Will, twelve, and Toby, ten. Kevin and I were their sole guests and they had us over to their cabin. Slender, bearded, and wearing wire rimmed glasses, Ben looked like the eccentric geology PhD hippie that he was. Eventually Kevin and I returned to our sleeping dorm, knowing that we'd set our alarm for 4:00 a.m. and that we needed to lie down and pretend to sleep.

"I'll lower you on the rope, and you put in an ice screw at halfway and build an anchor at the bottom and I'll down climb on belay," Kevin directed.

Cold waves of spindrift swept the steel-gray ice like windblown white sand drifting across polished ashen marble. It was the middle of November and -5° F. Kevin and I stood in the pied troisiéme position, the rope from our harnesses tight to a double-screw anchor 600 feet above the bergschrund on the Skyladder route on Mount Andromeda. Night was coming so we had to be going. We hadn't made the route.

I sat back on the rope and watched my new, gleaming, and knifepoint sharp crampons bite into the chrome-hard ice like a dog's teeth into brittle bone. Small arcs of fractured ice shot from the points looking like stone hits crunched into a windshield. We were climbing on a single eleven-millimeter rope that was 165 feet long and the only option known to us for rappelling was to leave an ice screw, double the rope, and do 82.5-foot rappels, it would have meant leaving all eight of Kevin's Chouinards to get back down the four ropelengths we had climbed—$200 worth of ice screws.

Kevin climbed down methodically front point, front point, ice ax, ice ax, 165 feet, 330 feet, 495 feet. He never faltered and I was humbled belaying in his rope foot by foot. I could not do what he was doing. I wasn't as good as him. Yet it was trying for him and I was learning Kevin held nothing back:

"Not too tight, Blanch! This is touchy, man. I don't want you to pull me off!" And I'd relax some rope.

"There, that's better, keep it like that."

When he got to the anchor I said, "Good work, Kev. That was amazing man."

"Thanks, Blanch, if we just keep doing this we'll get down this thing." And we did.

Ron came home for Christmas break and Humblini joined the clan of Zoltan, Klugan, and Bugaboo Blanch. Stewart ate himself into a turkey-and-dressing coma on Christmas Day. He slept until the middle of Boxing Day confessing that he'd had to lay on his back on his mom's floor and hyperventilate to deal with the fullness. "I felt like a python who had just swallowed a goat!"

December 29, 1979: We'd roll into a new decade in three days time. The four of us stuffed our waist-high bloated packs into Ron's Pinto station wagon and then we all piled in and I felt the car settle low and heavy. Cold, windblown shoulders of asphalt, chalk white drifts of snow draped over the frozen foothills like sailcloth, the Rockies stratified in blacks and whites locked solid in frost. Ron drove for three and a half hours, the four of us arguing, joking, laughing. Kevin, Stewart, and I dozed on and off.

"I don't know, Blanch. That system sounds screwy to me," Stewart said.

"No man, trust me, I saw it in Chouinard's book, *Climbing Ice*. It's the way to go."

Yvon's words and passion had resonated in my bloodstream. I wanted to climb ice. Pity that I wasn't more astute with the pictures, because I'd erroneously concluded that the climbers in one of Ruedi

Homberger's photos had a full ropelength between them while moving fourth class up some beautiful pleatings of névé.

"How in the hell does it work?" asked Ron.

"OK, again, Klugan takes all of the screws. How many do we have?"

"Klugan has eight; I, Zoltan, own two; Humblini counts two in his possession; and you, Monsieur Blanch, have zilch. Twelve, we have twelve screws," Stewart replied.

"Right," I said, "Kev leads off with all twelve screws and places one at half rope and then another one when the rope comes tight to you, Zoltan."

"One hundred and sixty five feet is a long way to fall if Kev blows it placing the second screw, or anyone thereafter for that matter," Ron observed.

"He's Klugan, he won't fall," I replied.

"It's ok you guys. Blanch and I did it on the way up Skyladder last month. It'll work," Kevin stated.

"Ooh yez! Ve hav Got's gift to climbing ve do, Das Klugan." Stewart joked, holding his finger up in point, enjoying his parody and chuckling.

"Anyways," I continued, "Stew starts up when the rope comes tight and he trails a second rope to Ron. When Stew gets to a screw he shouts up to Kev to place another one so that there are always two screws anchoring the rope. Ron starts up when his rope comes tight and he trails the third rope to me. Stew, you and Ron just have to unclip the rope above and clip in the rope below, I'll collect all of the screws. Ten screws should be enough to get us up the ice face and onto the Photo Finish sérac. Trust me, it works."

Early winter snows had been sculpted into drifts by the westerlies and the snow clung to the cement abutments that barricaded the snowcoach access road like the drape of a robe carved from white marble. My boot hovered over the edge of the first drift and I eased onto it. The crust collapsed and my foot thumped to ground in a shin deep posthole. Two postholes later the crust carried my boot and I braced both hands onto my bent knee and grunted upright. I walked on top for nine steps toward the next arc of wind-scoured black asphalt. Four feet from the edge of the drift my back foot broke through and shot to the ground and the mass of my pack yarded me back onto my ass with force.

"Fuck!" I grunted. Behind me Stewart cackled.

Kevin stepped to the fore, "Here, Blanch, let me battle this shit for a bit." We all took turns punching holes into the plaster-hard crust, the stiff edge of it rasping down the line of my shin like I'd stumbled into a sheet of half-inch plywood.

The parking lot at the end of the road sat barren and broad and the arctic cold of the day imposed an air of abandonment onto it. I sat on my pack in the lee of the boarded-up curio shop, the lot's sole building. An anomalous small garden of stunted spruce and low growth lay in an oval outside the front door and it was bordered by cinder-block-sized chunks of black limestone that someone had lifted and carried from the lateral moraine ten yards away, where the bull-dozer and paver had quit and the mountain sloped up. I pulled on my old down jacket and pondered how someone had planted and tended that small garden and got it to grow in a place where all other life on that scale failed.

"This fucking pack is pissing me off," Kevin growled and he shucked it from his back and let it hammer onto the pavement beside me. He found the offending hard edge in the back panel with his mit-tened hand, then stomped on it like he was driving a spade into hard ground. "There, that ought'a fix it." He beamed in self-satisfaction sit-ting down on it.

We pitched Ron and Stewart's tents one kilometer farther up on a bedrock bench with a meter of chalk-hard snow drifted onto it, the soaring black cliffs of the northwest ridge of Mount Andromeda above.

Irreverent, ribald jokes hurled between the open portals of the tents as we cautiously passed hot drinks and food back and forth while air that had been chilled over the Arctic flowed in low and pushed on us to yard the tent flaps shut with a yowling of the zipper.

"...No, we don't have to worry about crevasses. Humblini will take care of that. If there is a crevasse within a hundred miles Humble will find it and fall into it." I stated, "He's a crevasse magnet."

"Blanch speaks the truth you guys, shit always happens to me, never to him. Rockfall, too. It always hits me, never him. I hate him for it," Ron lamented.

I was extraordinarily aware of being camped below an alpine climb. My heart beat waves of possibility into my blood and I felt like I was standing at the threshold of a space that was vast and intimidating, yet calling. In my mind I saw Walter Bonatti bivouacked on the North Face of Les Grandes Jorasses in winter. I wanted to be in that picture.

We walked away at 4:00 a.m.

Wonder was the brand of our headlamps and it was an appropriate name in that it was a "wonder" that they worked. Ahead of me three pale sepia-tinted lights bobbed along like karaoke balls. Slices of cold, white snow bordered the black slots of the crevasses. Deep blues flashed in the feeble sweep of my headlamp then immediately sank back to black. This edge of the Andromeda Glacier fell in two directions and was crosshatched with a shattered grid of crevasses. Kevin found the same rib of dirty gray ice that had provided us passage one month earlier. Kevin, Stewart, Ron—their headlamps rose in an ascending procession, dim torchlights climbing into the night in series and following a path up the mountain like it were a songline threaded into their blood. I followed, gravel and ashen ice fragmenting from the bite of my crampons and rattling away into the darkness of the downslope crevasse like copper coins chiming into the underworld—that blackness one and a half meters to my right.

A half hour later, and we had gained the flats of the glacier when a trap door of snow sprang open under Ron's feet and he thumped waist deep into a crevasse.

"Fuck!" he screamed.

"Humble is in a crevasse!" I bellowed, lunging backward to tension the rope and then driving my weight onto it by digging my heel spikes in and thrusting with my legs.

Yellow beams slashed left and right. Stewart yelled, Kevin yelled in confusion, and then understanding, and I felt the rope tension to life around my waist. Ron waded out of the manhole. We continued into the gradual illumination of the coming dawn.

My rope system was ridiculous. Kevin was four hundred and ninety five feet, and two hours, up the face before I started across the bergschrund!

Pitch after pitch of gunmetal gray ice. Time passed. Our calf muscles were seared in lactic acid and ached at the edge of muscular failure and each of us would charge the last bodylengths to the ice screws to gain the step that Kevin had chopped and get a foot sideways and pant away the burning in our calves.

Late afternoon, Stewart, Ron, and I were standing at our second proper anchor 1,200 feet up the face. Above us the leading edge of the ridgeline glacier arced for 1,500 feet from the ice slopes of the North Bowl to the Photo Finish route that had been climbed by George Lowe, Jock Glidden, and Dave Hamre in 1972. The sérac looked like a tidal wave frozen in time, its top edge melding into a sky that had eroded from blue to the color of ashes. Kevin led up and right searching for the exit Rene Boiselle and Ray Ware had used when they'd made the first ascent of this North Bowl route in 1976. He didn't find it. By half a ropelength Kevin had placed six ice screws.

"Shit, if Doyle is putting in that many screws it must be hard," Ron said.

One hundred and thirty feet out Kevin's breath was raging as he fought to get in another ice screw. "Watch me here!" he shouted and the three of us at the anchor locked our eyes onto Kevin.

He clipped the screw and retwisted his right hand into its wrist loop and then he pulled up and locked off on it and reached to swing his left tool. An hubcap-sized chunk of ice fractured free and Kevin fumbled with it and swore and screamed "Ice!" and the chunk skittered away to leap and then bound toward us. It spun faster with each crunching impact and was soon roaring as it sliced through the air toward us.

"Oh shit!" Stew blurted.

"Don't worry, it'll hit Humble," I wisecracked, while tracking the projectile and trying to time my dodge yet panicking when the chunk outstripped the speed of my eyes and reflexes. It ripped past my inside shoulder and made an impacting sound similar to a five-pound ball dropped from the eaves into a large paper bag filled with dry pinecones.

"Fuck!" Ron yelped, "Fuck! Fuck! Fuck!" And he folded at the waist tucking his right hand against his stomach groaning low and powerfully trying to deal with the pain.

"Are you ok?" I blurted.

"Ohhh! Fuuuck!" he growled through clenched teeth, eyes clamped shut.

"We'll take care of this, Blanch," Stewart commanded, "you watch Kev."

Above, Kevin's panting was audible and his swings came rushed and many like a prizefighter teetering toward the bell throwing punches spontaneously. And then he pulled over and kicked up out of sight and the rope soon pulsed with the rhythmic cadence of step kicking.

The pitch overhung for several bodylengths and seconding it took me close to an hour. Kevin was sat on his pack, a saddle of snow braced between his legs where he had dug down and braced in his heels. Both of his ice tools were driven into the snow behind him and his rope hitched to their heads. He'd yarded hard on the rope, gifting me assurance, by bending forward and locking the rope off around his waist in a hip belay and then leaning back and letting the rope bite into his waist. I thought of Hemingway's character, Santiago, in *The Old Man and the Sea*, saw the taut, braided brown line that tied the old man to the great fish. Westerly winds raked the ridgeline above us. The wind held snow that it had scoured from the oceanic expanse of the Columbia Icefield. Nearly forty square miles of ice sat to the west of us. When the wind broke Andromeda's ridgeline it decelerated and dropped much of the scoured snow onto Kevin and me.

"We have to get Stew and Ron up here," Kevin said.

"Humblini's hand is hurt. It was already blue and swollen when I left the anchor. He's going to come up last. I'll dig in too and we can both pull on the rope."

"Sounds good, Blanch. I need the help. Let's do it."

Kevin and I, and then Stew, hauled hard on the rope as the daylight faded and the cold and the wind and the snow amassed and immersed us in a whiteout.

We hit the ridgeline at dusk and desperately staggered into the west wind trying to make it to the top of the Skyladder where we planned to get down just as Kevin and I had one month before. But we couldn't see, and the wind slugged into the left side of our bodies. We couldn't find our descent, and ended up huddling with our backs to the wind, the wind shoving and wobbling us at 11,000 feet above sea level on one of the longest nights of the year. Four young men buffeted onto the edge of an immense fear.

"If we stay here we are going to die," Ron shouted and the wind slapped him into me as it rotated a harsh rasp of sandpaper snow across our faces and needle pricked our eyes. Ron's ruddy cheeks glowed watery in the pale light of our headlamps, a halo of frost wreathed the edge of his hood and the wind ripped the clouds of his exhaled breath into streamers.

"I did a ski tour up the Athabasca and down the Saskatchewan glaciers last spring with Dick Mitten," Kevin yelled into our freezing faces. "There is a straightforward ramp off the backside that leads down to the Saskatchewan Glacier."

"Are you sure, Kev?" Stewart pleaded through chattering teeth.

"Yes. It'll work. We'll have to walk all night to get out to the road, but it will work."

"You're dead certain?" I asked. I could feel the night and the cold closing down tighter around me. Our situation seemed so serious, losing control so close.

"Ya, ya. It'll work," Kevin barked. "I saw it. You guys can trust me on this. Trust me."

We staggered back to where we'd topped out and began climbing down the backside of Mount Andromeda—to us, an unknown side of Mount Andromeda.

The wind abated with our loss of elevation. Sometime around midnight Ron fell waist deep into a crevasse and my leaden pace jolted into a powerful thrash back upslope to tension the rope. Ron backstroked and kicked and fought his way onto his feet. Kev's "straightforward ramp" became a labyrinth of massive and terrifying crevasses. Ron plunged armpits deep into one of the monsters and we pulled and he swam. We screamed to each other across the span of rope and agreed that "this is fucked!" We had to retrace our steps to the summit and find the Skyladder.

Slowly I turned back upslope. Each of the three steps that it took for me to change direction were feeble and teetered on the verge of my ability to balance. I felt a ragged and raw form of exhaustion and when I stepped uphill into the first of our downsteps my body went into shock and revolted at the cellular level. All I wanted to do was to lie down in the snow and go to sleep.

Fifty meters upslope the wind had drifted in our tracks. A series of faint shadows the size of a cupped hands marked the line of our right footfalls; our left tracks were gone. Within a hundred steps all trace of our passage had been erased. I felt abandon, heartsickenly lost, and afraid.

"I can't make out our tracks anymore!"

"Oh fuck," Ron sighed and he sank to his ass in the snow.

I stood dumb and anxious staring at the snow bounding over my boots, burying them, the unending snow. And then Kevin was beside me.

"We have to keep moving, Blanch. I'll go in front for a while. We can trade off when we get tired."

"OK, Wally," and my gaze fell back to my boots.

"We'll be OK, Blanch." Kev placed his snow-matted mitt on my shoulder. "We just have to keep moving."

He plowed off into the night with the rope summoning each of us to follow in series. It felt good to be taken care of. Kev's touch had transmitted a small spark of hope.

At 2:00 a.m. we were back in the teeth of the wind and I was in the lead. I would stagger punch-drunk with exhaustion for fifty steps and collapse backward onto my pack. My three partners would arrive and do the same and we would all pass out until one of us would chatter to consciousness and panic and shout to all "C'mon, guys! Get the fuck up! We have to keep moving!" and then we would repeat.

At 3:00 a.m. we had no idea where we were. The wind and the cold and the dark had compressed our world to the feeble island of light that Kevin's and my headlamps illuminated in the driving snow. Ron and Stew's lights had gone out.

"Blanch, get up, man!" Kevin was shaking my shoulders. I sputtered and jerked and realized that I was shivering and that I couldn't feel my hands or feet. I struggled to get up and swing blood back to my feet and hands.

"This fucker could kill us," I shouted. "We have to dig in."

Stewart erupted, "I'm not going to lie down in a snow bank and die!"

"Stew, what the hell else are we going to do?" Kevin countered. "We can't walk anymore."

The only tools we had to dig with were the adzes of our ice axes and our helmets and we took turns in our pit, two at a time, hacking at the chalk-hard snow with an adze and then scooping and scraping with the edge of our helmets held like we were gathering pails of grain.

"It looks like a coffin," Stew stated staring down into our six-foot-long by three-foot-wide and two-foot-deep trench.

"Fuck that, Buroker," said Ron. "Let's get in it."

We braced our backs to the wind and our feet to the opposite wall. Knees drawn up, shoulder to shoulder. With all of our clothes on, our packs held little and we emptied them placing anything with insulation value under us. Ropes, slings and empty water bottles, rigid with a patina of encased ice, all lined the bottom of our pit. We put our feet into our packs and I extended the top flap of my Berghaus Cyclops Roc rucksack and pulled hard on it to get it under my quivering butt cheeks.

"Loosen off the laces on your boots," Kevin instructed. "It will help with circulation."

Algid snow as fine as dust accumulated onto any lee and within six minutes my lap looked like it was coated in volcanic ash. The quaking of my shivers started from my core and I felt my invaluable heat bleeding into the cold that scrapped over my shoulders and surrounded me from the waist down like a frozen sea a hundred fathoms deep. The last time that any of us had anything to drink had been at noon the day before. A tacky paste lined the inside of my mouth and clung to the edges of my tongue like curing glue. In the inner pocket of my down jacket I found some food that I'd forgot I had—a granola bar and a block of cheddar cheese the size of a deck of playing cards that bore the imprint of my teeth and was frozen as hard as marble. I broke the bar into four equal pieces.

"Hey! I found some food. Eat this, it'll help. We need all the calories we can get."

Stewart was inert, but crackled to life on the offering of sustenance. He grabbed at the three-quarter-inch section of particleboard-dry granola and wolfed it into his mouth with an ice and snow matted

Dachstein mitt. Too much for his parched gullet, he hacked into convulsions that looked like dry heaves. I slapped him on the back and he coughed up the harsh cube.

"Buroker, you greedy bastard, take your time man. Chew for Christ's sake," I admonished.

"Jesus, I thought that I was choking to death, but I need the calories. I don't want to die here."

"Take your time with the cheese, man. Your survival does not depend on it," I replied.

"It damn well might."

I handed him a chunk that I'd cleaved from the block with my knife. Crystals of frost had fractured from the cheese as I levered on the blade. Minute gems of ice studded the edge of the rock hard cheese like quartz crusted to a limestone fissure.

Then followed hours of suffering. No matter how small I made the hole for my nose and mouth, nor how I sheltered it, pellets of icy snow sifted in to melt against my face, then freeze and accumulate as ice on my whiskers. I was full of the young man's fight and thought of the storm as a fucker who was trying to kill me rather than something that I had to endure, as in later years.

I dozed and I shivered and every time I lost feeling in my hands and feet I'd will myself to rise from my lethargy and swing my extremities until blood burned back into them. By and by I succumbed more to lethargy and surrendered and sat for longer periods before I truly feared frostbite and would rise to fight again. Kevin and Ron did the same, but not as often. Stewart didn't move all night. Even though we sat shoulder to shoulder we were separated into our personal battles for survival. I was the only one not to suffer a degree of frostnip or frostbite.

The hour before dawn was the coldest and most fearful for me. I did not know if I would see the dawn and I thought of my mother and how I did not want to die and put her through the grief of losing a son. I prayed and asked God to please let me get off Mount Andromeda, promised that I would give up climbing. Why wasn't I warm in Sunshine's bed? The heat of her skin seemed so far from the cold trembling surface of my own.

I could not feel my hands again and knew that they were the color of chalk inside my mitts. My feet had been gone for a long time. The wind pushed particles of ice over my back indefatigably, like a conveyor belt dumping sand. Climbing was a crazy game and it was trying to take everything. Rising to my feet was a phenomenal hassle. It took ten long minutes to swing feeling back into my hands and feet.

Dawn came. Black bleeding to gray, gray heating to white. Kevin, Ron, and I shouted to each other from inside the insular cocoons of our clothing. And then we crackled to standing shedding platings of ice and sculpted sheets of snow. Buroker looked like an Andean sacrifice that had mummified. Cornices clung to every fold and he was buried in snow from the waist down.

"Buroker! Are you alive?" I shouted at the torpid form. A beat passed, "Buroker!"

"Hummpff." And some of the cornices cracked and were grabbed by the wind.

"Buroker!"

"Ya, ya, I'm OK. I can't feel my feet."

Kevin and Stewart removed their boots and held each other's frozen feet to their stomachs while Ron and I got ready to move.

We trudged on. The day began to lighten and the wind diminished to a light breeze. The bellies of the clouds lifted from the glacier and we could make out a horizon and then a col up and left of us. A tender glow of optimism rose within my heart, my feet fired into the throbbing burn of full sensation as I kicked steps toward the col. We were moving faster than we had in twenty-four hours, rushing for the col, trying to get there before the clouds took it away.

We stood shoulder to shoulder at the col. Windows of sight opened through the clouds revealing ridges of crevasses in a glacier far below.

"It's the Athabasca Glacier!" Kevin shouted. "I know where we are! I can see the ramp that Dick and I skied up!"

"Fuckin' eh, Wally!" I exclaimed and we all laughed and hooted.

We descended ramps, made traverses, down climbed. It was so exciting to get under the cloud ceiling and see the glacier stretch out to the thin black line of the road. We were going to make it. And then

Ron fell waist deep into another crevasse and I kept right on marching down the steps toward him.

"Aren't you going to pull in the rope?" he asked, bewilderment framing his green eyes.

"Just get out of the damn hole, Humble," I said as I detoured around him striding wide and light to avoid breaking through.

Regaining 1,000 feet to retrieve our camp was an act of will. We were all shattered and would sit for long minutes before turning back to the slog uphill, yet when I walked away from camp, free from the rope for the first time in thirty hours, I felt a lightness, like the mountain was radiating a new source of energy up through the broken plates of slate and through my boot soles and into me. I felt light.

At 4:00 p.m., we found a Parks Canada truck sat idling beside Ron's Pinto. The warden was happy to see us because he could call off our rescue. Mount Andromeda had fallen back into cloud.

"Hey, what's that guy doing with a refrigerator on his back?" Kevin blurted the question out as we drove through Banff in the dark of night.

"He doesn't have anything on his back Wally, you're hallucinating," I replied.

"Fuck, are you sure?"

"No, he doesn't have anything on his back," Stew added.

Each one of us would see things that were not there before we reached the Calgary city limits.

Takakkaw Falls is the second highest waterfall in Canada. In early January of 1974 Bugs McKeith, Rob Wood, Tim Auger, Jack Firth, Jim Elzinga, and John Lauchlan attempted to climb the 800-foot-tall skyscraper of ice. Six feet of snow fell and avalanches savaged the nine-mile approach. The temperature plummeted to -49° F, and then it rained. Elzinga made it out on day two, the rest of the party were trapped in the Yoho Valley of British Columbia until day seven when

Lauchlan was evacuated due to a broken binding. A couple of weeks later Wood, McKeith, Firth, and Lauchlan returned and made the first ascent of Takakkaw over two days using aid climbing tactics (étriers clipped into the bottom of their Terrordactyls). Coloradans Duncan Ferguson and Dave Wright free climbed the route in '77, and the next winter John Lauchlan skied in and soloed the climb in two and a half hours.

March 30, 1980. I'd turned twenty-one the day before. Takakkaw would be the hardest route that Kevin and I had attempted, it would be my ninth waterfall ice climb and in preparation for it I'd bought a second Forrest Sérac Sabre, a hammer. Now I owned a matched set. I was ready to draft on Kevin's coattails, yet ice climbing remained a tenuous affair for me. I just didn't understand it like Kevin did and I knew that if I'd tried to lead some of the pitches that he had during our recent ascents of the Weeping Wall I would have fallen. Hell, I did fall off seconding one of his pitches! But that had been with my Mjöllnir hammer, a short-shafted tool that worked about as well as driving nails with a feather duster.

With the bright blue shaft of my new Sabre clamped firm under one thigh, and then the other, I'd toiled for two hours to file away a half inch of steel from the pick's profile. Kevin had told me that was how Lauchlan sharpened his. The large mill bastard burned hot to the touch and the freshly exposed metal glinted like quicksilver. I took coarse sandpaper to the slick plasticized shaft, then coated it with Barge Cement and rolled a foot-long section of one-and-one-quarter-inch bicycle inner tube onto it.

"It's just like putting on a condom," Wally joked, "although you may not know anything about that, Blanch!"

Three hours of work resulted in a more functional pick and a shaft that I could hold on to.

I opened the door of my MGB and Jerry Jeff Walker's baritone belted "LA Freeway" into the blackness of the Yoho Valley parking lot.

We'd left Calgary at midnight and it was now 2:00 a.m. Kevin hucked our skis over the road barricade and then pranced a theatrical scissor kick over the barricade using the headlights as a spot light. He was happy and soon he was leaning both hands onto a ski pole until his Nordic binding clicked twice.

He swung a wolfish grin at me and asked, "Are you ready for this, Blanch? Are you keen?"

"I was born that way, Wally." But I knew that this would be the biggest route that we had tried and a shadow of apprehension trudged back and forth inside my chest at the same time as a tingling of anticipation tickled up and down my spine. I knew that Kevin could see both my apprehension and anticipation in my words, and in me.

He kicked off powerfully leaning into a strong stride. I kicked and the long, black Karhu ski that I rented resisted the snow like it was sand. Kev's headlamp pulled away from me like a train running out into the night. I kicked harder, and more often, but still lost ground. Every pore in my body opened and began to weep sweat. Steam was wafting off of me when I finally came onto Kev. He was sitting on his pack, his skis running parallel down opposite sides of it.

"These fucking skis don't want to slide."

"Kick 'em off, Blanch, we'll try waxing them. We're going to have to move faster to make it out of here in a day."

Takakkaw Falls had had several one-day ascents by then and that was the carrot that Kevin and I were aiming for. An important gauge of how good we were getting. I corked in more kick-and-glide wax and it made the horrid black skis slide better for a couple of kilometers and then the wax would wear off and I'd repeat.

A gray dawn muted by an overcast sky. Takakkaw grew from a ghostly line on the right-hand rockwall to a massive white tower that had a deep black open cavern at its base. Mist pulsated from that thundering blackness like dragon's breath. The melt water from six and a half square miles of icefield and glacier hammered down the throat of the falls. I understood why the Stoney Indian word for "magnificent" had been applied to the falls.

"I want to feed these fucking skis into a wood chipper and dowse the chips in gasoline and burn them and then flush the ashes down the toilet!" I spat to Kev.

He laughed, "Is that how you really feel?"

"Yes."

"Well, wait on that, Blanch. We'll need them to get out of here."

He'd stamped out a platform in the steepening slope and was changing into his climbing boots, Galibier Super Guides. I pulled out my brand new blue Gore-Tex jacket, the first piece of the hallowed miracle fabric that I owned.

"Wow, look at you, Blanch! Is that Gore-Tex?"

"You bet ya. Sunshine bought it for me for my birthday."

"She's a doll...has to be to put up with your ass."

"Ha, ha, whatever, Walter."

Kevin led. Stellar snowflakes the size of postage stamps began falling from the underbelly of a sky that was the color of lead. Soon the flakes ganged into clusters and all of the back rock turned into white and then streaked itself black again as ribbons of spindrift hissed away.

I traversed, rising and to the right above the black portal. The air resonated from the thundering of the water inside the darkness and the falling snow quivered to that resonance. The dragon's breath had settled into huge mounds of alabaster ice that sat rounded and knuckled along the lower edge of the dark hole like a giant's hands clinging to the sill of Hades. A primal fear rose inside me: The hard-wired fear humans feel exposed to the overwhelming power of water.

I talked to myself as I collected Kevin's precious Chouinard screws, "It's OK. Kevin did this. It'll be OK. The ice is getting thicker and soon you won't be over the water."

I dropped the screws down the front of my new anorak. My body heat would melt the cantankerous ice cores out of them. I reached high for one of Kevin's pick holes and my anorak pulled out from underneath my harness and I heard the clanking of metal and looked down to see the screws spinning like thrown circus knifes into the raging maw.

"Shit!" I bellowed.

"What's going on?"

"Fucking shit! My jacket came untucked from my harness. Five of the screws dropped."

"Can you get them back?"

"No, they fell into the hole. They're gone."

"Oh fuck...C'mon up, Blanch. We'll see what we can do."

Kevin led on making do. I felt every bit the greenhorn asshole that I was. Following the next pitch, the crux, I felt responsible for Kev's long run-outs.

"Don't worry about it, Blanch. We're doing OK. That was supposed to be the hardest of it. I think that we'll make it. You will, ah, buy me some new screws though, right? I mean, those things are expensive."

"It will be my pleasure, Wally. I just wish that I could have them here now so you didn't have to run it out so far.

"Ah, it's good for me. Good for my head. How about you just buy me three because we're up here as a team, you know?"

"Thanks Kev, but how about I pay for two and a half?"

"Ha, ha, very funny."

It snowed heavily and it snowed lightly, but it snowed all the time. When I looked up to Kevin on the fourth pitch I was smacked across the face: A huge cumulous cell of snow was billowing out from the face!

"Avalanche!" I screamed and then there was the roar and the blackening thump of the snow as everything went dark and the snow drummed over me like a dump truck full of sand.

Then it quieted to a patter and brightened to a gentle white hiss and I looked up to Kevin and felt pounds of snow crack and fall away from me. He was shaking the snow off of his shoulders like a dog fresh out of water.

"Are you OK?" I yelled.

"Ya I'm alright. Holy fuck, man! When I heard you yell and I looked up and saw it coming...I thought that was it."

"Are you going to come down?"

"No, I'm OK. I think that I should finish this pitch and bring you up and we can see how we're doing."

Desire outweighed prudence. We were washed by a couple more large spindrift slides but none of them as voluminous as the first.

Seven hours after starting I pulled over the top and there was Kevin's beaming mug framed by his snow-matted rag-wool balaclava.

"Fuckin' eh, Blanch. We did it!"

"Great job leading, Wally, fantastic man." And Kev launched into his long and lonely wolf howl and I gave 'er with a "Yaahoooo!"

Kev wanted proof photos so we took turns posing beside the piton/bolt that Lauchlan had placed the year before. It was a spade-shaped blade pin that John had drilled a hole through. "It's so cool. You can use it as a piton or a bolt hanger." John would excitedly explain to me four months later in Chamonix.

As Kevin rappelled from John's piton/bolt I watched it flex under each pulsation of load the transmitted up the rope. I know now that metal needs to flex to absorb load, but I'm still spooked watching that process. I suffered through an anxious rappel.

The black skis double-sucked in the new snow and I fought into the night trying to keep pace with Kev.

"Let's try scraping the things clean and then rewaxing," Kev suggested. He handed me his Swiss Army Knife and I started scraping with it.

"This snot is not coming off." I hissed.

"Here, let the old carpenter have a go." -

I watched Kev work the ski like he was hand planing a door. He was already a master with hand tools and it dawned on me that his superior ability on ice was directly related to that, both due to his adept manipulation of the axes, crampons, and screws, but also in his judgment on how far he could stress the various ice surfaces, perceiving where the breaking point was. Curls of black base material spiraled from the blade. "Don't get sentimental, it's a rental," I told myself.

The scum-sucking skis did better and we were soon recrossing the 300-foot-wide, 50-foot-deep avalanche debris below the northeast face of Wapta Mountain. Sheared tree branches reached from the debris like skeletal limbs.

Midnight, we reached my MG. Kev had to be at work in eight hours. I was a commissioned salesman so I could dog it, something that I was already doing too much of.

"I'll drive, Wally. You sleep."

One hour later we were closing in on Banff and I fell asleep at the wheel. As we drifted onto the shoulder the crackling of the gravel jerked me awake. Kev kept snoring. One month earlier Sunshine had treated me to a ski weekend in Banff and I remembered the motel's heated underground parking. I pulled in stealthily with the lights off and dropped the seat to lie parallel to a snoring Kev. Four hours of coma, then I sprang to and plugged Roger Miller's "King of the Road" into the eight-track.

left Mark Twight and I (left) exiting the top of the Welzenbach Couloir during our first attempt on the Central Spur of the Rupal Face. Nanga Parbat, Pakistan. Photo: Kevin Doyle

right Kevin Doyle cruising in the early morning on the north face of Shigri Peak, before the sun started the rocks and ice falling. Pakistan. Photo: Barry Blanchard

left above The magnificent Rupal Face of Nanga Parbat,
the largest mountain wall on earth. The Central Spur
is a sweeping arc of white starting below the summit and
running to the right. Pakistan. Photo: Barry Blanchard

left below I'm belaying Ward Robinson into the crush zone
of the Welzenbach *sérac*, and none too happy about it.
Nanga Parbat, Pakistan. Photo: Mark Twight

right All attitude and ability, Mark Twight, I, Ward
Robinson, and Kevin Doyle below the Rupal Face of Nanga
Parbat before we made our first attempt. Pakistan.
Photo: Hank Van Weelden

left Rappelling the Rupal Face of Nanga Parbat after the avalanche and storm, Pakistan. Photo: Mark Twight

right We were amazed to find a step of vertical ice at 25,000 feet in the Merkl Gully. I'm climbing toward Kevin Doyle while Ward Robinson waits. The tattered remnants of bleached-out water-ski rope from the Herrligkoffer expedition of 1970 dangle from the ice. Nanga Parbat, Pakistan. Photo: Mark Twight

next spread left Mark Twight down climbing from the crescent-moon-shaped glacier towards the Wieland Rocks during our retreat from the Rupal Face, Nanga Parbat, Pakistan. Photo: Barry Blanchard

next spread right Kevin Doyle rappelling through hell, dodging avalanches to get out of the Merkl Gully. Nanga Parbat, Pakistan. Photo: Mark Twight

right above Wally gorging himself on tuna, mayo, and Camembert on a baguette at the top of Les Grands Montets before descending to the Argentière Hut and the north face of Les Courtes. Chamonix, France, 1980. Photo: Barry Blanchard

right below Wally and I (left) chowing down in our Nanga Parbat base camp's kitchen. As Mark Twight recently observed, "I can't believe how much we ate back then." Pakistan. Photo: Mark Twight

left Gilles Claret-Tournier and I rest on the railings of the minute Chalet Le Boutonniere. Chamonix, France, 1980. Photo: Kevin Doyle

left I'm leading on the Bonatti Pillar on Le Petit Dru.
Our good friend Gilles, a valley-born local training as a
mountain guide, advised us: "It is zee mountains. You must
'ave mountain boots." We would have killed for our rock
shoes on the perfect golden granite. Chamonix, France.
Photo: Kevin Doyle

right T. P. Friesen at Camp VI on The Nose, two hours after
an earthquake rocked the cliff, and us. El Capitan, Yosemite,
California. Photo: Kevin Doyle

next spread Aiding the Great Roof on The Nose.
El Capitan, Yosemite, California. Photo: Kevin Doyle

PLAYLIST

AC/DC	*Highway to Hell*
Johnny Cash	*A Boy Named Sue*
Vivaldi	*Spring*
Louis Armstrong	*Zip A Dee Do Dah*

Chapter 7

CHAMONIX

THE CALGARY TRANSIT BUS stopped and started its way up the Seventeenth Avenue hill. Late spring sunlight slashed hot through thick safety glass and the accordion doors flapped open and shut as the diesel growled to pull away upslope. Urs Kallen's broad square shoulders filled the seat beside Kevin. They'd happened upon each other on the bus and Kevin had just told Urs of our recent ascent of Balrog, one of Brian Greenwoods masterpieces, plumb and bold up the south face of Mount Yamnuska. Urs had written in *A Climbers Guide To Yamnuska* that Balrog "is the most serious free climb yet made on Yamnuska."

Urs leaned his wide granite-block head toward Kevin and winked from behind thick square glasses, "I'm glad that you guys climbed the Balrog. That is good for Calgary."

When Kevin told me, I felt proud. I'd been working hard at my climbing and I thought that I could be good at it. I thought that I could become somebody through it.

"I'm going to the Valley and when I get back I'm going to Chamonix. You should quit your job and come to Europe with me, Blanch."

The magnificent north face of Les Droites.
The Jackson-Shea route is a continuous white
line just right of center. Photo: Kevin Doyle

Wally took off to Yosemite Valley. I kept climbing on Yamnuska. Many nights I lay in bed fretting over what I wanted to do with my life. I hungered to become, to accomplish, to be somebody. My salesmanship was forced and hard and I didn't want to prop up the façade of success any longer. The black Samsonite briefcase felt heavier than the dumbbells that I did chest flies with, my suits felt hollow.

"You should go to Europe, Bear." Sunshine's glorious golden hair was everywhere on the pillow, it framed her soft blue eyes like bluebells caught between shafts of sunlight.

I walked into my branch manager's office the next day. Peter's self-professed mission was to become a millionaire.

"I'm going to go to the French Alps and climb mountains," I stated without preamble.

"Fantastic!" Without missing a beat he was into the affirmative and enthusiastic. It surprised the hell out of me as I'd just quit, until I realized it was probably on page four of "How To Get Rid of Unmotivated Salesmen."

I found a ride to Montreal with a gal on the university ride-sharing board. She had a '69 Rambler. When we pulled into Indian Head, Saskatchewan, Josephine, my maternal grandmother, was visible in the second-story window of the 1905 brick building that housed the picture show on the ground floor. My grandmother rose early every day to play endless hours of solitaire. I'd decided to stop in to see my grandparents sixty miles earlier. I hadn't seen my grandmother in awhile but she recognized me instantly when I rounded onto the landing.

"Oh! It's Barry," she proclaimed and then she folded her hand and laid down the threadbare cards and got up to great us.

In the next room my grandfather sat dead center in an ancient floral couch watching TV. Time and cheap red wine had weathered his bold, handsome face. His once-proud nose was bulbed out with rosacea that the wine had exaggerated. A front-page news story of John F. Kennedy's assassination sat in a frame on the wall and I thought that that was probably the last time that Napoleon Amyotte, my grandfather, gave a shit.

Five days later I got on a Greyhound bus from Montreal to Port Authority in New York City. You only step into midtown Manhattan for the first time once in your life. I was dressed for the occasion, the baseball cap that Sunshine had given me read in big black letters: Rays Power Tongs – Pincher Creek, Alberta.

The gray-and-black Peter Storm oiled-wool sweater that my mother had given me for Christmas and then shrank, on first washing, to the point that the cuffs now rode a full inch above my wrists, my Cyclops Roc pack packed plump to the point of popping with four ice tools and crampons reefed tight to the back, and an old bowling ball bag plumb-bobbing on my arm, heavy with my climbing boots and everything else that I couldn't fit in the pack. Yellow cabs buzzed like bumble bees while streams of humans flowed past. I looked like a doe caught in the headlights.

"Do you need some help?" and it was like we were two people snapped into a still photo within the flow. He was a well-dressed blonde Manhattanite and he gave me directions to the subway and told me which train to take to JFK. I said, "Thank you."

"Not a problem," he replied and he walked back into the flow.

JFK. For US$330 Freddie Laker was flying me to London round trip. I landed at Heathrow, the second person in my family to have crossed the Atlantic that century. Me and a guy from New Jersey rode the tube to Tent City in East Acton. The next day I hitchhiked to Ramsgate and boarded the hovercraft to cross the English Channel to Calais, France. Salt spray spumed from under the huge craft like ocean waves battering the headland and then we glided onto the landing pad and settled to stationary. I felt the presence of my grandfather's past; he had landed at Dieppe thirty-eight years earlier, one hundred miles to the south-southwest. Napoleon had been young and strong and ready to fight.

France, and everyone but me was speaking and understanding French. As I walked to the train station I felt deracinated and vulnerable. I was a long way from home. Nothing like a long European train ride to get those thoughts out of your head, all thought out of your head.

"Chamonix, Mont Blanc! Chamonix, Mont Blanc!" The conductor's baritone shook the walls of the train and strummed a deep bass cord of excitement within my chest. Good lord, sweet Jesus, sumbuck, this was it! The mecca of alpinism! I shouldered my pack, grabbed my bowling ball bag and stepped out onto the shiny wet black pavement. The rain had abated and small arcs of mist rose from the road. A low-lying ceiling of pewter-colored cloud reached into dense green-gray timber and anchored itself to the trunks.

I couldn't stop looking up as I walked intuitively toward the center of town, a window in the clouds opened and I saw the black spearheads of the Aiguilles thrusting into the slate belly of the upper sky. I felt like a mouse staring up at the ramparts of the Potala. And then I smacked crotch first into a metal parking post and dropped the bowling ball bag and stumbled groaning as a couple of thirteen-year-old boys in school uniforms either asked me if I was OK, or called me an idiot, and I knew that I had to find Wally and gain some security. "Bar Nash?" I enquired, but the boys looked at me blankly. "Le Brasserie National?"

"Ah, oui, oui," they chimed and pointed up the street and then scampered away laughing.

I thumped my pack down close to the window where I could watch it and stacked the bowling ball bag on top. The Bar Nash, a lineage of English-speaking climbers washed over me with the weight of legacy: Whillans, Brown, Mac Innes, Bonington, Haston, Harlin, Kor, Chouinard, MacIntyre...The front door opened and I crossed the threshold into the sacrosanct hovel of Anglophone mountain climbing culture in the European Alps.

AC/DC's "Highway to Hell" belted through the stereo. Bon Scott had died four months earlier but his raw baritone cut through the cigarette smoke and thick English accents like a hot knife through bad butter. The Brits were drinking because it was raining.

"Like a cow pissing on a flat rock, as the French say, mate," one of the Brits told me, and he also told me that Kevin was camping illegally, and for free, in the Biolay. I left in search of Kev's yellow tent.

It had been two weeks since I'd seen Kev and one of the last things that he'd told me was that John Lauchlan and Dwayne Congdon would be in Chamonix representing Canada at the Rassemblement Internationale des Alpinistes—a biannual gathering of the best young alpinists from around the world sponsored by the French government through the Ecole Nationale de Ski et d'Alpinisme.

The trail was muddy and slick and I was paying attention to the footfalls of my bright yellow Nike Waffles when I looked up...and there was John Lauchlan, and right behind him, Dwayne Congdon. Strange to run into one of your hometown heroes on your first day in the shadow of Mont Blanc. I felt some of the nervousness that I'd felt when I'd approached John after his slideshows, or in the Yam parking lot, but a trail in the trees in France was foreign ground to both of us and the aura of his celebrity toned down a notch in my mind. They were out running in the rain, training, and they wore the embarrassingly too-short nylon running shorts of the day.

"John," I said, and it stopped him in his tracks and Dwayne bumped into him from behind. I saw his brow wrinkle in confusion and I added "I'm Barry, from Calgary."

"You're from Calgary." He was trying to place me, no doubt thinking that he should know anyone from Calgary climbing in Cham that season.

"I'm here to meet up with Kevin Doyle."

"Oh," and the light snapped on and his blue eyes relaxed, "you're with Kevin. Right, I got it now."

"Have you guys seen him?"

"Well yes..." John grinned. "We saw him in the Bar Nash last night and he was drinking...ah...rather heavily. I think that the weather has him down."

John introduced Dwayne and we chatted and they gave me concrete Canadian directions on where to find Wally, and Kev was there in the sierra gold Starship tent that he'd ordered from Early Winters.

"Walter!"

"Blanch!" And we were bear hugging each other and lifting each other off of the ground and backslapping and laughing. Two young men standing beneath hundred-foot-high evergreen trees on the outskirts of Chamonix with the complete horizon of their lives laid clean and calm before them like the looking-glass surface of a quiet boreal lake at dawn. It was so good to see him and to sit in the tent for two hours and hear everything about his travels and to relate all about mine.

"I picked this up at JFK and just finished it," I said passing him the paperback *Shibumi* by Trevanian. "It's an incredible read, and cool. I think that you'll like it man. You have to read it."

A June monsoon, neither Kev nor I had ever seen rain like that before. Waves of water pounding out of the sky while Kev and I darted between awnings trying to link protective cover all the way back to the cemetery. The Biolay, our illegal camp, was just on the other side of the cemetery and I suspected that the superstitious French left us alone because of that.

"Don't look up Blanch! You'll drown!" Wally hollered.

The Starship was a first generation single-skin Gore-Tex tent. Kevin had methodically seam-sealed each and every seam before leaving Canada but water found its way in nonetheless. The floor of the tent was waterproof and would not let the water out. We lived on the islands that our sleeping pads created inside the tent that "let water in but would not let it out." Day four, sodden, Wally and I were at the hardware store buying five meters of clear poly to jury-rig a lean-to over the tent with sticks and cord.

"This is the way hobos live," I said.

"Or bums," Kev replied.

It had stopped raining and Kevin and I were halfway up the Couzy route on the Aiguille de l'M with me in the lead when a trembling Galibier helmet surfaced below the belay ledge looking like a severely hypothermic albino turtle. Strapped into the helmet was one very freaked out Frenchman.

"*Je tombe!*" he wailed. "*Je tombe!*" And then he dead pointed for Kevin's ankle.

"What the fuck!" Kev blurted.

"Wally, are you OK?"

High above Chamonix, I'm happy to be on the Aiguille de l'M. Photo: Kevin Doyle

The rattling helmet was clinging to Kev's leg like it was a skid of the last Air America helicopter to lift off as Saigon fell.

"Wow, buddy, no!" I heard anxiety steaming in Kevin's voice.

"*Je tombe!*" Which I later learned from Kev was French for "I'm falling!"

"Fuck! Hold on, Blanch," and Kev's hands dropped my belay and grabbed the guy and hauled him onto the ledge like gaffing a 175-pound tuna and dragging it over the gunwale. Kev reestablished my belay and then followed the pitch fast. We both wanted to be away from that guy.

"That was just fucking bizarre, Blanch. I mean, I thought that guy was going to pull me off. He was in a blind fucking panic, man. I'm sorry I let you go, buddy."

"Not a problem, Wally, I could see that you had to deal and I was solid anyway. I'm glad you got him onto the ledge."

"Ya, so am I. He was run-out, of course, he would have went a ways...a long ways...that's for sure."

I ran, Wally read, we'd both head down to the Nash to talk trash with the Brits and nurse *une grande bière*, or two, for hours. We got to know Maurice, the owner, and his lovely daughter. Wally and I had committed to staying in Europe until our money ran out and we strived to expand the time between our trips to the bureau de change to turn our precious traveler's checks into francs. We compared the exchange rates of the various bureaux like anxious stockbrokers.

I learned to heel hook on the Pierre d'Orthaz boulder in Snell's Field and it felt so good to unlock the sequence to the American Leaper problem with that unorthodox move. I was becoming a better climber. Kevin and I drew a crowd, and got applause, doing laps on a vertical wall of ice at the Glacier des Bossons. Vertical ice climbing hadn't hit the mainstream of French climbing culture and on rock it was still the norm to climb "French free": vaulting between fixed pitons and mauling the pitons as hand- and footholds.

"Fuck, Blanch, this book is incredible," Kev stated, a vibrant intensity sparking from his hazel-gray eyes as he closed the last page of *Shibumi*. The novel had denounced Western materialism in favor of a Japanese aesthetic of simple and unobtrusive beauty that is subtle. Trevanian had written, "*Shibumi* has to do with great refinement underlying commonplace appearances."

"I want to be a man of *Shibumi*," Kevin said.

"Do you really think that we should be defining our lives from a spy novel?"

"No man, this is a great book. The best that I've read in awhile. Maybe better than *Siddhartha*, or *Narcissus and Goldmund*."

"I think that it's Miller time." Both the beer and Henry Miller flashed through my mind, but it was the beer that I was after.

"What man could argue with logic like that?" Kev wanted the beer too.

July, the weather turned fine and I got sick. Kev took off to the Route Major with Damian Carroll, but our lean-to was empty when he got back three days later because I'd improved and headed up to bivy in the ice tunnel of the Aiguille du Midi before going for the Boccalatte Pillar on Mont Blanc du Tacul with Mel Williams, a Brit who taught me, on that route, to hiss my "Bloody hells!" through tightly clenched teeth when I was really gripped. As I climbed I was intensely aware that I was gripping holds that had felt the hand of Gaston Rébuffat and Gabriele Boccalatte—heroes, history.

Gaston Rébuffat published *Le Massif du Mount Blanc: Les 100 Plus Belles Courses* in 1973, it was translated into English in '74 and published as *The Mont Blanc Massif: The Hundred Finest Routes* in 1975. It became Kevin and my grail. In the first pages Rébuffat opened a toolbox of advice, the nuts and bolts for being a safe and efficient alpinist. And for young men like Kev and me, intent on achieving, there was a hierarchy of numbers. The routes were cataloged in a spectrum from the easiest, the traverse of the Clocher and Clochetons de Planpraz at number 1, to the hardest, the Central Pillar of Freney, number 100.

I carried all four of my ice tools up the Swiss Route on the north face of Les Courtes (number 94) in July. Kev and I had crunched away from the Argentière Hut at 10:00 p.m. in order to climb the ice-and-snow route at night when it would be frozen and safer. Six headlamps sputtered to life behind us and followed in our tracks.

On top the next morning one of the headlamps, a Brit, asked me, "Right, what's up with all of the ice tools then?"

I replied that I was trying to figure out which ones worked the best. He then noticed Kevin's watch and asked what the time was so he could figure out how long the route had taken him and his partner.

"What does it matter?" Kevin challenged.

In a somber British manner he replied, "It is important." Kevin told him the time and he seemed to be happy about it.

"Do you know who did the first British ascent?" I needled.

"No, I don't, but I should."

"What's up with that anyway?" I dug deeper. "I mean, who cares given that a hundred Frenchmen have probably already climbed the route?"

A pregnant pause, "You don't keep track of first American ascents?"

"No not really, but probably because we're Canadian." I savored my reply.

"Ah, right, sorry about that. You don't keep track of first Canadian ascents?"

"Ya, but only if they're first ascents. Like the very first people there," I said.

We all made our way off of the backside toward the old Couvercle Hut. By midafternoon, Wally had just made it to the lip of a salad-bowl swale on the glacier. We'd gotten ourselves trapped in a cul-de-sac. He'd used his "tricouni purchase," weighting his right toe like a figure skater to gain extra grab from the heads of the three Phillips screws that he'd twisted into the toe of the sole with his Swiss Army knife in order to anchor it and keep it from peeling away from the boot.

Standing *en pointe* at the last step the screws sheared through the ice and Wally screeched down twenty-five feet of glass-hard ice on his back, bouncing along on his pack, eyes wide and shock and panic stretched across his face. And then he hammered into the glacial talus at my feet and leapt up and exploded in a vitriolic tantrum that went on for a full two minutes of voluminous ear-splitting profanity. Then he clenched his jaw and attacked the slope hewing steps into the lip like his ax was a broadsword and he a berserker hacking on the battlefield. When I caught up with him five minutes later he was calmly weaving his way through the glacial maze.

"That shit really pissed me off, Blanch."

"Ya, I kinda thought that was what you were feeling there, Walter." We continued our long descent to Chamonix.

On the west face of the Aiguille de Blaitière (number 71) Wally managed to free climb the Fissure Brown, an offwidth so stiff that the French refused to believe that Joe Brown had climbed it after he made the first ascent of the route in 1954 with Don Whillans.

"Aye, but they dinna know the Human Fly," was how one Brit summarized it for me in the Nash.

I fought like hell on top rope, gained some "gravel in my gut," as Johnny Cash would say, from the Joe Brown helmet on my head and the Whillans harness around my waist—fight lad, fight.

Hours of rain, days of rain, and of downtime. Kevin and I passed weeks of time together in the leaky tent over our five-month stay in Europe. He could go to a place that allowed stream of consciousness talking, especially when he got euphoric and saw the world in van Gogh's colors, heard Vivaldi's notes, and felt the clay like Rodin. I've joked of my friend Kevin, "If it's in his head, it's out his mouth. Like there's a coal shoot linking the two and free of the social filters that restrict most of us from saying what is on our mind, and, unfortunately, in our hearts." I got to know him very well at that point in time.

"I'm telling Anna Christine that we should have an open relationship," Kev stated from his side of the tent where he'd been writing her a long letter.

"Hmmmm," I murmured. We'd both hung up our love lives when we left Calgary, not that we wanted to.

"I think that we should be able to see other people."

I'd been living that concept with gusto. "Variety is the spice of life," I blurted the platitude and my lust for sex edged closer to the center stage of my psyche. And love, and my desire for love, my ability to love, got pushed another step stage left. Wally licked the envelope and sealed his fate with AC.

Granite blocks the size of bread loaves bounded down the dirty stain of a couloir. Kev and I huddled close to the solid wall and watched gravel and mud ooze down the Petit Dru's intestine. Another volley clattered and crunched into the sidewalls igniting wee puffs of smoke with the acrid reek of pulverized rock. Long rappels with the black rope and the blue one, both of them eleven millimeters in diameter— an incredibly heavy system, but the only ropes we owned—sliding lazily through hand-sized aluminum figure eights that had been made in Wales by Clog.

We ran away from the Bonatti Pillar (route 92) and retreated directly down through jungle and vertical kitty litter to the Mer de Glace, the same route that we'd used to get to the Glacier des Drus, likely the only two fools to have done this in modern times. And then we got lost in the maze of crevasses below Montenvers. On the other side of the seven-foot-wide black hole that delineated our world a French guide was gaily whistling "Zip-a-Dee-Doo-Dah" as he pranced his clients along the "proper" route.

"Fucking Mer de Bullshit," I hissed.

Back at the Biolay, Kev and I regrouped for round two on the Bonatti, this time via the Charpoua Hut and a descent from the Flammes de Peirre.

Kevin and I traversed a glacier shaped like the inside of a vast white funnel on our way to the Charpoua Hut. The sun was hot, my pack straps dug down onto my clavicles. Stilted steps of snow rose from the established track like close-shorn tree trunks brindled and bleached by the heat of the sun. Between some of the steps the snow had melted away to glacial ice the color of ash and water wept over it. Ten meters downslope to my left sat a crevasse that could swallow a Cadillac bumper to bumper.

My next left step collapsed when I weighted it and my right hip splashed onto the wet ice and I began to slide. By the second yard I was accelerating and I instinctively sat on my ass to dig in my heels. Wet snow sprayed from my feet and lashed into my face as the crevasse charged. And then my heels bit into a six-inch-wide pre-crevasse and I snapped to a stop and panted fear. I was a yard and a half from the life-taking crevasse. It could have all ended for me then and I have often thought back to that day during the thousands of days I was destined to spend in the mountains.

Before coming to the Alps I'd passed two nights in planned bivies and three caught out in unplanned ones. (Over the next two years I would pass fifty nights in bivouacs.) Kevin and I huddled in the bivy sacs that he'd sewn for us. We were high on the route, just below the 150-foot vertical crack

It rained in the night and the next morning clouds clung to the Dru like snow loaded onto pine boughs. We continued, then opted for an escape to the right when a storm swirled into the Petit Dru. The summit was three hundred feet above.

By the end of August Wally and I had tallied eleven alpine routes between us.

"I think that we should go for the north face of Les Droites, Blanch." Kev snapped the Rébuffat grail shut and handed it to me from his side of the leaky tent. The route was number 99.

"Oh man, I don't know if we're ready for that, Wally."

"No, man, we can do it, Blanch. I saw Lauchlan in town, he and Dwayne climbed the Jackson-Shea on the north face and he told me that it is a waterfall route. No harder than Takakkaw. We can do it."

"Ya, but it's four times longer than Takakkaw. I don't know, Wally."

In early September 1955 Philippe Cornuau and Maurice Davaille spent six days on the first ascent of the north face of Les Droites. It was the hardest route in the Western Alps and saw only two more ascents over the next fourteen years with the best time being three days. In 1969 Reinhold Messner soloed the route in eight and a half hours accomplishing the greatest climb in the Alps since the Bonatti Pillar.

But who was I kidding? I was a city boy from Southern Alberta who had climbed all of his routes that season in cotton painter's pants and two wool sweaters. Three years ago I knew more about steer riding than I did about mountain climbing, how was I going to measure up to an überclimber like Messner? Thankfully Kevin didn't share my feelings of inadequacy. He didn't deify climbers, didn't deify anyone. He wrapped his strong hands around the conviction that what one man could do, another man could do.

"I saw Lauchlan struggle with the second pitch of Bottleneck Direct-Direct on Yam," Wally said. "I knew then and there that my heroes were human."

"Ya, but we're we talking about Reinhold Messner, Wally."

"Just another human, Blanch."

No matter how much I stared at the pictures of Les Droites in Rébuffat's book I just couldn't break it into pieces and hold it in my mind. Oddly enough it was John Lauchlan who solved the riddle for me, opening a door inside my head.

It was raining again and warm air surged over my face when I entered the Alpenrose Bar. French words hung heavy in cigarette smoke. I felt foreign for the hundredth time and then I saw John and Dwayne framed into the center of a crowded table, regiments of beer glasses, and two steak sandwiches the size of my forearm, before them. I smiled and John rose and threaded his way through the crowd to get to me.

His blue eyes crackled electrically and he sputtered and spat at me for five minutes telling the story of Dwayne and his recent third ascent of the MacIntyre-Colton route on the North Face of Les Grandes Jorasses. They'd managed the best time on the route and had won the covert competition for the hardest route done during the Rassemblement.

He was buzzing, yet he asked, as he always did, "What are you and Kevin's plans?"

I broke eye contact and stared down to my yellow Nikes, the ones that I'd laboriously stitched up by hand to save money and stay in Europe longer. My balled hands bottomed out the depth of my pockets and I shuffled my well-worn shoes.

"C'mon man, what are you guys thinking about?"

But if I said "Les Droites" our ambition would exist beyond the leaky tent and Kev and me, it would be in the world. I found some heart strength and looked to the ceiling and then back to John, I blew out like a horse.

"Well...we're kind of thinking about the north face of Les Droites."
I'd said it.

John locked on to me with sapphire blue eyes underlit by passion and I felt his gaze drill on back to the far side of my skull, nail me to the wall. There was no getting away now.

"Do it, it is perfect for you guys."

"Oh man, John, I don't know if we're up to it yet. I don't know if we're good enough yet."

"No, no way. You can do it. You know that Dwayne and I climbed the Jackson-Shea in July and I know it and it is perfect for you and Kev." He dropped his eyes to his sun-browned leathery hands and swept them up like they were surfing a wave.

"The lower face is just like doing the north face of Athabasca, and you guys have both done that. Then you do Takakkaw Falls." His hands mimed the planting of ice tools. "Then you top it off with Cascade Falls. You guys have already climbed all of that." His palms opened into a "so-what" gesture. "It's just three pieces of Canada on loan to France! All you have to do is put it all together in one day, you *can* do it, lad."

Go big or go home.   John Lauchlan

September 17, 1980, the Argentière Glacier wore the crust of a recent snowstorm and Kevin and I crunched on up following the tracks of a French guide and client, the only other souls in the basin, a staggering change from July when there had been hundreds upon hundreds. The Argentière Hut was deserted and Kevin and I sat outside studying the face and guzzling water, telling ourselves the whole time that we were drinking martinis, "shaken, not stirred." Later we piled gray wool blankets onto ourselves and pretended to sleep—it wasn't until years later that I could sleep before a big route.

We strode into the cold at 10:00 p.m. and the surface of the glacier felt like hard plaster. A full moon bathed the whole of the Argentière Basin in a soft, feminine light. At midnight I pulled over the bergschrund following Wally's footprints up a fragile, fresh apron of snow that had drifted down off of the face during the season's first snowfall a week before. I could feel the vibrations of my footfalls transmit through the shafts of my tools. The bottomless black of the bergschrund ran like a gargantuan sabre cut to the left and to the right of me. I prayed for the snowbridge to hold.

Above me the face reared in a sweep of silvery ice the color of the surface of the moon, and then it slammed into the black bulkhead of the upper wall and I sighed and bowed my head and breathed out fear. I smacked my Sérac Sabre into the first of the ice and the shaft resonated like I'd just planted the tool into wood.

The rope took me to Kev and we decided to switch off our Wonder headlamps and to climb the ice face simultaneously without ice anchors or belays. We saw by the soft glowing light of the full moon and that milky light luminesced from the pale snow with a tenderness that took me back to an early morning and dawn light washing Sunshine's naked back. The crunch of my ice ax, sounding like papier-mâché being crumpled under the heel of my hand, bought me back to the frozen 3,300 feet of Les Droites and I felt my scrotum contract. "It's time to go big," I told myself.

The gas flame blue of the new day found us high on the face. Spindrifting snow had scoured away the crisp Styrofoam coating leaving long sweeps of iron-hard ice. Climbing the ice was far more difficult and insecure, no longer was there firm snow to grab and hold the one crampon that we would place sideways. We began to belay. The route unfolded as John had said it would, ropelengths of alpine ice, cruxes of waterfall ice, immaculate granite, beautiful climbing. The crux was a vertical curtain of silver ice that you could see through like window pane ice on a frozen lake.

Kevin's body trembled on the lead and he spat, "Watch me, Blanch," and the air around me compressed into a sphere with me and my clenched and crossed arms at its center. Kev grabbed the edge of the curtain like it was a surfboard and pulled his head to the inside where he found a fixed piton that he smacked mightily with his North Wall hammer and then clipped and climbed out to power up over the lip.

Back at the Biolay with a broken nose, after the north face of Les Droites. Behind me is our tent that let water in, but wouldn't let it out. Photo: Kevin Doyle

"Off belay!" echoed authoritatively across the basin, filled the basin. John, Walter, Reinhold, all of my heroes quietly slipped into the back of my mind. At that moment in time Kevin Doyle was my hero.

At 2:00 p.m. we'd been climbing for fifteen hours and were one ropelength away from the Brèche—the top of the route. Kevin was 160 feet above me and just about to anchor when he kicked in his right crampon and a circular plate of ice that had failed from one of his tool placements, yet stalled there, skittered away. He didn't sense it and therefore didn't call it and the chunk bounded down the gully gaining speed and rotation and I looked up and took it square in the face.

Blackness buckshot through with needles of white light, the sickening and muffled crunch of my nose breaking transmitted through my skull and not my ears. I wailed and folded onto my anchor line. I opened my eyes to a veil of tears and my bright red blood splattered across the sleeve of my anorak.

There was lots of shouting between Kev and I, was I OK? I didn't know, it was my nose, I couldn't see how bad it was because it was my nose. I'd need a mirror. I climbed toward Kev, the blood on my jacket freezing to crinkle like flexed wax and thick drops of fresh blood blossoming pink on the firm snow. I worried that my nose had been broken, and then I worried that I would be scarred ugly.

"Oh man, that doesn't look so good, Blanch," was all the succor I got out of Wally. But he cleaned the half-inch-long avulsion with snow and then pressed a band aid tight over it and led the last pitch to the Brèche. Sixteen hours of climbing and we stood into the sun and it felt so warm and kind. My arms hung at my sides like yard-long kielbasa, it felt like I had bench-pressed my body weight about a hundred times.

The straw in the old Couvercle Hut felt heavenly. It was midnight and Kevin and I had been on the go for twenty-six hours. We parsed out the rough wool blankets and I swaddled myself in mine and collapsed into a deep, deep sleep.

Nine hours later I awoke to the awareness that I lay on a space that alpinists had lain on for decades upon decades and that some who had lain here had been the progenitors of alpinism. I knew what the word meant now. Further, I realized that no one in my upbringing had told me that I would ever be able to push my body, and my being, for twenty-six hours. None of the parents told me, none of my Phys Ed instructors, none of my teachers. Lauchlan and Bonatti were not superhuman, they just had a lot of heart and had decided to use it. I felt a part of a long line of mountain climbers. I also knew that I was unprecedentedly thirsty and I could eat a horse.

Chapter 8

EUROPE

LATE IN THE AFTERNOON Kevin and I tramped into the Biolay and I dropped my pack to the foot of a hundred-foot-high evergreen and sat down on it. I was lean and hard, 160 pounds. The striations of my forearm muscles etched hard lines in my sunbaked skin. I felt so light, like I was floating on freedom. The horizon of my future stretched out in front of me a clean open plain. Everything was possible. I wanted to climb mountains, I'd found my calling. Kevin and I swore a pact to climb in Yosemite in one year's time, but first we would stow our climbing gear and light out to see some of Europe.

The Bar Nash was quiet on our last night there, only a half dozen Brits to take the piss with, one being a cocky raven-haired beauty who I'd flirted with some. I was gobsmacked when she snuck up behind me and cupped her hands over my eyes and pulled me tight to her chest. It was the first time that I'd been touched by a woman in four months.

Simple men, we read through *Let's Go Europe* and decided on the two things that we most wanted to see: the hippy caves at Matala, Crete; and Dracula's castle in Romania. We drew a circuit through those two places and grabbed our Eurail Passes.

The passes got us onto a bus that would take us through the Mont Blanc Tunnel and on to the train station at Pré-Saint-Didier on the Italian side. When the black-uniformed border guard climbed onto

Me at Les Calanques on the south coast of France, where Wally and I went to rock climb and get our heads together before attempting Les Droites.
Photo: Kevin Doyle

the bus Kev and I realized that we'd left our passports in our packs stowed below. Shit. He asked us where we were from and when we said, "Canada," he pursed his lips and gazed at us from under a crinkled brow and fluttered his fingers in a dismissive mannerism and said that it was "OK" we could come into Italy.

We argued politics with four retired, rotund communists in Bologna who all wore Greek captain's caps and sipped grappa at a patio restaurant in the warm autumnal night. The Adriatic beaches were deserted and we walked far along them and swam in the midday sun that was still warm enough. In Brindisi we bought deck passages to Corfu and two jugs of Chianti that had woven-straw handles and each weighed over a kilogram. We got drunk on deck and crawled into our sleeping bags. Waves broke over the bow that night and all the deck folk fled down into the restaurant. Kev and I got separated during the scramble, he just managing to snag his jeans, with wallet in the back pocket, before they were washed overboard. Tipsy, he stumbled below and opened a door to a vacant sleeping cabin. He passed the night in clean, dry linen while I got shoehorned in with the rest of the young and the wet.

On Corfu we rented Vespas and Kev spun out trying to catch me on a corner high on the island. The machine spun viciously on its side, throttle open, with Wally trying to get a hand on it looking like someone trying to sneak up on a pit bull from its blind side.

Kev's twenty-second birthday was celebrated in Olympus, the birthplace of the Olympics, a place were we could pick pomegranates and lemons out the front door of the tent. We made plans of returning to that quiet restaurant to celebrate landmark birthdays in our futures, milestones that have come and passed now without Kev and I back in Olympus, yet often in each other's company.

I got off of a bus in Athens and watched it pull away with the Stephen King novel that I was halfway through tucked snug into a seat pocket. I took it as a sign and quit King and Robert Ludlum cold turkey, started to work my way into Henry Miller and Hemingway.

On Crete we hiked a gorge then hired a fishing boat to take us to a remote beach where we slept in a cave and lived without clothes for a couple of days just like the half dozen Germans we shared the beach with.

The hippie caves in Matala smelled of centuries of human urine so we slept on the beach in our bags and started each of our days with a fix, a Hellas Fix beer. That lasted for about a week, including one wild Greek wedding where we danced in a line with the men to the twang of bouzouki players.

Back to Athens and the Acropolis and then north through Yugoslavia, which seemed like a socialist country because Josip Broz Tito had stood up to Joseph Stalin. Many offered to buy our American dollars.

Romania under Ceausescu was the darkest and most desperate feeling country that I have ever been in. It was like the coal dust that darkened the miners also darkened the sky. Dracula's castle, however, did not disappoint. We removed our shoes and put on slippers to preserve the ancient wooden steps, crouched low to get in the old low doorways, saw some of the pikes that Vlad Tepes had people impaled on. Far below, the Turcu River flowed blue through Bran Pass, a strategic trading link between Transylvania and Wallachia, and, at times, the frontier dividing Christianity from Islam.

The state-run restaurant below the castle was small, the wooden table and chairs old and worn, but in good repair. We ordered sandwiches and beers and they were robotically delivered by the state waitress while Wally was in the john. Two yellow banana peppers the size of my little finger were the only adornments added to the table. They looked hot.

Cautiously I put one to my mouth and punctured it with a canine tooth. Incendiary. My mouth exploded into flame. I felt like I'd just swallowed napalm. My eyes overran with tears and I held my mouth open, trembling in a painful panic, and grabbed my beer and guzzled half the bottle. Didn't help. I rammed bread into my burning mouth but it hit the inside of my cheek with the pressure of a smoldering briquette. Tears streamed from the corners of eyes wide open and I groaned open-mouthed obscenities, "Huck, huck, huck."

Five minutes later I had myself composed when Wally returned. He sat down and took a long pull of beer. The fire-hot peppers sat in a small white saucer between us.

"Man, I bet those things are hot," I said. "I'd like to try one but I don't do so good with hot stuff."

"Oh, they don't look so bad. Here, gimme one of those, Blanch." I passed the plate to him.

"I can handle hot," he said, and he grabbed one of the yellow peppers by its stem and chomped down on the whole thing!

"Ya, these aren't so bad..." And his eyes stretched open wide and his face fell slack in shock at the same time as it burst tomato red. "Holy fuck, Blanch! Ah! Ah! Give me that water!" and he pitched the whole glass back. His eyes were swimming when the glass hit the table.

"Oh fuck, oh fuck. Gimme that bread man, gimme that bread."

I was choking on laughter that I couldn't let out. I half-clenched my bulging eyes like I was trying to swallow multiple sneezes, yet I wanted my eyes open to see Wally, it was so good.

"Oh fuck!" he cursed between wolfing down water, bread, and beer. "That's the hottest thing I've ever tasted." And he began to cry and laugh at the same time. "I guess it was kinda stupid to eat the whole thing, hey, Blanch?"

Six years later in a tent that we shared on the Rombuk Glacier below the north flank of Mount Everest I finally admitted to Kevin that I'd set him up. His eyes welled up with tears again, tears of laughter.

"If one more person gives us the runaround I'm getting back on the train and heading to Austria," I said.

We'd been walking the streets of Budapest, Hungary, for four hours futilely searching for a youth hostel listed in *Let's Go Europe*. Sure enough, the next guy we asked pondered our request scholastically and with much solemnity then handed us a platter of bogus directions rather than admit that he didn't know. We got back on the train.

"Holy crap, Wally, you can get beer here...McDraught!" We were at the counter in a McDonald's in Vienna, the first Western-style fast food that we'd had in over a month. Mickey D's back in Alberta did not have beer on the board. We ordered Big Macs and beers and were soon talking with a Czech guy who hauled us off to a back room in an

Climbing on the south coast of France at Calanque d'En-Vau. Photo: Kevin Doyle

expensive restaurant where a group of men met every Friday for lunch with the sole purpose of speaking English. Two young Canucks climbing the Alps and bumming around Europe were a novel distraction to the rigors of running IBM in Eastern Europe or being a diplomat at the UN. And the UN bar was the next stop, courtesy of the Czech guy's wife's employment there as a translator.

I felt like I'd stepped into Chalmun's Cantina in Star Wars. There were Africans in caftans, Japanese in business suits, Russians, Filipinos, Americans, a dozen different languages. Kevin chatted up a Russian actress and ended up leaving with her to go back to her place and discuss the merits of plot, and nothing more.

My evening got wild and lawless. Brett was a wide, beefy Texan who captained freighters around the Mediterranean. His Filipino wife translated at the UN. Brett and I went on a tear through half a dozen bars and ended up karate sparing in the park well after midnight, then accelerating his BMW into four wheel skids around the Ringstrasse at 3:00 a.m. When I made it back to my sleeping bag in the hostel at 9:00 a.m. the neck pouch that Kevin had sewn me was gone and with it my passport, traveler's checks, US cash, train pass, and plane ticket home. I was buggered. Getting a new passport would take a week and Brett offered to have me stay at their apartment. Kev and I agreed to split up as he wanted to make it up to Norway and I was now a vagrant.

I made frantic phone calls home to get money wired to me. "Son, I couldn't even raise a hundred bucks," my father, Norman, said, the weight of failure audible on his voice. "That's OK dad, thanks for trying. I'll be OK." Which was a lie, I felt very small and vulnerable.

My buddy and mentor from Pitney Bowes, Richard, came through with $500, but I would have to pick it up at a bank in Geneva, and I'd have to hitchhike to get there.

Brett and I continued to party and on about day three of my wait we were driving around when I pulled a brochure out of the Beamer's magazine rack. The central part of Vienna was pictured in a cartoon layout with busty and scantily clad women leaning out of windows and leaning against streetlamps.

"Wow, what's this Brett?"

"That's the hooker map to Vienna, Hoss."

"You mean there's a map?"

"Hell yes, Horse. It's all legal here, and government controlled."

"Wow."

"You mean to tell me that you've never paid for it, Hoss?"

"Well, ah, no."

"Hell, son, my treat. C'mon, let's go."

The absurdity of gifting a twenty-one-year-old male—me—cart blanche in a brothel when he's cresting a tsunami of testosterone after five months of abstinence is one of the definitions of high comedy. A beautiful and lithe black-haired Nordic gal with pale blue eyes came to me at the bar and we began talking in stilted grade school English. She wore a baby doll negligee and, in my eyes, her flat strong stomach shimmered with moonlight. I had permission to touch and she felt like velvet. When I looked to Brett he winked and jerked his broad forehead toward the back hallway. She took my hand and led me to a red-velour room with a red bed, champagne on ice beside it, and a porn film playing on a TV. I had a marvelous time, a number of times.

She was five years older than me and I knew that she relaxed a bit with the simplicity of my young desire, yet in both of us there was a darkness that lay under the façade of the physical fun, we each held wounds and the wounds recognized each other and they were so much deeper than the male fairytale of a red-velour room.

My new passport in one hand, I shook hands with Brett and thanked him for some wild times and left him to continue raging a bull's swath through the china shop of life. I hitchhiked to Munich and slept in the Englischer Garten where a Bernese mountain dog woke me in my sleeping bag, his moist black nose sniffing my face, his well-dressed "daddy" waiting and grinning five steps away—a good Munichite and dog doing their part to rid the city of vagrants like me.

"You don't speak French?" the well-dressed and immaculately groomed male teller asked me from his side of the blue glass in the bank in Geneva.

"No," I replied.

"But you are Canadian. You are a bilingual country. You have a French name. I assumed that you would speak French."

"I'm from western Canada, not many people speak French in Alberta."

He dealt out my $500 with the deftness of a croupier and I spent it all on trains back to London, and a hostel there.

The next day I walked into the Canadian Embassy and borrowed $100 to get me out to Heathrow where Laker Airways had a replacement ticket for me. In Port Authority, NYC, I bought a Greyhound ticket to Montreal and went straight to the Royal Bank of Canada when I got off of the bus. They called my branch in Calgary and signed off on a short-term loan to get me home.

I was so broke when I got home that I moved back in with my mom for several months. My uncle, Ken Baker, was a home delivery supervisor at Alpha Dairies and he got me a job delivering milk door to door. I became a milkman: up early Monday, Tuesday, Thursday, and Friday. I'd run my route and be off in the early afternoon to train on the basement wall of the university, or do long uphill runs, or both. Three days of the week I would climb. Reinhold Messner's book, *The Seventh Grade*, was having an effect on me, as was the recently published *Waterfall Ice, Climbs in the Canadian Rockies* by Albi Sole.

Messner hammered a philosophy of dedication into me and Sole gave Wally and me a hit list.

PLAYLIST

Jimi Hendrix	*All Along the Watchtower*
Jerry Jeff Walker	*Up Against the Wall Redneck Mother*

Chapter 9

BACK HOME

"YOU GUYS CAN'T CLIMB HERE TODAY." She was abrupt and physically wide in her blue Canada Goose Arctic parka. "We're shooting a film."

I saw Wally's spine straighten. "I'm happy for you," he said, "but you're not a warden so I don't think you can tell me where I can or can't climb."

And then Big Jim Elzinga walked into the Weeping Wall parking lot. Jim is six foot four and as blonde as Dolf Lundgren. Kevin knew him, but it was my first time meeting him. I felt the aura of the hero when we shook hands—Jim was John Lauchlan's main partner. Jim explained that the film was about their ascent of Mount Snow Dome and he got a good laugh when we told him that we "were the guys" who had spent the night out on top of Andromeda when he and John were making the first ascent of the Slipstream route. The abrupt gal was the director/producer and John was on the Lower Weeping Wall getting duffel bags of snow dumped onto him to get inserts of spindrift.

Kevin and I were on our way to the Upper Weeping Wall with the intent of climbing the Lower Weeping Wall to get there and then bivouacking below the Upper. Our first grade 6, the hardest grade in the range. We agreed to use Snivelling Gully for our access as it would be well to the side of where they were filming.

John smiled hugely and waved one ax at us when we walked by and then he put his head down for "Action!" and took another duffel bag load of snow.

On Corkscrew, south face of Yamnuska. Don't clip pitons like I clipped this one: If I had fallen, the leverage would have broken the carabiner.
Photo: Kevin Doyle

They all left with the setting sun and Kevin and I stomped out a platform tight to the rockwall and under an overhang so we would be protected from anything falling in the night.

The next day tested my Messnerian resolve when I followed Kevin's lead up a 10-foot-high exfoliated petal of ice 500 feet up the route, 30 feet from the top. It was all that I could do to cling to my tools while my forearms cramped, feeling like spikes were being pounded through them, and my body quaked with the exertion of pulling onto the lip by planting my picks pointing up into the inner concave skin of the ice petal. Only Kevin could have done that lead, I couldn't at the time and none of my other partners could have either.

Midwinter. I breathed crisp air in and out and locked off and reached full arm to swing my Sérac Sabre. The inner tube that I'd glued onto the shaft was nicked and slashed and aluminum shone through the chipped blue paint where I'd pounded on the tool to drive it deeper into the rock or ice or snow on mountains past. Now it *thunked* in as if I'd driven it into telephone poll and the vibration of security resonated in my forearm like a finely plucked guitar string. I was alone and moving up the 900 feet of grade 4 ice on the Professor Falls with precision and control. I felt competent and good. Three hours of concentration and performance and I pulled over the top.

The route's name was actually a short sentence: The professor falls. Eckhard Grassman, a colorful German math professor from the University of Calgary fell repetitively trying to second John Lauchlan's leads clinging to Chouinard Zero ice axes without wrist loops.

I untwisted the one-inch tubular webbing from my wrists and sheathed the Sabres into my harness and ran out to my MGB. I was the first in our wee clan to have done a big solo and I was giddy. The MG roared to a pay phone in downtown Banff and I tried Kevin, but ended up getting Stewart.

"Zoltan, I just soloed Professor's."

"And you just couldn't wait to tell us, could you, Blanch?" Touché. Stew called them as he saw them.

"Well, ah, no," and I laughed. I'd been called out.

I froze, the moose froze. Funnels of frozen breath streamed from her flared nostrils, my exhalations rose slowly, small white clouds in the beam of my headlamp. Her eyes reflected the light like road markers and she stared at me for three bellowing breaths and her breath matched mine and then she turned and pranced off through the three-foot-deep snowpack. I trudged on in Wally's postholes. He was already at the base of Polar Circus, 2,000 feet, one of the four grade 6 waterfalls listed in the guidebook:

> At the time of writing, it has still not been climbed in a single day.
> Albi Sole, Waterfall Ice

I had a dinner and a breakfast in my pack, Kevin had the stove and pot, we both had bivy gear and planned to match the route's best time of one and a half days. We raged onto the ice, dispatching pitches like we were doing laps on the university climbing wall, then jogging the snow slopes to get to the next ice pitches. At 9:00 a.m. we stood below the truncated roof of the Pencil. Blocks of aquamarine ice sat in the snow and their glassy fracture planes reminded me of the toppled columns Kevin and I had seen at the Acropolis.

"Blanch, I think that we can do this thing in a day. I know we can. Let's ditch the bivy gear here." Excitement and resolve flared in his hazel green eyes and there was the radiance of his knowing, the gift that he had for seeing himself to scale on the side of the mountain, and measuring precisely how hard and far he could push his being against the mountain, and if that would be enough.

"I think we can too, Wally." And we did, March 5, 1981.

Wally sold his Mercedes and bought a 1975 olive-green Toyota SR5 pickup. "It's better for my work, Blanch." The truck had a fiberglass capper and on March 16, eleven days after our one-day ascent of Polar Circus, it surged up the Big Bend on the Banff-Jasper highway and sped past the Hilda Creek Hostel to the Columbia Icefield.

Opposite the Dome Glacier, Wally pulled onto the shoulder and we climbed into the back to fake sleep. At 3:00 a.m. we crunched off toward Slipstream, our third grade 6 ice climb that season. Seventeen hours later we were back at the truck—no bivy, a single road-to-road push on Lauchlan and Elzinga's testpiece.

Years later Sharon Wood would tell me "that's when I started hearing about these two hot young guys, Blanchard and Doyle, who were ripping up the range and doing the big climbs in record times."

My dreams were in the process of becoming my reality. Training focused my physiology and I could hold on for a very long time and get oxygen out of the atmosphere and into my bloodstream better than all of my partners save for Kevin—I know now that I did get more oxygen into my blood, but Kevin was able to endure more pain.

April 4, the first rock route of the season: Wally and I headed off to Corkscrew, a 770-foot long, 5.8/A0 route on the south face of Mount Yamnuska. Kevin raged up the approach, sprint and stop, sprint and stop. I marched behind, steady fast footfalls. Clods of shale mud clung to our runners like gumbo, adding pounds of weight to each lift of our feet. We edged onto the uphill sides of our shoes, like we were setting a ski, to keep from sliding downslope. It didn't always work.

Lloyd MacKay had drilled a nine-bolt ladder across an over-hanging blank wall during an early attempt on the route in the mid-sixties. In 1967 Don Vockeroth, Hans Fuhrer, and Brian Greenwood aided across Lloyd's ladder and made the first ascent of Corkscrew. Kevin and I agreed that I should take that pitch to gain some aid climbing experience.

I crossed the bolts well, and Wally said, "I don't care what they say, Blanch, you're a good man to climb with."

Further into the lead I was nervously searching for gear on runout 5.8. "Wally! There's an empty bolt hole here!" I yelled, clinging, staring into a perfect round hole that looked like it had been shot into the wall with a .22.

"Oh yeah!" Wally wailed. "Laurie Skreslett fell off there and ripped out the bolt!" Great.

Two pitches higher I had numb hands; dumb hands. I squeezed too hard on insensible holds while snow blew, then changed to sleet before spitting into drizzle. Nonetheless we finished in good time and drove back to Calgary to the house that Stew and Kev had moved into. Klugan and Zoltan partied too late and kept Al Pickle and me waiting too long early the next morning. In retaliation I opened their fridge and Al and I ate all the good stuff, the expensive stuff.

A legion of trembling aspens swayed from strong gusts in the Yam parking lot. The sky was overcast, and looked like the underside of a slate-gray quilt. The four of us sparred verbally, politically, as motivations waned on the pulsations of hangovers. Al and Wally took off to the Mini Gonda, a short, challenging climb close to Banff that didn't require the 1,600 feet of elevation gain that it took to get up to Yam. Stew and I pounded up the trail, which had thankfully dried from the gumbo-fest of the day before, to Belfry, 5.8+, 1,000 feet, Brian Greenwood's first climb of Yamnuska in 1957.

Below the crux crack I set up a belay that incorporated an upward pull nut just as Stew had been taught on the Aspirant Guide course that he'd taken a year before and failed.

It was Stewart's lead, and he looked at me quizzically, "What? Do you think I'm going to fall, Blanch?"

"No, I'm just trying to be a good guide aspirant."

Stew moved away from the belay. His climbing was awkward and clunky and he was sixty feet out when I heard him yelp, "Holy fuck!"

I saw the slow weightless revolution of his hands leaving the holds and then he blurred into free fall. I wrapped the rope tight across my gut and heard my heart drum twice before I was lifted and snapped tight to the upward pull nut. The fall was surprisingly easy to hold.

Stewart hung inverted and limp fifteen feet above me, the white orb of his Galibier helmet held between the biceps of down-reaching arms that were bent passively at the elbow, hands lightly cupped like he was holding on to either end of a baguette.

"Stewart! Are you all right?" An anxiousness plumed inside me for two long beats of his unconsciousness and then he moaned and started to right himself. He had an abraded hip, but nothing was broken, so he sucked it up and went back up and finished the pitch.

He'd fallen forty feet and ruptured the mantle on my rope, three of the inner kern strands had been severed.

"Edelrid, when reliability counts," I joked, quoting an ad from the climbing mags.

The damage to the rope was twenty feet from one end so we cut it off and Stew tied back in. I led the next pitch.

"I need to lead to keep my head," Stewart said. And it wasn't pretty, but he took us to the top. "Thanks for saving my life, Blanch."

Then he gave me a genuine strong hug, and promised to give me fifty dollars toward a new rope, a promise that he later tried to renege on. It had been a serious fall and Stewart was a lucky man...but he was still Stewart.

A wire-meshed window stood at waist height on the door to the Men's room. "It's to see if anyone is getting knifed," Wally told me as we crossed the open floor of the Cecil Bar.

The Cecil had been a decent hotel when it was built in 1912 and during its subsequent ownership by Alfred Edward Cross, the pioneer for whom my Junior High School had been named. The Cecil served some of the cheapest beer in Calgary in the sixties when the Calgary Mountain Club (CMC) was formed, and it still was cheap on this, my first CMC pub night. I joined the "drinking club with a climbing problem" that night. By 1981 the Cecil was well into a skid that would see it bottom out as cesspool of prostitution, drugs, and murder. The City of Calgary closed the hotel down in 2008. But on that night in 1981 I sat down and drank cheap beer with local legends: Urs Kallen, Albi Sole, Chris Perry, and Trevor Jones.

Two days later, on Good Friday, a lot of the CMC took off for the annual Easter rock-climbing trip to Leavenworth, Washington. Kevin and I stayed behind to make the second ascent of Chris Perry and Trevor Jones's Goat Buttress, a bold 1,230-feet prow of limestone that defines the edge of the Goat Wall just south of Mount Yamnuska. The route was graded 5.8/A3, and Jones and Perry had bivouacked halfway up four years before.

Wally and I carried bivy gear. I was lost on acres of compact slabs and it was bad. One hundred feet of rope lay to the rock without any gear. I was scared. I knew that if I fell, I would die. I couldn't see a way up and I was past the point of down climbing. I quit willing myself upward because my feet quivered on the holds and my hands trembled like traitors.

Kevin had given me his bolt kit and I shouted asking how to use it. He yelled back and talked me through and I got the self-drive halfway in before it seized on the rock powder that I hadn't been blowing from the hole. I tied it off, handle still attached, and finished the pitch. It was not my finest.

The next day, and Wally was on the A3 crux and the rock was horrid and he was panicking because the piton that he had weighted was shifting. I heard fear in his voice and the fear was pissing him off. "Fucking shit rock! Watch me, Blanch. Keep a close eye on me, man."

And in an act of brilliance he slotted in another pin and tapped it tight and clipped his other étrier to it and divided his weight between the two poor pins. He looked like a cowboy standing high in the stirrups. I followed on Jumars and the pitons sprang out with gentle taps of my hammer.

Four days later, 8:00 a.m. on a Wednesday and I listened to Stewart call in sick to his work as a counselor at the Spy Hill Jail, where I'd visited Tim Shatto when he was doing time. I was cinching a rope tight under the lid of the pack that Stew had bought "for cheap" in a trekking shop in Kathmandu during his "walkabout to find myself."

"Ah, Blanch, it's just like George Burns says," and he pointed his index finger toward the ceiling to accent the glee sparkling in his eyes. "It's not so much about the golf when one sneaks away from work to play a little golf. It is more about the sneaking, one must sneak!" He thrust his finger higher and cranked his smile up to ten.

I pulled away from him on the approach to Yam. I was always trying to best my times, see how long I could hold my heart rate over 200. Push, push, push. And then I waited slathered in sweat and steaming, sitting on my pack at the base of the cliff. No Stew. My heart rate settled, no Stew, I began to shiver as my skin dried, no Stew. "Where the fuck is he?" I hissed, and I stood and yelled back down the trail, "Buroker!" A distant reply came from the east.

He was buck naked and sitting in the lotus position when I arrived beneath Red Shirt. The devious bastard had taken the short-cut, effectively ending the debate we'd been having on whether to climb Direttissima, to the west, or Red Shirt.

The route went well for me. I felt in control, not rushing to find the holds. Rather I had time to hold on and figure out how to move smoothly and securely. That wasn't the case for Stew. Who could blame him after his fall on Belfry two and a half weeks earlier. I led the traversing down climbing slab that had freaked out Humblini three years before. I put in as many pieces as I could to make it less scary for Stew, but he was trembling as he crossed the slab. Shell-shocked eyes, lips held like shutters over rows of teeth parted one finger's width, small stretches of his inner lip clinging to the enamel of teeth that looked skeletal.

I worried about him taking the next pitch, the crux, 5.8, but he closed his eyes and dropped his chin to his chest and breathed for two minutes and then he floated the moves perfectly.

"Ninety percent of this game is in your head, Blanch," he said when I gained his belay. I'd been training my body two to four hours a day and I knew that helped, that through the discipline of that I was becoming a better climber. Yet I knew that Stew was right. If I could ever hold on to the jewel of inner calm as I walked through the valley of death I would be able to really climb. Hemingway had called it, "Grace under pressure." And I'd glimpsed it in Kevin, but only glimpses, like mercurial flashes of firelight blazing across the shadows on the back wall of the cave.

"Right you are, Zoltan, right you are."

The rest of the route went rather well and Stew and I snuck off to the Cecil that night, and the route went even better in its telling there.

April 29, the last Wednesday of the month. Jeff Marshall was a com-pact and powerful young climber that Kevin and I had met at the university wall. Big square wire-rimmed glasses and a long black ponytail often bound over by a bandana headband à la Jimi Hendrix. Jeff worshipped Hendrix's music. Kevin and I shackled Jeff with the nickname 'Junior,' which we pronounced in thick French accents, "Joon-whaaar."

Necromancer, 5.8/A2, 1,300 feet, had been added to the west side of Yam by Jon Jones and George Homer in 1971 and in the decade since no one had been able to free climb it.

Jeff was up there bellowing out "Yahoos!" and "Free!" like he'd just won Lord Stanley's Cup and that pretty much told me that he'd manage to free the aid traverse on the eighth pitch. As I traversed the cleanly cleaved wall toward him I could see that the small, triangular handholds had been exposed by the fracturing of rock when pitons had been pounded out. The holds looked like chisel sculpted black marble, and moving over them was absolutely exhilarating. Junior and I ran off the top of the route. The first free ascent of Necromancer! Our first, on Yamnuska! Our feet didn't touch the floor when we strode, chest first, into the Cecil that night.

"Oh, Bear, we can't fit through there," Laurie, the girl with hair the color of sunshine, said. It was the wee hours of the morning and we had just quit dancing at her best friend's wedding. Laurie looked golden in her maid of honor dress. She'd folded it up under her in the passenger seat of my MGB. Twin metal posts stood like a miniature field goal in front of us, blocked the egress of the sly parking spot that I'd ferreted out close to the Big Four Building at the Calgary Stampede grounds where the wedding had been held. The posts were two inches in diameter and waist high, looked to be about five and a half feet apart.

"Hang on, Sunshine!" I hooted and my brain felt as tingly and light as the champagne that we'd been guzzling by the glass.

I slotted the MG dead center between the posts, but the car was six feet wide. The rasp of metal being compressed drummed through the door panels and then "popped" back as the car was extruded from the posts.

"Oh, Bear," Laurie laughed, and then put one hand over her mouth and rested the other on my shoulder and her touch felt warm.

I felt like a dolt. My car now bore the transverse stripes of an alien metal, it looked like its snapdragon yellow body had been clawed by a large predatory cat.

"Kevin wouldn't have done that," I said.

"If he'd has as much champagne, he might have." Laurie arched her eyebrows and nodded her forehead to me and smiled radiantly.

"No, he can judge distances to within the half inch. I've seen him do it. He can look at a span and say that it's forty-two and three -quarters inches, and when I measure it with a tape measure it is, or it is within a half inch."

"Bear, even I could see that we weren't going to fit."

"Yes, but it was so close. Damn champagne."

Laurie's parents were away on vacation and we drove to their house and spent the night and the day and the next night lazily making love and recuperating over Chinese takeout then sleeping wrapped around each other.

July 4, 1981, ten years and three days since the first ascent of the Kahl Wall by the bold climber Don Vockeroth, and the route had yet to be freed. Wally and I blazed up the approach and vaulted up the lower wall. I watched Kevin on the first crux pitch scan the next two yards of rock leading rightward to the edge of the overlap he was under-clinging. A vertical crack led up from there. Darting eyes told me that he had cataloged the next two underclings and three small breaks from vertical that would be his footholds. I knew that he'd already seen himself moving through, his visualization prescient to his performance.

He deftly clipped a fixed piton and yanked his hand from the task brusquely, like the rope and carabiner were hindrances to his will.

"Watch me, Blanch," and he began to breathe deeply and rhyth-mically as he moved across the five holds powerfully and precisely. He caught the edge of the vertical crack with his right hand and his forearm swelled with the pulsing of blood through blue and green veins as distended as girdling roots. His left hand jabbed into the red

Strawberry Mountain chalk bag that he'd bought in the Camp 4 parking lot in Yosemite earlier that spring. The deep bag swallowed his hand to midforearm and like a prizefighter pulling back a punch he yanked his hand out. An aura of chalk dust ignited against the oblique sunlight like a starburst. Kev got both hands into the crack and pasted his feet high, the axis of his hips was out from the wall, a position that we called "ass over space."

He flowed through the next three bodylengths with a balletic grace worthy of Muhammed Ali or Rudolf Nureyev. There was no hesitation between recognition and execution. Time became the cadence of his deep breaths and the fast flow of the rope. My good friend had become an animal of the wall, he'd given himself entirely to his intuition and it was inspiring to watch. Twenty minutes later he shouted down, "Off belay!" I applauded.

And then it was my turn. A clean water groove augured into immaculate gray limestone like the blood gutter in a medieval broadsword. Below me the rope hung in space like a sail. I pushed down panic with my breath and reached and pulled and reacted. A long hour saw me belayed at the base of the linear corner.

"Come here, my little brown friend," Wally said on top, and then we bear hugged long and strong.

I said, "The Kahl Wall free, Wally! Fuckin' aye, man, fuckin' aye." In retrospect they were strange words to mark our best day ever on Yamnuska...and then again maybe they were perfectly timely and appropriate.

———

"I think that I've got low altitude pulmonary edema," Bill Stark said, and then he thumped his pack onto the broken slate of the moraine and sat on it. Five foot eleven and as wide as a door, Bill was one of our crew from the university wall. We called him 'Captain Fist' because he was the only one of us whose hand was wide enough to stick a challenging fist jam at the Bearspaw—a very small sandstone outcrop in a ravine just west of the city limit. Kevin could climb it too, but with exotic wide hand jams that neither Stew, Ron, or I could manage.

It was July 12, 4:00 a.m., the sun was just heating the eastern horizon. Bill and I were at the edge of the Little North Athabasca Glacier on our way to the north face of Mount Athabasca, but now Fist was feeling off and not into continuing.

"I still want to do this, Fist," I said.

"If you want to go by yourself I'll wait for you here."

An hour to the bergschrund, another two hours of planting my Sérac Sabres into concrete ice, kicking one foot in on front points, and the other sideways, saw me at the crux. It felt absolutely amazing to solo the bodylengths of 5.5 that stepped vertically from the 1,000-foot ice face into the 500-foot-long ice gully leading to the summit. I felt the whole world pulling at my back, yet I moved up quietly and confidently. I'd become an animal of the wall myself. It felt mythical to look across to the Hourglass route, 300 feet to the right, and see myself there in my rental gear with Ron and Dick and Carl two years earlier. Five hours after leaving Fist on the moraine he was there waiting for me. Heaven knows what he did during that time.

Three weeks later, August 8, a Saturday, I soloed Red Shirt in two hours. I felt in control. As I ran back down to my car I felt like I was accomplishing something in my life and that made me want to climb harder, train more.

That Friday, after work, Kev, Tim 'TP' Friesen, Chris Dale, and I drove four hours west to the Bugaboos parking lot and bivied. The next morning we approached the west side of the South Howser Tower.

"That is God showing off," I said to Kev. It was noon and the four of us were standing beneath the Beckey-Chouinard. It is one of the finest prow climbs in North America and it rose above us like God had smithed a Celtic sword and laid its blade broadside to the mountain with the tip piercing the sky. A southerly wind dragged across its edge and a massive turbine of cloud swirled slowly in the lee looking like a field of chiffon turning into an oceanic eddy.

"That is too beautiful man, too beautiful," Kevin said, and a serene look of contentment relaxed all of the drive and concentration that was so often set in his face. He was happy.

Captain Fist, aka Bill Stark, and I (sitting) near the top of Popes Peak one February day in the early 1980s. We'd just climbed the north face with Wally. Photo: Kevin Doyle

Pitch four I was anything but; I was awash in a sea of terror. I'd cranked like a fiend to pull over a cantankerous roof. Above it, four linear cracks grooved the coarse wall of granite and I had chosen the wrong crack. I fought my way from a fine hand-width splitter to a rounded out gutter that looked dirty and rusted. Single crystals bit into the trembling knuckle edges of my palm-to-sky right-handed first jam. Kevin's precious number three Friend was cammed into the crack thirty feet below. Out of options I prayed and pulled, floundered onto the belay ledge above.

"This is fucking hard, Blanch," Kevin shouted to me from the number three placement.

"I think that you should leave that in for TP," I yelled back (TP and Chris had brought a miserly rack of four Friends). I shouted down to TP, who looked suave and cool in his white helmet and white glacier glasses that he'd had on since dawn, telling him he'd be much happier saving his number three Friend for higher in the crack.

"Watch me here, Blanch," Kev said as he pivoted up to where I'd had my tipped out hand jam, where I'd talked with God. He wrapped both palms onto the black, algae-stained curve of the gutter and pulled his right foot up to waist level, rotating his big toe into the bowel of the gutter and then he pulled powerfully into a slapping lay-back that he controlled with oppositional forces that met at his spine.

"That was fucking serious, my little brown friend."

"I was gripped out of my tree, Wally."

Below TP had cranked the roof and jammed to the number three.

"TP," Kevin shouted, "take it easy. The crack rounds out and gets serious up here."

"I'm doing OK," TP replied, and he continued up, but his breathing deepened and he struggled to place the second number three.

Ten feet below us he ripped off the white glasses and they bobbed under his chin on their keeper cord. Wally and I saw the eyes of the hunted jerking back and forth anxiously seeking an escape. He looked comical, and endangered.

"TP, I can lower you a rope," Kev said.

"No, no, I'm OK." TP sputtered, looking far from OK. He trembled and pulled and wobbled onto the ledge. "Jesus!" he said.

Chris grew up in Wales and had done a lot of hard climbing in Britain before immigrating to Canada. He once told me that he and his climbing partner, Robin, knew when the climbing was getting hard because they'd have to put on their glasses to see the "wee" footholds.

Chris pulled over the roof and then stepped left and climbed easily to where he had to force a traverse right to clean the first number three. "You were supposed to step left onto a horn after the roof," he said when he got to us.

"Fred Beckey and Yvon Chouinard slept here twenty years ago," Wally beamed.

On the "Big Sandy Ledge" ten pitches up the route, Wally and I wriggled into the bivy sacs that he had sewn. Chris and TP grinned as they pulled sleeping bags out of their packs. Wally and I were shocked. They'd bought a rack of only four Friends, but sleeping bags! Kev and I shivered through a cold night, but enjoyed the security that our full rack granted us when we finished the ten pitches leading to the tip of the sword in the sky the next day, Sunday.

Then we all rapped off and ran back to the cars. Each of us was at work on Monday morning, swollen hands, faces bloated and sunbaked, tired feet laboring to gain stairs, but hearts as light as feathers.

Wednesday morning Steve Langley had his 1978 white Chevy Nova barreling down the rough gravel road that led to the Ghost River. I sat in the passenger's seat. The doe exploded from the ditch and sailed into the right front headlight. She hit with an abrupt and sickening *thud*. I saw the fender fold and she was bounced off as Steve stomped on the brakes. It took the car tens of yards to grind to a stop, bellowing dust. I stepped from the passenger door and saw her fumble to her three working legs then thrash off into the timber, her left hind leg swinging behind her in an alien alignment like a broken branch dangling from a tree trunk in high winds.

"There's nothing we can do for her now," Steve said. Hair and blood clung to crumpled metal. I felt sick, yet we climbed back into the car and continued on to the south face of Phantom Tower, 5.8, 1,000 feet.

Late in the afternoon Steve led the last pitch. He climbed from my view at thirty feet. The sun was warm and I had a ledge to lie on. I fell asleep a moment later still paying rope out from around my waist and didn't wake up until I felt Steve tugging hard on my harness. He'd pretty much climbed the whole pitch without a belay!

"Good thing that I didn't fall," Steve guffawed, his eyes stretched wide beneath arching brows.

We stopped at the first ranch on our drive out and called Fish and Wildlife. We told the officer where we'd hit the doe and he said that he'd go in and track her and put her down if she was still alive. We should have driven out immediately and reported it the morning that we hit her.

It was Friday, two days after the south face of Phantom Tower and a week since the Beckey-Chouinard. I'd picked TP up after work in my MG and we'd motored out of Calgary listening to Jerry Jeff Walker decry the attributes that comprise a "Redneck Mother." We were headed for the northeast ridge of Howse Peak and figured on sleeping in the MG, then climbing half of the route Saturday to a bivy, finishing it off on Sunday, and descending to cold beer in the creek because the Beer Store would be closed. The route had been opened in 1967, Canada's hundredth birthday. I would have been an eight-year-old second grader in Calgary.

"If it was done in '67, how hard can it be?" TP had asked me over the phone earlier that week.

"Don Vockeroth was on the first ascent, man. That guy did not fool around. He got after it. I heard that Greenwood once followed one of his really bold leads and accused him of being a dinosaur: 'Big body, small brain.'"

Brian Greenwood's name was written across the Rockies in capital letters, and if he sat on Odin's throne in my pantheon, then Vockeroth was Thor and when he hammered pitons he wielded thunder and lightning. In my mind his hammer was Mjöllnir.

The phenomenal Beckey-Chouinard lies
on the west side of the South Howser
Tower—a sword point thrust into the sky.
Photo: Kevin Doyle

I'd been to the library Thursday afternoon and photocopied Don's route description from the 1970 *Canadian Alpine Journal*. Blocks of pitches were laid out in paragraphs...the article was many paragraphs long.

TP had land leases to lawyer Monday morning and I would be getting up ungodly early to run my milk route. We had the weekend to climb and climbing was my fountainhead. I dreamed of becoming as good a climber as Don Vockeroth or Brian Greenwood, maybe even Walter Bonatti. And I was trying to get there like Reinhold Messner had—by doing a lot. I was living my life on the template laid out in the pages of Messner's alpine manifesto, *The Seventh Grade*. One question that nagged me...did Reinhold drink beer? He hadn't mentioned it in his book, but Bonatti had in *On The Heights*.

The first guidebook that I'd bought in the late seventies was a *Climber's Guide to the Rocky Mountains of Canada—South*. There is a postcard-sized black-and-white picture of Howse Peak: the sweeping black walls adorned with lattices and ledges of pearl-white ice to the east, and decked by a lone glacier overhanging a 2,000-foot-high black cliff to the north, and both flanks cleaved into sunlight and shade by the northeast ridge as if it were the leading edge of an enormous ocean liner.

We ate bananas and pita bread long before dawn with the engine running and Waylon wailing on the eight-track. Also yogurt and orange juice bought from my milk truck (I was my own best customer for yogurt). TP and I clomped into the dark forest with the beams of our Wonder headlamps bouncing in front of us like bingo balls.

Dawn, the walls of Howse Peak wrapped around us like the wings of a gargantuan eagle squaring off for a talon hit. We were two hours from the road, already crossing a glacier, and the landscape had fulfilled the wanting of my dreams—it was alpine, and it was wild!

Midmorning, we had begun to climb anchor to anchor. The first crux was a bulging prow of gray limestone off of a broken shale ledge. Clumps of moss campion huddled around TP like a corral of turtles, their backs brilliant with lavender and violet. My Galibier mountain boots set well onto the small incut edges and my hands were finding the right holds. I pulled and climbed knowing that this bulge would have taken me more time, and gear, to figure out were it on the south face or Mount Yamnuska, yet there I was on Howse Peak allowing my confidence and belief to carry me over holds that would otherwise stymie me, holds that I could, may, fall from. I was going for it. I looked down to see my full leather boot rocking onto a highstep, I could see the divisions of my quad muscles snapped tight like creases into my new brown woolen knickers, my densely packed, twenty-five-liter pack pulled out on my shoulders as my lungs heaved in air. And then I flowed through the moves and pulled into balance. I felt light, I felt like Walter Bonatti.

"Yeehaa! TP! That was just fucking wild, man!" My voice echoed back twice from the magnificent sweeping walls and glaciers that ringed our northern horizon for two kilometers before melding into the slopes of the White Pyramid and Mount Chephren.

"Great! You looked really good up there. Now find a good belay and bring me up!"

We climbed higher. The sun began to burn, and then it swung behind the dark tower of Howse, leaving us to chug down mouthfuls from our water bottles, mine a dented red aluminum one with a wire-tensioned stopper that I had bought in Chamonix the summer before.

Midday I fought for fifteen minutes desperately trying to top out one of several 100-foot-high bands of black limestone by stepping into balance on a shallow shattered ledge of shale. It was like trying to exit an attic window onto a steeply pitched roof that was stacked with serving platters, many of them broken. The fingers of my right hand ached and quivered as I delicately piled enough of the shale plates onto one place overhead and was able to press my hand onto it and rise into a teetering balance on everything loose. I waded up the ledge and stitched together an anchor of nuts and pitons at the next steep, and thankfully solid, band.

Tim led through and we moved together for 800 feet. The first crux, where I'd felt like Bonatti, was now 1,500 feet below us and we'd just come to the end of the first paragraph of Vockeroth's route description. There were another three paragraphs to go!

At dusk, I pulled out the amazing one-pound down sleeping bag that I'd borrowed and laid back onto my pack, rope, and spare clothes. Stars shone overhead, TP snored, I was warm. I soon realized that before my trip to Chamonix I had spent two nights in planned bivouacs on the sides of mountains, then in the last year I'd bivied five times. I was living, and sleeping, out my dreams; Reinhold would approve.

The next day, Sunday, we climbed another 1,500 feet...two more of Vockeroth's paragraphs. There was a final paragraph to go when the day began to dim.

"I think that I can get to that water over there," TP stated.

"It looks a long ways away TP, and the ledge looks like total crap."

"We need water. I have to have water or I won't be able to go on." I'd come to know the redheaded resolve in his voice, he was going.

"OK, I'll belay you."

He advanced slowly kicking steps into rock that looked like broken ashtrays, arrowheads, glass beads, and dirt. Much of it fell from his feet like isothermal snow to cascade 3,000 feet and accumulate as colluvium at the base of the wall. For every three attempts at a piton placement he gained one, but one hour later he returned with our water bottles full.

I added another bivy, albeit unplanned, to my growing list.

By the middle of the next day, Monday, I'd gone without food for twenty-four hours. TP revealed a half-pound brick of cheese and began rationing quarter-inch-thick slices to me. I wolfed them down like they were potato chips then sat salivating as I watched TP slowly chew his thirty-two times each, Swiss Army knife in one hand and the rest of the cheese in the other.

"TP, can I have my next piece now?"

"It's taken me ten years to teach myself to eat this slowly," TP replied contemplatively.

"I'm happy for you, but I'm fucking starving. Give me my next piece, man."

At 3;00 p.m. we hit Vockeroth's final period and added our names to the few on top of Howse Peak. George Lowe and Jock Glidden were signed in after Don, Lloyd MacKay, and Ken Baker.

Heroes all, and though I didn't know George at the time, three years down the road I would be climbing with him in winter on the northeast face of Mount Chephren, three kilometers north of where I stood, an early attempt at what would eventually become The Wild Thing.

TP and I careened headlong down the back slopes of Howse Peak. "There has to be a trail down there," TP stated. Neither of us had a map.

Anxious and lost, we glissaded a glacier then stumbled left and right over talus and shale connecting shallow ground, avoiding cliffs. Alpine meadows ended too soon in a maze of forest. We bush-whacked for a long time and eventually caught views of a warden's cabin, and then we stepped onto the trail.

At 9:00 p.m. dusk came and we bedded down on the porch of the warden's cabin. My stomach churned in on itself, it felt like stone grinding on stone. My new knickers looked fuzzy and they'd lost their sheen, the waistband sagged. The highway was fourteen miles away.

Tuesday morning we were up with the dawn, desperate to get out, the burden of having missed work for the second day running worried TP. Hours of forced marching with hunger folding my stomach in half. The haze of the sunlit forest seemed overexposed because my brain wasn't getting enough sugar.

Midday we ran into a guy and gal who looked like Wavy Gravy and one of his groupies gone back to nature. I told them that we'd been climbing and had run out of food. They dug into their packs and came up with a plastic bag full of caramels. TP and I fell on them like ravenous dogs on diced meat. I couldn't get the wrappers off fast enough. By the time I stuffed the last one into my mouth they'd formed a golf-ball-sized lump that clung to my teeth and made it hard to chew.

Wavy and his gal were aghast. They'd obviously never witnessed such an attack before. Whatever other food they'd thought of sharing was now being stuffed back into their packs, and they had gone quiet and were avoiding eye contact. I think they felt threatened because Wavy said, "Well, I guess we better get going, good luck," and they shuffled away...quickly.

The caramels gave me a boost and I was soon far ahead of TP. An hour later I came to a trail junction at the north end of Mount Sarbach. The left trail went down and seemingly toward the highway, the right one up in the direction of the mountain. I pounded off down the left and forty-five minutes later came to the confluence of the Saskatchewan and Mistaya Rivers. I could see Winnebagos lumbering up the highway on the far side of the rivers, but there was no bridge to get there. I waited, no TP. I backtracked a bit and looking down realized that mine were the only boot tracks, all the rest were horse's hooves. I'd missed the hiking trail, this is where horses forded the river!

The Saskatchewan was brown and wide and pumping, the Mistaya blue and fast, but narrower. I stripped from the waist and lashed boots and clothes to the outside of my plump pack. Then I held it over my head and waded into the Mistaya. On my third step the current grabbed my upstream hip and wrenched me through two pirouettes and my head went under and my feet lost the bottom and I felt the power of the current pulling me in, dragging me under. Then my toes stubbed and stumbled into the bed and I thrashed free and lurched onto shore with my lungs heaving for air. I still had my pack and I sat on it for long minutes of shivering and swearing until the sun pushed the cold from me.

I didn't know where the footbridge was so I started bushwhacking up the Mistaya. It was cruelly comical to see the Winnebagos within slingshot range and not be able to get there. A half hour of hard work and I came to vertically walled canyon. The Mistaya was green, deep. and raging thirty feet below. The water thundered, filling the air with spray. It looked, and vibrated, like the bottom of Niagara Falls. Two pine trees had fallen in intersection over the canyon, bridging it. I needed this trial to be over.

I stomped hard on each tree, they quivered with tension. I stood sideways on the lower tree and balanced my hands on the upper that sat at waist level. I slowly and precisely shuffled out over the maelstrom. Spray and thunder. Halfway over the trees crossed and I had to straddle the upper tree to get past it. When I set my weight onto it—*Crack!*—and I dropped six inches and my lungs shot out a "*Huh!*" The tree didn't break and I slowly eased my weight off of it to stand again on the lower tree, and continued to shuffle across.

The guardrail. The blessed metal guardrail. I heaved my pack over, it thumped heavily onto the asphalt. The first vehicle that passed by my outstretched thumb was a Winnebago, but then there was a motorcycle slowing to a stop with TP on the back. At the trail junction he'd studied the evidence and followed the boot prints. The guy on the bike had picked him up and offered to help. He doubled me back to my MG where I told the warden who was standing beside it that, "No, we were OK, we didn't need a rescue." I drove back for TP and my pack, then returned for the beer with the warden gone. We drank the beer and then hurried back to Calgary and our waiting jobs.

Chapter 10

YOSEMITE

SATURDAY, SEPTEMBER 12, Wally, TP, and I piled into Wally's pickup, which was tight with gear, and hit the road for Yosemite. We engineered a space in the middle of all the packs, milk crates, and coolers—our road bed—and for the next thirty hours one of us was driving with someone riding shotgun as the third guy slept in the back.

Crossing the spine of the Sierra Nevada, Kev and I spotted a sign indicating a curving descent for the next thirty-three miles. Wally's hands clamped tight onto the wheel, opened his eyes wide to psycho, teeth gleaming, and then he stomped on it and hooted, "Yeehaw!" I cranked up "Sympathy for the Devil" and within four careening, care-free, tire squealing turns TP was pounding on the back window, having been tossed around like a martini in a shaker. Kevin and I laughed and laughed and slowed down for five miles, and when TP was settled, Wally pinned it again.

We pulled into the Valley. The full moon washed all surfaces presented to it with a soft luminescence like all had been dusted with snow. TP had come up front and was wedged between Kev and I on the bench seat. Kev called out the cliffs as we motored slowly under them.

I knew what was coming up and my heart stepped up a beat and my skin tightened and tingled and Kev said, "Are you ready for this?"

Wally geared up for the great roof on the headwall
of the Salathé, El Capitan. Photo: Barry Blanchard

And there it was, the universal touchstone image of ascent: El Capitan. It glowed in the moonlight like a defining feature of the planet.

I gasped, "Holy crap, El Cap."

Wally pulled into the meadows and we piled out leaving the doors wide and the speakers pointing at the great stone. We cued up "Gimme Shelter" and Keith Richard's sultry rhythm guitar washed over the pale swaying grass and we listened and looked, rewound and listened and looked again. The feeling of lightness that I'd had sitting in the Biolay campground in Chamonix one year earlier when Kev and I had descended from Les Droites rose from the ground and into me through the soles of my feet. I felt so good, so happy, so excited.

"We are going to climb that bad dog, me buckos," Kevin beamed.

"It looks amazing," I said.

"First we have to find a campsite," Tim added.

And we did, in Camp 4. The next day we commenced our Valley lifestyle of free climbing most days and going for the walls when we felt it was right.

Frank Sacherer was one of the pioneers of the modern free climbing movement in Yosemite. An intense individual who believed that if a move was 5.9 two feet above a piton, it was still a 5.9 move when the piton was forty feet down. Sacherer's mercurial thrust on the Valley free climbing standard lasted from 1961 to 1965. Sacherer Cracker, 5.10a, 150 feet, was one of his routes at the base of El Cap. In my mind I held a black-and-white image of him on the route. I believed that I'd seen the image in a magazine but I couldn't identify which magazine, or when.

"They say that Sacherer was the best free climber in the Valley in the early sixties," Kevin said as we sat and looked up at the perfect crack, both of its edges scoured clean of lichen for one human arm width leaving a sidewalk of pristine pale granite rolling up the cliff— a sidewalk with a crack down its middle. I wondered if memory and myth had intertwined in my mind, and my want of an image of Sacherer had created one.

"Isn't there a shot of him on this route in one of the magazines?" I asked.

"Ya, ya, I think so," Kevin replied.

TP pursed his lips and crumpled his brow then he shook his head and snorted and said, "I don't remember one."

In 1968 Frank Sacherer finished a PhD in physics and in 1970 he went to work at the European Centre for Nuclear Physics in Geneva. Sacherer was killed by lightning while climbing the Shroud on the north face of Les Grandes Jorasses in 1978. All of this I would learn about the man in the future, yet standing at the base of the Great Stone with the sun pressing heat into my back I looked up and imagined him there.

TP led the pitch and I came up second and both he and I battled with the finishing offwidth. It looked like we'd been strapped into straight jackets. Wally amazed us. He climbed the wide crack with a right-arm chicken wing, thumb-down edge grab with his left hand on the left side, a right knee jam and the top of his left foot pushing against the left edge. He padded up to us in seconds looking like a terrestrial acrobatic seal.

"How in the hell did you do that, Wally?" I asked and he pantomimed the positions. I'd entered the steep Yosemite learning curve.

The next day we went to the English Breakfast Crack, 5.10c, 150 feet. The first pitch was mine, but I didn't know how to deal with the flaring chimney at its end. The granite seemed as featureless as the backside of a headstone. I pushed like a son-of-a-bitch on my knees, rasped them over the granite in desperation. Halfway through the flaring chimney I felt like I'd come off of my skateboard at high speed and rode out the asphalt frog-legged. I'd pushed my kneepads to my ankles and once I was in the chimney I couldn't find a way to pull them up. I climbed onto the belay with burns the size of hamburger patties on the inside of both knees. It felt like I'd placed my knees on a barbeque and held them there.

"Should we use knee pads?" TP shouted up.

"Yes! You should use knee pads."

Back in Camp 4 Kevin gave me tincture of benzoin and I dabbed it onto my burns and it felt like napalm, but then the camphor sweet smell of care hit my nostrils and that placebo ameliorated the fire on my knees.

"Tomorrow let's rest and get ready for Half Dome," Kevin said. We'd been in the Valley for four days and climbed ten pitches.

"Do you think your knees will be up to it, Blanch?" Kevin asked.

"Let me see how they feel tomorrow. I think that they'll be OK if I wear knee pads. The tincture is helping."

"How do they feel?" Kevin persisted.

"Like the rug burn I got with Laurie one night in the spring."

"Ah! Pleasure and pain, pleasure and pain. This is the same, my little brown friend. The pain of ecstasy!"

Two days later the three of us hiked up the back slopes of Half Dome. The sun was high and hot and Kevin and I had stripped down to running shorts. TP kept clothes on for protection, his skin being as white as skim milk. My head was down, footfalls ahead, I looked up and there was a guy who looked like Jesus Christ: slender, nut brown from the sun, a walking staff in hand, and wearing khaki cutoffs and leather sandals.

"Hey man, there's a bear behind me," he stated in a laid back Californian drawl. He sounded like a surfer. And five feet behind him, ambling through a corridor in the granite, was a very large black bear!

"Holy shit!" I blurted and scampered off the trail into low bush and dry dirt.

The surfer Jesus followed me, we turned to see TP raise his baseball cap and recognize instantly that there was a bear lumbering toward him. Tim vaulted from the trail and came to cower with Jesus and me. Kevin was several strides behind and we all watched as he raised his eyes and mistook the bear for a dog. Wally's eyes smiled and his hand came up to pet and then an electrical jolt shot up his spine and his eyes popped wide as his jaw dropped open. He jumped from the trail and hustled into the huddle. The bear padded down the trail not ten feet from us. He didn't even turn to look at us, just walked on by.

We stood silent for a couple of minutes.

"Do you think he's gone?" TP asked. We ventured out onto the trail, no sign of the bear.

"I thought that it was a big black dog," Wally's voice was giddy with adrenalin. "I was going to pet it."

"Good thing you didn't," Jesus said, and we stood on the trail talking down the rush. Eventually Jesus wished us a good day, nodded, and walked off in the direction of the bear.

Half Dome dominates the upper end of Yosemite Valley with all the solemnity of a burlap-cowled head. The serial overhangs of the Visor thrust out like the peak of the mountain's cowl that had been pinched by God and pulled forward. Inside the face portal, and in the early morning light, the northwest face fell in shadow as dark as an obsidian mirror.

June 28, 1957, the Visor shelved out over the top of Royal Robbins, Mike Sherrick, and Jerry Gallwas. It was the trio's fifth day on the northwest face and they feared that the stacked overhangs would block their exit. And then they were granted the miracle of a "Thank God" ledge—a catwalk of clean golden granite that narrowed to the width of a concrete parking block and gifted them an escape from under the crushing weight of the Visor. They watched the sun set for the fifth time from the summit. The northwest face was the most difficult wall climb in North America.

TP was a one-year-old when Robbins, Sherrick, and Gallwas stood on top of Half Dome. Kevin was born the next year, 1958, and me the year after. Twenty-four years had passed since the first ascent and the route had seen hundreds of repeats. Knowledge amassed as mystery retreated like mist leaving the surface of a lake. A lot was known. The northwest face of Half Dome had become the Regular route and it was now formulaic.

We followed the formula: approach and rap in, climb six pitches and bivy, climb to Big Sandy Ledge and bivy, top out, and descend.

Day two, I wore my only rugby shirt. It was bumblebee colored—yellow bars on black bars on white bars. The thick wick-like fabric of the wristbands had been scraped to threadbare tatters from the rasp of limestone and granite. A red bandana was tied around my forehead—Apache style, just like Ron Kauk wore his, white painter's pants that were cooler when the California sun pounded into them, and kneepads, always kneepads after the English Breakfast Crack. All together, the de rigueur armor of a Valley climber. I'd pasted a cuff of denim-colored canvas around the ankles of my EBs with barge cement and then painstakingly stitched the edges with Wally's Speedy Stitcher. It was the same tool that I'd used to repair my Nikes in Chamonix the year before. The canvas would protect my EBs, make them last longer.

I traversed from Wally and TP and came to a tombstone-clean, wide crack that looked really difficult, but when I reached in to figure out how to jam it my hand found a positive edge, just like I'd reached the width of a gravestone to clamp the back of it firmly. I laughed out loud. I wouldn't have to jam, and that made the climbing four grades easier!

"Hah! There's an edge in here! Wally, take my picture. It looks like I'm jamming a 5.11 offwidth."

Thank God Ledge: Wally related some Valley lore, "There use to be some bongs banged into the crack here and then a guy was going across, and he'd clipped into them all, when an earthquake struck and the whole wall shook and the plate that forms the ledge vibrated more and the bongs popped out like watermelon seeds squeezed between your fingers. Buddy nearly came off when the weight of the bongs hit his rope."

Standing across Thank God Ledge is one of the classic Valley challenges and it can be equated to trying to walk a tightrope while someone gradually pushes hard on your right shoulder. Each of us tried and we took great glee in goading each other on to the point of toppling backward into the void.

I was last man across and I stepped onto the near end of the ledge and started. Soon the ledge narrowed underfoot and the upper wall pressed to vertical. I pasted my chest to the wall and began shimmying like a mime stuck to an imaginary wall of glass.

"Ya, Blanch, you got it man, keep with it, buddy," Wally encouraged me from the far end where he and TP stood anchored, bringing in my rope. I sucked my body in tighter, got the points of my shoulders to touch, smeared my right cheekbone onto the hot granite and stood on tiptoes with my heels over the edge of space. The void pulled on my shoulder blades like when I was thirteen and balanced backward on the edge of the six-foot diving board and Jon, the joker, pushed me in the chest. I slithered six inches further.

My body began to lever out, "Oh fuck!" escaped from the left corner of my mouth, the right corner being pasted to the rock, slobbering. Wally and TP choked on suppressed guffaws, then burst into laughter as I crumpled into the wall trying to get low enough to grab the crack beneath my toes, but I wasn't flexible enough to touch it! I lurched in thuggish desperation and clamped on to the edge of the crack with both hands just as my body bounced off into space. I caught myself with a lung blowing exhalation, "Huh!" My thighs slapped into the wall. Wally and TP crumpled into their harnesses quaking in spasms of laughter. Kev had to reach and wipe tears from his eyes.

We joined masses of hikers on top. They'd all come up the steps of the Cable Route, the way that we would be getting down.

"Well, if that's a big wall, then it's the third one we've done this month," I said feeling arrogance rise in me.

"True for you and TP, Blanch, but I wasn't with you guys on Howse Peak, not that missing out on that extended adventure troubles me. But I've only done two when I add this to the Beckey-Chouinard."

"Let's get down and get some beer, and then hit the Sweet Shop at the Awhahnee tomorrow," TP concluded.

Mornings I would rise early and run the trail to El Cap to see the sun hit the top of the Wall of Early Morning Light. Wally and TP slept. TP could do that for a long time...noon even. Tension born of impatience welled up in Wally and me as we waited, chomping at the bit, to get to our chosen climbs for the day.

"Where the fuck is TP?" I spat one morning while sitting on the tailgate of Kev's truck. We were all incredibly self-centered young men, yet less so Kevin. He had the Christian regard to care for the stranger and a gift for empathy, but much of the time that had to be provoked.

"I don't know," Kev replied, "I'll go see if he's up." And he stomped off across the parking lot.

TP resolved to run with me one morning and he did get up and we started, but about a half mile out his footfall landed on a redwood cone the size of a softball and twisted his ankle. He limped back to Camp 4 to sleep it off.

Watching the light of the new day creep down the Wall of Early Morning Light is sublime, and the next day it slowed me out of my powerful strides and wiped clean the fantasies of conquest surging through my head. I stood panting, slack-jawed, watching the sun descend onto the Great Stone, and some of the lightness that I'd found in the Alps came into me through the soles of my trainers and I felt good and clean and blissfully optimistic.

Four days after descending from Half Dome we fixed ropes to Sickle Ledge and the next day we launched onto the greatest rock climb in the world, the Nose of El Capitan.

"Hey guys, do you know that Warren Harding started up the Nose four days after Robbins climbed Half Dome? We're on the same schedule. That's kinda cool, eh?" Kevin said.

"Let's hope that it doesn't take us a year and a half like him," TP countered.

Kevin had taken the plans for a haul bag to Calgary Tent and Awning and got them to sew one up out of vinyl coated nylon, and "at a good price too, Blanch." I clipped some one-inch webbing into the haul loops to create shoulder straps and then leaned into the eighty-pound load, much of which was water.

"You look like a giant walking bottle of horseradish!" Wally chortled.

Five minutes into the trail I bumped up against six guys with shoulder slings manhandling a blue plastic wrapped cylinder the size of a deep-freeze up the trail toward El Cap.

"What the hell is that?" I asked, thumping the haul bag, which I'd already taken to calling "the Pig," down onto the trail behind me.

"And down," the guy at the front left corner instructed, and all six of them squatted in unison and set the cylinder to the ground like ancient Egyptian slaves. The guy closest to me answered in a slow Southern accent, "That there is a 3,000-foot nine-millimeter rope."

"Holy crap," Wally blurted. "Are you going to fix El Cap?"

"No, we all are going to set the record for the longest continuous rappel and rope ascent ever."

"Huh," TP exhaled. "You don't climb?"

"No sir, we're rappel and ascent experts."

"How are you going to get it up there?" TP asked.

"We got a team on top lowering a haul line down right now. See," he said, shielding his eyes and pointing to a streamer of orange flagging tape that fluttered out from the wall about halfway down the steep southeast face.

"Wow," I said. "Well, we're off to climb the Nose. Do you mind if we go around you here?"

"No, not in the least, gents. Please do."

The streamer eventually touched down and for the next several days we watched it rise slowly and then we lost sight of it when it was high up the wall and it went behind the prow of the Nose.

We swung leads and I got the pendulum into the Stoveleg Cracks, it was my first big wall pendulum. I climbed up for half a ropelength and then had Kev lower me down about forty feet. Kev and Tim were huddled in the Dolt Hole a further forty feet below.

The epic first ascent of the Nose spanned eighteen months and was spearheaded by Warren 'Batso' Harding. Harding and various partnerings of seven other men spent forty-five days on the wall and fixed 2,600 feet of rope in siege-style tactics. Then through the night of November 11, 1958, Batso hand drilled twenty-eight bolts to finish the final blank, bulging headwall and at 6:00 a.m. on the twelfth he, Wayne Merry, and George Whitmore staggered onto the top of El Cap. The Nose was the first route up the Great Stone.

Kevin had read, and reread, Harding's book, *Downward Bound: A Mad! Guide To Rock Climbing*. Batso was Wally's guardian angel in the Valley and when we got to Dolt Hole Kevin told TP and me the sad story of William Andrew 'Dolt' Feuerer hanging himself at Christmastime in 1971. And then Wally handed me the rack and pointed up to the pendulum point.

I hung on the rope and started sprinting back and forth across the face. Wally and TP yelled "Yahoos!" from the Dolt Hole. At the low point of each return, when my velocity was greatest, I had to time a hurtle jump to clear the yard-wide flank of the open book corner that I'd climbed up. A hilarious image of Wile E. Coyote slowly smack, smack, smacking into the side of a desert tower on the end of a rope slipped into my mind from the cartoons of my youth. And then I sprawled out at the right apex of my swing and caught the edge of the stove legs with my right hand (*Beep! Beep!*–the Roadrunner).

The rope hauled mightily on my harness, and in the opposite direction. If I let go I'd go bounding back across the cruel granite just like Wile E. "Slack! Slack! Slack! I need some slack!"

The rope gently eased my hips into line with my right hand and I punched in some jams and hung there panting the adrenalin away. That night, September 27, we slept on Dolt Tower, eleven pitches up the route.

TP insisted on replicating every picture from the Nose that he'd photocopied, and carried with him, out of George Meyers's classic book, *Yosemite Climber*. It was a pain in the ass for Wally and I at the time, but it has given us something to gaze back on from our advancing years—like TP lying on top of the Texas Flake pretending to sleep like Royal Robbins.

"TP! Start coming up!" Wally bellowed.

"No. Take my picture first," TP replied.

"Oh fuck, another picture. OK! Then will you come up?"

"Yes, then I will come up."

Kevin was preparing to do the King Swing when we all heard the growing sound of a large rock fall. We jerked our heads up and saw a human body hurtling away from the wall. I was instantly horrified—a human being was plummeting toward death—a tremor of terror vibrated my jaw and I reflexively grabbed for my anchor line and ducked, TP and Kev too. Then a streamer of color stretched from the falling man's back and exploded into a bright square parachute. The *Snap*! of it reached our ears seconds after we saw the parachute pop and then we heard a maniacal staccato laugh spiked to an unnatural pitch on an overwhelming rush of adrenalin. He sounded like a hyena.

"Holy sweet fuck," Wally said as we all eased to standing and let go of our anchor lines, "I thought that guy was going for the big ride."

"That was bloody freaky," I added, laughing nervously.

TP lowered his chin to his chest and shook his head back and forth while blowing the image out through his nostrils.

That night we bedded down at Camp IV, twenty pitches up.

The next day I looked up to the Great Roof and felt like a bug clinging to the stem of a golden calla lily.

El Cap exposure is on a different scale, and as I aided across the horizontal underbelly of the roof my core trembled whenever I weighted anything I doubted, like crackling sun-bleached webbing that flexed

Kevin floating up Wheat Thin on the Cookie Cliff, Yosemite. Photo: Barry Blanchard with the air of mummification. I felt like I was climbing up the outside of a weather balloon. And then I cleared the edge of the roof and made the nervous steps from étriers onto free holds. I've always been anxious stepping out of étriers. There is a shift that happens within my sense of balance and it is always momentarily disorienting, like when you step off of a high-speed walkway at an airport.

I howled when I clipped into the anchor. The pitch, like so many on the Nose, was perfect. Clean, beautiful lines that swept us into the air and made me feel like a bird. Comically a small green lizard clung to the underside of the roof and as I passed him he did reps of twenty upside-down push-ups!

The sky was pure Californian blue and it was magnificent to see Wally wrap his powerful hands around the surfboard edge of Pancake Flake and layback the stone masterfully. He looked like John Bachar to me.

TP led to Camp V and, as Wally and I readied the Pig to haul, one of El Cap's insane updrafts screamed over us and raked our haul-loops overhead like a bouquet of kite strings. And then the wind let go and all the rope smacked down onto us like churned, three-color spaghetti. It took us a half hour to untangle the ropes, a task that would have taken longer were it not for Kevin's savant-like ability to see patterns and unlock them.

"Here, Blanch, you hold these two loops open so I can pass this one under then pull it over that ganglia at the other side."

I led to the Glowering Spot.

"Harding broke his hammer here," Wally said. "When Wayne Merry came up, Batso was crouched in here glowering foully, like an evil gargoyle."

Kevin took us to Camp VI and I felt a rush of relaxation flood over me, stepping onto its horizontal tabletop. Camp VI is a one-hundred-foot-high detached pinnacle with a small, beautiful, triangular island of flatness on top of it. A foot-wide crack forms one of its sides and separates it from the wall. Climbers past had managed to fill this deep crack with garbage and human feces. Flies swarmed from it and it reeked if you got close.

"People are fucking disgusting," Wally spat. We set up a comfortable bivy and ate the last of our food and the dregs of our rationed water—two quarts per man per day stored in rinsed plastic milk and window-washer jugs with clip-in loops tied through the handles. Tomorrow we'd climb the final five pitches and descend to the comforts of the valley floor.

Crackle, crackle, crackle. Soon after it got dark—with the three of us bone tired and worked—we were fast asleep. *Crackle, crackle, crackle.*

"What the fuck is that?" I asked groggily, my mouth cobwebbed with tacky spittle.

"I think it's a pack rat," Kevin said, snapping on his headlamp and catching a glowing pair of reflector white eyes. He hissed and kicked at it and it scampered into the shit crack.

"If it chews on our ropes we'll be screwed. We are going to have to keep scaring it off," Kevin said.

And we did through long hours of exhaustion. Then toward dawn I felt the whole pinnacle start to shake and vibrate and I thought, "Wow, Kevin must be really pissed at that pack rat to shake the whole pinnacle." But then I realized that El Cap was shaking too!

"Earthquake!" I screamed, bolted upright, and grabbed our anchors. TP and Wally were right there.

"Holy fuck!" TP exclaimed. Camp 4 danced, El Cap trembled, and the whole Valley, with all the cars and buildings in it, vibrated. And then it stopped. I heard the hiss of one baseball-sized rock out to our right, and then all of the dogs in the Valley began to bark and howl.

"That was a fucking earthquake!" Wally blurted. We later learned that it was a 5.5 centered in Mammoth, about thirty-five miles away as the crow flies.

"Fucking eh, man," I said. And the three of us laughed nervously in the same adrenalin-spiked pitch as the base jumper had a couple of days before.

"I only heard one rock fall," TP said.

"If that happened in the Rockies the whole range would come tumbling down," I said. "The Rockies would get turned into a high prairie."

"I think we better get up off of this wall," Kevin concluded.

By midday we came over the rim.

Kevin said, "Come here, my little brown friend," and he clamped his strong arms around me and lifted me off the ground, then he did the same to TP.

A lanky guy with straw-blonde hair ambled over to us from a camp where a winch sat idle. He had on khaki shorts and a Whillans harness, a foot-long brake bar bounced on the outside of his thigh and he had a walkie-talkie in his hand.

"Howdy," I said. "How is the big rappel going?"

"Well, it's not. We got the rope to within a hundred feet of the top and the parachute cord we were hauling it with broke."

"The what broke?" Kevin asked in disbelief.

"The parachute cord."

"You were using parachute cord to haul the nine-mil up?" Kevin checked the facts.

"Yes sir. It was rated strong enough but we figure that the wind load must have exceeded it. We don't know what we're going to do now."

"The rope fell?" I asked to confirm my amazement.

"All 2,800 feet of it."

"Into the trees?" I asked.

"Yup, they tell me it's one hell of a mess down there."

We packed up and waddled off well out of earshot, then sat to relive the conversation and release the laughter.

"Can you picture 2,800 feet of rope silly-stringed into an acre of hundred foot high trees?" Wally exclaimed. He buckled into convulsions with his arms wrapped tight over his gut.

"How about the noise it must have made? And the ground crew running for cover?" TP added.

We laughed until it hurt too much to laugh any more. Late that day we were back in Camp 4. The next afternoon we were at the Sweet Shop in the Awhahnee Hotel, just like we'd done after Half Dome.

"Is this some kind of contest?" A well-dressed middle-aged hotel guest had leaned over from his table. His expensively dressed wife sat across from him. Plates that had held club sandwiches, burgers, and cheesecakes that had Kiwi fruit on them were stacked three to four high in front of each one of us. Empty float glasses and banana-boat cups formed an armada, telltale tongue tracks up the insides of them all.

"Well, not exactly," TP replied. "It's just that we climbed El Capitan yesterday and it took us four days and we're hungry."

"But if it was a contest, that guy there would be the winner," Wally said, pointing at me, my parfait glass up to my mouth.

"Humpff," I replied through a mouthful of ice cream.

"You guys climbed El Cap?" the guy asked, his eyebrows on the rise. His wife smiled winningly and leaned in, all ears. And for the next half hour we told them about our adventure and answered their questions.

"You boys order whatever else you want, and don't worry about your bill. We've got your bill. And thank you for telling us about your climb."

"Wow," I gasped, and I glanced to TP and Wally and saw dumb-founded grins of acceptance.

"Well, thank you so much," I said.

Like the Bar Nash in Chamonix, the Camp 4 parking lot was a mecca of climbing culture. We were cooking on TP's Coleman camp stove set on the tailgate. Parked next to us were two comely lasses from Arizona sporting a sticker on the bumper of their Toyota that read, "A Hard Man Is Good To Find."

"What I wouldn't give to be found about now," I whispered to Wally.

"I hear ya Blanch, I hear ya." But we remained lost.

John Bachar walked through the parking lot. He was the best rock-climber on the planet and heads turned and people whispered into friends' ears from behind cupped hands and pointed to the blonde god. John stopped to talk to some folks, and then he bent down to grab the top of a parking block. With smooth, slow, and controlled movement he pressed up into a perfect handstand that he topped of by doing the splits with his legs flat and horizontal forming a T.

"That is impressive," Wally said.

A little later a square-cut man who looked as solid as the granite that surrounded us walked toward us from a green International Harvester Scout. He had black shoulder-length swept-back hair and a full black beard. He looked like a wild-ass hardman, yet when he spoke his voice was soft and warm, his eyes clear and calm.

"Is that Genesis you guys have on?"

"Ya, it is. Do you like it?" Kevin replied.

"I really do. I love those guys. I'm Mugs, Mugs Stump," he said, offering us his hand, which was firm and conveyed a reservoir of power. You could feel it in his grip.

Once Mugs learned that we were from Calgary he told us about making the first ascent of the Emperor Face of Mount Robson. We were rapt. Before he walked back to his Harvester he invited us to a climbers' dance that night in El Cap meadows.

A bright moon; El Cap glowing in soft silver light; climbers from five continents communing for something tribal, primal. We drank red wine and beer and talked and joked. Dope smoke hung in the air, "Anarchy in the UK" on a blaster. Not our kind of music—where were the Stones? Jerry Jeff Walker? Huddles had formed, then Elvis

Costello's ballad "Alison" came on and some of the women, bold and beautiful, began to dance. And the words to a Jimmy Buffet song about pretty sisters dancing in the ocean drifted through my head.

The ice broke and more climbers, women and men, stepped into the dance. I caught a snapshot through the dancers of Alison Osius rising to statuesque, firelight warming her face and framing her in a shimmering orange glow as it dappled the bodies around her. She looked like Meryl Streep and I felt the string pluck of desire strum inside my chest. Of course I didn't go to talk to her, she seemed quartered within her peers. I stepped into the dance, and danced, and danced. Energy whirlpooled.

I carry another timeless image of one of the big Aussies standing next to the blaster and bellowing out the words to "Mirror in the Bathroom" as the rest of the tribe danced in the moonlight. It was a perfect night.

In the morning we drove to San Francisco and checked into a hotel for the night. TP had to fly home and get back to work the next day. We went out on the town that night and, around about our third bar, we were moderately liquored when we met a couple of Danish gals who hauled us off to another bar where, unbeknownst to us, men were dressed up as women.

"Wow, some of these women are hot!" I said to TP.

"I think that's a man," TP replied.

TP left in the morning and Wally and I returned to the Valley and our rhythm of free climbing and rest days. Other Calgarians showed up. Jeff 'Junior' Marshall was pushing his climbing too hard and sailed for sixty feet off of the Cookie Cliff and when Kevin and I tallied up the amount of air that he'd logged that year it was over 200 feet. We took to calling him Dr. Risk, and we worried about him.

Stewart Buroker appeared and it started to rain. More rain in the forecast sparked the Valley exodus and Stew, Kev, and I fled to the wine country and ended up drinking Robert Mondavi's Zinfandel and eating ten-for-a-dollar avocados by a beach fire north of the Golden Gate. We stayed with friends of Stew's in Mill Valley and at a music festival the next day we bought Dr. Risk a classic propeller beanie that we promptly graffitied with jibes like "Fly Risk Air" all in an effort to embarrass the man into a more conservative, and survivable, approach to his climbing.

Back in Yosemite, October 19, Wally and I climbed to Heart Ledges, eleven pitches up the Salathé Wall. Our second night was passed comfortably on the pickup-sized, perfect island-in-the-sky on top of El Cap Spire.

Day three and we are firmly entrenched in the rhythm of the wall. Lead, mostly on aid, but free climbing when you can and relishing the challenge of the immaculate stone. Then you labored like a dumb beast hauling the Pig, and the Pig had an evil mind of its own, ever seeking the fall line, even if that was under roofs twenty feet off of the climbing line—one learns a lot about hauling on a wall. Then you belayed, and next you jugged to clean the gear out of your buddy's lead and babysat the Pig, and helped to deal with any shit that the Pig had gotten into. Nothing happier—or more tear evoking—than a pig in shit.

Late in the day I aided up a flawless corner. Golden granite polished to a ceramic finish passed on my right. Crystal shards embedded in the polish twinkled in the oblique light. I worried about the time, everything was oververtical and overhanging and there was no place to bivy without a hammock or portaledge. Wally and I had neither, and there was one hour of daylight; we had to bivy soon.

"Wally, I think that we should rap back down to Sous Le Toit. It's just one ropelength down and at least we can sit there tonight."

"No, Blanch, give me the rack. I'll fire the Roof, quick, and then you lead the headwall pitch and we'll make it to Long Ledge. We'll be way more comfortable sleeping there tonight. We'll be able to lie down there."

The wall was already beginning to glow in the golden hour of dusk, the hour that the photographers love.

"I don't know, Wally. We've only got an hour. I think that we should go down."

"No, Blanch. We can do this, believe me, we can do this. Trust me." And the Irish/Scotsman won the argument, then took forty-five minutes to lead the roof.

The photography was perfect. Long shadows draped across the Captain from my right to my left, colors glowed. The exposure was insane and there was no way for me to keep my heart out of my throat as I swung around under my jugs, busting a gut to get the overhanging pieces out. I fumbled the last Roof piece and I immediately hurtled out over the 2,500-foot void feeling like I'd just jumped backward out of an airplane. And then I swung back under the Roof, and then out again. I screamed profanities the whole time. Wally got the stroboscopic effect of me coming into view bellowing and shaking my fist, then the quietude of my disappearance, followed by the image of my reduced rage that grew smaller with each return until he could only see my first shaking from below the roofline.

"That scared the ever-loving shit out me, Wally. And now it's getting dark, fuck!"

"We can still do this, Blanch, get out your headlamp."

"Are you fucking shitting me?"

"No, man. We have to do this, we can't stay here."

Silence.

"And, by the way, your Roof swing was hilarious to watch from here, buddy."

"Thanks, Wally."

I twisted my headlamp on and started up. Within fifteen feet I knew I was going to kill us both if I continued, so I came down.

"Looks like we're spending the night here, Wally."

Over the next hour we arranged our bivy by headlamp. I emptied everything out of the Pig and fastidiously clipped it all into the wall. Then I shimmied in. It felt like squatting down in a forty-five-gallon oil barrel until your knees dug into one side and your back into the other. In an effort to keep warm I cinched the draw cord down around my neck. The headwall is ninety-five degrees—five degrees over vertical— so my shoulder touched the wall but the rest of me hung out from it. Wally pulled his diaper-wrap butt bag, a sling designed to sit in, tight around his ass and then braced his kneepads against the wall. We were so raw, worked, and exhausted that we did manage to fall asleep, but every time we did our heads would roll backward and wake us right up.

"I'm going to anchor my head to the wall," I said.

"That's a great idea."

We girth-hitched slings around our foreheads and clipped them in snug to the wall and as ridiculous as it sounds—and it does sound so—we were able to catch snippets of sleep before the burning from the bite of the sling would wake us up and we would have to massage our foreheads, and then repeat.

With the dawn light I watched Wally remove the cinch from his forehead and the crumpled red skin there looked like the compressed and corrugated skin around my hips after a day of wearing elastic-waist boxers under tight jeans and a belt. I had to laugh.

My hands had swollen stiff and bent with a pudgy resistance. My skin was deep, deep brown and dry, and my joints were in no particular hurry to move. It took us an hour to sort ourselves out and then I started back up the headwall pitch.

I cannot imagine the amazement that Tom Frost, Chuck Pratt, and Royal Robbins must have felt when they pulled over the Roof and saw one perfect linear crack cleaved into the bulging breast of the headwall. I was in awe. I used every last piece of our rack to get up that perfect 150-foot pitch. In my mind I can still see a size-three stopper slotted in sideways—one of my last pieces to the anchor. I

Long shadows and golden light: a photographer's dream. Twenty minutes of daylight left and I'm just coming up to where Wally treated us to a bivouac on the over vertical headwall of the Salathé Wall, El Capitan. Photo: Kevin Doyle am amazed to this day by how much you learn about protection by doing a wall.

Late that night I was in the Camp 4 bathroom doing a sink bath to get some of the grime off. I felt like I'd been dipped in cooking oil, and that was four days ago. A jovial husky man came in chuckling and asked, "Hey, did you see those guys bivy on the headwall of the Salathé last night?" and he laughed and jiggled as he pointed Percy at the porcelain.

"Oh ya, yes I did." And I hollered out to Wally, "Hey, Wally, come on in here man. There's a guy who wants to talk to you. Just wait, my buddy Wally will tell you all about it."

Wally drove for home soon after and I hooked up with Randy Slattery, a fellow Canadian, to drive down to Joshua Tree and climb some more. Randy had completely rebuilt a 1957 Chevy Apache, baby blue on white. It was a beautiful truck and I felt mighty fine cruising down the east side of the Sierra in it.

We stopped in Joshua Tree to buy groceries, and to try and scrounge some free water. It was strange to be in a place where water was a commodity.

Cruising into the national monument the Joshua trees stood ranked out across the high desert like legions of zombie triffids rooted in place. Granite domes squatted on the landscape like herds of grazing dinosaurs.

Randy and I got a site in the Hidden Valley campground and were welcomed into the vagabond community of climbers hanging out there. For the next two weeks we climbed every day and I was amazed to see my finger pads ripple into red achy flesh by day three, and this after over two hundred days of climbing in the last year including the thirty days that I'd just logged in Yosemite.

"It's because of the size of the crystals," Drew told me. He and his girlfriend Susan were camped beside us. Susan didn't climb and would read and hike and mind the camp while Drew came out with Randy and me.

Every night Randy and I would light his Coleman lantern and read for hours at our picnic table: *Trinity* by Leon Uris, *Zen and the Art of Motorcycle Maintenance* by Robert Pirsig, *A Farewell to Arms* by the big man. *Trinity* became more poignant to me because Claire and Calvin where camped across from us and they were from Belfast and from different sides, yet they'd fallen in love and eloped to the United States to marry and to rock climb. I talked to them about the Troubles.

One night the six of us headed into Joshua Tree to do chores and then go to the Winner's Circle Bar and Grill to shoot some pool and drink some beer. We were having a good time racking 'em up and plugging quarters into the jukebox. Susan was sitting at the bar watching the rest of us circulate around the pool table. There was nobody else in the bar on that Sunday night in early November. A guy in black leathers who kind of looked like a husky Dwight Yoakam, after Dwight had lost some hair, walked into the bar and sidled up to Sue. Drew had his back to this and his head down making a shot. I walked over and heard the guy make a lewd "Hey, baby you wanna..." comment to Sue. She cringed and leaned away.

"Hey, buddy, that's my friend's gal you're talking too," I said.

"I wasn't talking to you," he growled.

"You need to back way the fuck off."

"Are you telling me to fuck off?"

"Yes, sir, fuck off!"

"You wanna step outside?"

"I'd love to."

I followed him to the front door and let him out and then closed the door behind him and walked back into the bar.

Buddy didn't like that and he stomped back into the bar. Verbal posturing ensued, then Randy snapped.

"You wanna fight? Let's go." Randy marched behind the guy and the guy turned at the threshold and sucker punched Randy. I saw Randy's head snap back and then he charged forward like a fighting bull. Calvin was quick out the door and when I hit the street I saw Randy over the guy and the guy rolling across the pavement like an oil barrel and Calvin scampering along at his head smacking him when he could. It was all over in about a minute when Calvin and I hauled Randy off and left the guy to rise to his feet and leave. Randy was pure rage, I could feel the heat and the vibration of it as soon as I touched him.

"Whoa, take it easy, man. Let's get back inside. Buddy won't be bothering us anymore."

But he came back through the door. "Takes two of you cowards!" His eyes and his posture were pointed at me. The bartender reached beneath the bar.

My turn to snap, "OK!" I grunted and thrust myself out of my chair and strode toward him. And then we were out on the street and he threw a punch to get me in a headlock and it seemed so schoolyard to me. I ducked and brought my knee up and tackled him onto the street. I punched into his arms for a couple of hits and tried to stay on top of him as he squirmed across the asphalt on his shoulder blades.

The silver glint of the blade cut through the night like it was the scythe of the reaper. My fight instantaneously turned to flight and I jumped off of him and pressed my hand to the pain beneath my left pec. He scrambled to his feet and ran to his bike, a Honda. The blade had changed the level of consequence, and retaliation. The fight had become lethal. I lifted my hand and saw the slash in my shirt, and then I saw red and charged and tried to kick him off of his bike.

My foot glanced his back, and he wobbled, but the rear tire already had power and he straightened and sped off.

"Holy fuck, you're cut," Randy said.

"I...I...I know," I was trembling uncontrollably and could not calm my jaw. "He had a knife, but he had it pinched between his thumb and first finger so that only about an inch of the blade was out. He didn't want to kill me, just wanted to hurt me."

"They won't let us back in the bar. Let's see how bad the cut is. Did he cut you anywhere else?" Randy asked.

"I don't know."

I had a four-inch-long incision along the lower crease of my left pec. Several inches of subcutaneous fat was exposed and it looked like yellow cottage cheese. There was a small cut on the back of my left shoulder and a scratch line across the top of my head where my thick hair had protected me. We rinsed the cuts with water and cleaned them with Betadine and then we drove back into the desert.

I couldn't afford to get stitches so I closed up my big cut with Steri-Strips and kept climbing. Long reaches opened the wound every day and it healed with a raised ridge of scar tissue. It was one of the only physical confrontations of my adult life, and the scar is a souvenir—and reminder—of one of *the* dumbest things I've ever done.

PLAYLIST

The Rolling Stones	*Jumpin' Jack Flash*
Led Zeppelin	*Stairway to Heaven*

Chapter 11

THE **CASSIN**

I WAS PLENTY BROKE when I rolled back into Calgary. My uncle Ken got me back on delivering milk with the dairy and I moved into a communal house with Sean, a fellow salesman from Pitney Bowes, with whom I'd maintained a friendship, although the friendship was largely based on partying.

Jason Maitland was a strong climber from Calgary whom Kevin had climbed with in Yosemite two years earlier. Jason was studying outdoor pursuits at the University of Calgary and wanted to climb the Cassin Ridge on Mount McKinley in alpine style. Kevin, Bill 'Captain Fist' Stark, and I all jumped at the invitation and we immediately started to have expedition meetings to plan our trip.

I was in charge of food, which pretty much guaranteed we'd have too much. I went to work at collating menu plans from previous expeditions and making spreadsheets for a five-day repeating menu on the route, heavier food for when we were on the glacier. Kevin and I spent hours in my mom's kitchen baking Logan bread and cutting it into one-man/one-day rations and slathering it with butter.

"Wally, use the butter like a Catholic priest uses guilt. Trowel it on, man," I told him. We stowed the bread in plastic bags and froze it.

We got a small expedition grant from the Alpine Club of Canada and the loan of some gear from the Canadian Himalayan Foundation. Jansport gave us a pack each and a couple of two-man tents and that was uniquely rewarding in that it was the first sponsored gear that any of us had ever been given. The pack was made out of a heavy, durable, red nylon. I saw it as a token to my ambition.

Stepping above the clouds on the Tent Arête of the
Cassin Ridge, Mount McKinley. Photo: Kevin Doyle

An eagle soared against the outline of the sun, an ice climber sat on his haunches blowing warm breath into cupped hands—the artwork was clean blue on white and it had been created by John Lauchlan. I was standing at the bulletin board in the Mountain Equipment Co-op when John's artwork caught my eye, a poster advertising an Instructor Hiring Clinic with the Yamnuska Mountain School. I took down the number and talked with Bruce Elkin on the phone, signed up, and paid my seventy-five dollars.

Friday night I pulled my MG into the Yamnuska Centre, a part of the Rocky Mountain YMCA. The south face of Mount Yamnuska sat like a castle four and a half miles to the north-northwest, across the Bow River.

Bruce Elkin greeted me with a sincere handshake and warm welcoming smile. His pale blue eyes twinkled and I immediately felt at ease with him. Six feet tall with a barrel chest, shoulder-length blonde hair, and a manicured mustache that had earned him the moniker of 'Custer' with the Stoney Indians who lived across the river.

Chris Miller was the other course leader and I was well aware that he'd made the first ascent of the north face of Mount Cromwell, at the Columbia Icefield, with Jim Elzinga, two winters before: After three days of -13° F, when Jim dropped Chris at his home, Chris had immediately gone to take a hot bath. His girlfriend, Sharon Wood, came out of the bathroom, her face drawn and pale, "Chris's toes are black." Chris had recovered with no loss of flesh and his handshake was firm and friendly, but he had an air of professionalism and was reserved compared to Bruce.

Bruce presented the history and philosophy of Yam. He outlined the structure of the courses and the need to expand the pool of instructors.

The next morning six participants went off to the Canmore Junkyards with Chris. The Junkyards has long been the first-time ice experience for anyone learning to ice climb in Southern Alberta. The name is from Canmore's early history when a road was bulldozed above the area and the not-so-good rednecks in Canmore took to dumping stuff, including some cars, off the road and over a cliff into the area.

One of my fellow potential ice climbing instructor hires placed her crampons onto the ground with the spikes facing up and proceeded to try and fit her boot between the spikes. "She ain't getting a job," shot through my head. I know that Chris was shocked, I could see it in his body language. He had to step in and redefine that the clinic was for hiring skilled instructors, not to teach people how to climb ice.

Having said that, he did teach me some of the nuances of the rearmost points of the crampon when he casually faced out and walked down a slope of twenty-five degrees. Most of my ice climbing was focused on the steepest ice and the largest alpine faces. I'd learned the front point well, but that day I learned to roll onto my normal points with my full bodyweight—stuff that I had only read about in Yvon's book but never been able to practice. I was excited when I finally did it like Chris.

Sunday afternoon we had one-on-one debriefs. Mine was with Chris and I confessed to him that I was looking for a career. In my head I knew that my climbing was going well, that I was becoming someone. In my heart I had a need to be proud, and bring pride into my family.

"Can I make a living at this?" I asked.

"Well, there is not a lot of bucks in the business, but given your skillset you should be able to support yourself."

They offered me a job; Bruce beamed and Chris smiled. I would start as an apprentice on a basic ice course the next weekend. The first people that I ran into were John Lauchlan and James Blench. They walked into the Yamnuska Centre dining room in their climbing clothes with medium-sized packs, ice tools, and crampons strapped tight to the outside.

"John!" I gushed. I'd seen him once since Chamonix and that was when he and James presented a slideshow on their amazing climb of the south face of Gangapurna.

"Barry! Jump and fuck, lad, how the hell are you?"

I'd never actually met James and John introduced us, and then they told me that they had retreated from a bivouac in the Stanley Valley after last night's storm had doubled the snowpack. I told them that I'd just got an apprenticeship to teach ice climbing the next weekend.

"Cool, you'll be working with me," James said.

We chatted some more and then John's parting words to me were, "We'll have to get out sometime soon, lad."

On February 5, 1982, John approached Polar Circus via head-lamp. He intended to make the first solo ascent. Halfway up he was "turning the pencil," a passage that requires a large boomerang ascent and traverse. John plowed steps across a 300-foot-wide avalanche slope. The *whumpf* and the black line of the fracture must have taken his breath away, and then the slab accelerated and mauled him and swept him over a 150-foot-high cliff. His femur was shattered on impact and he lost his mitts. Broken, bleeding, and alone he crawled four hundred feet downslope to the top of the last steep ice pitch. His hands wouldn't work and he pounded in his ice tools as best he could. When he weighted them on rappel they pulled out of the ice and John's heroic heart stopped beating when he hammered into the snow 130 feet below.

February the sixth was a Saturday and Wally and I, unaware of John's death, motored away from Calgary in the wee hours. We were heading for a climb called Curtain Call, a waterfall at the Columbia Icefield. We had the Stones on loud and when we came onto Polar Circus it was still pitch dark but we saw the bob of headlamps and soon saw two guys throwing gear into the back of a station wagon. Kev pulled up. Jim Elzinga and Albi Sole stood and shielded their eyes against our headlights.

Kev and I hopped out but Jim and Albi were moving slow.

"Hey, how's it going?" Kev asked.

"Pretty fucking shitty, mate," Albi spat.

"Whoa, what's up?"

Jim and Albi locked eyes and held it for a couple of beats, and then Jim said, "John Lauchlan is dead. We just came down from find-ing his body." The cold air bit harder, my lungs expelled. The dark night sank into black.

"You're kidding," Kev said.

"No," Jim answered. And then he took a full breath and let it hiss out. "He was trying to solo Polar Circus. Something went wrong. When he didn't come back we came out here and climbed up in the dark. We found his body at the base of the first grade 4 pitch. He'd tried to rappel off of his ice axes but they pulled."

The world lost words. We all blinked and breathed. It was the first time that death had walked into my life.

"What are you guys doing?" Jim asked.

"Ah, we were heading up to do Curtain Call," I said. "It's probably not a good day to be in the mountains?"

"No, it is definitely not a very fucking good day to be in the mountains," Albi barked.

I felt stupid for asking, selfish for diluting a sacred space with my vaulting ambition. I felt like an asshole.

"I think that we'll just head home," I muttered.

"Ya, we're going home," Wally affirmed. "I am so fucking sorry, you guys. Poor John."

"Me too, I'm sorry as hell," I added. Kev and I drove away.

"Here, Blanch, take the Stones," Wally said, hitting the eject button. "Give me some Led Zeppelin. Let's put on some Led Zep for John." John had been a Zep-head.

"Right, Kev, that's good. That is good." And we cranked it up loud.

One week later all of the Yamnuska Mountain School, most of the Calgary Mountain Club, and many of John's friends and family got together on the second floor of an old sandstone building in downtown Calgary to remember, and to celebrate, the life of John Douglas Lauchlan. We danced and danced.

If we all are stars in the night sky John was a comet that blazed across our twinkling and, all too soon, blazed beyond our horizons. He was twenty-seven years old and since his death not a week goes by that I do not think of him.

Kevin and I had just screwed up the approach to the north face of Mount Kitchener and skied back to his truck. We came upon Urs and TP hanging out in the van waiting to start their attempt on Slipstream. Urs kindly filled in the holes in our knowledge and the next weekend Kev and I set up our tent on the glacier below Kitchener's 3,700-foot north face.

It was early April 1982. We planned to fly to Alaska at the end of the month for our attempt on the Cassin Ridge. Big Jim Elzinga had shuffled some Sunice salopettes to us out of the largess of the 1982 Canadian Mount Everest Expedition. They were red with white piping and Wally and I felt, and looked, like pros in them.

"Oh, Blanch, you've got to see this man. This is beautiful," Kevin said.

I stepped out of the tent and was staggered by the northern lights. Flares of sapphire and jade, streamers of gold, radiant energy sweeping through a quadrant of the night sky like fire seen through the curtain of a waterfall.

"That is just beautiful, man," Kevin said, and I could see his heart opening to it. He swooned into the sublimity, allowed the light to surge into his chest. It was 12:30 a.m. and we planned to leave at 1:00, but we just couldn't pull ourselves from the lights. We brewed more tea and poured it into our one-liter measuring cups and stared at the lights agape.

A thousand feet of spindrift-scoured snow, ribbed and runneled and darkened to smoke in the moon shadow of the face, above it a sweep of armor-hard ice. I took our ten screws and we climbed fourth-class terrain with one screw between us all the time. We reached the hundred-foot-high cliff that separated the upper couloir from the lower. The corner climbed by Jeff Lowe and Mike Weiss on the first ascent was cloaked with a standing wave of snow that looked like a behemoth can of whipping cream had exploded over the top of the corner. We wouldn't be able to get through it. Jeff and Mike had climbed the route in the summer with no snow on the rock. They did, however, endure constant rockfall and named the route after Grand Central Station in NYC because the regularity, and volume, of the rockfalls reminded them of the trains coming and going.

Fifty feet right of the corner, a finger of the couloir reached into the rockband. A thin strip of cinereous ice brindled with bone white and translucent diaphanous green traced a slender thread through overhangs of rock trimmed with lines of white snow. During the storms, avalanches thunder from the upper couloir and snow clings to any lee and lengthens to drape the cliff in clean lines of white.

"I think that I should try to climb there," Wally said, pointing to the ice strip. He grabbed the rack and launched.

The depth of the ice dictated his speed. When there was enough for the first tooth of his pick to bite his movement was constant. When the ice thinned he climbed slowly, or stopped to search for gear—Chouinard screws turned in one and a half inches and tied off, marginal knifeblades, and then a good one. One hundred feet took an hour and a half.

And then the ice ended below the breakover, the last overhang. He balanced front points on rock and for long calf-searing minutes he swept the snow from the small sheaved edges of limestone. Having revealed the best two holds, he bit his Dachstein mitts and one at a time stuffed them inside his jacket. Then he licked his bare fingers and spot-froze them onto the algid rock.

"I'd lose a little hide when I pulled my hands off, Blanch, but it gave me more purchase, if you know what I mean."

"I do not, Wally, but that was an amazing piece of climbing, buddy. I think it's the best lead I've ever seen you do. I think that we are going to get up this thing!"

I'd followed the pitch on Jumars, at trick that we'd learned in Yosemite. It did accelerate our climbing, but ethically there was a burr, Walter Bonatti had never used Jumars.

I rode the jugs again, following the pitch to the "Cheeseburger." Halfway to Kevin, I shoved mightily on my upper Jumar and sank my weight into my harness. The Jumar raced down the rope and *cracked* into the lower one. I'd fallen two and a half feet and the fear knocked the breath out of me.

Snow clinging to the rope had compressed to ice on the face of the Jumar's cam. The ice grew thick enough to conceal the cam's teeth. I stood and took the jug off of the rope. That left me singly attached to the lower one. I could see that the lower teeth on the cam weren't masked with as much ice. Some of the teeth were still exposed and could bite into the sheath of a rope. I pushed the handle of the jug I stood on toward the rope, and past it, so that the lower teeth could get a grab. If the lower jug slipped I'd be going thirty feet to my last tie off knot, and I would probably bring the sheath of the rope with me. Maybe Bonatti was right, I thought, it might be safer to have both of us climb.

The Cheeseburger was a perfect disk of snow fifteen feet in diameter and seven feet thick. It weighed a number of tons and somehow sat in balance atop a rock pinnacle the size of a man somewhere underneath all that snow.

My lead got serious and hard up a steep short wall of stacked crumbling rock the size of alphabet blocks that I exposed by knocking away a four-inch-thick eggshell of snow. It all got better when I found three inches of a Warthog sticking out of the rock. I hammered on it and although it was ice protection it rang true.

"Watch me here, Blanch," Wally barked between huge draws of air. It was late in the day and we were one pitch from the top. Cornices the size of Victorian houses had blocked any escape from where we exited the rock so we'd traversed several ropelengths to the left to get out from under them. But Wally got bored with the traversing.

He was so close to the top, but the snow was vertical and ribbed with bulges. He had to stab the spike and shaft of his tools ten to twelve times to get them into the snow, and they had to be set at very positive angles. When he judged each placement good he'd wrap his hand around the shaft at the snow's surface. Each foothold had to be sculpted with multiple kicks and his forearms burned and the tools made small perceptible shifts within the snow. A fall would have been terrible. Then his upper body disappeared and he stepped high and from my view.

"Off belay!"

We descended the east ridge and the northern lights saw us back to our tent at 2:00 a.m. We'd been on the go for twenty-four hours.

Steven, my youngest brother, was fifteen and having difficulties in school. He'd found partying and was growing fond of alcohol and dope, and he needed money to get that.

My uncle, Ken, pulled me aside at the dairy one afternoon, "Two young guys approached some of the milkmen in a coffee shop today and offered to sell them milk tokens. It sounds like it was Steven and one of his friends."

Running my milk route involved selling, and accounting for, up to $500 in plastic milk tokens. I brought my token bag into the house with me when I finished work, as I always did, and when I checked it over a hundred dollars worth was missing. I confronted Steven and fell into a rage. He confessed.

"You never steal from me! Not from me!" and I hit him hard across the face with an open hand and I could see the fear in his eyes and then the regret and the tears.

"I'm sorry, Bear, I am sorry," he blurted in a panic, his terrorized brown eyes darting left and right like an animal cornered desperate to escape.

I cried too, "I should not have to do this, Steven!" I loved my brother and this kind of discipline should have come from the hand of his father, but he didn't have a father there to do that and neither had I. We were a young man and a boy trying to figure it out as best we could. And I will go to my grave wishing that I had done better that day.

Western Airlines had started a direct flight from Calgary to Anchorage and been good enough to sell us four tickets for the price of three. Somewhere Wally had found a duffel bag big enough for three of us to stand in, the exemption being Fist who was just too damn big. We stuffed the duffel with skis and bulky stuff and it took two of us to lift it. Western checked it in and it, along with us and all our packs and duffels, arrived in Alaska.

Denali Overland Transportation drove us to the frontier town of Talkeetna in a twelve-passenger yellow cab. We pitched our tents and waited to fly. Our pilot, Jim Okonek, and his wife Julie, were in their second year of operating K2 Aviation and we, being their sole clients at the time, enjoyed a fine spaghetti dinner at their house one night.

We sorted our gear and it was pointed out to me that I didn't have ski skins, and that I would need them. I'd always waxed my skis to that point, and I felt like a greenhorn dork. Thankfully we found a pair in Talkeetna and I used the last of my cash to buy them. And then I was told that my share of the flights in and out would be $250. I was flat broke and Jason had to phone his wife and have her put money on his credit card to cover the extra. They were both students and I owed him. I felt like a double dork.

Day four, Jim stuffed us, two at a time, and all of our gear into his Cessna 185 Skywagon and we took off. Brown tundra, spider-webbed with shallow gray creeks and sparsely picketed by stunted evergreens, gave way to braided gravel flats and four silt-colored rivers born from under the three-mile-wide terminus of the boulder-strewn Kahiltna Glacier. Trees and grass ended and we soared past lower peaks already alive with wet, snotty, spring avalanches running to ground on their southerly exposures. Jim climbed and Wally and I could feel the power of the prop vibrate the plane.

Wedding-cake layers of sérac passed close to the wingtip, serpentine ridges of snow that looked like some of the Samivel watercolors I'd looked long on in Chamonix. Jim began cranking on a lever that looked like a parking brake and we felt the skis *clunk* into place. A right turn lined us up onto the north buttress of Mount Hunter and I saw alpine perfection and then we landed on the east fork of the Kahiltna in the heart of the Alaska Range. My heart felt light, I was in awe.

For the next of week we toddled our way high onto the west but-tress in order to acclimatize and bury a cache at 17,000 feet for our descent from the Cassin.

The four of us sat outside cooking at the Motorcycle Hill camp and I'd just divided our pre-dinner ration of quick-cooking mine-strone soup.

"The noodles are good, eh? How do you guys like the noodles?" I asked.

"Noodles? I didn't get any noodles," Fist wined in a plaintiff plea while hunkering down over his one-liter measuring cup like he was cowling and protecting an infant. And it stuck: He became Bill 'I Didn't Get Any Noodles' Stark.

We all went to ride the exercise bike in the high altitude medical research tent at 14,000 feet. I had already left the tent when Dr. Rob Roach told Bill that I had the highest blood oxygen saturations that they'd seen. All the uphill running and training was paying off. Reinhold would have been proud.

After three nights in the 14,000-foot camp, we pushed up to 17,000 and buried our cache. Jason lost his peripheral vision during the descent and after talking with the docs at medical tent at 14,000 feet he concluded that he wasn't acclimatizing well enough to climb the Cassin. Captain Fist, always mercurial in his motivations to climb, succumbed to the siren call of a Belgian gal that he'd met in Talkeetna. He was also sweating the logistics of the three of us crammed into one tent. He decided to fly out with Jason, but not before he ate all the tins of corned beef that we'd left cached at the northeast fork of the Kahiltna Glacier. Kevin and I were on fire to climb and we would be using the northeast fork approach to the Cassin.

My new red pack was rammed full and close to splitting like a hot dog. I heaved it onto my right knee and fought to steady it and then threaded my right arm into it and grunted to standing. There was a tearing sound and the weight was gone and I windmilled to keep from falling face first onto the glacier. The bar tacking holding the bottom to the right shoulder strap had burst. I guess ninety pounds was too much.

"Wally!" At the far end of the rope he dropped his pack with an audible *whump*. "We're too heavy, Kev," I concluded.

"What do you want to do?" he replied.

"I don't know. How about making two carries?"

Our shouts reverberated from the walls of granite and bands of aquamarine séracs that squeeze the northeast fork. When the séracs calve big they sweep the corridor from rockwall to rockwall and climbers had been lost there buried under feet of shattered blue ice.

I knotted my broken pack strap while Kev corralled our six days of food and fuel in the snow. Under much lighter loads, we cramponed up an established track through a jumble of castle-sized blocks that the glacier had churned into existence and delineated with the deep, sagging troughs of bottomless crevasses. We kept the rope tight and ice climbed down into sways and up over steep short walls. Overhead, blue séracs reached into a sky that was one shade bluer. The ice was beautiful and terrifying in the same moment and we felt the urge to move. And then we could see the edge of the Cassin cutting into the sky. We made two carries up the fork that day.

"Fuck, there's something wrong with the stove," Kevin hissed.

A plume of blue flame shot from a fractured brazing one inch below the burner. Snow pressed into the pot minutes ago had become a damp gray, it should have been boiling. We wouldn't be able to continue without a stove. We were camped inside the bergschrund at the start of the Japanese Couloir and the air within our small dome tent became heavy and solemn.

"All right, we might be able to fix it," Wally said, and he took charge. I rolled tinfoil from a chocolate bar into tight, match-sized pieces and Wally tamped them into the fracture with the micro driver from his Swiss Army knife. An hour later the stove roared to life burning hotter than when it was new, but a seed of worry has been planted in our minds, would it keep on working?

Riccardo Cassin was one of the progenitors of the game that Kevin and I had come to play. In 1961 he led a team of five younger Italians and over the course of a month they climbed the ridge that now bears his name. It is a perfect line parting the 10,000-foot south face of Mount McKinley like a corner on the Great Pyramid of Khufu. In 1967 a Japanese team made the second ascent and avoided Cassin's initial rock ridge by climbing a thousand-foot-long couloir of snow and ice west of the ridgeline.

The next morning I delicately manipulated my weight up a snow-bridge draped over the bergschrund. Kev shouted encouragement. Up until then he had always been the one who "tiptoed up the cotton candy stretched over the gaping maw." It was my first big-time 'schrund crossing and when I kicked onto the ice face above I turned and beamed at him.

We had a 330-foot nine-millimeter rope and before we left Calgary Urs Kallen had said to me "You'll end up cutting that in half." We also had a 165-foot seven-millimeter haul line. The most expeditious technique that we could come up with saw one of us leading until the seven mil came tight, sinking a screw, hauling up the food bags and leaving them anchored, along with the pack off of our back, then continuing to the end of the nine mil. We'd anchor and rap the seven mil to retrieve our pack, jumar up the seven mil, and haul up the food bags. The second would jug the whole length of the nine mil. It was one of the dumbest systems ever conceived in mountaineering and should never be repeated.

Wind came, clouds grew overweight with charcoal-colored bellies, the ceiling dropped, and it began to snow. The storm caught us five hours up the couloir. I was leading when the first avalanche hit.

The oncoming roar set my heart rate bounding and I clenched into my tools and shouted to Kevin. I caught a terrifying glimpse of the wavefront charging down the ashen ice like a tidal surge and I ducked my head and took the hit. A heavy *whump* onto my shoulders and I trembled on my front points and then the pressure and the drumming of the snow and the fear of there being chunks dried my breath to feeble draws of sand-tasting wind. There were no chunks, it was just spindrift from the storm. It hissed away and I shook the mantle of its passing from my bowed head and shoulders. Only then did I accept that I hadn't been swept away.

It took us ten hours to climb the couloir. The storm and the spindrift continued, and the avalanches went from being a threat to being a nuisance.

"Oh fuck, here comes another fucking spindrift!" Wally yelled, and then he disappeared in an onslaught of raging white.

A large golden block of granite sat at the top of the Japanese Couloir and it was littered with an archeological sedimentation of fixed rope. They'd been piling up, layer on layer, for twenty years: different colors, different brands, different thicknesses and constructions, all from a number of nationalities. It was the first time that Kev or I had seen anything like it.

"That's ugly man, just really ugly," Kevin said in disgust.

We traversed to the left for a half ropelength and gained the small, perfect tent ledge that Cassin's team had created by stacking rocks. We pitched our tent. The storm battered us all night and was still there in the morning.

"I think that we need to keep climbing if we can," Wally said.

"I agree, Kev."

I led over granite that looked like the decaying façade on a Celtic ruin. All of the rot was welded in place by a patina of ice. I rappelled from the anchor and jumared with my pack, the ground being too shallow and too coarse to haul.

Two pitches higher we gained the Tent Arête and opted for two carries across that tightrope in the sky. The storm got mean. Ice shards raked across our faces and the gusts shoved at us, tried to topple us off of the slender ridge. We retaliated by swearing at it, threatening it like it was a human. Challenging it to fight. We were young, and plenty capable of being dumb.

During our second trip across the arête the storm began to break up and we caught brief flashes of the sun, momentary rushes of its heat. Powdery storm snow on steel gray ice commanded attention, but to balance on the edge of a storm as it quits the sky two miles up was phenomenal.

We camped at 14,000 feet on the large, flat ledge of a hanging glacier. Stress evaporated in the warmth of the sun. Kevin and I bundled up and stayed outside for a long time gorging ourselves on food and drink and the mountain set about us like a glowing cathedral.

In the morning Kevin exploded up the hanging glacier, setting a pace with his full pack that I was hard-pressed to keep. All the pores in my skin dilated and I was in a sauna sealed by my outer shells when I caught him. The rockband at 15,000 feet rose from blue ice in front of us, its tawny clean stone shrouded in the mist of a coming storm.

The climbing was amazing. Dihedrals cleaved into bronze-colored rock, sweeps of stone as angular as quarry cuts rising for a hundred feet. The occasional fixed piton provided protection and I placed one large cam in addition, the only rock runner we placed on the route.

Mist thickened to storm and again the wind raked ice shards over us savagely. Kevin and I fought hard and long. Our endurance faltered and my joints felt rusted and my mouth felt lined with cardboard. Pushing the Jumar up the rope into the pounding wind felt like a prizefighter throwing the last feeble punches before he's knocked out. In dusk and desperation we lashed our tent to ice screws on a sloping ledge on the edge of the Cassin. Inside we piled packs, food, and rope in an effort to gain some horizontal. We were too exhausted to cook. We'd climbed for thirty-eight of the last forty-four hours. I pried my feet from frozen supergaiters and boots with my diaphragm cramped and my breathing compressed. Then I wrestled into the small sleeping bag that Kev had lent me and zipped it into my bigger bag. It had been the only system that I could afford that was warm enough.

The first violent gust of wind flattened the tent and pulled the nylon over my face like a stretched plastic seal. The tent fly ripped from all of its anchor points save one, and spun into a streamer that flapped like a mad tentacle on the outside of the tent. Light flooded in with the dark brown and purple fly gone. I swore and clawed my hands free and swam my way to sitting against the pressure of the nylon. Compressed air shrieked over stone and pounded on the walls of our tent like we were inside a drum. The scream and the pressure pulled back and then roared in for another hit that drove my face into my knees. Frozen condensation from our exhaled breath vibrated in the small open space in front of me as the wind mauled us and I feared it reaching under the tent and throwing us off of the mountain.

"Blanch! We have to hold the shape of the tent! It'll blow apart if we don't hold the shape!" Kevin screamed from somewhere only eighteen inches away.

For the next three hours we battled the wind. I wrapped the draw cord to the snow portal around my hand like a leather rein. Kevin did the same with the cord to the door. We leaned our backs into the wind and yarded on the cords and tried to keep the dome of the tent established. The wind pummeled us. It was like large men were running at the tent and hurling their weight and speed into our backs. I felt the hits in my ribs, in the surges of breath beaten from my lungs.

Our hands went numb from the choke of the cords and we coordinated when to rest and regain our grips so that one of us was always holding the shape of the tent. Our breath stood as mist in front of our faces and the tension in the air was visible in it as the mist jerked and quivered to the slapping of the tent walls. Eventually the violence and frequency of the hits diminished and we dressed and packed paranoid of another hit.

"Ah fuck, here comes another one," Wally spat, dropping his hands from his coat zipper and thrusting his back into the windward side of the tent.

Eventually we stepped out. The sky had blown clear. We saw the wind howling off of the south shoulder of the mountain, clean blue ice hazed in a mare's tail of ice crystals being raked off and sublimated away. We stood exactly even with the shoulder, 15,500 feet, exposed, unprotected...so very lucky to not have been blown away.

All three tent poles were deformed and one had fractured like a bone. Six inches of seam had split and the fly had snapped all of its anchoring toggles save one. We made makeshift repairs and climbed away.

Three pitches of mixed ground led us into the large glacial couloirs that form the top half of the route. We dragged the ropes behind us, slowly cramponing up side by side.

At 17,000 feet we found a good platform and pitched our crippled tent and set about catching up on fluids and food. The first thing that we ate, as always, was the Logan bread. That evening is one of the precious gems that I've sifted from over thirty years of mountaineering. Wally and I were truly happy. We were exactly where we'd dreamed of being, strived to be.

The tops of cumulous clouds tumbled by at thirty miles per hour and we caught flashes of sunlight afar. The lowlands of the range had fallen into shadow, and the granite shoulders of Denali glowed. The movement of the clouds gave me the illusion of motion, like I was sailing through the sky.

"Pretty damn cool, eh, Blanch?"

"You betcha, Walter. Beautiful man, too beautiful." We slept long, hard, and well.

"Urs said that we'd do this," I hacked my knife through the middle mark of the nine mil rope, coiled up half of it and left it sitting on a ledge below a granite bulge. "I guess we can't curse the rope fixers as much anymore," I said.

"No, Blanch, no we can't."

Kev and I tacked up firm, wind-hammered snow. Twenty steps left, twenty steps right, breathe, and breathe, and breathe. At 18,500 feet I hit a wall. Flashes of pain rang in my skull every time I forced twenty steps.

"Wally, I need to stop. I'm getting a stab of pain across my temples every time I push." I heaved in more high and dry air. "My balance isn't good. Feels like I could fall. I think that we should camp here."

"Blanch, I've been pushing past that for the last two days." His face was drawn from the effort of breathing. Frost haloed the edges of his hood. "Let's just keep pushing. We can make it to the top."

"No, Kev, it's just not safe enough. I'm too out of control here, really man."

"OK, OK, Blanch, we'll stop."

We camped in the lee of a boulder. I was woken up in the night by a pounding in my head, the kind of headache that I only ever got when I drank too much. I downed a couple of Tylenol and drank a liter of water and sat breathing deeply and massaging my temples. The headache went away, but it was back when I woke up in the morning.

Our frozen breath had formed inch-long frost feathers on the inside of the tent. We cautiously moved everything to one side and carefully scraped the frost onto our shovel blade and threw it out the door, then we did the same on the other side.

My headache went away with drinking and sitting. We left the rest of the nine-mil rope and a frozen can of kippers there and climbed into our sixth day on the route. Visibility pulsated between a whiteout and a misty hundred yards. Stretches of plaster-hard snow were interrupted by rock moves on boulders imbedded in ice. Breathing was a chore and we had on all of our clothes including big down jackets, neoprene overboots, and two balaclavas each. Our packs were finally light enough to climb comfortably.

Visibility contracted to twenty feet when we crested the summit ridge. Kevin led with our only set of goggles (his) and our sole pair of ski poles (also his). He used the ski poles as white canes, and he halted abruptly and often when he could no longer sense the ridge. I followed close on his heels practically blind in my glacier glasses. I had to put my faith in him and his incredible drive and unwavering desire.

Then he overstepped the edge and was hauled away like a claw had surfaced from the underworld and yanked him down. He tumbled into the whiteout limbs splaying, torso churning, carving a swath into the white.

"Kevin!" He stopped abruptly thirty feet down spread eagled in the snow.

I lowered him an ax and an end of rope and I stepped back onto the south face to belay him up.

There was no higher ground: a cluster of wands, pickets, and rope—the summit, and we couldn't see ten feet. It was just like the inside of a Ping-Pong ball. There was no cattle track to lead us down the west buttress because no one had summited in over two weeks.

We staggered off blind. Two hours later we were down climbing into the night when Kevin fell again and I caught him on the rope. We hadn't the slightest clue where we were and the cold bit through all of our layers. For three hundred feet we got excited thinking that we could see a tent below us in the dusk. It was an old spool of rope half-encased in ice.

Finally we stopped and started hacking into the thirty-degree concrete-hard ice. We swung until our hands opened and the ax fell from our grip and our heads sagged onto the slope. And then we swung some more. After three hours we had a ledge that was three feet wide and six feet long. We jury-rigged the tent with two of its three poles and crawled in.

The wind started. It blew minute ice shards through the nylon and a fine dusting of snow steadily accumulated on top of our sleeping bags. We brushed it off, but it kept coming.

"If our bags get wet we are really going to be screwed," Kevin said.

"I'll go out and get the fly and we can lay it over us in here like a blanket," I said.

I backed out into the coldest temperatures that I have ever encountered: colder than Everest, colder than K2, colder than Antarctica. I had bare hands, a mistake. In fifteen seconds my hands were numb and I couldn't contract them. I clamped the stuffsack holding the fly between the heels of my wooden hands and ripped it from the ice screw. On my elbows I burrowed back into the tent. I'd been out of the tent for forty-five seconds. The tips of my fingers blistered white with frost nip, they would peel for the next month.

We spread the fly over us and spooned as close as we could.

The morning was clear, but brutally cold. We figured that we were at 19,500 feet on the Farthing Horn. The West Buttress route, our descent, lay a half mile to the west at the Archdeacon's Tower.

The highest point in North America, the summit of Denali, and we couldn't see ten feet. I had every piece of clothing on and I was still shivering.
Photo: Kevin Doyle

It took three hours to pack up. Our hands would work for all of fifteen seconds before they had to be rammed back into expedition mitts and swung aggressively through full circles to force the blood back. I hit the head of my Chouinard Zero ice ax with my hammer and the last two inches of the pick fractured and fell into the snow.

I swung my feet through huge pendulous arcs that bought my foot level to my waist in front of me, and then *swoosh* behind. Hundreds of repetitions, but my toes remained cold steel inside my boots. For the next three hours I worried that I would lose them. They burned to life as we walked into the 17,000-foot camp on the west buttress. I had to sit on my pack and hyperventilate to deal with the pain of their return. Tears ran from the corners of my clenched eyes.

Wally and I dug up the food cache and ate all of the chocolate and Logan bread and then we scampered down to the 14,000-foot camp and the air felt so thick and full.

"Yeah, Blanch, I can do another freeze dried," Wally said. It would be his fourth: The equivalent of eight adult meals, if you believe the package. I quit at three—six adult meals—but Wally pushed on to four, and that slapped him into a food coma.

Twenty-four hours later Kev and I walked into Peter Habeler's large camp at the base of Motorcycle Hill. He was guiding a big group of European clients and Kev and I got invited in for tea. Peter had set the speed record on the north face of the Eiger with Reinhold Messner and then they'd gone on to climb Hidden Peak in alpine style and do the first ascent of Mount Everest without supplemental oxygen. It was like getting ushered into Valhalla to chew the fat with Thor.

"Where are you coming from?" Peter asked with an Austrian accent right out of *The Sound of Music*.

"We were on the summit two days ago," I said.

"Really?" His eyes popped, "Which route did you do?"

"We climbed the Cassin Ridge," Wally said. "We were six days on it."

"You've climbed the Cassin in this weather! You've done a great thing!" Peter gushed.

Eventually Kev and I stepped out, and stepped into the WWII-vintage white wooden skis that we'd borrowed from the Yamnuska Mountain School. The skis were unturnable and I straight-lined off down the Kahiltna Glacier, waving goodbye to Peter where he stood outside his kitchen tent. I was going warp seven when I finally escaped his view and promptly bit it.

We got onto our good skis, Lovett mountain tourings, cached where the northeast fork branched off. They were only slightly more turnable. Our sleds became top heavy with the addition of our cache and mine toppled sideways soon after starting. Wally was a thousand feet ahead.

"That's it, Wally! Just fucking leave me here. Don't worry about all of this heavy shit, I got this heavy shit. Asshole!"

The acoustics were perfect and Wally answered me in a calm voice, "What seems to be the problem, Blanch?"

"Oh, I didn't know you could hear me. Sorry, but my fucking sled is tipping over. I'm carrying too much."

"C'mon up here, Blanch, and we'll sort it out."

Later that day Kev and I skied to the airstrip that we'd left three weeks before. Annie, who ran the airstrip, ran out of her tent and laid a couple of cold beers on us. It was a tradition for summiteers and we were the first in over two weeks. Over a hundred people were waiting to fly out. It was finally a bluebird day and the first plane in brought Walter Cronkite and his wife for a brief landing.

The legendary anchorman stood on the glacier in his Hush Puppies and Kev and I got introduced. Walter and his wife wanted to know about our climb and we gushed away to the master orator. They got back in the plane and flew away from a hundred anxious faces, some of whom had been waiting for over ten days to get out.

The next plane in was Jim's red K2 Aviation Cessna. He'd come to pick up his clients, Wally and me, and we could feel daggers of envy and hate as we stepped into the plane without having set up our tent. "Fly the friendly skies next time," shot through my head.

Wally used his Visa card to get us a room in the Fairview Inn, an early 1900s two-story hotel that had been built when Talkeetna was a mining and railroading town. We showered and went down to the bar where an Alaskan with a ZZ Top beard and a welder's cap took a long look at Wally's sun-bronzed face with its dramatic stenciling of fish-belly-white eyes from where his glacier glasses had blocked out the sun. The guy smiled and belted out, "You look like a raccoon!"

Three days later Wally and I were back in Calgary.

Chapter 12

CANMORE

HOME, AND I WAS BROKE AGAIN. I sold my MG and borrowed my mother's small white Nissan truck and moved out to the Rocky Mountain YMCA to start my summer's work with the Yamnuska Mountain School. The move did little to increase my monetary wealth, I lived in a closet that was used to house cleaning products, but my life was richer because my door opened onto the Front Range of the Rockies. I was living in the mountains and earning my living by teaching rock-climbing and mountaineering.

It was a fine summer and in the fall the mountain school was divorced from the YMCA. James Blench, Dwayne Congdon, Bruce Elkin, Chris Miller, Janet Powers, Marni Virtue, Sharon Wood, and I all moved to Canmore. Bruce was the director and we set up our office in one of the bedrooms in the house that Bruce, Carla Smith— a physiotherapist working at the hospital who had taken a rock-climbing course earlier in the summer—and I rented. It was one of the only houses in town to have an indoor pool.

Not really snow, not really ice: Sn'ice is insecure to climb and very challenging to protect. I'm ascending the Elzinga-Miller route on the north face of Mount Cromwell. Photo: Kevin Doyle

In 1883, when the Canadian Pacific Railway (CPR) was being pushed across Canada, a division point was set in the Bow Valley between mountains that would come to be known as Chinaman's Peak (renamed Ha Ling Peak in 1997) and Mount Lady MacDonald. A roundhouse and water tower were built. In 1884 CPR director Donald Smith gave it the name Canmore. It is a Celtic word that means "big head," a nickname of Malcolm III, King of Scots, who lived in the late eleventh century.

Queen Victoria granted a coal mining charter in 1886 and the Canadian Anthracite Coal Company opened their first mine in 1887. Canmore incorporated as a town in 1965, population 2,000. Canmore Mines Ltd (a 1938 amalgamation of the Canadian Anthracite Coal Company and the Canmore Coal Company) ceased coal production on July 13, 1979. In ninety-two years, 15,573,900 metric tons of coal had been extracted.

Canmore was still getting over being a coal-mining town when I moved here. It was an economically depressed little town of 3,500 souls. Bruce, Carla, and I lived in Teepee Town, the traditional camping grounds of the Stoney Indians, which lay on the far side of the rail line. There was dancing to live music at the Canmore Hotel, known to all in town as the "Hilton." Some of the old miners enjoyed afternoon beers there along the south wall, "miner's row," the deep, rasping coughs of black lung interspersed with sips of lager.

I made just enough money to pay for my rent and food, drink some beer, and try to meet girls. I had lots of time to train and climb.

Most of my success came in my climbing. Wally and I made the second ascent of the Elzinga-Miller route on the north face of Mount Cromwell (IV, 5.7, WI 3, 3,300 feet, the route that Chris Miller had blackened his toes on) over the three days of Canadian Thanksgiving. A crisp and supportive crust coated the glacier like the glaze on a pastry. Wally and I jogged toward the wall, the beams of our head-lamps bouncing. The heat of my blood felt empowering, an eagerness surged in my limbs. My body wanted it. Dawn light showed us a sys-tem of ledges ramping in from the right that avoided 500 feet of difficult rock-climbing taken on the first ascent. We dashed across the ledges unroped, feeling, and looking, like Reinhold Messner and Peter Habeler in our Ferrari-red salopettes.

Kevin Doyle embarking on one of the most incredible pieces of climbing I have ever witnessed. When the wisp of ice ran out, he pulled his mitts off and licked his fingers and allowed them to spot freeze to the rock to gain more purchase! The Grand Central Couloir, Mount Kitchener, Canadian Rockies. Photo: Barry Blanchard

left Traversing the Tent Arête on the Cassin Ridge of Mount McKinley, Alaska, 1982. Photo: Kevin Doyle

top Toiling under far too big a load in the Japanese Couloir of the Cassin Ridge. Mount McKinley, Alaska. Photo: Kevin Doyle

left Tim Friesen planting ice picks and crampons into the exit bulge of the Andromeda Strain—ice that had never been touched by man. Canadian Rockies. Photo: David Cheesmond

right I'm following the exit ice bulge during the first ascent of the Andromeda Strain. Mount Andromeda in the Canadian Rockies, 1983. Photo: David Cheesmond

next spread left Following Gregg Cronn's lead through the yellow band on the north face of Mount Alberta. A mitted hand holds snow-covered rock, the pick of my ice hammer torqued in a crack, crampon points set precisely on snowy edges: some of the joys of mixed climbing in the Canadian Rockies. Photo: Gregg Cronn

next spread right I'm aid climbing in my Euro-style étriers on the second headwall pitch on the north face of Mount Alberta. Canadian Rockies, 1983. Photo: Gregg Cronn

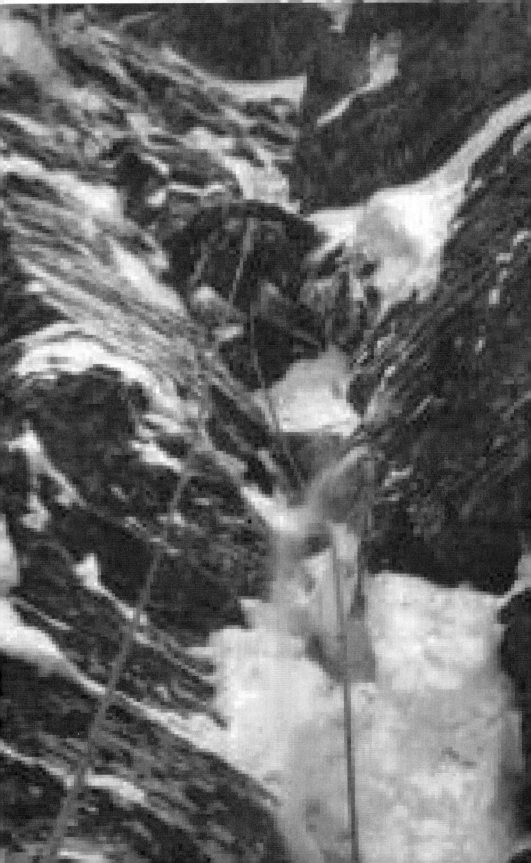

previous spread left The thin ice on the east face of Mount Fay. I'd somehow convinced myself that the tied-off icicle, the size of my thigh, I had clipped to twenty feet below was protection. Canadian Rockies, 1984. Photo: Barry Blanchard Collection

previous spread right James Blench leading into the storm on day two of the second attempt on the northeast face of Mount Chephren, a route that three more attempts and three years later would become the Wild Thing (1987). Canadian Rockies. Photo: Kevin Doyle

left David Cheesmond transferring a piece as we climb into the storm on the north ridge of Rakaposhi. Pakistan, 1984. Photo: Barry Blanchard

right My teammates sitting like beasts at 23,000 feet on Rakaposhi. From left to right: David Cheesmond, Steve Langley, Tim Friesen, Gregg Cronn, and Kevin Doyle. The next morning Kevin, Gregg, and I headed for the top (wasn't to be) while Dave, Steve, and Tim descended. Pakistan. Photo: Barry Blanchard

left The Fox, David Cheesmond, on Rakaposhi. Pakistan.
Photo: Kevin Doyle

right David Cheesmond looking toward me as I sit in the
mouth of the cave that we found halfway up the North
Pillar of North Twin. A hailstorm lashed the face that
night and we were as snug, and dry, as bugs in a rug.
Canadian Rockies, 1985. Photo: Barry Blanchard

left After five days on the face, I walk onto the summit
of Twins Tower and the top of the North Pillar of North Twin.
Canadian Rockies. Photo: David Cheesmond

right above The Black Hole seen from the summit of Mount
Alberta. Twins Tower is the massive dark spear point just
left of center. The white peak to its left is North Twin, the
one to the right South Twin, and to the right and lower
is West Twin. Mount Columbia is the large pyramid in the
background. Canadian Rockies. Photo: Barry Blanchard

right below Le Grande Fromage aiding out of our cave
on our fourth day on the North Pillar of North Twin.
Canadian Rockies. Photo: Barry Blanchard

left Dave Cheesmond jamming splitter limestone on our first day on North Twin; yes, it is seeping wet. Canadian Rockies. Photo: Barry Blanchard

right En route to the west ridge of Mount Everest in 1986, Kevin Doyle lets the wee ones of Shigatse look through the expensive camera that Leica had lent us. Tibet. Photo: Barry Blanchard

top Robert Redford's little brother, Ward, goes alpine.
Ward Robinson on the first day of our first ascent of the
north face of Howse Peak in the Canadian Rockies, 1988.
Photo: Barry Blanchard

bottom Early morning day three on the north face of
Howse Peak, Ward Robinson heads back to his high
anchor. He'd taken a twenty-five-foot fall leading the
pitch the night before. Canadian Rockies. Photo: Barry
Blanchard

A ten-foot-wide strip of ice lay against the cliff like a curtain of chainmail that had been dragged from ocean froth and draped down the castle wall. It reverberated in detachment at my first vertical swing and I tensed my core into a plank and kept my heels low while reaching high to find the rounds of ice that had anchorage to the rock. Nowhere was the ice thick enough to take a screw and the consequence of a fall grew more dire with each placement that I committed to.

"Take it easy up there, Blanch," Kevin shouted, concern deepening the timber of his voice. "Can you get anything in up there?"

"I'm trying, Wally, I'm trying."

A flake of rock the size of a rifle stock protruded from the edge where the ice was gray and paper-thin. I stuffed a fist-sized cam deep into the cleft between it and the wall. The cam bit into rock and I took confidence in it and that eased my fear from that of being pulled off of the wall to that of a fall. I breathed and pulled. Higher I crossed the top edge feeling good, knowing that I climbed well and with grace.

An hour later Kevin and I were fourth-classing up a ramp of alpine ice guttered to the edge of the hanging glacier that forms the top half of the route. Petals of blue ice sheared in series against the interface of the flowing glacier and the static ice face. The ice petals looked like the fronds of a fern. Some of the petals fractured out and exploded down the face as Wally and I charged.

We came so close to getting up the route and back to our tent in a day. Darkness trapped us crossing the innumerable rock gullies that ripple the western flank of Mount Engelhard like the folds of a Victorian skirt. We sat back-to-back on our packs and shivered through the long hours until dawn. The night fear came, and we talked to deal with it. Fear forced Kev and I into deeper intimacy. Had we been better with love and trust we might have been able to get there without the fear and threat.

"I hardly remember my mother," Kevin confessed in the hour of the wolf, 3:00 a.m., both of us quaking like jackhammers from the cold. "She died giving birth to my younger sister. I miss her so much." And he choked a bit. "My dad married his secretary, and she is my mother, and I love her, but I miss my real mother so much."

"Mama Paulette is a tigress," I chattered. "She is absolutely ferocious defending her children. I've seen it. You could be Muhammed Ali and if you threatened her children you'd get shredded, wouldn't stand a chance. I got to see my father some, growing up. He tried, just never enough."

It was comic trying to keep up with Wally as he vaulted out of Woolley Creek the next day in his blue leather Pumas.

"If I'm late for Thanksgiving dinner my family is going to kill me. Let's go, man, let's go."

One month later Chris Miller and I did the second ascent of Humble Horse on the north face of Mount Diadem (IV, 5.7, WI 4, 2,000 feet). Big Jim Elzinga and Jeff 'Junior' Marshall had put the route up seventeen months earlier. We descended the other side of the peak into the Woolley Valley. I was so happy to finally face out and then walk away from the mountain and onto the flats of the glacier. I started jogging, pulling away from Chris.

The November snows stayed on the ground at this elevation, and the sculpted surface sat in regiments obedient to the wind. The snow gave little indication of crevasses, and my feet punched through a bridge and I dropped like I'd jumped off of a chair. My arms shot wide into a palms-down crucifix and the bottom of my pack smacked onto the bridge. The right side of my body canted into the crevasse and I stopped. I could feel my feet hanging in air and a vertigo-like feeling of tenuousness stopped me from moving anything.

Chris walked up.

"Hey man, I'm in a crevasse," I said.

"I can see that, Barry." A shroud of impatience darkened his face and he shucked his pack and methodically began flaking out a rope. I could see his frustration in having to deal with the hassle of my mistake.

"Can you throw me an end?"

The summit of Mount Cromwell, with Mount Alberta behind me. Wally and I nearly made it down, but not quite. Another cold forced bivouac.
Photo: Kevin Doyle

"Not until I'm anchored."

When the loop came I grabbed it and hauled myself up and out. The hole was black and deep.

"Sorry about that, Chris."

"It's OK, but let's rope up until we get off of the glacier."

"I'm definitely into that."

A 1,600-foot ridgeline connects the southwest summit of Mount Andromeda to the northeast summit. The ridgeline sits wholly above 11,000 feet and it is glaciated for the length of its run. The northeast summit is higher, 11,319 feet. Parallel ridgelines traverse each of the summits and joining the inter-summit ridgeline at right angles. The topographic image of the mountain looks like a big H. Kevin, Stewart, Ron, and I had endured the "trust me" epic wandering lost off the south side of the H four years earlier.

During the ice revolution of the sixties and seventies almost all of the attention of alpinists was focused on the snow-and-ice slopes of the northwest bowl. In the late seventies the vertical and over-hanging rock of the 1,800-foot northeast wall came into the limelight, especially the dust-colored ice of the Andromeda Strain. It presents

an interrupted couloir cleaved dead center into the black wall like an ax strike that stuttered midblow against thicker armor then bit less deeply below.

Many talented and experienced alpinists had tried the line. None had been able to get up the steep rockband that interrupted the upper and lower couloirs halfway up the wall. Some had tried to climb an overhanging snow-choked offwidth. It looked to be the best option, but proved difficult to impossible to protect. John Lauchlan had suggested cutting one-foot lengths of hockey stick to cantilever into the crack, a truly Canadian solution. I asked Jim Elzinga how a route that had yet to be climbed already had a name.

"Everybody has been up there lad, and no one has figured it out. It's become a huge strain, an Andromeda Strain."

James Blench would often take a dump when we reached the alpine walls. The Andromeda Strain towered above us as James squatted, the chest and hood of his sleeveless Farmer Johns pulled down and dangling like a diaper.

"Oh Fuck! Fuck, fuck, fuck!" he bellowed.

"What's the matter, James?" I asked, alarmed.

"I just dropped a fucking load in my fucking hood."

"You're shitting me." And I laughed.

"No, no I'm not."

"Shitty, man." And I laughed a bunch more.

James cleaned out his hood and we started.

We pulled fresh rappel anchors all the way up the lower gully (later I learned they were David Cheesmond's). James and I made the halfway ledge and bivied. It stormed, and in the morning we traversed left to an edge past the "hockey stick" offwidth. Around it I saw a snow-choked chimney, and then spindrift and storm sent us packing. We replaced the rappel anchors on the way down.

The fine north face of Cromwell above
Woolley Creek. Photo: Barry Blanchard

Dave returned the next week with Robbie Mitchell, a guy who'd been two years ahead of me at Viscount Bennett High School and been one of the only other climbers there. They pulled the rappel anchors out on the way up, and put them back in on the way down.

Wally was with me for round number two. We gathered the rappel anchors and bivied in the snow cave that Dave and Robbie had dug on the halfway ledge—after ejecting Robbie's frozen turd from it, and digging out all of the brown stained snow from under it.

The next day Wally launched into the chimney system. Two hours in he tried to continue straight into overhanging ground and there was fear and anger in his voice when he told me he was backing down. He'd gotten himself cornered and he jury-rigged three manky pieces to hold his weight while he unclipped his bolt kit and drove in the only bolt he ever put into the alpine environment. He got it most of the way in and it was marginal but it allowed him to lower off.

We replaced the rappel anchors on the way down. It was the last time that I ever carried bolts into the alpine.

———————————

One year earlier, before we'd left for the Cassin, Urs Kallen had said to Kevin and me, "You two have to meet this guy, Dave. He is really good, and he soloed the Cassin last year."

On a winter Wednesday in March 1982, when I was still living in Calgary, Kevin and I walked down the stairs to the Unicorn Pub. It was owned by the Irish Rovers, and the Calgary Mountain Club had moved pub night there after a murder was committed in the Cecil. Cheap beer was only worth so much, a life's blood spilled taints a scene for eternity.

"How good can this guy be?" I asked Kev. My success in climbing had stoked my ego and the mountains had yet to kick that out of my public persona.

Slender, medium height, with shoulder-length hair, a pointed beard that accentuated his aquiline nose like two arrows pointing down, gray eyes creased with laugh lines, and perfect, white teeth gleaming from a narrow boomerang of a smile: David Cheesmond looked like a fox. He sat calmly sipping a beer, some maps and pictures piled on the table in front of him. Kevin and I barged in, posturing, but David's calm stood us down and we were soon talking about climbing, the thing the three of us held paramount in life.

"The first time I put skis on in my life was here, man," David said, his South African twang strong, and he dropped a pencil point onto the Kahiltna landing strip. Kevin and I laughed at the fact, and the theatrics of its presentation. David lent us his map, and a precious topo of the Cassin route, the only one known in the climbing world at the time. It was wrinkled, worn, and creased like a treasure map. Kev and I walked away knowing a lot more about the Cassin and knowing that we would have to climb with Dave.

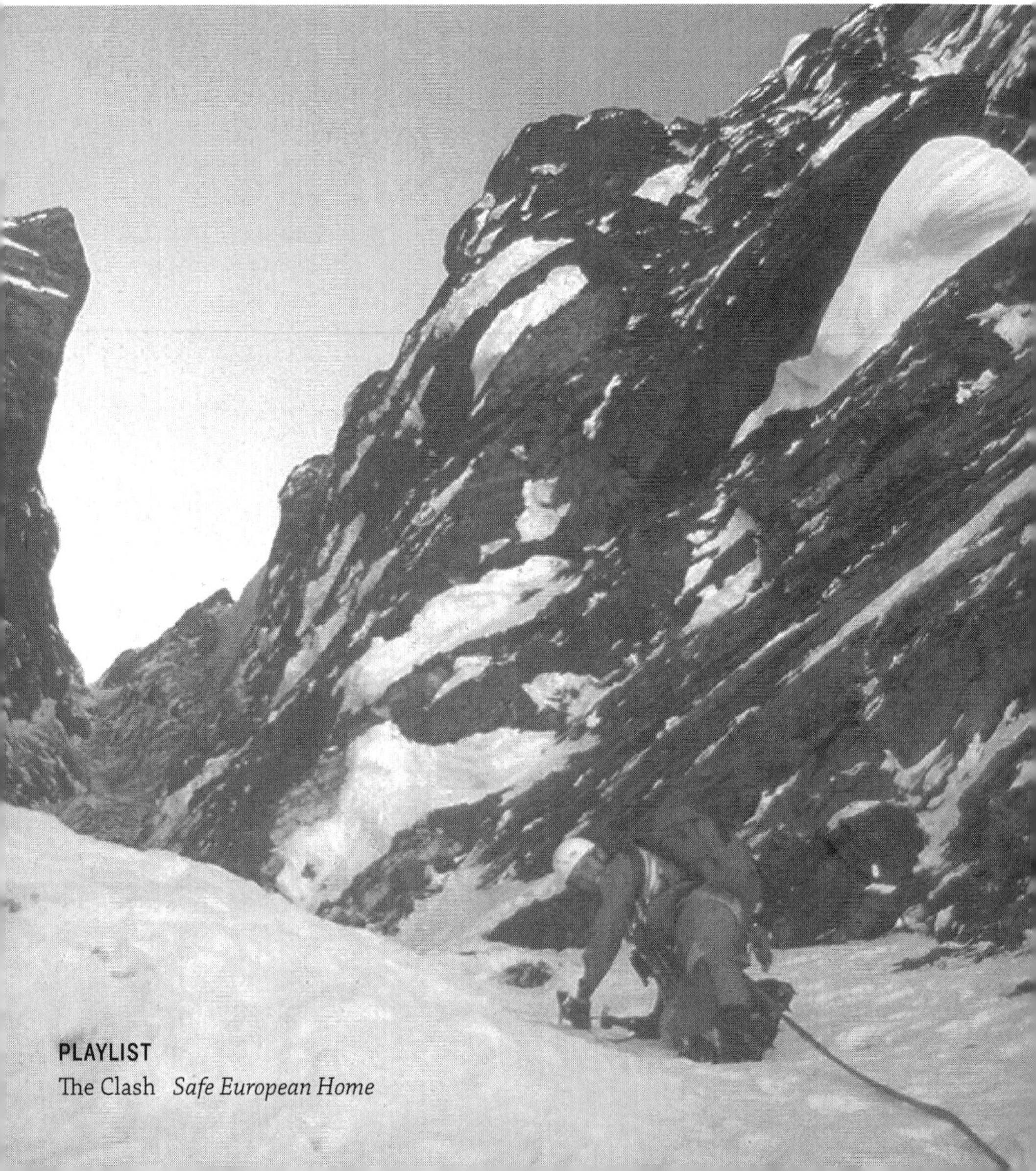

PLAYLIST
The Clash *Safe European Home*

Chapter 13

DAVID

"TIM AND I WILL PICK YOU UP AT 3:00 A.M.

in Canmore, man," David said over the phone. He and I were heading for our third rounds on the Andromeda Strain, but our first being partnered to each other. TP Friesen was our third ropemate and it was his first time on the route.

April 16, 1983, a bulwark of leaden cloud sat squat and unmoving over the mountains to the north.

"What did the Banff weatherman say?" David asked.

"You mean Lying Ralph?" I replied.

"Yes, Lying Ralph."

"He said three glorious days of high pressure."

"That doesn't look like high pressure to me," TP stated, pointing north.

"What do you guys want to do?" I asked, springing the trapdoor of retreat, yet knowing that I wanted nothing more than to be up there. A wave of wind charged over the glacier billowing snow like a herd of ghost horses. The horses hit raking ice shards across our faces and we turned our heads and shoulders into the wind.

The crux was over and the first ascent of the
Andromeda Strain was in sight. I was one
happy Alpinist. Photo David Cheesmond

"Right, man," David said. "It is supposed to be getting better. I think that we should head up and see what it does."

We climbed unroped for 900 feet. The weather didn't appear to be getting any better, nor was it getting any worse. The rack and ropes came out. Above us a clean open book corner. Spindrift, from the bulging wall that sat above the corner, had driven a vein of plaster-hard snow into the spine of the open book. I led and the climbing was superb classic alpinism. Front points set on small, square-cut edges of limestone, my tools delicately tapped into the plaster vein. The pitch placed us onto the halfway snow ledge—an amazing shelf that bisects the entire 5,000-foot width of the face. I traversed to the chimney. It took twenty-five blows from my hammer to picket my Sérac Sabre ax into the hard snow and it became a principal part of my anchor.

"Right then, Barry, you are keen to lead and given that you watched Kevin here that makes sense. Tim can belay you and I'll see if I can get us a snow cave there," David said, pointing to a VW-bus-sized cream roll that was somehow adhered to an overhanging wall above and the forty-five-degree snow ledge below. In my mind I saw the whole thing tumbling away when he touched it.

"Be careful with that thing," I said

"It will be OK, man. I have a plan. We won't go anywhere even if it does shear."

Dave had a PhD in engineering and he had already been a passionately obsessed climber when he graduated with his first degree from Durban University, in his South African homeland, at the age of nineteen. At the time, he was off to make another ascent of Mount Kenya (he would go on to climb the mountain seventeen times) when he called the university. "They told me that I could graduate with honors if I came back for the ceremony, but I said that a normal degree would be fine, and I went and climbed Kenya and that was my honors, man."

The right wall of the chimney was sheer, cleaved slices of lime-stone, wads of snow drooped from any wrinkle or imperfection. Angular overhangs jutted from the left wall like the undersides of boats. A stack of shattered rock was pressed between and it looked like a coal seam once I uncovered it from a blanket of snow. Everything was smothered in snow. Firm dollops the size of beach balls bulged out overhead and I spent tens of minutes chunking at their underbellies with my adze.

Snow cascaded onto my hood and shoulders with each swipe. Sugar grains of it sifted into my collar and it melted. My mitts got wet, and then refroze into gauntlets that I had to bite to pull off and expose my liner gloves to the frozen rock. When my fingers lost feeling I pulled my mitts back on.

I prayed that the dollops got carved down before they sheared from the rock but a couple fractured free and tumbled over me as I screamed to TP and David below. One felt like a safe clunking onto my shoulders and I compressed into the étriers that I stood in and gasped for the piton to stay.

And then there was a clear yard of shelving rock and I stood into the top rungs and wrapped a liner glove onto a frozen flake the size of an ashtray and slammed and slammed the pick of my Sabre at the crack tight to the right wall. Tremors of effort shuddered through me as I stepped high and wide, crampon points on an edge, breath raging, and my heart hammering. I heaved my left foot onto the snow above the roofline, grunted like a bull, and thrust into an alcove not knowing if gravity would grab me and haul me off backward.

I caught my balance and stood trembling and breathing in and out, in and out. My forearms burned from the cling of keeping myself there. It was some of the hardest alpine climbing that I had ever done. The chimney felt as hard as the 5.9 ones on top of the Balrog route on Mount Yamnuska. I had ascended via a medley of free climbing, aid climbing, and mixed climbing, whatever was the fastest and most secure—a technique that we would come to call "free as can be" in deference to the free climbing ethic that we held close while rock or waterfall ice climbing. Up there not falling was far more important; you could die so easily falling in the alpine. And climbing as fast as we could would minimize our exposure to what the wall, and the weather, could throw at us. Seventy-five feet took me two hours.

At 7:00 p.m. dusk was coming on. TP lowered me and I saw that the weather had come around, few clouds in a clear blue sky, the temperature already falling like a stone. Tomorrow would be perfect alpine climbing with frost locking everything in place. But my mind felt like burnt toast and my body like it had been ridden hard and put up wet. I'd processed as much adrenalin in the last two hours as I had in the rest of the season. I felt small, scared, and intimidated— a hollow husk.

David's snow cave was incredible: fifteen feet long and three feet wide, room for the three of us to stretch out, and a roof over all of our heads. He had a pot of soup already on the boil.

"I'm fucking fried," I confessed, knowing that they could see it in my face. "It looks harder above my high point. I don't know if I'll be able to climb it."

"Oh, Blanch, the climbing will look easier in the morning. It always looks easier in the morning," David said, and he smiled his fox smile. "Here, man, have some hot soup."

The minestrone billowed steam into the vault of our cave and it was so hot and salty and good. I felt a warm expansion in my chest like the armor ratcheting open, loose, and free.

The climbing did look better in the morning and more importantly I felt good. A small, bold voice within me said, "You can do this." It was the same voice that had spoken out from my bloodline when I was a small boy lying in bed trying to find my way through my Aunt's brutal beating. That voice has pushed me forward a number of times. It comes to me from the strong lips of strong women and men stretching back 500 generations, the length of time that my blood has been in North America.

The sky was blue. The air was deliciously cold and perfectly calm. The climbing wasn't overhanging, but there was less protection and it was harder to find. Forty feet higher I left the corner where Kevin had continued into no-man's land. A three-foot-high apron of forty-five-degree snow led out right, and the only way that I could come up with to cross it was to front point as low as I dared (too low would stress too little snow and the ice might fail and I would skitter off) and stab my picks in at waist level and hold my upper body in by wrapping my hand over the head of the tool. It felt similar to manteling onto the tiles to get out of a swimming pool.

Thirty feet out from the corner a snow-choked crack led up to where the angle eased. A pendulum fall back into the corner would have shattered me and there was no protection between me and the corner. I couldn't find anything for my right tool in the rock above and in growing desperation I thrust my forearm down behind the firm top edge of the snow, chicken-winging my arm between the backside of the snow and the rock. Snow fell away and there at my right elbow was a solid black crack that looked like it had been drawn by a felt tipped marker.

A long, shallow-angle piton rang true so I added a second long, thick-waisted knifeblade. Twenty feet higher I found a good fist-width crack splitting a bulge of black limestone. I anchored. The last eighty feet had taken me two hours to climb.

David jumared the pitch with his pack on his back and mine hanging from a long runner clipped into his crotch strap. It was a hard physical act.

"Holy crap, Cheese, you brought my pack too. Good work, man."

"Yes, the freight train." And he put his head down and panted.

Two minutes later he was looking up the route and orchestrating our ascent. "I can lead into the ice of the couloir, and then you or Tim can take all of the screws and we'll fourth-class up the ice."

"I'm never fucking doing that again," TP spat when he reached the anchor. To save on weight we'd only brought one set of Jumars and TP had just prusiked up the ropes, a technique that he had little experience with and one that is definitely more complicated and challenging with a lot of snow around.

"The fucking prusiks wouldn't slide up the rope." His red complexion was fired with rage and his green eyes burned. He jerked his head sideways, "And my pack kept getting stuck in the goddamned chimney."

A travel pack that he had used to tour through Europe five years earlier sat on his back and it had a suitcase handle on one side and a rectangular metal frame sewn inside to make it stand like baggage. The shoulder straps could be concealed by a zippered panel on the back.

"TP, you're a fucking lawyer, man," David said. "Buy yourself a proper alpine pack."

"Ya, you cheap bastard," I added.

"I will, just as soon as we get off of this route."

Five-hundred-foot-high limestone walls rose to a spear point of the palest blue sky that was so close to being a shallow green. A canted boulevard of névé led a hundred feet deep inside the fold of Mount Andromeda. Higher, it split into twin flows of chrome-colored ice parted around a bulge of snow-plastered limestone. Above that, it looked hard as the rock reared and the ice thinned to nothing. Incredibly a bulge of pale emerald ice hung like a giant pointed jewel on the right wall. If we could get to it, it could be our passage to the top.

David led to the end of the névé, then I charged for four ropelengths feeling like a sled dog leaping into the harness. Dave and Tim could not follow fast enough. Dave took us up the left flow of chrome ice and TP got what would become one of the most iconic alpine pitches in North America—the exit ice bulge of the A Strain.

Like the leading edge of a bird's wing, a foot-high band of vertical snow arced from us to the emerald ice. Above it lay minutely stratified limestone, vertical and draped in angel's-breath snow; below, ice glazed edges in file, few of which would take front points. TP set his picks into the snowband and onto what lay underneath and was masked by the snow. He found the edges that would hold his front points and eased onto them with slow and precise transfers of his hips.

There was a thirty-foot belly of rope between him and Dave and I when he planted his right ax firmly into the ice. A fall would have been horrible and when TP clipped his first ice screw Dave and I sighed and relaxed into our harnesses.

The repeating pattern of TP's placements pocked the virgin ice like bullet holes shot into safety glass and the marring of that unex-plored surface gave me pause. It felt like we were defiling something,

something sacred. Then I reached high and dead centered the next bullet hole with my pick and climbed up into sunlight and the heat felt so good, so much like the benevolent warmth of life, of blood.

Two more pitches and David cut us through a small cornice and we rose to our feet on the shallow back slope. Packs and ropes were piled there and we walked up to the summit.

Five o'clock in the evening, April 17, we shook hands, smiling, and stood and pointed out the summits that we knew. All around us were beautiful, beautiful mountains. The sun was warm and I was with friends. My life felt good.

"Right, then, we must get down off of this thing." Cheese snapped me back to the task at hand, and we walked down to our packs and then on to several rappels down the northeast ridge toward the Athabasca/Andromeda Col.

The top of the col fell away like a breaking wave at Maverick's. I stepped into the slope and dug a shovel shear test just like James Blench had taught me. There was a clean shear a foot down.

"What does that mean?" TP asked.

"Nothing good," I replied.

And then Dave, who had stayed to coil a rope at the bottom of our last rappel, plung-stepped up to us and willfully past us and on down to where he turned to face in thirty feet below us and started to down climb. All of his actions saying, "Fuck that, let's just get down this thing." Tim and I followed the 'Big Cheese.'

"Whoever climbs that will make a name for themselves," Pierre Lemire stated, his Quebecois accent softened by several decades lived in the Canadian West. It was early July, three months after we'd climbed the Andromeda Strain, and Pierre was pointing at the route. I was a candidate on the Summer Assistant Guide Course, my first exam with the Association of Canadian Mountain Guides. A course that I'd heard sarcastically referred to as a "twenty-one day vacation with Rudi and Pierre."

Rudi Kranabitter had earned his mountain guide pin at the age of eighteen in Austria, his homeland. As I matured into the profession of mountain guiding I would come to recognize Rudi's skill set as one of the very best that I was ever to see. Pierre was his second. The exam was anything but a vacation for we four candidates, especially when one of us, Dean, an American that I'd met bouldering in Snell's Field in Chamonix three years earlier, failed on day number three. When Darro, Brian, and I did the math we came up with six whole days that we would be in the lead and given the opportunity to fail.

"Some guys climbed it this spring," Brian chirped.

"That was David Cheesmond, Tim Friesen, and me. We did the first ascent in April."

A pregnant pause and I knew that I'd either gained points in Pierre's mind, or lost them. My tally had not remained neutral.

"I didn't know that," Pierre said. "Congratulations."

I got the same congrats from both he and Rudi when I passed the course. My roommates, Bruce and Carla, threw a pool party at our house to celebrate. "Safe European Home" by the Clash was on the stereo; Joe Strummer's English lisp boomed from the speakers.

I stood in three inches of water that had been transported from the pool into our sunken living room by partiers soaked to the bone. Sixty people showed up and each and every one had been thrown into our indoor heated pool. I'd been dancing for three hours. A pair of hands grabbed my shoulders and I was spun around and there was Kurt totally naked, his blue eyes crackling electrically. "What a great party, Barry!" and he frolicked off back to the pool. Three other men were naked, and two women, everyone was wet. Thirty years later I still hear comments around town from middle-aged folks who remember the "pool party."

Chapter 14

GREGG

GREGG CRONN WAS A LEAN AND TALL AMERICAN
with elongated El Greco looks intensified by a black beard, a long
nose, and sad, black-bellied Benicio del Torro eyes. His eyes were
misleading because Gregg was so easy to laugh. He took such joy in
pitching his head back and laughing loud. Gregg was one of the first
people I knew who studied the science of athletic training and we ran
for long hours on the old roads and trail systems threading the forested
benches above Canmore.

And we talked for hours more within our tent pitched atop a
glacier while teaching mountaineering courses. Love, life, climbing
ambitions, social justice—I'd get him guffawing with my ribald irreverent humor. "Those dick-lick, conservative butt-knuckles wouldn't know
leniency if it came up and bit them on the ass," I once commented. And
Gregg kicked his forehead back and howled. We were close friends
when we left to attempt the north face of Mount Alberta during the
dog days of summer 1983.

My cheap canvas tennis shoes splashed into the frigid flow of
the Sunwapta River. It is a Stoney Indian name that means "turbulent
water" and this was my fourth time fording it. The first had been with
Albi Sole in early October nine months earlier when we'd came to try
the north face of Alberta, got dumped on with snow, and with the face
plastered, never left the glacier. Albi and I climbed 700 feet up the
Elzinga-Miller on the Mount Cromwell on the way out and that led to
my second crossing of the Sunwapta with Wally on our Thanksgiving

The closer you get to the headwall on the north
face of Mount Alberta, the more you feel like it
is going to swallow you. Photo: Gregg Cronn

ascent of the Elzinga-Miller. And Chris Miller and I had crossed on our way out from Mount Diadem in November.

I sloshed onto dry, rounded stones that had been sorted into a Zen garden by the flow of the river. My feet had lost feeling crossing the first braid of the turbulent water. I wrenched my shoes off with a sucking sound and toweled the icy water from my frozen feet with a hand towel that we'd brought for that purpose. It was 8:30 a.m. on August 22. The morning sun felt warm and good. Gregg and I levered our feet into mountain boots and tied our shoes and towel up in a tree. We thumped our way up the primitive path on the south side of Woolley Creek. My pack was heavy but my heart was light.

Islands of stunted spruce sat ringed by terminal moraines like a boreal archipelago. Gregg and I marched through the tattered tree line and onto the talus-littered glacier. I could see where I'd stepped into the crevasse with Chris but now the glacier was dry and there was no snow masking the crevasses and we walked around their closed-off ends.

The northern reach of the Columbia Icefield is marked by the glacially carpeted twin summits of Mount Stutfield; North Twin (12,237 feet, the third-highest peak in the Rockies) and Twins Tower. A shear limestone wall falls a vertical mile from the dark spear point of Twins Tower, the black wall arcs for one and a quarter miles to Mount Stutfield, forming a 180-degree amphitheater. It is the most phenomenal feature in the range and climbers joke that not even light possesses the escape velocity to get out of the "Black Hole."

Woolley Shoulder is the price of admission. Seven hundred feet of elevation toil, gained by wading up scree that sits at the angle of repose: thirty-two degrees of slope. Each staggering footfall slides back downslope half a stride, the foul foot placements see you skitter lower than you started. It felt like trying to ascend a sand dune made out of marbles.

"Jump and fuck! Is anything stable in this belittling slope?" I wailed. Below me, Gregg howled with laughter.

My supporting heel shifted and sifted deeper into the marbles and I pivoted downslope and slid onto my ass. Gregg choked on guffaws and spittle as I raged back to my feet, my pack pulling on my shoulders like a pair of strong hands. I stood panting.

Sweat dripped from my chin, splatting the fragmented rock at my feet, and there I saw a perfect trilobite fossil. I picked it up and the rock shadow of the animal fit in my palm. Gregg thrashed up to me, I handed the trilobite to him.

"Wow, it's perfect. It was alive five hundred million years ago," he said.

Gregg passed it back and I held it in wonder and in awe. "We should leave it here," Gregg said, and I placed it back onto the slope.

Scree laid back to talus, then broken plates of slate, and at the top a spine of level ground the width of a desk. I thumped my dense red pack onto the flat and held it with both hands. If it had tumbled back down Woolley Shoulder I would have committed suicide.

"Holy shit," Gregg gasped, "there it is." And he thumped his pack down too.

Across the hazy deep pit of the Black Hole, the north face of North Twin looked like a great black cape on a leviathan dark knight. I stared and breathed. The face was so steep and so black. It was the hardest climb in the range and its sole ascent by Chris Jones and George Lowe in 1974 had already amassed the weight of myth. I felt a wave of blood surge from my chest and roll on down to my fingertips. I knew that I would go to North Twin...when I was good enough.

"It's pretty amazing isn't it, Gregg?"

"Yes. It's hard to believe that two men climbed it," he replied.

To the north Mount Alberta stood proud, independent, and isolated. A dark bastion footed with a dusty flat glacier, the north face invisible inside a deep cobalt shadow.

We traversed acres of broken shale and made a committing full-rope rappel down onto the north face glacier.

At 6:00 p.m. we were on a patch of broken stone that sat on the sloping surface of the dry glacier. Gregg and I created horizontal platforms from scree and flat stones like cave men. Rivulets of water trickled over the bare ice close to our beds and we funneled it into our water bottles and pot.

The stove purred. It was our second night of Parisienne Leek soup, the first being the night before in Gregg's VW van parked on the side of the Banff-Jasper highway. I'd asked him if we had anything other than Parisienne Leek, mac and cheese, and breakfasts of Alpen. He'd held a smile for about one beat and then broke into laughter and said, "No, buddy, it was a rush food job."

The sun was oblique and kind and it stayed on us until 9:00 p.m. I'd been into Calgary to see a recent slideshow by Doug Scott and he'd answered a question on what he wore in the Himalaya, saying that he started with a base of two cashmere sweaters. My mom had bought me a cashmere sweater for Christmas the year before and I wore it next to my skin. Any other sweater would have irritated my upper body, but cashmere didn't. I pulled a second wool sweater over it, just like Doug. I'd bought a pair of navy blue nylon knickers for my guide's course and made a trip to the Ukrainian specialty store to get a red wool babushka from the elderly matrons there. The large, floral-patterned scarf was a di rigueur accouterment for all Yamnuska Mountain School guides. New gray Koflach double-plastic boots and knee-length wool socks, I looked like a cross between Clint Eastwood in *The Eiger Sanction* and a hippie.

Dusk had engulfed Gregg and me. The last long ribbons of sunlight touched the north face of Alberta: wedding-dress-white ice, abrupt and brutal black rock, and the glowing white bridal veil of the summit glacier. Overall the face was beautiful, yet as Gregg and I squirmed into our bags lying down at right angles to the face I felt a dread. Like a sword, I laid my seventy-centimeter ice ax along my side, between the mountain and me, and slept fitfully always aware of its presence.

"Do you think we should bring a repair kit for our crampons?" Gregg had asked me two days earlier.

"No, my crampons never break."

Now we were one pitch onto the wedding-dress ice and an Allen screw had come out of the front of my left crampon, making it useless. The full weight of "oh fuck" sank into my mind. It could have been the end of our ascent and I felt like an idiot. Gregg waited patiently, and with grace, as I tinkered away one of our precious cold morning hours, when the ice face is safest, using both of our Swiss Army knifes to remove a screw and nut from the pick of my Mjöllnir hammer, insert them into my crampon and get it twisted tight.

That done, I racked four of our five ice screws and raged onto the white pleatings of névé. One ice screw per ropelength and one to anchor, backed up with my ice ax pounded in with my hammer, and the Mjöllnir then smacked in as deep as I could get it.

The sun rose and the rockfall started. The humming of hornets, the basal whir of a circular saw, Gregg's eyes darted left and right under the brim of his Galibier helmet. A chunk of rock the size of a depth charge fractured from the northeast ridge 500 feet to our left. It roared like a jet engine gouging trenches into the white slope. From opposite ends of our 165-foot rope Gregg and I screamed. We were so exposed and so in need of luck, good luck. And then the summit slopes fell into shade and the rockfall stopped.

The verticality of the headwall reared greater with each ropelength we gained. Black rock soared over my head and I felt I was getting too close to a primal force of nature—a tidal surge, a rogue wave. My ice placements were competent and secure, yet I felt that my hold on the mountain was so tenuous, as fragile as a butterfly wing. Three ropelengths of shitty shale—the infamous "Yellow Band"—capped the white ice and my American friend led us into a mixed chimney, choosing it over an easier ramp of thin ice that had edges of shale sticking out of it like horns on lizard skin. The chimney took more time than the ice would have.

"What is it about you Yanks and rock?"

"I am a product of my environment, my friend, and it is why I live in a house while you live in an igloo." He laughed and laughed and handed me the rack.

It was early afternoon and all of the earth surrounding us shimmered in the warm haze of summer. Gregg and I stood lashed to our anchor in the cold shade of Mount Alberta. If I arched back into my harness and craned my neck I gained the horizon of the headwall and above it the sky was a pale aquamarine. When I pulled myself back into standing my head felt light, like I'd stood up too fast, and that lightness lasted for four beats of my heart.

"Which way do you think we should go?" Gregg asked. Four cracks presented options but the wall above was so steep we couldn't see if any of the cracks were continuous. I took off my crampons and started up the most promising-looking crack, but it wasn't the way and I lost an hour of hard climbing and one of our precious knifeblade pitons.

The yawning funnel of the ice face looked like the gullet of the underworld and a primal fear rose in me as I rappelled. Human beings were not meant to be suspended on ropes above the gyre of an alpine face. I felt so tentative and anxious.

"Well that was fucking real up there," I said.

"Are you OK?"

"Ya, I had to leave a knifeblade, but I think I saw where the route goes. I'm going to have to put my crampons back on."

I climbed to the leftover hard mixed ground feeling like Walter Bonatti, and on the last third of the ropelength I realized my dream of experiencing some of the terrain that Walter had. I found some of the perfection of the alpine as I palmed both of my hands into a crucifix to hold my upper body into the open book corner just like I'd done on the golden granite of Yosemite, a band of silver ice ten inches wide was inlaid up the spine of the corner and I precisely stacked my crampons one atop the other using all of the accuracy that I'd gained during my days on waterfall ice.

I felt competent and light and I looked down the half-mile sweep of the ice face and the wildness of my position charged into me and I felt a melding of myself into the spirit of alpinism. I was climbing like Bonatti!

And then I was out of rope and I anchored and hauled my pack on the seven-millimeter line that Kevin and I had carried over the top of the Cassin. As Gregg jumared the pitch, I constructed a shelf for our butts out of the ledge that I stood on. It ended up being about the size of a manhole cover. "This is going to be a rough night," I said to myself, and then Gregg yarded up to the anchor blowing like a quarter horse that had just run the track.

"I can't climb like that. You're going to have to do the leading," he panted.

"OK. But this is where we are going to have to bivy."

"Ugh."

Eventually Gregg and I were sat to the mountain. Our feet dangled over the void and for the first time ever I tied the stove in.

"Oh shit." One of my pile mitts stumbled down the yellow band then luged down the ice. Later, *clang, clang, clang* as the lid to the pot frisbeed into the night. We folded the foil windscreen into an origami triangle and crimped its corners down tight to the purring pot. At some point another one of our precious knifeblades got fumbled. "Crap."

"Oh well, it could be worse," I stated, "Walter Bonatti dropped his sleeping bag from the first bivy on the first ascent of the Croz Spur, and that was in winter."

"Don't even mention that stuff. Where's your cup? The Parisienne Leek is ready."

"Oh, yum."

What little sleep I did get I got between bouts of my ass going numb and my forehead starting to pound...we were sleeping with our heads tethered into the wall like Wally and I had done on the headwall of the Salathé but Gregg and I were facing out.

I felt like I was in Yosemite the next morning. The rock was so good. A laser-cut Al crack saw me high-stepping in my plastic-runged étriers. I'd bought the Euro style steps at the Hostel Shop because they looked like the metal ones that I saw in pictures of Gaston Rébuffat. I thought that I was the only North American who used them as everyone else I knew tied theirs from one-inch tape as Royal Robbins suggested in *Advanced Rockcraft*. I'd been called into climbing via the words of classic European alpinism, yet I'd learned much of what I knew on North American mountains.

The next pitch started with finicky placements and I struggled to stay in the stirrups of my étriers. Thirty feet up the crack I came to George Lowe's pendulum piton, the sole piece of gear we were to find on the whole route, the only trace left from the passage of four other men: George and Jock Glidden in 1972, and Kit Lewis and Steve Swenson in 1981. The pick of my Mjöllnir rattled as I pounded on the black piton. With the one screw missing that I'd pirated to keep my crampon together, the pick became looser and looser and I couldn't get it back tight without an Allen key.

"Gregg! Feed me out some rope." I lowered down and then powered right to gain a windowsill ledge. Fifteen feet of free climbing and I clung under a meter-wide roof formed by the clean cleaving of horizontal strata, a parting of sediments laid onto the floor of a shallow inland sea over 500 million years ago. Ripples of the ancient sea floor textured the roof that pressed down on me.

A crack separated the roof from the wall and I jiggled some protection into it and tried to climb around the right edge, but the free climbing was too hard. I set a piton by hand into the crack up the roof's right side and it stayed and I gently tapped on it until it grabbed the rock and then I struck a hammer blow and heard the plank-like gonging of the roof and felt the rock expand under the pressure of the piton. The roof was a detached feature!

My heart hammered as I continued to strike the piton. I clipped an étrier into it and my heart was in my throat as I breathlessly stepped up. Everything held, but I still couldn't find holds to pull on. I needed another placement. The first piton I tried gonged on the way in and pulled out like a nail from wet wood when I hand tested it.

A Long Dong is a seven-inch Lost Arrow piton that was marketed with a notch in its tip so that it could be used as a nut pick. It was a piece of gear that had two functions and I'd bought it, and now it hung on my harness amongst a cluster of our dwindling supply of pitons. The Long Dong was heavy and redundant as an extraction tool on an alpine climb because the picks of our axes had more reach, yet I reached for it and set it and began tapping it true, and then I hammered on it. The roof vibrated and gonged.

One inch shy of full depth on the dong and the piton that I was standing on shifted and my body dropped a half inch as my heart charged back into my throat. The last piton that I knew could hold a fall was twenty feet below. The dong had flexed the roof and loosened the bite of the pin that suspended me.

Frantic, I clipped an étrier into the dong. Fear shook my hands and feet and the metallic taste of fear dried my mouth. With a comic mix of flight-based jittering, and the will to fight into the higher étrier in a controlled manner that would not stress the Long Dong, I stepped up and the long piton held. Everything slowed down and I breathed.

Above the roof the vertical black rock was compact and I found a pencil-width hold on the horizontal crack that was the top fracture line of the roof. The roof was fractured along all four planes of contact with the wall—a freezer-sized block of limestone waiting to release and hurtle to the flat, chalk-colored glacier 2,000 feet below me. I stepped into my highest rung holding myself in balance with my left hand grasping the pencil width hold. The dong pivoted inside the crack and I dropped an inch and abject terror choked me. I clung and I prayed, my chest pasted flat against the wall like a foot soldier trying to escape sniper fire.

My world contracted to the one square yard of rock within reach of my right hand. There was an opening the width of a wink in the top-side fracture of the roof. Down my right side I could see a half-inch angle piton clipped on to my harness. The piton's spine had split from repetitive use leaving two tines that looked like a minute pair of trouser legs. I stabbed the tines into the opening and the piton set. I tapped it, then pounded on it and the spine kept splitting and the twin blades went in and rang true. And then the Long Dong scratched a fraction lower and I panicked. The eye of the split piton was out of the rock one inch. I made three wraps around the shaft of the pin with a sling, clipped an étrier into it, and quivered to standing.

A good, thin crack came into my reach and I sank my last knife-blade piton into it, cursing obscenities of fear with each hammer blow. I stood into the pin and breathed out the taste of rust and blood as my heart pounded down the seconds. The last ten feet had taken one hour to climb.

Above me was an ice couloir and I stood high in my étriers and sunk a bomber screw into polished silvery ice.

"Gregg! Tie my crampons onto the haul line!" For the first time in 700 days of climbing I strapped on my crampons while standing in étriers.

Forty feet of ice climbing and I anchored, hauled my pack, and chopped myself out a bucket seat to sit and look out and deal with my doubt. "What if the route gets harder? Will I be able to climb it? Can we get down?"

Black rock dropped sheer to the funnel of the ice face. Glaciers glowed overexposed in sunlight, the hazy folds of forest falling to the mercury-colored braids of the Athabasca River, jagged regiments of peaks melding into cloud on the northern horizon, the power of the

Rockies seeped into me like ground water as I sat strapped tight to the high black cliffs of one of the range's proudest peaks. My heart felt strong when Gregg arrived on the jugs. I was ready for more.

Forty feet of AI flew by in a flurry of Hexentrics, Friends, wedges, then good hand jams. The pitch ended with fabulous free climbing up a dihedral and a large ledge to belay on. Hauling was effortless as my pack swung clear of the face and came up through space.

It was 5:00 p.m. and heavy clouds surrounded us like the dark buildings of Gotham City. It was going to storm. Fuck.

"Do you think we should bivy here?" Gregg asked.

"If it storms this is only going to be harder in the morning. I think we should get up as high as we can while the getting is good."

"Can you keep leading?" Gregg's voice quavered with concern for me, and for him.

"I've got this, buddy, I can keep going."

Then came immaculate vertical limestone with large incut holds. My plastic boots worked perfectly on the small square edges and I climbed bold and strong with good protection. It felt so good. And our decision to continue was blessed with the best bivy ledge on the route—a clean, inward-sloping platform big enough for us both to lie down on. And then the storm started. Wind, hail, freezing temps, Gregg and I pulled our bivy sacs up over our eyes to sip the Parisienne Leek

soup and pray that the monsters would go away. Toward dawn the slapping gusts diminished.

In the morning, hail sat on anything that wasn't vertical. A charcoal ceiling hung at the top of the face like the underside of a manhole cover. We rose with the slow movements of the intimidated, the scared. The thought of retreating the face was repulsive.

"I think that we have to keep trying to go up," I said. Gregg's eyes looked spooked from within the cowl of his hood. Gray air hung all about him and the rock was zebra striped with ashen strips of snow, a dirty zebra.

"Do you think we'll be able to climb with all the snow on the ledges?"

A crack split the wall fifteen feet to our left.

"I think that I'll be able to aid that crack, it must be where the route goes from here, but I'm going to have to tension to it. I can't climb the rock with all this hail all over everything. Keep me tight."

"I've got you, buddy."

I tension-traversed to the left and sunk a wedge sideways into the crack and stepped into the rhythm of aid for half a ropelength. Above lay an apron of ice with rock spikes sticking out of it like inch-long silver ones on a dog collar. I grabbed the spikes and balanced onto them avoiding the ice with cramponless boots. Teetering atop the last spike of rock, ten feet of ice separated me from the wall. In a fit of nostalgic illumination I unholstered my Mjöllnir and began chopping steps just like I'd seen Hamish MacInnes do in black-and-white pictures. It was so much fun! I tilted my head back and howled like a wolf!

I loped up some mixed ground to a loose overhang and powered over it with a sequence of bold physical moves that flowed and felt good. Had I been intimidated, the same stretch of mountain would have taken much more time. "The mind is the most powerful muscle in the body," I said to myself.

Constructing an anchor made my head hurt, but half an hour later I'd brought three pitons, a Friend and two tied-off blocks into a focal point and hollered "Jumar!"

"I don't know how you can keep on leading these pitches, Bubba," Gregg stated, worry and gratitude creased his forehead and made his bottomless dark eyes deeper. "I can't believe that you were cutting steps up here!"

The north face of Mount Alberta; behind it on the left, the North Pillar of North Twin catches the early morning light. Photo: R. W. Sandford

"That pitch was amazing, man. It just kept getting more engaging. I floated the last overhang like it was a boulder problem in the basement of the U of C. It felt good, light, and the hail is melting. I think that we are going to be OK, buddy."

"All because of your climbing abilities, my friend."

"Thanks, man, now give me the gear and I'll get out of here."

I traversed right across a plumb vertical wall on a series of small face holds. My calf muscles throbbed from holding boots onto holds the size of the edges on matchboxes. Twenty feet right with no protection and my forearms burned like I was climbing 5.10 on Mount Yamnuska. Desperate moves up an open book to my first piece of gear. More bridging and stemming to harder climbing and I berated myself for not placing more protection. "This is not the place to be running it out, asshole!"

An ice-filled groove and I hauled up my crampons once again. The ice and rock were so good and the angle was easing back. My climbing became a joy and I realized that I was the only expression of joy for many a mile and thousands of feet.

Far below, Gregg was nervously monitoring the rope while trying to shove a Cadbury Fruit and Nut bar into his pie hole. I suspected that was making him happy, but that fell shy of what I was feeling. The ceiling had dropped and sunk us deeper into cloud. I belayed on an outcrop of ice mushrooms in the mist that could have been the top edge of an iceberg in the North Atlantic. Somewhere during the lead, the pick of my Mjöllnir had lost its last screw and fallen down the face. I told myself that we still had three functional ice tools for the summit ice field.

"I can lead this," Gregg said. A broad smile stretched across his face. He bridged up into the mist, one tool sunk into the ice-choked offwidth crack that was the spine of the corner, his long legs reaching for rock edges to set crampon points to. His yellow suit looked surreal against the cloud and softened black rock. I stood fast, worrying about stepping through a cornice along the whited-out summit ridge, and about being able to find the Japanese Route for our descent.

"Doesn't the mist add something to it?" Gregg asked, looking down.

"I'd actually rather that it would fuck right off, my friend." And he laughed and climbed out of sight onto the summit icefield.

The rope came tight, and then the haul line. I tied his pack onto it and lowered out as Gregg hauled.

I'd removed all of my anchor placements save for one Z piton nailed under a frozen block of limestone above my head. Ready to climb, I grabbed the Z pin and went to high-step. It *pinged* out and I was launched backward over the north face of Mount Alberta. The wall blurred in a rush as my feet bicycled wildly. I grabbed the rope to keep upright, but it stretched and I hit a ledge and fought to get my balance, but the rope stretched more and I fell farther. My feet hammered into a ledge, my forearm slammed something, and then the rope took my weight and I thrashed to get my feet under me on the vertical wall.

I was thirty feet down from the stance and I was freaked. My jaw quivered uncontrollably and my breath raged. I screamed until Gregg heard me and answered that he was OK, then I swept my body for breaks or wounds. Looking down I saw that my crampons had been wrenched through a quarter rotation on my boots and the spikes stuck out from the insides of my ankles like lineman's spurs. "Holy shit."

I got myself together and righted my crampons and climbed up to Gregg. Because of rope drag he wasn't even aware that I'd fallen and taken thirty feet of stretch out of the rope.

"You're fucking kidding me," he said.

"No, I wish I was. I went fucking plummeting back down the face. Scared the ever-living shit out of myself. "

"Holy shit," he said in a slow reverential tone. Gregg racked three ice screws and pounded up the ice into the mist.

Halfway to Gregg I watched the pick of my ice ax tear open like crepe paper at the second tooth when I levered it to get it out of the ice. I could see the end of the shorn pick still embedded in the ice. "Fuck!" And I shouted up to Gregg to lower me one of his tools.

We finished the face climbing with one ice ax each and using the *piolet ancre* technique of gaining two handholds from a single ax placement—one midshaft, one over the head—that we'd learned from Yvon Chouinard in *Climbing Ice.*

Our summit photos could have been taken in my back yard in winter with someone holding up a white sheet behind us, yet we were two young men so happy to be there. I thought Gregg was going to break me when he tried to hug me into his chest.

On July 21, 1925, six Japanese mountaineers, two Swiss mountain guides and one amateur Swiss climber stood on top of Mount Alberta for the first time after sixteen hours of intense climbing from their high camp at tree line. The Japanese route on Mount Alberta had the patronage of the Marquis Mori Tatsu Hosokawa of Japan and an ice ax engraved with "M. T. H." was left on the summit in his honor. Mountaineering myth transformed the ice ax into silver even though it was a normal ax of Swiss manufacture. It was found, and carried away to the American Alpine Club's museum in New York City, by John Oberlin and Fred Ayers when they made the second ascent of Mount Alberta via the Japanese route in 1948.

"No silver ice ax, Gregg."

"Nope, no silver ice ax, buddy. Let's get out of here."

The traverse of the corniced ridgeline 11,800 feet up Mount Alberta was as nervous for me as a tightrope walk over shark-infested waters. Gregg merrily hummed along in my footsteps.

We gained the black rock. A bivy corral marked the top of the Japanese route and there we spent the night.

In the morning, at the bottom of our first rappel, I realized, "Crap, I left my long ax up there."

"It's broken anyways, buddy, and it ain't silver, but it seems like a good resting place for it to me." (Seven years later is was still lying there, rusted and weathered, when Jim Elzinga and I made the first ascent of the northwest ridge of Mount Alberta. I carried my broken old friend home with me then.)

Gregg and I were one day overdue, and as I pounded down the lower reaches of Woolley Creek I heard the thumping of a helicopter coming in low. I sprinted into the open creek bed waving my arms and the ship saw me and it wheeled a tight turn and slapped away down valley.

A Jasper park warden was parked next to Gregg's van. "You probably want to talk to us," I said.

"Are you Barry Blanchard and Gregg Cronn."

"Yes we are," I replied.

"And you've been on the north face of Mount Alberta?"

"Yes we have."

"Did you make it?" Genuine curiosity perked his voice up from rote bureau-speak.

"Yes we did."

"Oh, that's great, really great. But you are overdue and I have to ask why."

"Well, it's just a really big mountain way back there and it snowed on us two days ago and that made the climbing harder and really slowed us down."

"I believe it, and that is all that I need to know. Glad to see that you fellas are OK."

Later, Gregg gave me a fourteen-by-ten-inch blow up of one of his fine photos of the north face taken from our bivouac on the glacier below it. On the back he wrote:

"Barry,

As I step though the rise and fall of this adolescent existence, Alberta will always be a masterpiece in my gallery of memories.

To the future! Gregg"

PLAYLIST
Juluka   *Scatterlings of Africa*

Chapter 15

MOUNT FAY

"I JUST SOLOED the north face of the Matterhorn," Kevin said. It was the fall of 1983 and he was in Europe and I was in Canmore. I could feel his tranquility over the phone line. He was in a very good place.

I gave him the blow by blow of the north face of Mount Alberta, "Wally, it demanded everything that I've learned in 700 days of climbing, and then it asked for more."

"And you came up with it, didn't you, Blanch?"

"Yes, buddy, I did." I, a ne'er-do-well half-breed raised on the wrong side of the tracks, had stepped onto the razor's edge...and danced!

David Cheesmond was also out of Canada on an expedition to the Kangshung Face of Mount Everest, his team made the first ascent of that remote wall in Tibet. I hungered for the Himalaya.

"I think that we should go to the north side of Rakaposhi," David had said at our inaugural team meeting earlier that summer. David, Kevin, TP Friesen, Chris Dale, Steve Langley, Gregg Cronn, and I where all keen to go to the Himalaya, we just needed to decide on a mountain to go to, and figure out a way to get there.

"It is only a one-day approach off of the Karakorum Highway and the north face is massive and unclimbed," David continued.

"How do you pronounce it?" I'd asked.

I'm leading the crux pitch of the Wild Thing on the northeast face of Mount Chephren. Twenty feet higher, Wally took over the belay from James, and I took a thirty-foot leader fall coming to rest just opposite them.
Photo: Kevin Doyle

"'Raka' like alpaca, and 'Poe' as in Edgar Allan, followed by 'she' as in a girl. Think of an alpaca with Poe on it's back dressed as a woman," TP said.

"Now there's an image," Chris stated, and started to laugh.

Rakaposhi it was. We divided up responsibilities. Le Grand Fromage was the leader; TP was legal; I got gear donations; Chris got fundraising and film; Steve was our treasurer; Gregg, being American, became our US representative; and Vern Sawatzky, a childhood friend of TP's practicing medicine in Churchill, Manitoba, signed on as our doctor. We all got after our various responsibilities.

I got drunk on the success of hauling in free gear with a form letter. I'd even written to a major Canadian publisher and scored a dozen titles on the history of Pakistan.

"I'm going for furniture next time," I bragged to Wally when he got home from his European alpine vagabonding.

The toughest thing to come up with was money and we soon realized that T-shirt sales were our greatest cash cow. I got a fledgling silk screening operation in Canmore to print our shirts cheap, but there was a problem with the first ten dozen shirts.

"Barry," Chris said in his Welsh lilt, "do we call them 'Pakis' or 'Pakas'?"

"Pakis, why?"

"Because our shirts read: 'Canadians to the Pakastani Karakorum,' which would be right if they were Pakas, but they are Pakis and our shirts should read: 'the Pakistani Karakorum.'" My six teammates laughed their asses off and howled.

"Shit, I guess I'll have to change that," I grinned.

"The first ten dozen will become collector's items, man," David added in kindness.

"I'm phoning to formally invite you on our Everest expedition in 1986," Jim Elzinga said over the phone and my heart ramped up. Everest! The highest mountain in the world! Where Reinhold Messner and Peter Habeler had climbed to the summit without supplemental oxygen. Where Messner had gone back and climbed it again without supplemental oxygen, alone. This was the big time and an expedition that I really wanted to go on, my chance to climb the big E.

"You know that James Blench, Dave McNab, and I left the 1982 expedition when Blair Griffiths and three Sherpas were killed."

"Ya, man, I can understand that."

"Well, we've decided that everyone on this expedition, which we are calling Everest Light, has to know each other and has to have climbed with all of the other team members. We don't want to repeat the mistakes of '82 and we believe that this strategy will accomplish that," Jim concluded.

"Sounds good to me. Are you going to invite Kevin Doyle?"

"His name is on our list, but he'll have to be voted in at a team meeting. Our next one is in two weeks time. Can you be there?"

"You bet, with bells on. I'm keen."

I'd gone from dreaming of climbing in the Himalaya to being a team member on expeditions to the Pakistani Karakorum in six months time and a national expedition to the highest mountain on earth in just over two years time! My life got busy, but I still needed to go climbing, and to try to meet girls.

Jackie had heavy dark hair and olive skin, eyes as brown as mine, but beautifully round and mysteriously hard to read. I kissed her in a foyer during a party, and she kissed me back with full lips and a soft and slow tongue. My hands glided down to her waist and hips and I lowered my face in front of her crotch and blew hot breath through her nylon running shorts. She took me home and we started seeing each other and climbing together.

A glowing strip of ice draped down over dark rockbands, linking patches of snow like a silver braid of pearls laid onto black velvet. I immediately thought of the Peruvian Andes or the Himalaya. I grabbed the eight-by-ten glossy from the piles of mountain photos and route descriptions sheaved atop David Cheesmond's desk.

"Where the hell is this?" I said.

"Oh shit, man," he said. Pale auburn eyes slashed left, then right, acute as a fox. He made a futile grab for the picture. "You weren't supposed to see that!"

"It looks so cool. Where is it? The Himalaya?"

"No, it's...Ah..."

"C'mon, man, you have to tell me. Please."

"Oh hell, OK. It's one of Urs Kallen's photos."

"You're telling me that this is in the Rockies?" The ice looked so linear, so perfect, a staircase into the sky. It looked great, as in the Greater Ranges. Could it actually be in our backyard?

"Yes. It's on the east face of Mount Fay."

"Mount Fay at Moraine Lake?" The scale wasn't adding up for me.

"Ya, man," David said in his cultivated South African English. "But not the Moraine Lake side, the east face, above Consolation Lakes. That face is much bigger."

"Holy shit! When do we go?"

The first snows of autumn had just, that evening, sifted small arcs of white onto the windowsill. We cracked a couple of beers and got down to planning for an attempt that winter. In my mind's eye, I saw David and myself cleanly inserted into Urs's picture. Perfectly present there, the two of us doing what we believed we were meant to do: Going up.

Later that night, Dave dropped me off at my mother's house on the far side of Calgary. In the morning, I'd board the bus back to Canmore.

My mother had five half-breed kids by three different men in seven years. None of the white fathers made it. All of them left, and it was as if the fabric of our family had become faded and patched by the time Steven came around. At seventeen, he was flunking out of school and already in trouble with the law. He'd been drinking at a party when an older man, who had previously done time, talked him into a robbery attempt and they got caught.

One of the good men I'd taught to rock climb was a gifted criminal lawyer. "It will make a strong impression on the judge if as many of your family as possible can be in court to support Steven," he said. When the judge asked if there were any family members present, my mother, brother, sister, and I all stood up. The judge gave Steven a term of probation, conditional on his staying in school.

It was late by the time I finally said good-bye to David and opened the door of my mother's house. Steven was still out.

"I don't know what to do with Steven," my mother said. Her forehead sank into her fingers, and her elbows trembled against the hard

The east face of Mount Fay with its silver strip of ice, dead center. Photo: Barry Blanchard sheen of the kitchen table. A deep sob shook her shoulders. I put my arm around her. I'd seen my mother cry before, but that was usually over Steven's dad. She'd always been a pillar for us, a tigress.

"Maybe he can come and stay with me," I said. The only way I knew how to help was to take him climbing.

Two days later, I found a place for Steven and me in old Canmore. Built in the 1950s, the cheap, blue house had seen some hard use. It sat on the westernmost corner of Tepee Town. My mother drove Steven up on the last day of October, and he enrolled in the local high school. We sat on borrowed chairs at a borrowed table and ate a lot of pasta with red sauce. My girlfriend, Jackie, called our house Sparta.

It felt good to see my little brother go out the door, walk to school, and start to make friends. I knew he was trying to step up, to be good enough, and I had hope. And although that hope would waver over the next twenty-two years, I realize now that I never really lost hope over those intervening years, no matter what my brother did.

By mid-December, strips of blue ice laminated the gray walls above our valley. Steven and I had been living together for six weeks, and we were doing OK.

"We should go ice climbing, bro," I said. "I think you'd like it."

His huge brown eyes glinted with what I took to be imagination and interest. Since I didn't have a car, Steven and I walked for two hours to get to the Canmore Junkyards instead of driving for ten minutes. We were doing the best that we could.

My brother stood at six feet, and he weighed 200 pounds, three inches taller and thirty pounds heavier than I was. He took pride in his physique. We'd hit the gym together, and while I trained to get leaner and harder for climbing, Steven just got bigger. He looked more native, and I'd joke that he was an "FBI": a Fucking Big Indian.

He did fine with the ice climbing, and I hoped it would capture him as it had captured me. "How do you like it, bro?" I asked.

"It's pretty cool, Bear," he said. He was poised midway on the ice-fall. "But it's scary."

"Fear can be your friend," I said. "It can make you stronger."

"I don't know, man."

The muffled crackling of water emanated through the blue ice. Far above the point where Steven stood secure on his crampons, came the roar of open water. The spray gave birth to mist, which slowly rose toward Chinaman's Peak and traced vanishing patterns against a stark, black wall.

In February, Steven said, "Canmore isn't working for me, brother." We'd been living in our hollow house cooking meals, going to the gym together, getting by. I made sure he went to school. I even tried to get him to run up the road above the Junkyards with me.

"Running isn't my thing, Bear," he said. "It's too hard."

Steven told me that Calgary had more going on, and he'd decided to move back to my mother's house. We walked to the bus station together.

"Thanks for all your help, Bear," he said.

"It's OK, bro. I hope Calgary is better for you now."

Our hug was a little clumsy as always: It felt awkward for me to wrap my arms around my brother's floundering. But then I got him close, and I felt my love for him, and I said, "Be good, bro." A glassy sheen of tears shimmered over my eyes.

"I will, Bear," he said. His voice quavered. "I will."

At 11:00 p.m., five hours after Steven stepped onto the bus, David Cheesmond and Carl Tobin pulled up to the front door of the blue house.

David sang along to the Juluka song "Scatterlings of Africa" on the cassette as we drove to Lake Louise. Strong guttural male voices issued the chorus,

"Yun! Bo! Ha!" and I saw lines of Zulu warriors pounding the earth with bare feet, spears, and cowhide shields, preparing for battle. The van barreled down the dark and deserted highway. Inside that sanctum, Carl and I joined the chanting. Our pact of ascent was a given.

"Bugger!" The toe bail on my binding snapped clean and cold as a frozen twig. I stabbed the broken skis into the snow and wrestled my second pair from the plastic sled.

Our plan was to ski, by headlamp, eight miles up the closed Moraine Lake Road and bed down in a cook shelter for four hours. We'd cache one pair of skis there to facilitate our return down the north side of the mountain, and at 8:00 a.m., we'd ski on the second set up a branching valley that led to the east face. We had just Saturday and Sunday for the climb, and Monday for the ski out. David had to be at work on Tuesday morning. Carl, who was on vacation, intended to ski back in later to pick up the set we'd leave below the east face. Now, down to one pair of skis, I'd have to walk out behind them from the cook shelter after we finished the climb.

The gray strip of road rolled through dark timber. I skied through clouds of exhaled breath, my skins creaking over the coarse, frozen track. A halo of frost grew on my chest. I hoped Steven was at home in our mother's house. It felt good to move through the cold, toward what I'd imagined Urs's photo to be: a beautiful alpine dream.

A day later, Carl yelled down to David and me, "I'm going to jump!" He was halfway up an aquamarine pillar of ice that dropped plumb from the apex of an outward-leaning, hundred-foot-high black lime-stone wall.

"What do you mean?" I shouted back. I didn't believe ice existed that Carl couldn't climb. I'd seen him shirtless in the gym, and his muscles were like plates of metal and cut-white marble: broad, flat, and efficient, none of the bloated bulk of the bodybuilder. "You can't fucking jump!"

"I can't hang on anymore! I'm going to jump. Fuck!"

David and I looked at our anchor of shallowly driven pitons and picketed ice tools. We were 1,000 feet off the deck.

Carl let go of his tools and jumped. I stopped breathing. David and I lunged into the wall as Carl sailed through the air and nailed a perfect gymnast's dismount on a snow ledge. Flexing his knees and thrusting his arms out, he stayed in balance and didn't even weight the rope. "Pure action superhero shit," I thought. Minutes of deep breathing passed.

Carl made his way back to us, and David turned to me. "Right then, now it's your turn."

To this day, that pillar remains one of the hardest trials that I've had on ice. I only got up it by clipping Carl's in-situ axes for protection, then weighting one of my tools, twenty feet higher, to place a screw. I pulled over the top with my heart hammering. It took the remainder of the day to get us, and our packs, up that blue column of ice.

I woke cold to the bone. The top of my homemade bivy sack had slipped down, and my shoulder had melted a hollow into the back wall of our cramped snow cave. Water saturated my sleeping bag. I punched my arms down my body over and over. The shivering came again, and I clenched my body into a fist. I had to find some warmth. I had to sleep. I prayed for dawn.

Finally, the next morning, the sun's heat radiated into my dark clothing. One hundred and thirty feet overhead, Carl was tacked on to a silver strip of ice. Higher up, a rock pillar rose like the handle of a sword affixed to a gleaming silver blade. The stone glowed in an aura of oblique light, and we envisioned it as a direct finish to the summit.

Then *crack*! The air vibrated with the whir of a large object accelerating. I glanced up: The belly of a cornice was bearing down on Carl.

"Avalanche!" I wailed, and the sky exploded. I dove forward, weighting my tools as the chunks thumped into the snow all around me. Something like a sledgehammer smacked into my right shoulder. Pinpricks of hot, white light scattershot through black. I slid six inches before my body snapped to and flexed harder into the slope. I stopped. The roar drew off down the mountain and hushed into a hiss.

Carl was still on the ice—white from helmet to front point—but still attached. Since he and David were both OK, we decided to keep going. But my shoulder blade was blue, stiff, and throbbing, and I was out of the leading. I hung back and followed, riding the Jumars on the steep sections. It was marvelous to watch how well David and Carl worked as a team. David's fox eyes twinkled, and he said to Carl, "Climb like a beast, man."

They hadn't mastered the mountain. Instead they'd come to know and accept their place on its side.

That afternoon the storm began, and that night I pumped my limbs inside our snow cave, willing myself to stop shivering. I felt cornered by the dark, the wall pressed against my back, and for a moment I wondered whether this was how the world looked to Steven, everywhere, all the time. Through my sodden sleeping bag, I felt only the bottomless cold of the mountain. I shivered and fought and prayed, once more, for the sun.

Heavy snowfall obscured Monday's dawn. Our dream of climbing the rock pillar was out. We simply needed to survive. Late that day, we traversed through the twenty-ninth hour of continuous storm, striving for an escape to the ridgeline of Mount Fay. Waves of spin-drift slapped across my face. Snow, fine as ground glass, pushed into all the openings in my clothing. Ice crystals pressed like cold metal against my neck and the insides of my wrists. I turned out from the mountain and began screaming obscenities into the driving snow, challenging the storm.

I wanted perfection in my alpinism, and I was given this. This is what you dream; this is what you get.

I spent what was left in my lungs and crumpled back into the slope. Carl caught up with me, waited for ten heartbeats and then said, "Hey, man, it don't gotta be fun to be fun."

Perfect. I had to laugh.

At dusk we dug one last snow cave. The fuel was gone. Dinner was a box of candies split three ways. Sealed within our white vault, we talked about life, and I told them about Steven. They listened and prompted me to continue. But a brother in trouble was too big a problem inside our cave, and the best that they could do was to be with me. They put me between them, but the cold still tried to get my core.

We hit the ridgeline early the next morning and spent all of Tuesday retreating. There was high comedy crossing Moraine Lake: I would lift my leg with both hands and scrape it onto the fluffy surface of the six-foot-deep snowpack. Carl would grab my hips and vault me over my foot, which would punch belly-button-deep into the snow, and then we'd repeat, hundreds and hundreds of times.

Out of the leading with a bruised and battered right shoulder blade, I ride the Jumars on the east face of Mount Fay. Photo: David Cheesmond

We finally got to Dave and Carl's skis cached at the cook shelter and I staggered out on foot behind them. The only food we could get in Lake Louise at l:00 a.m. on Wednesday was potato chips from the bar.

"Don't worry, man," David said. He leaned against the open door of the van. "It will all be OK. I don't understand my brother either."

I swayed up the steps to Sparta. Jackie was there, and she drew me a hot bath and gently helped me into it. The hallucinations were magnificent. Four hours of sleep, and then I had to move that same day from the house where Steven and I had lived for four months. All that time we'd spent there seemed suffused into the walls in a form of physical remembrance, like the faint patinas of evaporation that ring a Mason jar.

Ten days later I laid inside my sleeping bag for twenty-four hours inside a snow cave one-third of the way up the 4,300-foot unclimbed northeast face of Mount Chephren. Carl Tobin and George Lowe lay in the cave with me as snow streamed from the sky outside and massive spindrift avalanches rumbled down the face like passing freight trains. We felt the reverberations of the passing avalanches in the snow that entombed us.

George had pried five days out of his busy schedule to come up and climb with Dave Cheesmond and Carl. Both had been team members of his Kangshung Face of Mount Everest six months earlier, where George's ability and drive had cracked the overhanging buttress that foots the Kangshung. The team named the 3,500-foot vertical layering of tawny slate and obsidian black colored rock the Lowe Buttress in deference to George. David couldn't get time off of work and he and Carl vouched my climbing skills to George and I found myself tying in with the greatest North American alpinist of all time.

I was twenty-four and George was forty and when I suggested that he use the shovel blade to square the wall of our snow cave to the floor he barked in a high nasal voice that sounded like someone massaging a balloon with damp hands, "I know what to do!" It was the same squeaky voice that I'd heard earlier in the day when I got the immortal Lowe line from the eternally boyish George, "Barry! Can you get any pitons in up there?"

Carl, who called him 'Boy George,' had described George's voice as squealing brake pads and I could hear it. The persistent and bull-doggish George had put up new routes on many of the Canadian Rockies greatest faces: Deltaform, Temple, Alberta, Geikie. His 1975 first ascent of the north face of North Twin with Chris Jones had become as mythical as Beowulf slaying Grendel.

We got to know each other better inside the sanctum of our cave. "It sounds like you've done all the prerequisite routes," he said kindly when I proudly told him what I'd been climbing, especially so the north face of Mount Alberta where I had, like him, led most of the headwall pitches.

At the end of that stormbound day I negotiated for descending come morning. I would have just enough time to get back to Canmore to attend one of our Everest Light meetings. Carl and George acquiesced, but not before George said something prophetic to me, "You should stay up here, this is where it's at." George was willing to sit out the storm for as long as it took to get up the face. I felt that I was descending for a higher form of climbing. I was wrong.

Kevin got voted onto Everest Light and on April 5 he, James Blench, and I skied toward the northeast face of Mount Chephren for the second attempt. Starting in the couloir that Boy George, Carl, and I had, we transferred into a parallel gully about 1,000 feet up. Two thousand feet up the face we dug a snow cave. It started to storm that night.

Snow swarmed from the sky like cottonwood seeds as I squirmed up the opening chimney of the crux pitch. Thirty-five feet higher I tensioned left across a blank slab, my crampons grating like hockey blades on marble. I nailed up a thin overhanging crack on the adjacent wall standing in étriers. Arching backward from my highest knifeblade placement I got a fist-sized cam in, and then the piton sprang and with no warning I plummeted downward toward the highway. It felt like I'd been suspended by an electromagnet when someone had cut the power. I accelerated to the *pinging* of pitons sounding like ricocheting bullets. Thirty feet charged by in a rush. I hammered into the wall beside Kevin and gear clanged down onto me like a free falling length of chain.

"Holy fuck!" I spat, grabbing at the rigid rope to right myself.

"Fuck, Blanch, are you OK?" Kevin shouted. His strong hands locking his belay fast.

"Ya, I think so."

"Good, well do not do that again. OK, buddy?" My body vibrated with adrenalin. It was such a serious place to fall.

I went back up and melted the pitons into the crack with numerous powerful blows from my hammer. I managed to step from aid by pounding the pick of my Sérac Sabre ax in as a piton and aiding up it to mantel onto the adze then stand on it. A few feet higher I clung to a flake while free climbing. The flake fractured off and I was airborne again! I'd never fallen in the alpine before and now I was plummeting for a second time on the same pitch!

My right hand found the yellow étrier clipped to the bottom of my Sabre and I slapped into the wall and stopped. I'd managed to catch my fall!

"Blanch! You've got to stop doing that shit! I'm serious, man!" Wally wailed.

"I know, man! It's fucking hard up here! Just watch me." I didn't fall again and finally made it to a ledge to anchor and try and calm my frazzled mind.

Kevin and James came up on Jumars as snow continued to fall. Wally took the rack and attacked the offwidth crack above us. The rope kept paying out as he uncovered wide jams and holds beneath the masks of snow. He climbed with the confidence of a matador who knows he can't be gored. We dug our second snow cave on the first of two huge transverse ledges that cut clean across the northeast face of Mount Chephren from its southeast ridge to its northern one.

The bellowing roar of the MSR XGK stove had waned to a feeble sputtering whisper.

"I don't think that the stove is getting enough oxygen," I said, "I think we need to punch some holes through the wall."

"I can't see that," James said. "There has to be enough oxygen in here."

"I don't know, James." Kevin said.

"Trust me, you guys, there's enough oxygen in here," James replied.

I stabbed a couple of holes through the snow blocks that we'd chinked up to seal the portal of the cave and the stove raged to life like a signal flare.

"Well, I would have never thought..." James said.

"That's because your brain wasn't getting enough oxygen either, man," I said.

"No shit."

"You guys, we have to go down. It's been snowing heavily for over twenty-four hours," James pleaded from the arched vault of the far end of the snow cave. Our packs were packed and James sat on his like a hobbit on a low bench. Anxiety had raised his voice an octave and drawn gaunt lines around his sea blue eyes.

"Ya, but James, we could get this thing done," Wally stated. "I mean, I'll go down if that is really what you guys want to do, but I know that we can get up this, and that's what I am saying."

"Kev, James did his Level I avalanche course this winter. He knows what he's talking about with the snow. I think that we should go down."

I belayed James out across the snow ledge leading to the north ridge of the mountain, six ropelengths away. Kevin took slack on his rope and punched steps up left to where he arched his neck and set his jaw firm, and protruding, from the cowl of his hood. He looked like a gothic sculpture, like the Dark Knight staring into the gray gloom of the Gotham sky. Clusters of snowflakes fell like ash from a forest fire.

"It's there, Blanch," he told me when he climbed back to my anchor. "I saw it, man. There's a strip of silver ice up there. It's all there, man."

We traversed acres of avalanche-prone slopes crossing the ledge, trying to stay on the top edge stitching in as much gear as we could. Nothing avalanched with our passing. We rappelled a half dozen times down the north ridge and then walked out from the bulk of Chephren along a mile length of horizontal ridge. At the top of the biggest gully that fell from the ridge toward the Mistaya River, and the highway, we started bum sliding and minutes and minutes of elevation hissed by under our nylon-clad asses.

And then Wally, who was always the fastest on almost all mountain terrain, bum sliding not withstanding, was up on his feet and waving his arms wildly, "Stop! Stop! Holy fuck, stop!"

He was laughing when I ground to halt, like someone sliding into home plate, above him. Below was 150 feet of vertical blue water ice.

"Holy shit, Wally, I'm glad you didn't launch over that," I said giddily.

"Me too, Blanch. That wouldn't have been good. It would definitely wreck a guy's day."

We rappelled the ice, bum slid more, and then postholed into the timber. The postholing got increasingly harder as the forest floor flattened out and the snowpack swallowed us to the waist with every step. Wally and I broke four big boughs from an Engelmann Spruce and lashed them to our boots with prusik cords to try to make snowshoes. It was an act of desperation and it didn't work. James just kept wallowing toward the river, and then the highway.

My Galibier leather boots dug into the thick dry duff on the forest floor. Dust and sweat mixed with 99 percent DEET mosquito repellent ran into my eyes and I swathed the burn of it aside with the sleeve of my plaid shirt. I'd tied orange flagging tape tight around my wrists to keep the black flies from buzzing up onto my forearms and biting.

My boots, that I'd bought in the Hostel Shop in 1979, were on their last legs, but they scraped eight inches of duff away to reveal mineral soil and I slammed the thin, tempered-steel blade of my tree spade into the sandy ground then pried the handle back and forth to open a channel for the root plug of the seedling spruce that I held in my left hand. I bent over and pushed the tree in deep, then stood and stomped the soil tight to it with the heel of my right foot. I advanced five feet in a measured stride over the charred ground and I repeated the process. Tree planting, twenty-five cents a tree and I could put from one to two thousand seedlings into the ground a day.

It was my second spring doing this work around Ootsa Lake in north central British Columbia and I hoped to make my share of our Rakaposhi budget in the two weeks that I had to work. Kevin and Gregg had come north with me and were hoping to do the same.

The burned-out logging block looked like a war zone and Kevin and I marched row on row up and down it putting the wee trees in the ground twelve to fourteen hours a day. I was better at it than Wally and he pushed himself hard trying to keep my pace. One of the blackened and pulverized boughs tripped Wally and ten days of Irish rage exploded in concussive waves of profanity. He wielded his tree spade like a battle-ax arcing it high overhead and raining blows onto the offending branch until it was shattered to toothpicks.

"There, Blanch, that bough will never trip anyone ever again," he stated, smiling smugly.

PLAYLIST
Police   *Walking in Your Footsteps*
UB40   *Red, Red Wine*

Chapter 16

RAKAPOSHI

ON MAY 19, 1984, David Cheesmond, Chris Dale, Tim Friesen, Vern Sawatzky, Steve Langley, Kevin, Gregg, and I boarded a British Airways flight at the Calgary Airport. One of Kevin's sisters, Maureen, had a girlfriend who wore a large Rakaposhi shirt as a dress. A leather belt cinched her hourglass figure and bought the shirt to a miniskirt level. She looked so hot. The farewell kiss that she bestowed on each of us felt like we were going off to war and I marveled at what women will do for men who could be, potentially, risking their lives.

David walked onto the flight in his size twelve Koflach double-plastic boots and expedition outerwear and we all carried on our ice axes and crampons as a way of getting more weight on board for nothing.

"Sir, I think you should check all of this stuff," the flight steward suggested, a bemused knowing look in his eyes.

"No way," David replied. "I did that last time I went to the Himalaya and your airline lost my boots and climbing suit. Never again."

The steward gathered our ice axes and arranged for the captain to keep them in the cockpit. Fellow passengers looked at David like he was Ronald McDonald as he clomped down the aisle.

Our flight was bound for London, Abu Dhabi, Dubai, Karachi, and Islamabad. We had a three-and-a-half-hour layover in Heathrow.

"I'm having the breakfast of champions," Steve announced. Then proceeded to down six pints of Guinness Stout and sleep all the way to Abu Dhabi.

Gregg, aka King, jugging above Camp III
on the leviathan north ridge of Rakaposhi.
The Hunza River is visible 14,000 feet below.
Photo: Barry Blanchard

Guys with dark turbans and machine guns lined the tarmac there and Israeli nationals were not allowed to leave the airplane. Kevin, Gregg, and I chose to stay onboard too, in protest.

"I didn't want to see their fucking country anyway," I said.

Rawalpindi was hot when we landed and the airport was as chaotic as the market scene in *Raiders of the Lost Ark*. Our wee Welsh teammate, Chris, was a geophysicist and had connections through the oil industry. One of his colleagues, Mel, who was overseeing some drilling in Pakistan, met us at the airport in a Suburban and ushered us through sweltering dust and diesel fumes to Mrs. Davies Guest House. The last remnants of the Raj: worn wooden table markers with gold-leaf numbers painted on by hand in a precise and bold font, yard-high window fans that blew air over trays of water to cool our rooms from the 117° F outside, claw-footed bath tubs. (Steven happily submerged in the one in our room declaring, "Baths, squire! In the colonies we take baths.")

Five in the morning was the only time it was cool enough to do anything. Mel told us that would be when he was up getting ready to golf. Gregg and I started running in the mornings. Wally hung in with us for the first couple of kilometers the first morning, but begged off after that. David, Tim, and Chris hired a 1957 Morris Minor taxi one morning to videotape Gregg and me running, Chris sitting in its open trunk and shooting from there. The early rising Pakistanis—all males— gazed on us like we were from another planet, and an insane planet at that.

The Canadian government flew a Hercules to Pakistan twice a year as part of a UN agreement and the ship was half empty most of the time. David had arranged for us to get some free freight with the Canadian Army. A month before we left, Kevin and Chris went to a car wash with ten fifty-gallon blue plastic barrels that had contained herring and pressure washed them for a long time. The soldiers had enthusiastically received our stuffed barrels at the Canadian Forces Base in Calgary, inventoried them all dutifully, and there they were waiting for us at the airport in Pakistan.

Sourcing fuel for our MSR stoves was far more challenging and our liaison officer, Captain Fahrid, an immaculately groomed man of medium height and weight who looked like a dark version of Freddy

Mercury, eventually got us some jet fuel from the airport. Other than that we had regular leaded gasoline.

The Canadian embassy in Islamabad warmly received us, and they hosted a reception for us where we met the ambassador and his wife. The embassy staff gifted us a life-size cardboard cutout of a Royal Canadian Mounted Policeman dressed in full scarlets. He was a promotional prop sent out to all our embassies. Dave immediately dubbed him "Lance Corporal Caruthers."

"Why Caruthers?" I asked.

"Yes," Dave answered in his high South African accent, "because when a call of distress comes from the front line the answer is always, 'Send up Caruthers, we must have Lance Corporal Caruthers!'"

It became our battle cry and was uttered often over the next two months. We thanked the ambassador and his staff for a fine evening and left to ready for an early departure the next morning. Our five days of formality with the Ministry of Tourism and packing preparations were done; tomorrow we would start toward the Karakorum Highway.

"It's a whorehouse on wheels," Steve exclaimed as we hopped onto our Silver Bullet bus two hours before dawn. Hand-tooled tin facades paneled the old Bedford bus with all the audacity and extravagance of the cow-horn Cadillacs I'd seen in the Stampede Parade when I was a boy growing up in Calgary; those Caddies had silver six-guns for door handles. The Pakistanis call the Beddies "Jingle Buses." The man hours put into metal and plastic adornments, paintings, and plush cloth and vinyl was hard to comprehend. But the eight of us (Fahrid travelled with us) and all of our barrels and duffels fit in and off we chugged into the Punjabi Plain.

Steve was the first to get butt sick. "I'm not dealing with this," he quipped popping a couple pills into his mouth.

"What did you just take?" I asked.

"Imodium, it's a bowel paralyzer. I'll keep popping them until my guts deal with whatever's rotting them. I'm not living on the toilet."

"I don't take any drugs that I don't have to," I stated naively. At that point in my life I had been to Europe and Mexico and I hadn't gotten sick in either.

Ten hours into our boiling bus ride I got the shit kicked out of me, literally. There was a bubbling percolation that quivered my lower guts then it felt like a tenpin bowling ball had been hurled at my midriff as my bottom fell out. I hobbled to the front of the bus clamping my ass cheeks shut and pleading for a stop. I squatted in the low bush beside the highway, liquid feces splattered out of me like a garden hose fit with a wide spray nozzle. Each contraction and blow out felt like I was being cored, again and again. Five minutes in I was hyperventilating to deal with the pain of what felt like tassels of barbed wire being pulled through me.

I sprinted from the bus a dozen more times before we stopped for the night at an inn built on the site of an ancient caravanserai. Pale as wax and drenched with sweat I trembled in the corner of the restaurant battling each mouthful of salty soup and sip of flat cola. The rest of my teammates gobbled down rice and chicken and joked and laughed...at me. Chris and Steve giggled as they came in close and shot portraits of my agony. I came to believe in Imodium during that dark night of the butt in Pakistan.

The next day I ran from the bus for the eleventh time and squatted and groaned. My anus was raw from repetitively wiping away the acidic burn of my spraying. I wiped and swore and rose to my first view of the planetary bulk of Nanga Parbat.

"Holy crap," I blurted, then smiled at the irony of holding a roll of crepe-like toilet paper in my hand. It was my first true smile in a day.

We jingled and chugged from the Indus River to follow the Gilgit River close to Jaglot. My teammates ate a hearty lunch in Gilgit and I tried plain white rice and flat Coke. Standing in the courtyard of the hotel restaurant I looked west to the Hindu Kush then did a quarter turn to look south into the Himalaya, another quarter turn and I was looking east to the Karakorum, three of the greatest mountain ranges on earth.

Our Beddie backtracked to the Hunza River and the southwestern end of Rakaposhi came into view. For the next hour, as we rounded onto the northern flank of the mountain, fluted ridges, buttresses, and hanging glaciers elongated and amassed on a scale that most of us had never seen before, save for David and Steve who had been in the Himalayan mountains of Tibet and Nepal.

At Ghulmet we got out of the van and gawked slack-jawed at the summit. It lay seven horizontal miles away and 19,000 feet above us. The face was near twelve and a half miles wide and the north ridge sliced toward the top like the leading edge of a colossal triangular yacht sail. Stepped glaciers and séracs stacked either side of the ridge like the blocks of the great pyramid of Khufu that have lost their façade of limestone casting and sit bare as a skeletal staircase. Rakaposhi is said to mean "Shining Wall" in the local Burushaski language and it indeed glowed white with glaciation as our team stood and gazed.

"Oh my God!" Gregg exclaimed, and then he started laughing.

"It looks pretty damn big," I said. We'd come with the idea of climbing a new route up the north face, if it looked feasible. From where I was standing counting a half dozen sérac barriers, it was looking suicidal. The north ridge had been attempted in '71 and '73 by expeditions led by Dr. Karl Herrligkoffer, the same guy who had led the 1970 expedition to the Rupal Face of Nanga Parbat that saw Reinhold and Gunther Messner summit, and Gunther lost to an avalanche on the descent. The north ridge of Rakaposhi was climbed in '79 by a Japanese team from the University of Waseda who fixed 16,500 feet of rope.

"I don't like the look of those séracs," Wally said. "If you ask me, the north ridge is the line, that's the way to go."

"Yes, it is beginning to look that way," David said. "But I think we should get up close and take a better look."

Fahrid arranged for us to camp in a field right on the Karakorum Highway and we pitched our tents and began organizing our porter loads. It was May 26, 1984. The next day both Kevin and Gregg erupted with butt sickness. Gregg shared a tent with me, and his Italian lineage and Latin blood came to the fore as he suffered. Plaintiff wailing and moaning bellowed from his side of the tent as he lay on his back thrashing left and right, his long arms slapping out like strands of kelp beached by waves. One would have thought that he was gut shot—which in a sense he was.

"King, do you have to make so much noise?" I asked. I was feeling better, having passed some solid feces just that morning.

"I'm suffering, man! I believe in being in my suffering."

"But I'm suffering now too, because of you!"

"Aaahhhaaa!" And he thrashed into a horizontal crucifix of moaning agony.

"Nuuurrrssee!" Steve sobbed from close by outside doing his best Dudley Moore impersonation.

"Fuck off, you guys! I'm dying over here! Aaahhhaaa!"

Black flies filled the air and buzzed mightily around the growing mound in our shit pit.

"Just takes one of those little shit-eaters to land in some dung and then settle in your food," Wally said, and then he pulled his nylon running shorts out from the wedgie they'd gained on his butt crack.

David, Steve, Tim, Chris, and Vern all busied themselves with weighing and numbering porter loads, while much of the male populace of Ghulmet, the young and the old, squatted and watched for hour upon hour.

On the morning of May 29 we were ready to make our one-day approach to base camp. The shortness, and cheapness, of the approach was one of the reasons we had chosen to come to Rakaposhi. We had all of our loads numbered but realized we hadn't come up with a way to number our porters with the same load number.

"Right, then," David said. "We will mark the load number onto the porters' foreheads with felt-tipped marker."

All around our kitchen tent jaws dropped lower than they had when we saw the north face of Rakaposhi. Ninety seconds of dumbfounded disbelief passed, and then I asked, "Are you fucking serious, Cheese?"

"Yes, it will be a failsafe way of accounting each porter to his assigned load."

"Ya, but this isn't South Africa, man, we can't mark numbers on peoples foreheads with magic marker."

"Ah...yes...yes, I suppose that's right."

Wally's cheeks went crimson and he started shaking with laughter, "You honestly wanted to write numbers on our porter's foreheads! Ha! That is too..." and he couldn't finish because he buckled at the waist crying with laughter. It was contagious and we all cracked into guffaws that left us bent at the waist with our arms wrapped around our guts and tears rolling down crinkled crimson cheeks. We settled for recording each porter's name beside his load number in a book that Fahrid managed.

The midday sun was high and hot. In a dimpled hollow of runneled and retreating snow the lead porters shucked their loads and squatted.

"They say that this is Base Camp," Fahrid translated.

"No way," David chirped. "Base Camp is 1,000 feet higher!"

More porters lumbered up and dropped their loads. David argued in translation through Fahrid.

"This is crap," David related to the rest of us. "The porters are saying that this is German Base Camp and 1,000 feet higher is Japanese Base Camp and they want more money to carry up there.

"But they've only done a half a day of work," TP stated drawing his chin back toward his chest.

It was noon and we already had a porter strike. Doubly so because it was obvious that the porters had agreed to play this card long ago and they got the last laugh because after an hour of argument we decided, "Fuck it, we'll carry the stuff up there ourselves."

Six days of good weather passed shouldering loads and slogging up 1,000 feet of snow. I listened to *Synchronicity* by the Police on my Walkman for many a trip.

A hard hour or two up and we'd empty our packs and sit on them like sleds for a wild, hollering two-minute ride back down at twenty-five miles per hour. By day two we'd scraped a one-and-a-half-foot-deep luge track into the snow and Wally and I were commonly launching for up to twenty feet off of the three jumps in the track. Getting down was a blast, getting up was a lot of work. Dave, Chris, Tim, and Vern did a couple of trips a day, while Wally, Gregg, and I managed three loads a day. Then I found lightness in the exertion and the altitude and went for four and my back went off for the first time in my life. A hard nub the size of the tip of my ring finger extruded just left of my lower thoracic spine. It felt like a metal rod had been inserted down my spinal cord. Vern examined me and called it "one big fat muscle spasm."

"I'll give you some muscle relaxants and you shouldn't carry anymore loads until it calms down."

"Do you think that I've screwed up my trip?" The poison of that thought lay like ether inside my skull and I willed a calm onto the panic rising in my soul. Would I exist if I could not climb?

"You should be fine in a couple of days, you just have to let the muscles come out of spasm."

Wally and Gregg brought up the last couple of loads and on June 3 everything was in our Base Camp, 12,000 feet on a snowy knoll bulging off of the eastern moraine of the Ghulmet Glacier. To celebrate we stood Lance Corporal Caruthers up in the middle of camp and beside him the mascot TP had packed into one of our barrels back in Canada: a pink flamingo.

The next day we found a way onto the glacier and a good line of travel up its lateral trough to where a broad couloir ascended several thousand feet to gain the north ridge proper. A jutting rockband the size of a six-story building leaned out protectively from the foot of the couloir and we established a dumping-off point there as the altitude smacked all of us and going all the way to the ridge on those first trips wasn't happening. We pitched one of our wee Integral Designs tents there and named it Cache Creek after a truck stop on the Trans-Canada Highway in southern British Columbia.

––––––––––

"I didn't know what the hell it was," Chris grinned a Cheshire, and continued, "There was a hell of a racket and I climbed out of my tent and saw a shadow at the food barrels and I thought it was someone ripping us off so I shouted 'Hey! Get the fuck out of here!' And that is when it growled and I crapped myself and dove back inside the tent."

"Ya," TP added, "It growled, and then you could hear it crashing off."

"We went back out with headlamps, but it was gone," Chris added. "We could see its paw prints in the snow and see where it bit into our cookies. It ate five packs! It must have been a Himalayan brown bear."

"You have got to be shitting me. How in the hell can it survive around here?" Wally said.

"I shit thee not. It must have enough space," Chris replied. "And I think that it may come back as it likes cookies."

"I like cookies," I said.

"So do I," Chris added. "Fahrid went down to the valley this morning with our kitchen boy to get a shotgun. Chef Ali figures the bear will come back too." (Chef Ali was our jovial cook.)

And Yogi did visit us the next two nights running and ate a bunch more of our food. Fahrid never did get a shot off, which spoke to his judgment as a captain, knowing that discharging a scattergun in a tight camp at night could only end badly.

The north flank of Rakaposhi is massive and we'd decided before we left Canada that we didn't have enough experience to climb it in alpine style. We brought 2,000 feet of rope and planned to climb in "capsule" style, meaning that we would fix our rope ahead of us, ferry all our supplies to a new camp at rope's end, and then clean our ropes from behind us and repeat. June 9 we established Camp I at 15,400 feet on a broad glacial ledge on top of the ridgeline.

Chris was not doing well with the altitude and on June 15 we all said goodbye to his cherubic ginger mug as he'd decided to leave the expedition and salvage his vacation in Britain. He is a practical man and it was a practical decision yet saddening for all of us because we lost one-seventh of our team, 15 percent of whatever we were.

The next day the six of us: David, TP, Steve, Kevin, Gregg, and I occupied Camp I. Vern would wait in Base Camp with Fahrid, Chef Ali, and our cook boy. Gregg, Wally, and I hauled up the last of our fixed line, there was no longer a lifeline to Base Camp; we were committed to the ridge and that felt liberating and exciting.

Our three yellow and green turtle tents sat on the snow platforms that we'd dug for them. Two human heads stuck out of each one, all spellbound by the sun setting over the Karakorum and Hindu Kush. Shafts of orange light fanning through a quilt of red-tinged gray cloud, jagged peaks stabbing through the underbelly of the clouds and pointing higher into the darkening sky. Several planets and the brightest stars were already visible, harbingering the night.

We were all feeling the raw rush of being small humans on the edge of a huge mountain and our banter was jocular and ribald as Steve had declared us in the "sexual" stage of the expedition; when all we want to talk about is what we will be doing to our wives and partners when we get home. Next, he tells us, will be the "anal" stage and we will talk, at length, about our bowel movements, or lack of them, and how we yearn for normality. Lastly is the "oral" stage when we won't care if we ever have sex again, or if we ever have a solid dump again, all that will matter in life is eating the food that we want to eat.

"But Steve, how can you go to strip shows?" Gregg asked. "Don't you think that it is degrading for the woman?"

"No, not at all. I think that it gives them a sense of worth." And he said it in a monotone with a straight face and we all laughed at the audacity of it and then there was a pregnant pause and Wally came cackling and bounding out of his tent completely contained in his sleeping bag like a massive blue Gore-Tex salmon jumping back to the source. He managed three pogo stick leaps before he flopped into the snow laughing and panting. Everybody howled with joy. Then Wally thrashed out of his bag, sprinted sock footed through the snow, and dragged a reluctant and resistant Steve from the tent they shared and into the snow. Kevin was like a messiah of joy and Stephen Robert Langley was his prophet, a reluctant one, but a prophet none-theless. In that magic moment Steve became, 'Steve Langley, The Reluctant Prophet.' Amen.

Gregg looked like a man slowly succumbing to quicksand. He and I were off to carry loads to the end of our fixed line, and then fifty feet away from Camp I the bridge over a crevasse fragmented under his feet and he fell to his right hip, He slowly began sinking in, the weight of his pack like a pair of strong hands trying to drag him under. We

Me at Camp I on Rakaposhi the night that Steve was christened 'The Reluctant Prophet.' Photo: Gregg Cronn weren't attached to the fixed line yet and Gregg grabbed it and took a wrap around his left forearm and then he got his ax into his right hand and flailed at the crusty ice above the crevasse. I stood stupidly and watched; going any closer could see me in it too.

"C'mon, King, you can get out of that thing," I encouraged him.

"My pack is dragging me in," he panted, anxiety and exertion slurring his words.

Then he got a stick with his pick and grunted and heaved mightily and was able to scissor his legs back to the surface and thrash backward out of the hole.

"Shit, man, that was spooky," I said. "Let's stay clipped in with a jug attached from now on, eh?"

"Ya," he panted, "it's not always the falls or the avalanches that get people."

He was right. In my mind I saw Gregg slowly going under, weight overcoming his grip strength and then the plummet into the black cold slot that for all intent and purpose was the underworld to us as we stood staring into the dark portal his hips had etched. Blue sky above, a cold death below, I squatted and picked up the fixed line and clipped in my locking carabiner and snapped my Jumar on tight.

We occupied Camp II, 17,500 feet, on June 16 and Camp III, 18,300 feet, two days later.

The apex of the ridge, at Camp III, was a defined arête of ice that looked like a serrated knife when we could see it. Cream-roll cornices the size of cargo vans clung to, and masked, much of it. At the end of our 2,000 feet of line, one of the migrating cornices was the only game in town for a camp. The prevailing wind was from the east and the cornices slowly rolled to the west, or they fractured and failed and fell away catastrophically. We pitched our three tents on the horizontal top of last year's cornice where it sat, having crept down the ice ten feet.

This year's cornice stood proud above us like a massive rooster's comb. Three feet in front of our tents all of the cornicing had fallen away and we rappelled from our ice anchors to gain the ice of the ridge and progress.

After a couple of days atop our cream roll we were feeling pretty good about ourselves. Our Canadian flag had three feet of hoist by six feet of fly and we'd hung it from ice screws above our three wee tents. Our line was fixed out ahead and we were into our rhythm of getting up in the morning and fixing, or carrying, all day long, every day; and then my foot punched through the floor of our camp and I discover that we had a basement! The cornice was hollow! David and I drilled in a half dozen more ice screws.

Every night at 6:00 p.m. we would check in with Vern over a brick-sized walkie-talkie that David had bought at Radio Shack before we left Canada. Vern would have six cassette tapes keyed to his picks of the day. Duck tape held the push-to-talk button open on his walkie and he would play the songs over small speakers hooked up to his Walkman: "Vern's Hot Six Pack at Six."

The day that I discovered the basement on our cream roll camp was our last day there and when Vern cued up "Red Red Wine" by UB40 we all jumped to our feet and began dancing on top of our panel-van-sized cornice. It somehow stayed put via a contact bond to the sloping ice of the mountain as the sun blazed golden and low from the west. I felt like I was partying onboard a space station.

We occupied Camp IV, 19,500 feet above sea level, on June 23, and two days later Camp V, 21,500 feet. The storm started that night and by morning we were immersed in the gray with snow falling constantly. Steve and I lay in our tent, the highest of the three, with the edge of Gregg and Wally's tent three feet horizontally from us yet five feet lower. Dave and TP's tent sat below with the same rise and tread. All six of us within arm's reach of each other but each couple isolated like survivors in separate life rafts.

For two days spindrifting snow pissed down onto our tents with the consistency of a statuesque marble cherub urinating into a European fountain. Our tent largely sheltered the two below. We'd wait until the dull gray line of accumulated snow was in danger of collapsing our tent and one of us would suit up and step out into the storm to shovel the tent out. And the dull gray line would again start its hourglass creep up the dull yellow Gore-Tex.

In the heat of the day, snow would melt to droplets and one would gain enough mass to run down the skin of the tent gobbling up all other droplets in its path. Water found its way into the tent seams and into the tent where everything was damp. My mind felt like a dishrag that froze in the night and cracked with the fear of never escaping our sinking tent.

Midday on day two I snapped. The gray line was slowly pressing onto my left shoulder, crowding into my face.

"Fucking fuck this shit!" I bellowed and then I spun to face the line and began pounding it with my fists and smashing it back with my forearms like I was an ancient pugilist, my forearms wrapped in cestus. I wanted to kill the storm. Within forty-five seconds I collapsed and I just wanted to breathe.

Steve waited another forty-five seconds and then he asked me, "So what was it like growing up in Calgary, Barry?" I had to laugh at myself.

"Right, then, we will not have enough food and fuel to sit out any more storm days," David yelled over the patter and hum of the storm. "We will have to start climbing into the storm if we are going to have any chance of making the top."

"Send up Caruthers!" Steve bellowed from inside our damp gray tent, and then he choked on his chuckling.

The knife-edge perfection of the ridge ended against a bulkhead of tawny rock that towered over our camp for 1,500 feet, not that we could see it anymore. It took us three days to fix the rockband and all of our fixed line was left in place there to facilitate our retreat.

On June 30 we climbed toward our Camp VI, 23,000 feet, the six of us were divided onto our two lead ropes, three men per rope. We had been on the ridge for fourteen days and it had been storming for the last seven. Now the storm was intensifying.

The wind mauled us as we hacked out tent ledges tight to an exceptionally steep wall of ice one hundred feet high. I knew that if we tried to hold the tent open to erect it, it would balloon and be sheared from our frigid hands. I anchored my end of rope and squirmed inside the tent to keep it pressed to the mountain like a bivy sac. Steve jabbed the two aluminum poles in and I extended them and arced them into place.

Closing the small Velcro tabs around the poles took minutes. The wind raged and shuttered the tent like a flag in a gale. Frost fell in quivering fields onto my hands. I'd lose the ability to hold the Velcro and have to scrape my damp, senseless hands back into gloves and wait until I could feel again. We finally got the tent up and Steve scraped his way in.

I was dehydrated and hungry but there was no way to cook inside the tent as the fumes from the jet fuel were poisonous. The wind screamed and lighting the stove outside, and then keeping it lit, was impossible. It was difficult to see out there. Steve and I settled for chewing on snow and laying in our bags and holding our arms against the walls of the tent to help it keep its shape as feathers of frost grew and shattered and sprinkled down on us.

Midnight, the winds abated and I was able to get the stove started outside our tent door. Two hours of brewing and eating, the glow of my headlamp and the blue-orange flare of the stove the only halos of light in the suffocating blackness of the night storm. I twisted the burner off and turned the pot upside down and placed it over the stove burner to protect it. A stuffsack full of ice chunks weighed the pot down.

Two hours later the wind came screaming back and I heard and felt it turbine against our tent bulging the fabric inward and raining frost shards onto us and then I heard the pot and the windscreen lifted and slapped against the tent before clanging off down the dark black mountain. Gone forever.

Discus-sized hunks of ice the color of white marble sheared from each and every tool placement I made. It was dawn and it was cold, -13° F. The ice climbed like frozen glass; I had to swing and swing and eventually the sensation of biting insects left my hands and they just went numb. I had to warm them or they would be frostbitten.

The screw whined like the dry axles of a passing freight car and I had to brace the pick of my ice ax into its eye and crank like I was breaking the bite of a lug nut. Twisting the last inch in I saw the shaft of the Chouinard bend, but I got my rope clipped in and given that security I spent minutes swinging one arm, and then the other, until blood blazed into my fingers with a pain that felt like my hands had been laid on a barbeque.

David shouted encouragement up to me, "You look like Jeff Lowe up there, man!" It was a twist on a favorite punch line of his— we'd be climbing and David would look down and say, "Look! It's Jeff! He's coming up, and he's soloing!" (A jibe at one of North America's best, and most publicized, alpinists.)

The explosively fragile hypercooled ice demanded thuggery and I was coming up with it. Although it wasn't graceful it was effective, and I knew that I was climbing appropriately and climbing well. That made me feel competent, especially having my ability equated with Jeff's.

"Thuggery under pressure," I gasped on an outbreath.

Midafternoon, the eighth day of storm, and we were inside the Ping-Pong ball, 23,600 feet above sea level. Base Camp was 11,000 feet below us. I was leading up broad slopes of snow past the occasionally exposed bulk of blue ice that looked like sunken hulls jutting up from the sea. My left-hand tool plunged through a bridge and my chest smacked into the edge of a crevasse. I righted myself and thumped a hole into the bridge with the broadside of my ice ax and then I peered into a huge cleaved and vaulted chamber that sliced back into the glacial flesh of Rakaposhi. "Holy shit guys! You have to see this!"

One hour later we had our three wee tents set up on the snowy floor of the ice cavern. Smooth walls of ice rose in increasing separation for fifty feet to where a snow ceiling spanned fifteen feet wide looking like the under side of a breaking wave captured in a still photo. We'd walked seventy feet into the crevasse and it was perfectly calm and polarly cold, -13° F.

A tranquility settled over us all. It felt like we'd been entrenched in a war and found a mystical door in the trench wall and stepped through to a candlelit cathedral. We'd exited savagery and entered benevolence.

"This place is absolutely amazing," Kevin beamed, his eyes wide open in awe. "It feels holy to me."

"It would feel a whole lot more holy to me if it wasn't so fucking cold," Steve leveled.

The next morning, July 3, we stepped back into the storm.

"I'm worried about TP," Dave said to me, "I think that he's getting altitude sickness." TP had started to slow down, and his cream white skin had changed to chalky. He looked ill.

The storm mellowed to a haze with light snowfall. We'd tied both our ropes together and were ascending as a ropeteam of six. Kevin was leading with David tied in a half ropelength below and me, Gregg, TP, and Steve equally spaced along the line. Glacial features bulged and jutted from the slope and Kevin had traversed to a gully between a bulge and a fin. The metallic clang of his hammer smacking a snow picket rang through the haze like the gonging of an ocean buoy.

The ridge proper was 1,000 feet above and as I looked to it I saw a massive zigzagging line slice across it like it was being cut by a giant pair of tailor's scissors. And then all the snow below the cut line began to slide.

"Avalanche! Avalanche! Avalanche!" I wailed. And then I saw the white surge of it smack into Kev and he disappeared and the rush of the snow roared by. The rope to David went limp and David disappeared in a charging white wall.

I dove down onto my tools and the snow pounded into me and pushed me downslope and every muscle in body tensed and clawed into the mountain. The surge parted around me and thundered off down the mountain and diminished to a roar and then a hiss. David was fifteen feet lower than where he had been and clean lines of failure etched out from him at forty-five-degree angles. The top six inches of snow had slid and I could see everyone except Kevin.

"Where's Kevin!" I wailed. "Where the fuck is Kevin!" I couldn't see my beautiful dear friend Kevin. I panicked, "No! Kev! Kevin!"

There was one anomalous mound of snow in the debris field one hundred feet below David. Suddenly it burst like a killer whale breaching the ocean and there was my fighting Black Irish buddy raging at the world because the avalanche had taken his pack complete with his new camera, sleeping bag, and much of our food and fuel. He was ready to kick someone's ass, looking for a fight. I loved his rage then, loved the fact that he was there matted in snow like a dog and livid and wonderfully alive.

I choked on a sob and said in a quivering voice, "Kevin, oh thank God, Kevin."

We continued and late that day came onto a rounded shoulder of Rakaposhi where the north ridge melded with the east, 24,300 feet.

"I need my sleeping bag liner," TP said, and he looked fragile. The creases in his face were deeper due to dehydration and altitude sickness.

"OK, fucking fine, TP. I'll just use Steve's and Gregg's," Kevin countered—David and I had left our sleeping bag liners lower down. Kev got two of the three liners that were there and the plan was to have him cram into a tent between Gregg and me and hopefully keep warm enough.

"Steve and I have to take Tim down," David said the next morning, "He's got cerebral edema and I think he could die if we don't get him down."

"Fuck," I said.

It was cold and windy, but the sky had cleared. The summit blade of Rakaposhi sliced into the sky and it wore a latticework of fresh white snow. Runnels from point-release avalanches ribbed the snow slopes below and the summit had never been so close yet seemed so far away. We all talked and decided that "the young tigers," as Steve, the Reluctant Prophet, put it, would go for the summit. We had two liters of fuel left and two ropes. David, Steve, and Tim took one liter of fuel and a rope and started back down and it was heartbreaking to see them move away.

The six of us had been living on the edge of Rakaposhi for eighteen days and it felt like we'd left the world below and entered an insular and separate reality of living, eating, and breathing climbing. Now we'd split and half of what we were was returning back to earth.

Gregg, Wally, and I left our tent set up and took a shovel blade. Our plan was to dig in at the base of the summit rockwall and go for it the next day. We began plowing a trough through fresh, knee-deep snow.

Three hours later Gregg battled up a steep black rockband using two points of aid and some impressive mixed moves. Kevin and I jumared, and then Kevin took over, clearing the snow from in front of his chest with scything cuts from the shaft of his ice ax held horizontally by the head and the spike like it was a bark peeler.

Cumulous clouds billowed from the west ridge and then they rounded onto the north flank and crowded in on us like a gang of bulging bullies. Visibility dropped to a couple hundred feet and the summit disappeared. Kevin forced his way over a steep snowbridge, a large black crevasse yawning underfoot. We'd traversed 1,300 feet and there were 1,300 more to the summit rocks: 24,800 feet. Deep basal notes resonated through the snowpack as Gregg and I kicked into Wally's steps. I could feel the snow vibrating.

"This slope is fucking groaning it is so overloaded!" Gregg said, "It's going to avalanche. We have to get out of here you guys."

"Do you really think so, King?" Wally asked.

"Yes. You can see how much loading has gone on. I think that it is too dangerous."

"Well, I don't know about that. You may be right, but I'm not convinced and that is what I'm saying. What do you think, Blanch?"

"There's two feet of new snow here and we can't see anything. I don't want to fucking go down, but I think we have to."

That night we rejoined David, Steve, and TP at Camp VI, 23,000 feet, the base of the steep ice cliff where I'd felt like Jeff Lowe. The next day we made it down to Camp IV, 19,500 feet, where there was a duffel bag of food. We burned the last of our fuel gorging ourselves, yet we all woke hungry the next morning.

Almost all of our fixed line was left in place on the rockband between 21,500 and 23,000 feet. We'd stripped one 300-foot piece and were now able to do 300-foot rappels with it and our two lead lines tied together to create the other side of the rappel. We chose to rappel the fall line off of the ridge to gain the Ghulmet Glacier and an easier descent down walkable snow as opposed to the sideways down climbing we'd been doing along the ice edge of the ridge. Getting all six of us down each 300-foot rappel took at least an hour, even with two of us simultaneously rappelling both sides of each rap. We had long waits at the anchors as the first ones down engineered the anchor below.

Clipped into the side of Rakaposhi we came up with a list of the twenty greatest places to eat on the face of the earth, and then we listed the best thing to order in each and every one, and our descriptions of the plates, and the sensual experience of eating them. We waxed poetic or hilarious in hyperbole.

"The fries at Peter's Drive Inn are so good that I have to squeeze out a half a bottle of ketchup in advance or I just can't keep up with the ketchup application because I go at them two handed and it's kind of like a conveyor belt, you know, one of those ones that you see dumping gravel into little mountains. It's kinda like that, but with french fries." I said.

"We are in the oral stage gentlemen," Steve said. "If the weather doesn't clear our expedition will be over."

"Ya, but this fucking storm has to end some time. And when it does we will be able to blitz up this thing," Wally said. "Especially given the fact that we have the rockband at 21,500 fixed."

Late in the day we found the lowest point of rock available, built an anchor and Wally and I simu-rapped toward the bergschrund.

"Shit, the 'schrund is still below us," Wally cursed.

"We can get the guys to tie off the 300 footer and drop us the lead lines," I said. "We can rap off of the end of the 300 footer and that should get us over the 'schrund. We can leave the 300 footer here, we won't need it for the glacier."

And it worked, and an hour later the six of us were tying in to our two lead ropes anxiously trying to make sense of the insanity of the "canon" above us, a massive arch of electric blue ice that shot out several tons of ice every five to ten minutes.

"OK, now!" Wally shouted as blocks of blue ice bounded downslope, gouging trenches into fans of pulverized ice and snow. I sprinted into the killing fields—sérac carnage that can only be described as a war zone. We ran and ran and my heart hammered and my pores wept, there was still 1,500 feet to cross when the rope behind me came tight,

"We don't have to go so fast," TP shouted.

"Oh yes we do, TP, and if you don't come I'll fucking drag you!" And I could see the pain of exertion stretched across his face, but my urgency was stronger and TP pounded on until we left the last of the debris behind us and trotted out onto the undisturbed surface of the Ghulmet Glacier.

TP marched up and shucked his pack, his breath raging in and out. He'd pushed himself and he wasn't happy. I felt sorry that I'd made him go harder when he slowed, but the deadly vulnerability I felt under the canon cornered the animal in me and I'd sprinted to survive.

Dust-mottled snow curled into the blackness of crosshatched crevasses and Wally charged into the labyrinth, his jacket tied by the sleeves around his waist and hanging down like a hula skirt. He looked comical, but he commanded our descent through the maze of trenches and black cracks like General George S. Patton.

"No, no, it's that way." Kevin had stopped for the twentieth time to survey the spider's web of dirty snow and cobalt holes in front of us. His right arm pointed to the pattern that only he had discerned, and it was correct, the one way through.

Dusk caught us on the glacier and we set up the three turtle tents one more time. It was the twenty-second night that we'd spent on Rakaposhi since we'd committed to the ridge on June 16.

Early morning, July 7, 1984, Vern and Fahrid jogged up the moraine to meet us. Vern bear hugged each of us and lifted us off the ground and we dropped and sat our packs and David began telling our stories. But we were all too hungry for that so we rose and clomped down to Base Camp were the snow had all melted and small flowers were in bloom smelling so much like life!

Chef Ali sizzled paratha after paratha—pan-fried chapattis— and we smeared peanut butter on them hot and dripped honey on top and I couldn't eat them fast enough. And then he made us a huge pan of eggs, potatoes, and onions and I wiped my plate restaurant-standard clean with a chapatti and lapped all the residue off with my tongue, just like a dog. Then there were tins of corned beef fried in the egg pan and quart-sized tins of fruit cocktail. We ate for two hours while David told our story and we all jumped in with tangential narratives.

When the air warmed I stripped down and peeled off the Lifa underwear that I'd had on for twenty-three days. A mummy-like layer of white skin dandruff came off with it and I felt like a snake shedding its skin. My top held its shape off of my body like there was a head-less manikin inside and the bottoms smelt feral, like the smell of the night mammals at the zoo. Vern had started a bon fire and I walked over to it and threw my underwear in and both pieces exploded into flame and then zapped down into golf-ball-sized blobs of blue goo.

Plans were made. Gregg, Chef Ali, and I descended to Chef Ali's one-room tea shop cum restaurant that doubled as an inn by night: the Rakaposhi Inn. We arranged for porters to retrieve Base Camp the next day. Vern and Tim were heading home and the other five of us planned on sightseeing up the Hunza for a couple of days. If the storm continued we'd head home too.

Black flies buzzed around my face as the yellow dusty haze of dawn began heating the new day. Gregg and I lay on hand-planed and chisel-joined cots that had hemp rope woven in one-inch squares to form a sleeping platform. The flies were such a fucking hassle that we draped bandanas over our faces to keep them out of our noses and ears. We knew that would work until the heat came on and then even the bandana would be too much to have on our faces.

My joints felt like sandpaper and my blood pulsed thick and sluggish. Everything was raw and my eyes felt like there was salt in them. Vern had mixed me up a combination of topical anesthetic and anti bacterial cream to numb and heal the open sore that stretched from one side of my lower lip to the other.

"I think that it is from the sun reflecting off of my teeth when I had my mouth open wide to breathe, which was most of the time," I'd told him. My lip burned when food touched it and without the anesthetic I couldn't eat.

The tiled floor of the Rakaposhi Inn was dusty and the walls whitewashed plaster. Rain stains blotched the ceiling and I stared at the lichen-like patterns and felt like a failure. I'd wanted so badly to succeed on my first Himalayan expedition. I wanted it so badly.

"Do you think that we pushed far enough, Gregg?"

"Oh ya, I do. David thinks that we pushed too far."

"How do you know?"

"He told me at High Camp. He said that he didn't know if we'd make it down," Gregg replied.

"You're kidding, the Big Cheese said that?"

"Ya, he thought that we'd gone too far."

"Fuck." And I paused for thirty seconds, "I know that it's wrong but I feel that we are expected to make the top."

"Well, maybe the weather will come around."

"Ya, maybe."

"Yes, after this last month we should certainly be acclimatized enough. We could write the first attempt off as a one-month reconnaissance of 90 percent of the route."

"It's too bad it's the last 10 percent that counts," I concluded.

On July 9 magic happened. We got the first clear view of the north ridge in sixteen days. July 10 dawned perfectly blue from horizon to horizon. The Cheesmond Comet ignited, and I sat in my tent in our roadside camp drinking black tea with milk powder and coarse-grained sugar watching David stride to the food barrels and slash some scribbles in his blue Chinese notebook. Then he was off to his tent to grab his camera and snap a few pictures of Rakaposhi "while the light is good, man," and back to the food barrels and more notes. The next day the five of us hiked back up to Base Camp and pitched our tents.

The horrid sounds of tent zippers ripping open in the night and then the retching, and King's moaning. Gregg was butt sick again, and so was Steve. Morning saw them descending for England where Gregg would stay with Steve's family until it was time to go home.

David and I stumbled along behind Kevin retracing our faded descent tracks toward the canon. I felt wasted and hollow, David was running on willpower too. He and I convinced Kevin to stop and camp on the glacier and run the canon before dawn. If we could ascend the line of our rappels we would avoid our first three ridge camps and that would chop several days off of our time.

July 13, 1984, the canon was quiet and the weather perfect. David, Kevin, and I climbed 4,500 feet to gain our Camp IV, 19,500 feet. The next day we made it to Camp VI, 23,000 feet, then High Camp on the fifteenth. On the night of July 16 the three of us crammed into one tent at 25,000 feet. We were right up against the summit rockband and it felt like the whole of the earth swept away below us, the Hunza River a dirt-colored thread at the bottom of the atmospheric haze 20,000 feet below. Eat, sleep, prepare, I strived to be as efficient as possible, as good as I could be. We would be going for the summit the next day.

"This is so fucking disgusting, man. I hate this fucking shit," Kevin hissed.

He squatted down in the polar cold of the predawn, his right arm and mitt wrapped around the rope, his left hand holding the butt zip of his salopettes open wide as a gaseous spray of shit sputtered from him. He was there for minutes.

"I can't lead with this cock sucking shit going on. You'll have to gun for it, my little brown friend."

The climbing was harder and steeper than it looked, and I linked two pitches of technical sand-colored stone. All of my clothing was on me including my parka and balaclava yet the morning sun contained so much radiant heat that I could climb with bare hands and watch them brown like gas station hot dogs rolling on heated steel rods. The juxtaposition of my body's chill and my hot hands was fascinating to me.

The second move off of my high anchor was a mantel and I had to go at it several times before I found a hold with my right hand and could pull myself into balance and heave air in and out of my lungs. When my breathing calmed, I stood my crampon points onto a horizontal edge and pulled up. Fifteen feet above was an alcove where I thought I could get gear.

I pulled into the alcove and brown stone pressed against my chest and there was no way to stand in balance. A knifeblade went in one handed as my breathing ramped up and my legs began to quiver. The carabiner snapped shut and I stood into balance in a sling and let my breathing calm. My bodyweight was held by the piton, but I didn't trust it to hold a fall. Ice filled a finger-sized crack in the back of the alcove and I pounded a Warthog in halfway and equalized it with the piton.

Seven feet to the left of me an open book corner led to the summit ridgeline of Rakaposhi, but both of my tries to gain it ended at the point of losing control and falling. I called down for tension and Dave held me fast as I thrust sideways against the taut lines of rope. Controlled and calculated bridging up the corner, I marveled at how

A half hour after rising the morning he returned from climbing Rakaposhi, Kevin looks a little more like himself, with his face swollen only a half inch. It was a full inch when he first stirred. Photo: Barry Blanchard much the climbing felt like the South Face of Mount Yamnuska—and then I was in a small amphitheater of straw-colored rock and wind carved snow, on the ridgeline, and all of the difficult climbing was below me.

"Off belay!" Wally and Dave howled from below.

The black pyramid of K2 sat on top of the western horizon like something not of this earth, a black obelisk that was part of space. Broad Peak and the Gasherbrums were outlined too, but so much lower, part of the Karakorum. I wondered how Voytek Kurtyka and Jerzy Kukuczka were making out, and then I began to fret because clouds were rising out of nowhere and amassing everywhere.

Dave took the lead over the lip of the amphitheater and on to a forty-degree slope. Hip-deep unconsolidated snow that acted like coarse-grain sugar forced him to trench a channel from boulder to boulder. Slow laborious toiling. At 2:30 p.m. Kevin and I joined Dave at an outcrop of rock. The atmosphere was tearing over the mutinous blade of Rakaposhi. Everything was gray and the incendiary bursts of lightning were spontaneous to lung-quaking thunderclaps. We agreed to continue for another hour.

Strong winds tore at my clothing and the draw cord from my hood stabbed at my face. More muscular gusts smacked into us and I couldn't see a thing. The snow had become supportive underfoot though, and we continued traversing up toward the summit. My torso rose above the ridgeline and *Zap!* I was hurled onto my side like a blindsided check while playing hockey. David and Kevin both got jerked off of their feet over the next 300 feet and we realized that it was a static charge from passing clouds that was zapping us and smacking us to the ground.

One hour later I was sitting under a large rock with the blizzard raging. David arrived, "I've fucking had it, man," I spit. "This isn't any fun, it's not fucking any anything. It's an empty experience." I felt cheated and depressed and defeated. Empty.

"You're right, Blanch. This isn't worth it, and Kevin is hurting. Let's take some pictures to document our high point and let's get out of this."

"Fuck."

And then Kevin arrived, "No you guys, no. Fuck the fucking storm. We can do this. Let's do one more ropelength. I'm OK, I'll be OK. Don't give in now, we're too close."

Sick as a dog but as willful as a mule and bold as lion, Wally pushed water uphill and David started up.

Four in the afternoon on July 17 saw us at 25,546 feet above sea level. David, Kevin, and I were huddled five feet below the summit of Rakaposhi, electrical charge ticking into the penultimate rock and sounding like an excited Geiger counter. None of us dared to touch the top because we knew we'd take a big hit, probably the biggest of the day, possibly the last in this life. We grinned against the gale and hugged each other. We'd fucking done it. We'd climbed the north ridge of Rakaposhi! Yah!

That night we regained our bivouac at the base of the summit rock-band. The storm clouds collapsed and retreated with the setting of the sun. The next day we retreated to the base of the steep ice wall and slept there, 23,000 feet. July 19, the next morning, we started early and rappelled the ropes that we left fixed on the rockband and at dusk we stumbled over broken plates of rock into Base Camp. We had down climbed and rappelled 11,000 feet in one day. In the last hour I'd felt some power radiate into my feet from the shattered pieces of Rakaposhi I walked over, a lightness. But when I hit Base Camp I collapsed into my pit.

"Holy shit, Wally, your face. There's something wrong with your face," I said. Morning light, my first view of him, and his Adonic features were bloated and bulging. His face had swollen out one inch.

"It's the same with you, man," he replied, "and look, Cheese has got it too."

Our inflated faces began to return to normal with us getting up and walking and within an hour the edema was gone. Afterward, when I related the story to my friend, Dr. Jim States, a man with a lot of high altitude medical knowledge and experience he said, "Well you came pretty close to giving yourself a stroke so don't push that hard again."

Later that day we arranged our sleeping bags in a classroom that Fahrid had arranged for us to spend the night in. I stepped onto the scale that we'd bought to weigh our porter loads. When I arrived at the road head on May 26 I'd weighed 165 pounds, now I was 130. All of my muscles had wasted and the Levis that had been tight on me flapped like the voluminous white pants that all the Pakistani men wore.

PLAYLIST

Monty Python	*The Lumberjack Song*
Stan Rogers	*Northwest Passage*

Chapter 17

THE **NORTH TWIN**

I WENT LOGGING THAT FALL, 1984. The work was steady and physical. My Jonsered 920 chainsaw (I ran two with one as backup) was bright red and weighed about twenty-five pounds when it was all gassed up and powering a thirty-six-inch bar. A ridge of callus the color of chalk developed on my left palm and there was a day when I grabbed a hot cast-iron frying pan from the airtight stove inside the wall tent where I spent the workweek and I smelled my flesh burning seconds before I felt any pain.

I liked the work, the physicality of it, smelling like a pine tree at the end of the day, I even liked the thick and lugubrious fetor of chain oil, gasoline, and diesel that clung to my filthy bucker's chaps. Frank, my boss, had been on the US Nordic Ski Team in the seventies and we would run the logging roads after work. Our fellow loggers thought we should be taken away in butterfly nets and shared that with us.

I left the bush at Christmas and returned to my life of climbing and guiding in Canmore. My first wife and I married on Groundhog Day 1985. Our union didn't work out and she has asked that I omit her from this book and I have chosen to respect that.

David, aka 'The Big Cheese' or 'Le Grande Fromage,' showing off his jamming gloves at our last bivouac on the North Pillar of North Twin. Photo: Barry Blanchard

Tim Pochay showed up for the four days of staff training with Yamnuska Mountain School that June. He was the same age as me, twenty-six, and strong and keen to climb. As a young man he'd taken a fall onto his face while learning to climb at Wasootch Slabs and an inch-long linear red scar fell from the left corner of his mouth to near his chin where the rock had parted the flesh against his mandible.

"If I had the same on the other side I'd look like a ventriloquist's dummy!" Tim beamed and smiled and bobbled his head, yet behind his dark smiling eyes there existed a black intensity. Black as hell.

Our schedules allowed us three days off at the end of the first week of July and we headed into the Bugaboos. We stopped at the Hind Hut to hand copy several topos from the official climbing log—I felt like I was transcribing treasure maps. Then we continued up to camp at Applebee Dome.

The next day was beautiful and we climbed the magnificent Sunshine Crack on the north wall of Snowpatch Spire. The route was first climbed by Alex Lowe five years earlier and I got the second pitch—a damp 5.10 offwidth—and I had to use all of the techniques that Kevin had taught me in Yosemite plus some of my scrappiness and will to survive.

"That was fucking bold," Tim said, puffing onto my belay.

The tenth pitch is a hundred-foot-long fist crack and Tim evenly spaced the four cams we carried that would fit into it as he led. Some of the falls would have been horrific, but the crack was as incredible and as perfect as the lone crack splitting the headwall of the Salathé on El Capitan.

Viewed from Bugaboo Spire, across a col from us, it etches the profile of a long-stemmed wine glass. Tim and I where hanging at the junction of the stem and the bowl.

"It's a fucking great thing that I know how to jam cracks!" Tim spat when I panted up to him, his eyes burning black.

I took the rack and hand-railed right to gain the vertical line of the bowl. The crack ended shy of the rim—the top of the route—and I pinched and crimped and prayed, and gingerly pulled over. Tim and I sat on a flat clean ledge the size of a pickup truck, I felt like I'd pulled over the edge of the earth. We were grinning with glee, wide-eyed with exhilaration.

We woke raw the next morning but the sky was bluebird so we headed off to the east face of Bugaboo Spire. Tim and I gained the Balcony, a large horizontal ledge, via a chimney formed behind a rock tower that has since fallen into Crescent Glacier. The Balcony led us to the route.

The east face had been opened by Ed Cooper and Art Gran in 1960, we hoped to free climb it as Mike Tschipper and Tom Gibson had managed to do for the first time in 1980. I got the first pitch of the route and my body felt like it had been battered. I went at a layback around a roof twice before giving up on it in favor of face holds to my right that led to the same belay. I clipped a long sling to a fixed piton at the roof and clipped the left hand of my two nine-millimeter ropes into it. The rigid shafts of three cams stuck out of the crack leading back down to Tim like aluminum fence posts. My red, left-hand rope clipped into the second, and the brand new purple rope I'd bought in Banff two days earlier ran through the first and third cams.

The face climbing was slow and deliberate and there was no protection and the red rope soon hung with the belly of a skipping rope twenty-five feet to the pin.

"How is it going up there, man?" Tim asked.

"I've got one more move and it backs off. It'll be OK."

"Can you get any gear in?"

"There's nothing here, man, fucking blank. Watch me."

I slammed the heel of my right hand against a chunk of granite that looked like the end of a bread loaf and it was solid. I wrapped my right hand onto it and rocked my head to look at my left foot. As I grunted to get my foot onto a hold I heard the sound of grating rock then felt my right hand move an inch. My eyes jerked back and I saw the hold come out of the wall looking just like a loaf of bread coming out of the pan. I shouted, and then I vaulted backward into free fall. The sky charged away in a roar of air and I hammered into a ledge seventy feet down, head first, my Galibier helmet muffling the crunch of rock and my eyes going black until I heard Tim screaming.

"Barry! Are you alright! Are you alright?"

Groggily I grabbed for my ropes and felt the tight sinew like rigidity of a bundle of cords. "Yeah, I think I'm OK."

I righted myself and saw the sheath of the red rope in tatters. It had separated from the white core strands in three places and foot-long white sections of the inner ropes glared like tendons exposed from a flayed human wrist. Two feet of the purple rope hung limp from my harness and the end of it was melted and looked like it had been chopped clean by a hot cutter.

"Holy fuck," I sighed, and then I shouted up and over to Tim, "Are you alright?"

"No, man. My hands are fucked. You need to get up here."

The ropes had run through the crotches on both sides of the middle finger on his right hand and stopping them had burned most of the flesh away. Two white grooves glared like marbled meat. The rock that I'd pulled had buzz sawed through the air and melted a hole through the lid of my pack and then impacted Tim's left hand and it was red and hot and already going to blue.

"Let's get the fuck out of here, Poch. We need to go to the hospital in Golden. We can pull the ropes and rap on what's left of the purple and pull it down with the red as a tag line," I said.

"I can't leave those three cams up there. That's a couple hundred bucks."

"Fuck the cams, man, we've got to get out of here. Look at your hands."

Tim's eyes glittered dark and intense and he said, "No, at times like this you got to come up big." And he climbed up and retrieved the cams.

When we hit the glacier his right hand had contracted into a closed claw.

At the emergency room in Golden, Tim got his burned hand cleaned and dressed. An X-ray revealed no breaks in his left hand and he was given ice for it. I had a concussion and had to be woken hourly that night. We walked out and drove back to Canmore.

Two weeks later I guided the Red Shirt Route on Mount Yamnuska and it was my first time back on rock since my fall. I over-gripped the rock and got scared out of my mind on the exposed sections. My climbing became an act of will, yet by the finishing pitches my mind, my body, and my body's memory had relaxed.

That night my phone rang and David Cheesmond didn't even say hello, he just wailed, "George is coming up for the Pillar! And he's bringing Alex!"

For three years the North Pillar of North Twin had risen from the mists of my dreams like Excalibur piercing the surface of the Lake. A black-and-white photo of the face from George Lowe and Chris Jones's 1974 first ascent hung above the bench in the room where I trained with weights. In my mind's eye I saw the Twin during the

The north face of North Twin, a great black cape of a peak. Photo: Barry Blanchard

hours that I spent running uphill, it was there when I was guiding, and it came to me in the night. Chris's and George's faces stared out to me from the dog-eared pages of my tattered ten-year-old copy of *Ascent*—heroes' faces. Two men who turned from the fire and crossed into the wilderness to call down the dragons. Bamboo-shafted ice axes, woolen knickers, Dachstein mitts: the strained, set gaze of men engaged in a lethal struggle. I'd come to believe that Lowe and Jones's 1974 ascent of North Twin was the hardest route yet climbed—globally—by two men with "a rope, a rack, and two packs."

The Big Cheese and I had been planning to try the unclimbed North Pillar, about 1,500 feet to the right of George and Chris's route, ever since we'd arrived home from Pakistan the year before.

"Oh shit!" I spat into the phone. The Pillar was the Holy Grail of the Rockies, and to hear that George and Alex Lowe (unrelated) were coming to try it was like spotting Arthur and Galahad cresting the horizon. We had a saying back then about George's gifted, amped sidekick: "If you bring Alex, it's cheating!"

David pleaded plaintively, "George, I've been looking at the Pillar for three years."

"Oh, yeah, Cheese? Well, I've been looking at it for ten!"

The Lowes arrived in the rain and walked in through the rain. Rain ushered them past the Twin and on to Mount Columbia, where they climbed the north ridge in the rain, shook hands on top, and walked out to the highway, where it was still raining.

"We've been saved by the rain," David told me over the phone after George and Alex had left.

The dog days of summer were blue and David and I trudged over Woolley Shoulder on July 29. We carried light packs, as David had left a full rack, two ropes, and food in the Mount Alberta Hut earlier in the month after he and Sean Dougherty had descended into the Black Hole to attempt the west ridgeline of North Twin in its entirety.

I crested Woolley Shoulder and there it was, a concave obsidian spear point stabbing the sky. I felt my lower abdomen draw up. The skin of my scrotum contracted and tingled.

"Oh man," I sighed.

Dave and I picked his stash up at the hut and under heavy loads descended to the southeastern branch of Habel Creek and crossed over it on the same snowbridge that he and Sean had. The glacier at the foot of North Twin is fed by tiers of séracs and icefalls that calve from North Twin and the west summit of Mount Stutfield. We pitched our small yellow tent, one of the ones we'd had on Rakaposhi, on a beach of gravel below North Twin, a glittering and clear emerald tarn set into glacial ice three steps away. We were in the gut of the Black Hole and collapsing séracs thundered constantly; their reverberations tapping the taut walls of the tent like the drumming of human fingers.

The next morning we charged onto the face and sprinted up ledges of snow, scree, and shale, cowering breathlessly against steep bands of rock as the sky screamed with rockfall. Anchored to the base of the first 500-foot-high band of vertical rock David gleefully stuffed his feet, adorned in electric-pink socks that his wife, Gillian, had given him, into the Boreal Fires that he and I had both bought in London on our way home from Pakistan a year before. It had been the first pairs of the hot new sticky Spanish rock shoes that we'd seen.

"They have to be cheaper here," the crafty Cheese had reasoned. They were ten bucks cheaper when we saw them at the Mountain Equipment Co-op in Calgary a week later!

Now David bellowed the Monty Python line to his gay pink socks, "I'm a lumberjack and I'm OK!" Then he danced around the water weeping from a splitter offwidth and logged his first masterful lead of the day, completely focused on the task at hand, oblivious to the roar of rockfall that was scaring the absolute crap out of me.

Late in the day we gained the protective bulge of the Pillar, and the rockfall ripped down far out from the face, well away from us. I felt that I'd barely survived Dieppe.

"Did you hear that?" David asked, twisting to me at the belay.

"Yeah, I definitely heard someone." I yodeled and got a "Yahoo!" in response.

"Holy shit, there's another party on George's route!" he said, pointing across the hazy expanse of the face. The climbers were at the base of a steep black band.

"Here, man, look at this, man. Free water!" David beamed and held up one full quart of water in an opaque plastic water bottle. We were arranging our first bivouac on the face and he was so proud of the black garbage bag and candy-striped Dairy Queen straw/spoon collecting system he'd engineered. I smiled at the image of Cheese in Dairy Queen, pirating away his milkshake straw because he saw in it a piece of a system. Collecting the quart had taken the better part of an hour, but it meant that we wouldn't have to melt as much ice and we would save fuel.

The next morning a small tent sat on the glacier at the base of the wall and we shook our heads in disbelief. Three parties on a face that is usually seen by more grizzly bears than humans? Then we realized that it was the party on the Lowe-Jones route retreating and we both sighed at the loss.

"Cheese, we are definitely alone now."

"Yes, Blanch, that we are."

It was July 31 and the pale morning sky was clear and the air was warm. The first lead, and I followed some moderate cracks to a large shale ledge that cuts across the base of the pillar running from one rim of the wall to the other. The rock was horrible, like bulldozed piles of jackhammered sidewalk. Getting an anchor took time, a half dozen pieces, and a bunch of rigging. David waded up the rest of the crap to steeper rock and a better belay and then it was my turn.

To save on weight we'd brought just one pair of rock shoes. I had no problem fitting my size eight feet into Dave's size tens. They climbed about as well as flip-flops. Thirty feet up I cranked on some small face holds and heard a sharp snap like a dry twig breaking and then I was in the air and managed to grab a sling in flight and slammed to a stop.

I can still see the softball-sized foothold that I'd broken spinning out into space, accelerating, and nailing David in the right thigh where he sat facing out and belaying. He swore mightily and rubbed his leg and swore again, then caught himself, realizing, I was sure, that he was being self-centered—in the Cheesmond book that equated with being rude, even if you had a big, bloody contusion gaining heat with each beat of your heart. He shelved his pain and looked up and yelled to see if I was OK. I lied and said that I was, and that I was sorry for nailing him. I'd sprained my left ring finger, which was turning blue and swelling.

David lowered me to the belay and rubbed his bruised thigh, blew out through pursed lips and asked for his rock shoes. From then on I led all the ice, and whatever rock that could be climbed in double-plastic boots, and he took all the steep rock, about twenty-five pitches in total. He finished my lead and when I asked him what grade he'd give it he repeated the line he'd used the day before, "Ah, it was 5.10, man." And as the hard pitches amassed it would be the suffix that would change between a and c. "It was 10a," he added. Late in the day David powered up the last lead of the middle rockband, a solid vertical-to-overhanging hand crack. "5.10, man, 10b."

I traversed left and sunk some secure screws into the dirty ice of the second icefield. It looked like a cinder box had been dumped onto it. The rounded spine of the icefield bulged then arced toward the sheer rock of the pillar like the back and neck of an immense sea ray, its skin pocked with rockfall and stained black on one side with limestone sediment that had been deposited there by water.

I hacked through to cleaner ice and chipped chunks of it into a stuffsac. The sky had faded as gray as the ice in my sack, ice that would be our water supply for the night. David and I came together on a broken pedestal of shale a half ropelength below the ice face. Everything was slanting and we spent an hour building narrow plat-forms from plates of rock. Across the void of Habel Creek, Mount Alberta looked so proud and independent and defiant, and above us the North Pillar of North Twin hung with the oppressive air. It formed a barrier in my mind, one that felt overwhelming.

"We're in a good position, man," David said. "Tomorrow we'll find a way through it."

"It's getting to the point that we have too. I don't know if we have enough gear to get down from here."

And I sat tending the stove. My hands were calloused and baked brown from a summer spent living in the sun. David smiled his sly-fox grin and we watched the evening light fade to black on the bastions of Mount Alberta.

Later, I lay in my bag with my harness on; both of us tethered to rock gear and, higher yet, ice screws. My wildest dream had become my reality. I was inserted into the black-and-white picture of the Twin that hung in my weight room. Then sleep mugged me, but my dreams where so vivid that I jolted from them thinking that I was still in them, that they were reality. Then the chill of the Black Hole touched my face like cold obsidian and anchored me in the night, and to the wall. I would close my eyes again and slip back into my dreams as easily as stepping through an open door. It was like my day mind and my night mind had melded and all of my hours pulsed with the engagement of life.

Yet the dull and cool light of dawn found my body groggy and slow to start, like all my lubricants were sluggish and the line pressure slow to make running levels. But the mountain was locked up in frost and there was no rockfall, yet, just like Walter Bonatti had written about. David and I took his advice and took advantage of the freeze. I kick-started my body by kicking into the crisp ice. I needed the machine to perform, demanded it, and I crunched up 400 feet quickly and methodically to anchor into the rock of the headwall.

David pulled his Fires over his pink socks and started dispatching pitch after pitch of steep limestone. "l0a, man. l0b, l0c..." Ropelength upon ropelength. I was jumaring and climbing in the wake of a genius. And then it was getting dark again and a black-bellied juggernaut of a cloud scraped over the spear point of the Twin and cyclonic gusts smacked us as the mist descended.

I jugged to David, who was anchored to a small ledge in the middle of nowhere, and asked, "You got any idea on how we chop a bivy ledge out of solid rock?"

"I think we must go and check that out, man," David said, pointing up and right fifty feet to a black hole in the wall. I traversed toward the hole.

"Oh man! Yessss!" I hollered. "You won't believe this, Cheese! We have a cave to bivy in! Yahoo!"

It was perfect. Room for two with a flat floor of ice to melt for water, a cam-sized crack in the roof to drape our tent like mosquito netting and then crawl in. For the first time in sixty-four hours we untied from the rope.

Outside our sanctum thunder bursts shook the wall and the small triangular portal to our cave flashed a pure blinding white on the explosions of lightning. Rain lashed limestone like waves crashing onto headlands. Cheese and I looked at each other and laughed. We could not have been luckier. I felt like an Apollo astronaut snug in the command module.

The storm passed and we slept, and in the morning David stepped through the portal and began to climb.

Our ropes, one blue, one purple, arced from my waist to David in a clean hyperbolic sweep. He was thirty feet up an overhanging crack and he hadn't been able to get any gear in. I cowered and quivered, braced in the threshold of the cave. If he fell the load onto me would be terrible, possibly enough to tear us from the wall. Images of other falls onto the belay sheaved through my mind: my friend Al watching the loaded rope snap his femur, accounts of anchor failures with both climbers going to the bottom, forever.

My anxiety stepped up with each inch of rope I paid out and I knew that David was locked in a lethal game of chess and that he played as he always played—cool as a cucumber and methodically slinking into each move. Grace under pressure: It was interesting to see how much of that state required cunning. My breath was becoming as dry as the Sirocco, and then David got three pieces in and I let out an audible sigh of relief.

Our packs lowered out into space and David hauled them the entire ropelength without touching the wall. All of the ground was vertical and overhanging and the gravity of the Black Hole grew with every foot I gained shoving my upper jug up the blue rope. I was as high and exposed as I had been on Warren Harding's bolt ladder at the top of the Nose, but now sérac walls arced from me like the arms of galaxies. The glacier below where I'd slept four nights ago, that had seemed so massive and incomprehensible then, had become a dirty sheet of paper on which I could easily see the areola of rockfall and the regiments of crevasses lined up like standing waves in a ripple tank.

"l0c," David said when I got to him.

Halfway up the next pitch the wall reared well over vertical and David stepped into étriers to aid the last half of the rope. The blue rope snapped taut to each consecutive piece as I jumared and cleaned.

And then the floor fell out of the elevator and I plummeted five feet and jerked onto the rope as a black shadow swooped by my shoulder and I choked on the fear of it being Dave. It roared through the air spinning and screaming, and exploded against the lower wall and sprayed the glacier with impacts to distant to hear.

"Barry! Barry! You have to get off of the rope!"

The principle piece of David's anchor, a number three Friend, had failed and my weight had fallen onto his harness. My hands shook and I thrashed the jugs up and clipped into the next pieces and got my weight off of the rope. David added more gear to the belay—in my mind it could never be enough—and I was a nervous wreck committing myself back onto the rope.

A seven-foot scar of pale limestone sat like an X-ray image of broken bone on the right side of the fist crack. The Friend, and my weight on it, had pushed the fractured slab free.

"I'm glad the backup nuts held!" David exclaimed although it was hard to hear him over the ringing of the pitons I was adding to the anchor.

Three hundred feet higher, a curtain of water drops fell free from the apex of the face two hundred feet left and behind me. Oblique sunlight fired the droplets into a glittering mosaic of diamonds and I felt calm and secure and fulfilled. Stan Rogers' rum barrel deep baritone quivered in my throat with the solemnity of a hymn to birth and I belted out the chorus of "Northwest Passage" loud and proud to David, and to the Black Hole.

Ah, for just one time I would take the Northwest Passage,
To find the hand of Franklin reaching for the Beaufort Sea;
Tracing one warm line through a land so wide and savage,
And make a Northwest Passage to the sea.

David led on, placing his hands and feet onto rock that had never felt the warm-blooded touch of man. We etched our line onto the wall with the ardent heat of our hearts, ropelength after ropelength.

Late in the day it looked like the angle backed off above and I took the lead in my Koflach plastic boots. A crack turned to an ice-filled chimney and I hacked footholds into the ice and climbed to a desktop-sized ledge. David continued to fix a rope at the top of what proved to be a huge pillar improbably attached to the wall. The rock above was vertical and blank, but he sussed out a flake to the right before descending to me and my slim ledge; home for the night.

I spent much of the night trying to wedge my left butt cheek into a crack while balancing my feet in the backpack, slings, and rope hammock I'd concocted to suspend them over the void. Rain squalls and melt water dripped onto us through the night. Our situation sucked. And then it got horrifying as a large rockslide crashed into the night somewhere left of us and sparks flew like tracer rounds and the gunpowder reek of pulverized rock hung in the air.

"Fuck!" I spat, "This has to fucking end."

"Yes, we have to get off tomorrow, man. We're out of food."

"And running out of luck. We're running on empty, Cheese."

"Yet again, my friend, yet again."

I hung at David's high anchor, nervously paying out the rope inch by inch. David had climbed from view around to the right. The whole route came down to this pitch, the one piece of the route that we couldn't see features on through the binoculars six days earlier. I'd paid out 130 feet of rope when everything stopped and David yelled back, "Watch me, I'm going to fall!"

My heart rate doubled and I could hear my pulse inside my skull, but the rope stuttered out, and then it paid out and then David was shouting "Yahoo!" And I knew that he was off of the wall and I smiled wide and white and tears of relief squeezed from the corners of my eyes.

"A 5.l0 finger crack! l0d, man! I thought I was off," he blurted when I jugged over the apex. The final pitch proved the hardest free climbing of the route! "All we have to do now, Blanch, is keep a cool tool for twelve hours and we out of here, man."

I laughed, and slapped high, high fives with the Big Cheese, then I jogged up two ropelenths of shallow loose stone to merge us onto the northwest ridge first climbed by Hank Abrons, Pete Carman, and Rick Millikan in 1965. David and I held the holds that those men had held and at midday we stepped onto the summit of Twins Tower and I was so very incredibly happy to be there.

A beautiful, perfect arête of snow and ice cut from the summit of Twins Tower, where David and I sat sipping collected water through Dairy Queen straws, to our exit across a glacial bench on the eastern summit slopes of North Twin. The arête looked like the top edge of a scimitar. Fritz Wiessner and Chappell Cranmer had been the first to traverse it en route to the virgin summit of Twins Tower in 1938, a time when Wiessner was the best alpinist in North America. George Lowe and Chris Jones had climbed across it in a storm eleven years earlier. I siphoned energy from history as David and I plodded toward the west peak of Mount Stutfield.

One last night in our wee yellow tent right on big, broad glacial summit and one final thunderstorm to illuminate our sanctum electrically as it quaked from the explosions of thunder. I could name places that I would have rather been during lightning strikes.

Eighteen hours later David and I sloshed from the Sunwapta River and thumped our packs onto the highway beside his van. I placed my hands on my knees and blew out like a horse. My body felt hollow and raw, like much of my core had deflated. All I wanted to do was sit.

Three slow days later I tied-in with new clients and started climbing again. Later that week I went to visit Kevin in Calgary.

Kevin's basement suite felt dark when I closed the cheap, sandwich-constructed door behind me. The old, orange shag carpet lay witness to a passage of time that did not favor it. Wally was sitting in the middle of a Salvation Army couch and he was crying, told me that he'd been doing it for most of the last couple of days.

"I don't know, Blanch. I just can't figure it out. Why the fuck are we here?"

I didn't know. But I did know that I loved Kevin so I put my arms around him and I held him while he cried, and he let me. Eventually we drank some beer and although it didn't solve anything it shifted our space, made it less intense.

Chapter 18

EVEREST

"DAVID IS A NATURAL LEADER," I SAID.

Jim Elzinga's brow furrowed. "What do you mean exactly?"

"There's never been any question about it on our climbs. He has, by far, the most experience of any of us, and he always has the big picture in his head. Always knows where we are on the side of the mountain and where we need to go to get higher."

"Ya, Cheese is good that way. You just want to follow him," Kevin added.

"Or be told where to go by him," I chirped. "The Big Cheese definitely knows how to use, and get the most out of, the young tigers."

"Ya, he's like the Magus," Wally continued, "only a good one. Not like that guy in the novel, more like a benevolent puppet master, or an orchestrator."

"What novel?" Jim asked.

After some debate among our 1986 Everest Light team, David was not invited on, largely because he hadn't climbed with many of the other team members. I could hear the bewilderment in his voice when I told him over the phone, and it sucked. Sucked for me to act like a spokesman and not be able to tell all to my buddy—and I'm embarrassed for having done that now. But the Big Cheese shook it off, rolled with it, and even assuaged the messenger—and that is why I followed his leadership back then. He would never expect, or ask, for anything that he would not or could not do himself. And he was kind, he put himself in your shoes—even though I fell short of his virtues, I loved him for them.

Kevin, Jim, Albi, and I jump for joy and relief
on hearing that Sharon and Dwayne are OK
after making the summit of Mount Everest.
Photo: Bob Lee

Our team was finalized: James Blench, Dave McNab, Dwayne Congdon, Laurie Skreslet, Albi Sole, Dan Griffith, Chris Shank, Sharon Wood, Dr. Bob Lee, Wally, me, Jim Elzinga (our leader), and our base camp manager and chef, Jane Fearing. David Cheesmond, the most accomplished and capable climber in Canada at the time, joined an American expedition heading off to the north ridge of K2 and a second American trip heading to the north side of Everest that fall.

Everest Light came down to the wire. Jim burned the midnight oil for three years striving to find a sponsor and put the whole thing together. Contingencies were made for a smaller team of those who could come up with enough cash to pay their own way. I couldn't afford, or find that kind of money, so I wouldn't be going.

Finally it was a chance meeting on an airplane between Al Wiggan, the head of Hayhurst Communications, our Calgary-based advertising firm, and John Barratt, Senior VP with the Continental Bank of Canada, that landed us our sponsorship two months before we were set to get on the airplane. The Continental Bank of Canada became our flagship sponsor and they conducted an internal promotion with their branches endeavoring to regain three-quarters of the deposits that they were at risk of losing during the recession, when many Canadians wanted their money in the big banks.

China was a trip. In Chengdu, a city of nine million people that few of us had ever heard of, Wally and I marveled at row upon row of black Flying Pigeon bicycles, hundreds and hundreds of them all aligned on their kick stands like endless rows of dominos. All identical.

"How in the wide world of sports do you figure they tell whose is whose?" Wally asked, scratching his head.

"They execute bicycle thieves here," Dave McNab grinned. "That's a big incentive to get it right!"

Almost all of the people we saw still wore the communist khakis of blue or gray pants with white shirts and the country felt spookily compliant, homogenous.

We shuffled our armada of Everest Light duffel bags through airports where they would sit in a pyramid that looked like sandbags stacked around a machine gun bunker. The stewardesses on our Civil

Aviation Administration of China flights threw cardboard-boxed lunches at us like it was below them to do so. There was always some bright plastic prize in the box: flowers, good luck charms, key chains. Our seats cost many times what the Chinese paid for their seats. All of our land costs were administrated through the Chinese Mountaineering Association, the CMA, an institution we started to refer to as the Chinese Money Association. Secondhand Boeings, Soviet jets bought from Aeroflot, "Who maintains these things?" James asked me as we took off for Lhasa.

Touring the Potala was sublime. We joined the tight flow of Tibetans shuffling through the Jokhang Temple, and it affected us all. The accumulated air of incense and butter lamps hung heavy like carpet in the dimly lit space—thirteen centuries of it. There were Tibetan pilgrims who had prostrated themselves every bodylength from wherever they've walked from in Tibet—they where matted with dust and protected by thick leather aprons, on their hands they had shoes made from wood and leather, and leather wraps padded their knees. They chanted on each prostration, inch-worming their way to the Jokhang. I felt their piety like living skin inside the temple.

Danny spent a morning in the market buying 800 eggs. Our Chinese cook showed him how to hold an egg between two others to see if it spun. If it spun a certain way our cook wouldn't buy it. We packed the eggs in straw inside cardboard boxes and they became a treasure in Base Camp.

Our first sight of Everest was magnificent—a broad perfect pyramid that stood so much higher than anything else, including the fourth-highest peak on earth, Lhotse, crouching behind the Big E's northwest shoulder. We'd pulled over on a high pass on our last day of driving from Shigatse into base camp. Dust and diesel and Tibetan prayer flags spun from a high cairn of stones like a large psychedelic spider's web. Behind, in the distance, Everest was a black-and-tan-banded triangle draped with slender white couloirs of ice that looked like Buddhist prayer scarfs. The great peak pointed into the sky and was throwing a plume of snow kilometers long, with most of that snow sublimating into the high thin air.

"I didn't expect it to look so handsome from this side," Wally said. "It's a really good looking peak."

Base Camp in the Rongbuk Valley sat at about 18,000 feet and within an hour of getting out of the truck and starting the physical work of erecting tents I felt the distinct pain of each and every cell in my body not getting enough oxygen and all of them letting me know about it. I hurt.

The hurt haunted me the first time I went to the site of our Camp I on the flanks of the Rongbuk Glacier. I pushed too hard to get there and just shy of camp my mind felt like a helium balloon that had lost its tether to my body. My balance shifted and I leaned onto the tops of my trekking poles like they where canes. I began to shiver and I couldn't keep pace with Big Jim and Wally. My pace diminished to a crawl and it was all that I could do to keep upright and keep moving.

Wally and Jim nursed me back to Base Camp by headlamp. Sharon offered to get in a sleeping bag with me to warm me up—I must have been suffering from acute mountain sickness because I said no to that! I was given hot quarts of water and I placed them in between my thighs and under my armpits and against my stomach as I lay in my sleeping bag, all in an effort to warm my arterial blood and my body core.

I was hacking in the wee hours when I saw traces of blood threaded into my thick sputum. "Fuck, Wally, I think that I've got pulmonary edema!"

He rousted from his side of our shared tent, and the eminent neurologist, Dr. Bob Lee, made his first tent call in twenty-five years.

"No, I don't think you have pulmonary edema. I think that you rup-tured a blood vessel in your airway from all the coughing," the doctor gave his considered opinion.

I rested a couple of days fretting about my health. If I wasn't acclimatizing I wouldn't be able to climb. All of my hours of training and getting better as a climber would end with me staying low, or going home. I'd be a failure. But then I started carrying again and my body came around and I felt good.

"OK," I said to myself, "I can climb this peak."

Fixing 7,000 feet of rope up the west ridge of Everest and establishing five camps took the communal effort of our team eight weeks to accomplish and Everest beat all of us down over time. A hard march of physical attrition, but one that meted out some good memories.

Wally stomped across the wind-strafed surface of the Rongbuk to our Camp II at the base of the west ridge while Jim, James, and I stood watching his determined progress. Fifteen feet down from the tent platform where the three of us were standing, Wally swept his new Leki trekking pole high overhead like it was a cutlass. The pole snapped when the basket impacted the glacier and Wally hissed, "Fucking Baptist upbringing!" and marched to our cook shelter— a room carved into the glacier and roofed with trusses of skis and an orange storage tarp. He left Jim, James, and I choking on stifled giggles in his wake.

Later in the trip Dwayne and I climbed together a lot because we were both still relatively strong. I was forcing seven to eight quarts of fluid into me a day because it is what Messner had decreed. Dwayne and I were in one of the tents at Camp II, on our way up. Groggily I reached for my pee bottle in the night and filled it up with one quart of piss, then I fell asleep before I'd screwed the lid on tight and kicked it to the bottom of the sleeping bag where it would act like a hot water bottle for my feet. A half hour later I rolled onto the open bottle and jerked to consciousness in a wet sleeping bag swearing my head off and bolting Dwayne from sleep too.

"Barry, Barry! What's the matter? Are you OK?"

"Fucking fuck, fuck, fuck! I just dumped my whole motherfucking piss bottle inside my fucking sleeping bag! Fuck!"

"Oh, God, I thought there was an avalanche or something. Can I help? Is there any on my side?" Dwayne asked.

"No, but shift over that way, man. Fuck."

I mopped my bag out as best I could and then crawled back inside. In the morning I wiped it out and hung it over the tent to dry, and left it there, as per our system, for the next of my teammates to use.

Chris Shank and I met on the fixed ropes at about 23,000 feet one day, he descending from a carry, me going up with one. The sun had cracked his lips to the point that they looked like the Mojave Desert floor. I could see the glint of fresh blood in several of the fissures and he had both his nostrils packed with swaddles of toilet paper crusted with dry blood. He'd pulled the surgical mask that he'd cut a silver-dollar-sized hole into, to facilitate spitting, below his chin to talk to me. He reasoned that the mask trapped some of the humidity of his expelled breath.

"How's it going lad?" he wheezed and then he convulsed into a lung-ripping spasm of hacking. He'd pulled some muscles in his ribs because of the spasms and I saw tears squeeze from the corners of his eyes.

"Chris, how can you keep doing this, man?" I asked him.

He got beyond the coughing and composed himself, "I can bear any amount of pain for one day. And if I can bear it for one, I can bear it for two."

Wally had bought a copy of Ayn Rand's novel *Atlas Shrugged* and a lot of us read it and, it being a big book that no one wanted to carry in its entirety, it got quartered into sections along its spine. I spent a lot time and energy tracking down the sections to finish it.

"Has anyone seen the section that starts with 'White Blackmail,' page 392? Over," I asked on a radio call from Base Camp.

"Yes, Bubba, it's here in the side pocket of the tent. Over," Albi replied from Camp IV, 6,500 feet above me.

The stalwart Chris. Photo: Jim Elzinga

"Oh crap. Can you bring it down with you? Over."

"I'm not coming down, but I can give it to Woody, she can relay it to Dave at Camp II. Over."

"Yes, please, please. Don't forget. I need to finish this book. Over."

One day Wally and I where heading down from Camp II. We were a month into the trip and both well acclimatized. Wally stopped and stared up the Japanese Couloir to where it linked with the Hornbein Couloir.

"This is stupid, Blanch. Why are we doing all of this work, why don't we just climb up this thing. Just go for it?" he asked.

"Cause we signed on to a team and now we have to be team players."

"Ya, but we could just climb it, you know what I mean." And I believe that Kevin could have, and that he saw that then, before the days wore him down. A couple of months after our team left the mountain Jean Troillet and Erhard Loretan did just that. To the top, and back, in forty-three hours.

We had three teams, A, B, and C, and we'd revolve through weeks of work on the mountain and three-day rests in Base Camp. Wally and I fell into the ritual of making thirty-six-egg omelets on our first morning down. Three pounds of cheese and a pound of Tulip canned bacon (one of the finest inventions in the history of man, one pound of bacon in a can). I turned to get the bacon that I'd cooked to add to the monster omelet one morning, but it was gone!

"Wally, where's the bacon?"

"Oh that bacon, I ate that bacon, Blanch," he replied.

"The whole pound?"

"Uh, ya. I was hungry. What can I say?" And he arced his eyebrows comically and gave me his vampire grin.

The next morning Wally and I had our tent door open and saw Sharon and Jane slowly rising to elbows inside their tent. Both their manes of flowing blonde hair were backlit by early morning light.

"God, they look like lionesses, Wally."

"Yes, Blanch, they are beautiful women."

"Damn straight on that, Walter, damn straight." Desire and longing sat on the haze of a radiant dawn.

All of China, a country over half as wide as Canada, was on one time zone—Beijing standard time. Most of us found it too depressing to see that we were getting up at noon Beijing time so we made our own time zone and it felt a lot better to be admiring Sharon and Jane in the soft morning sun of 8:00 a.m.

I went alone one day across the kilometer-long traverse from Camp IV at 24,500 feet to Camp V at 25,500 feet, and back. It was one of the strongest days that I've ever had at altitude and I felt like I was the athlete that I was at sea level. Alone in the tent at Camp IV that night I started thinking of sex and decided to conduct an experiment purely in the interest of studying human sexuality at altitude. My pulse exploded to over 200 beats per minute and it scared the hell out of me. I thought that I might have hurt myself.

And then it was time for our nightly radio call and Jim's voice came on in the tortured low reptilian hiss that it had become due to a chronic throat infection. We'd taken to calling him the Grand Imperial Lizard.

"How's it going up there all alone, Bubba?" Jim wheezed.

"Well I just scared myself on a date with Mrs. Thumb and her four daughters. My heart rate went through the roof, I thought I might have hurt myself, over."

There was absolute silence for thirty seconds and then the radio crackled to life with laughter howling in the background. Jim tried to talk, but couldn't so he passed the radio to Woody.

"Are you telling me that you...ahem." Sharon couldn't find the words or wasn't willing to say them.

"Yes." More outburst in Base Camp.

"Well, oh my, oh dear. I hope that it was good for you, dear."

Dwayne and I got the job of building an igloo at Camp V. Jim wanted a bombproof snow shelter at each camp on the mountain. It was sick physical work and I could see it drain Dwayne every time he handed me a snow block and stamped back to cut another.

"I have to go into the tent for awhile," he would say about every third block and I'd stay out there shoveling and sculpting.

We got the igloo up, then both of us collapsed into the relative comfort of the tent.

That night I said, "You know what I could really eat right now? A hot dog, I could really eat a hot dog."

Dwayne, who tried to force himself to eat anything up there, and usually ended up throwing it up, said, "Oh shut up, man! I could so eat a hot dog right now."

And then he fell asleep and I lay staring at the grid of ripstop nylon on the roof of the tent counting one-millimeter by one-millimeter squares until I gave in and took a Halcion sleeping pill. We each had our high altitude crosses to bear, mine was insomnia.

The wind began to scream in the night and it thumped at the walls of our tent in spite of the corral of snow blocks we'd erected to above the height of its roof. We couldn't move back to Camp IV and by midmorning we ran out of fuel and I thrashed out the door to get another gas cylinder from out beside the igloo, twelve feet away.

The wind flattened me against the snow wall as soon as I stood. It was like I'd been taken to the boards by an NHL enforcer. Streamers of wind clawed into the sky from Nepal. They looked like high-pressure water jets and rocks the size of playing cards were being shot thirty feet in the air and then hurled violently into Tibet. The shrieking roar of the wind was deafening and overpowering and I instantly felt cornered. I couldn't even stand. I grabbed our two ice tools and flattened myself onto the plaster hard snow of Everest and then reached and planted the tools and dragged myself to the fuel and back.

"How was it out there?" Dwayne asked.

"Fully fucking Monty Python, man."

The storms took their toll and a lobby began within the team to switch our objective from the West Ridge Integral—what we'd come to climb—to the Hornbein Couloir. We had an impassioned meeting and the democratic process prevailed. We'd have more chance of success in the Hornbein.

"I'd rather fail on our harder goal than succeed on an easier route," James stated.

By early May Everest, and her storms, had kicked the crap out of most of us. Sharon, Albi, Dwayne, and I were still relatively strong and at a team meeting it was decided that Dwayne and I were in the best position in the rotation to make the first summit attempt. It was hard for me to believe that those words had been spoken. An ancestral pride burned inside my chest and I went to my tent feeling giddy, proud, and as excited as I had been walking onto the stage of the Jubilee Auditorium in Calgary to receive my high school matriculation from a politician who said to me, "Life is a banquet, son, don't settle for a boloney sandwich." I felt like I was a success, like I was good enough.

"Bubba? Can I come in and talk to you?" Woody asked from outside.

"Sure, Woody," and I unzipped the tent flap and she crawled in.

"I'd like to make the first summit attempt with Dwayne-o," Sharon said.

She and I knew she had a chance at becoming the first woman from North America to summit Everest and that would mean a lot more back home than just another bloke, like me, reaching the top. We also knew that the American team sharing Base Camp with us, and attempting the Great Couloir, were hoping to have Annie Whitehouse make the summit. A wisp of competition and opportunity hung between our teams.

A lead brick plummeted from my throat, through my chest, and smacked down into my guts. Too good to be true, I took a breath and looked into Sharon's eyes.

"OK, Woody. I'll switch with you and I'll make the second attempt with Albi."

"Holy smokes, are you sure, Bubba?"

"Yes. I owe you this. You took on my responsibilities in the fall so that I could go on my honeymoon."

"Ya, but that wasn't worth what I'm asking."

"It was to me, Woody. I owe you this. It's fine."

For a moment it felt like that politician at my graduation had yanked the table cloth out from under the banquet, and then Ayn Rand's philosophical treatment on work and fairness, as presented in *Atlas Shrugged*, was forefront in my mind and my decision felt good, right. I owed it to Woody. I've since come to value the poetry of Rumi far beyond the objectivism of Rand, but I am closing in on fifty-five and it is appropriate that I travel out of my head and into my heart.

May 18, 1986, Woody, Dwayne, Wally, and I crunched into Camp V.

"Hey Dwayne-o, Wally and I will be the first people to use the igloo that you and I built!" I called toward the tent where Sharon and Dwayne, the summit team, would be sleeping. Wally and I were carrying in support.

"Ha, ha! That's great, Bubba. I wouldn't want to think that all of our hard work was for naught."

"Oh crap, it's full of snow." Swirled in as hard as concrete fill, snow filled the space from wall to wall. It took Wally and I an hour to chunk the plug of snow out, and then we got in and bed down and the winds began to strafe our camp like P-5I Mustangs charging pylons in an air race.

The next morning the four of us threaded oxygen masks over our earflap knit caps and neoprene face masks. We shouldered heavy packs and rode the fixed lines out to where they ended at 26,000 feet and then we left them and climbed unroped into the Hornbein Couloir.

The amount of clothing I had on, the size of my double boots inside neoprene overboots, and the restriction of my peripheral vision with goggles on and two hoods over them made me feel like an astronaut. The mountain seemed distant and detached through my eyes yet I felt its firmness every time I planted the pick of my Chouinard Zero and kicked in my crampons.

Midday I was in front and just below the first narrowing of the Hornbein. I held the Zero in piolet ancre with my right hand at the spike and my left wrapped over the head. I saw a tiger-clawed cloud bulge out from the west ridge, then a gust charged across the north face like ocean spray with a discus-sized plate of rock surfing its wavefront. The wind slammed into my right flank and I was flipped I80 degrees to look out on the tawny plains of Tibet. I panicked and kicked my body back square to the mountain, slammed both sets of front points in, and curled my chest and head onto the beautiful Zero ice tool whose aggressive teeth had remained sunk into Everest for the duration of the hit. I breathed and breathed and looked around for Wally, Sharon, and Dwayne. They were methodically climbing up, none of them having taken the focused fist of the gust like me.

Wally caught up to me and said, "I can't breathe through this fucking thing." An eight-inch icicle clung to the exhaust ports of his oxygen mask and I reached and held it and cracked the ice free with smacks from the hammer of my Zero. "Ah, that's better, Blanch!"

It was 8:00 p.m., and I knew that Wally and I had to skedaddle back to Camp V. I finally came onto an apron of snow that would work for a tent, 26,800 feet above sea level. Wally, Sharon, and Dwayne arrived and I cranked my oxygen from four liters a minutes up to ten and grabbed a shovel and went at chopping out a ledge like I was

The summit pyramid of Mount Everest, with the west ridge facing the camera.
Photo: Barry Blanchard

391

Superman. Wally and I emptied our packs, left our oxygen bottles, shook hands with Dwayne and Sharon and wished them good weather and told them to "knock the bastard off!" using our best Kiwi accents. Then we hightailed it back to Camp V.

"Bubba, you've got some frostbite on your face," Kevin said to me.

"What?" I held my sunglasses up like a mirror. A clean quarter moon of black skin had been stenciled onto my right cheek where that sliver of flesh had been uncovered between my goggles and oxygen mask.

"Holy crap," I said.

Then next morning we headed down, passing Danny and Laurie, who were coming up in support, at Camp IV. Wally and I crunched into Camp II midmorning and joined the long anxious vigil of our summit team. It was May 20, just before 8:00 p.m.

Sharon came on the radio, "It's pretty windy but we're twenty feet from the top."

"Do you guys see five guys jumping up and down getting mauled by a big blonde guy?" Dave replied.

"You guys, we're all really proud down here. We're all in tears," Jim joined in.

"We're pretty happy up here," Sharon agreed.

"Don't forget that photo. Do you want us to keep supper on for you?" Dan asked.

And I said, "Talk about good work. There are two people standing on the summit of the world. Kevin said he could make out a guy with brunette hair and buckteeth and a girl in a bikini. For Christ's sake, put some clothes on, eh? Congratulations, Dwayne and Sharon, on your first Himalayan summit. It's the right one. If my lips could stretch that far, I'd kiss both of you."

Dwayne replied, "I wish I had more time up here, it's quite outrageous."

"Must feel good to be above Makalu. How was the rock-climbing?" I asked (Dwayne had narrowly missed making the summit of Makalu in 1984).

"I don't know—5.4, 5.5, just like home."

"Just like guiding on Yam'," I replied.

Twenty feet stretched to two hundred and they didn't summit until 9:00 p.m., but none of the rest of us knew that because the antenna to their radio worked itself loose and got lost. It was -13° F out and they were extended and began a zombie-like descent into the night.

Dwayne's oxygen ran out and he fell well behind Sharon. He wanted to jettison the useless oxygen bottle but couldn't for fear of hitting Sharon below. It is telling of his mental state that he didn't think of anchoring the bottle to the mountain and leaving it behind.

Sharon hit Camp VI at 2:00 a.m.; Dwayne staggered in at 3:30. Dwayne had been on the go for nineteen and a half hours and they were both shattered, yet they knew they had to hydrate. The stove exploded in a fireball when Sharon went to light it and they both leaped from their stupors and thrashed out either end of the tent into the cold black night. Sharon lost her eyelashes and singed her brows. The inside of the tent was a scorched wet mess from the fire-ball and water that got spilled, but, by the grace of God, it hadn't ignited in flame and they crawled back in and fell into sleeps resembling comas.

"Wow, here's the antenna," Dwayne said when he saw it in the bottom of his pack the next morning. Finally, after many anxious hours for the rest of us—working ourselves up to fenzy of worry and then talking ourselves back down and repeating—we heard from them and got the story of their night.

"I'm a real doll," Sharon said, concerned over the loss of her eyelashes.

"We still love you and think you're beautiful. Over." I replied.

"You can make an attempt but only on the condition that there is a team of two at Camp IV or V to back you up," Jim stated.

"OK," I said. We'd just finished an emotionally charged meeting with Jim pushing to quit the mountain on Sharon and Dwayne's success and the fact that we'd had no injuries. The rest of the team said no, that Albi and I deserved a chance. Our permit ran out on May 27.

James, Kevin, and Chris started from Camp II with Albi and me. Chris fell into coughing spasms soon after and looked at me and said, "Sorry, it just hurts too much now." I watched one of the toughest guys I've ever met start down the ropes for the last time.

At Camp III James stated the obvious, recognizing that ground that had taken him ten minutes to climb a month ago had just taken an hour, "I thought I could do it, but I can't. I'm done."

I was so strong and so ready yet I felt my chance being pulled through my fingers like a gossamer thread. Below Camp IV, I waited for Kevin. He came up with tears in his eyes and said, "I'm sorry, buddy. I just can't do this again. I've puked twice in the last hour. I have to go down."

Albi and I got established into Camp IV and talked. I believed that Jim would tell us to go for it.

I picked the radio up at 8:00 p.m., "Hey, Jim, Albi and I are feeling great and we are ready to go for the top."

"That's not the deal we made. There's no one to support you."

"Ya, I know, but right now this is about the safest mountain that I've ever been on. We've got fixed ropes most of the way up it and camps in place. I've never had that behind me before. It's as safe as it can be. We can climb it."

"I think that it is too much to risk, and it is not the deal that we made."

My voice began to crack and I felt myself go to the emotionally overwhelmed place that I'd seen my mother go to when the world had swamped her. My hands began to quake, and I left the radio silent.

"What do you think, Albi?" I asked.

"I say that we just do it, mate, he can't stop us from down there."

"Jim, you have to let us try." And my shoulders heaved and I clenched my eyes but the tears came.

"No, as the leader I'm ordering you to come down. You gave me your word."

I looked at Albi and he shrugged his shoulders and shook his head.

"OK! OK! I'm coming fucking down!" And I threw the radio hard into the vestibule and I cried and cried. An hour later I was heading down the lines.

"I'm not going down," Albi said and he spent the night alone up there and descended the next day.

I had time to think while making my way down. I didn't agree with Jim's decision, and in all fairness to him it was the hardest one he had to make while we were on Everest, but it was a banker's decision, not a climber's. He could hand the Continental Bank of Canada an amazingly successful outcome, why risk that? I still don't agree with it, but I'd signed on to be a team player so I had to play by the rules of that game, and the rules of my friendship with Jimmy.

I walked into Base Camp and went to him and said, "I don't agree with your decision, but I love you."

I knew that I would never sign on to another large, siege-style expedition again. I would return to my fountainhead—alpinism—and try to get up the greatest walls I could in partnerships of two, three, or four, two ropes, a rack, and the packs on our backs. I decided that I would try to climb the Rupal Face of Nanga Parbat in alpine style and that I would return to Everest and attempt it in alpine style. Wally was keen. When I asked Sharon she said in a tired voice, "Oh, Bubba, don't ask me now, ask me later."

Wally and I got so very drunk on Chinese beer in Shigatse, way beyond the tipsiness of our teammates, that first night back under a roof. Way, way beyond that. I fell into the dust of the main cart track at 2:00 a.m. and vomited onto a pile of yak dung. My brother Wally helped me up and we staggered back to the motel and passed out.

From Lhasa, Jim and I traveled out to Beijing to do the initial paper work with the CMA, and so that I could book a permit for my return—post-monsoon 1988. We rendezvoused with the rest of the team in Shanghai and then we got on the plane and flew home. I was on fire to come back as an alpinist.

August 28, 1986, 4:00 a.m., stars pierced the black firmament in clusters and rows and I could see the luminous arm of the Milky Way. My clients, Mary, John, Marvin, and Tom, and I walked away from the Whyte Hut at the northern end of the Wapta Icefield at 5:30 a.m.

"Not as cold as a couple of days ago," I said as we roped up to cross the glacier. It was day five of our mountaineering course and we were off to climb the northeast ridge of Mount Baker, a 10,407-foot peak that is the north guard of the Wapta.

The sky was brilliant blue but the ridge was icy blue and we wore crampons. I cut some steps and belayed from ice anchors several times. It was not the gimme it was when it was covered with supportive snow and I'd just kick steps up and down it as on some of my previous ascents. Coming down the ridge would be a chore.

We summited at noon and I went over to check out the east face as a possible way to get down more directly and hopefully before the snow on the glacier sagged deeper into the crevasses. It looked good so I tied my folks into the end of the rope at seven-foot intervals and started belaying their down climbs for three ropelengths. It was slow going. I descended to my crew facing out and moving quickly.

The angle of the face had backed off and I decided to switch from a belay to a lower to speed things up. It was 2:30 p.m. I stamped out a platform in the forty-five-degree slope and then used my boot to stomp my seventy-centimeter ice ax straight down into the compressed snow. I clipped a Munter hitch locking carabiner into the webbing at the head of the ax, threaded a Munter hitch with an extra wrap into the 'biner and locked it shut, then I stood on top of the ax ramrod straight and took a shoulder belay on the rope. Tom weighted the rope, then Mary, John, and finally Marvin.

I began to slowly pay rope over my shoulder and into the Munter hitch. Marvin was about ten feet down from me when the ice ax jerked and sheared ten inches through the snow, and then it exploded into space and I grabbed hard onto the rope with my left hand and leaned into the slope and screamed, "Self arrest! Self arrest!"

I saw the rope tighten with line tension, watched its diameter compress below my left hand and I heaved at it and the rope pigtailed into rigid spirals above my hand and I watched it entrap my thumb like a constricting snake. I was hauled off and I let go to the inhuman pull on my hand. I felt my thumb pop and heard a *snap* and then I was fighting to self-arrest.

Moist snow hissed under me and I got my elbows in and was decelerating and then I felt the rope suck my harness hard onto my hip bones and I was catapulted into space and smacked into the slope only to be yarded off of it again like a water-skier wiping out at high speed and ludicrously fighting to hold on to the tow rope.

And then the rope went slack and I was on my ass and rocketing toward the bergschrund. I clawed my heels in and braced my legs and flew over the upper lip of the bergschrund. My crampons hammered into snow and I stopped and stood bolt upright.

Heavy, heavy snow poured in behind me like I was standing below the chute of a concrete truck. The weight of it was the weight of the grave and I screamed, "No! No!"

I fought like a wild animal to push the snow away from my back while frantically reefing on my feet to get them out of the concrete. And then the snow pattered to a stop and I could see Marvin's head and shoulders and John's too. They were both calling out for help. I couldn't see Mary or Tom.

"Oh fuck, oh fuck!" I said, knowing full well how dangerous a burial in the snow could be.

I went into hyperdrive, clawing at the snow encasing my feet. The snow was dense and solidly bonded and I ripped my helmet off and gouged at he snow with it.

Both John and Marvin were encased in place and facing away from me. I shouted to them, and Marvin answered and John asked, "Can you see me, Barry? Can you see me?"

I told him that I could, and finally I yanked one foot free and damn near broke the other yarding it out of the snow.

I leapt down to John and snow flew as my heart hammered and I dug as fast as I could. I got him out and told him to dig out Marvin and began hacking and heaving on the rope to have it lead to Mary and Tom.

John got Marvin out and together the three of us dug for Mary and Tom. It took an hour to uncover Tom's face at the bottom of a yard deep hole. I put my head down into the hole and put breath into his lips. They were cold and blue, and his eyes were dilated and unfocused. My artificial respirations produced no response and Tom had no vital signs.

I left him and went for Mary. We found her a half hour later under nearly six feet of snow. My artificial respirations couldn't start her breathing again. I cut her helmet off then cut her pack straps and we were able to pull her out and lay her flat and I attempted cardio pulmonary resuscitation, but she was dead, as was Tom. John had a broken ankle that I needed to tend to and I had a fractured thumb.

We had slid 300 feet down a slope that relaxed from forty-five degrees at the anchor failure to forty degrees at the bergschrund. The snow that our bodies scoured from the slope was what buried us. A Canadian Army group who where sharing the hut with us responded to our signals for help.

Marvin recited a prayer over Mary and Tom and we descended to meet the Army group who had radioed for a rescue. Soon a helicopter was overhead.

The hand surgeon in Banff reconnected a severed tendon in my thumb and reconstructed the shattered end of my proximal phalange with a couple small loops of wire, but the thumb has never been the same, nor have I.

I moved out of the mountains that fall, and back to Calgary. My dear friend Bruce Elkin pulled some strings and got me in to see a very good psychiatrist. I needed to heal my body, mind, and soul.

If we were allowed to relive one minute of our lifetimes I would chose the moment I decided to change to a lower.

Chapter 19

WARD

THE FIRST TIME THAT I MET WARD ROBINSON

was in the mid-1980s. Albi Sole and I had stopped in Banff on our way back from climbing in the Lake Louise group. It was winter and the streets were icy and meter-high snowbanks lined the curbs and they were dirty with gravel and salt.

Ward was living in a three-level ski condo with three other people and when I was led into his room to meet him he was sitting cross-legged on his bed, stitching red nylon patches onto his tattered blue salopettes by hand. "I need to keep them going so that I can keep climbing," he said, his Mediterranean-blue eyes holding mine, yet soft under his straw-blond hair, his jaw was wide and muscularly rounded and I thought, "Wow, this guy looks like Robert Redford in Jeremiah Johnson."

It is funny how you meet a certain few people in this life and know that your spirit and theirs are kindred. It was like the alpinist inside me had instantly tied in with Ward's inner alpinist yet our timid and clunky selves needed to complete some ritual of etiquette.

"I hear you're keen to get out into the alpine," I said.

"Climbing mountains is all that I want to do right now."

"We should get out some time."

"Anytime, man, anytime."

And we started to do some ice climbing together, getting out more and more...until my clients and I slid down the east face of Mount Baker.

The northeast face of Mount Chephren. I spent fifteen days on five different attempts to finally put up the Wild Thing. Photo: Barry Blanchard

Calgary was good for me. I rode my mountain bike, or ran, six miles to my work at the Mountain Equipment Co-op and six miles back in all weather right through the winter. Riding my bike in -30° F, I'd be dressed in much of the same clothing that I'd worn to the high camp on Everest.

I went to rehab for my thumb and eventually got forty-five degrees of flexion back in the joint and the hand surgeon said, "That's pretty damn good, considering you totally shattered that joint. Destroyed it."

My occupational therapist was kinder and said, "The joint at the base of your thumb will become more mobile to compensate. Some people only have forty-five degrees naturally. You'll be able to do everything that you do, no worries, you'll see"—her words have proved true over time.

My psychiatrist gradually, and gently, led me to understand that my decision only became a mistake when there were negative consequences. He encouraged me to learn from it and to grow because of it, and not just in the context of climbing systems but also in the larger context of my life.

Mountains, and dreaming of mountains, kept me on the surface. It was like my climbing was a surfboard and if I clung to it and tried to sit it well I wouldn't sink to the bottom like Kevin had—not that I didn't sink.

I trained hard in the weight room at the YMCA and put a black-and-white photo of the Rupal Face on my closet door. I applied for a permit for the face for the spring/summer of 1988 and I got it. I began organizing expeditions to the Rupal and Everest, both in 1988. My partners would be Albi, Wally, and Ward.

In the fall, when the temperatures dropped and the Rockies locked up in ice, and my thumb could take it, I started climbing again. The first twenty days that I got out, mostly on ice and often with Ward, Wally, Stewart Buroker, or Jeff Marshall, my thumb got in the way of my swing like a Ping-Pong ball had been taped to the front of my Stubai ice tool and it clunked into the ice often, a foreign object. I learned to place it along the back of the shaft and that kept it out of the way and eventually it would wrap the shaft so I wouldn't hit it against the ice anymore.

Early one morning I met Ward in Banff to go ice climbing. He handed me a copy of Climbing Magazine folded to an article, "Kiss or Kill" by Mark Twight.

"Have you read this, man?" he asked

"No, I haven't seen it yet. Is it good?"

"It's absolutely fucking amazing. I read it four times in a row."

"Really?"

"Yes, man, you have to read it."

And I did that night, and I read it again for the next five nights running. It was a manifesto screamed out to my generation of alpinists, like it had been sung by Joy Division's lead man, Ian Curtis, in his haunted baritone—a call to arms.

In January 1987, Jeff Marshall, Jim Elzinga, David Cheesmond, and I made my fourth attempt to climb the northeast face of Mount Chephren. We climbed slower than Kevin, James Blench, and I had on my second attempt. (Kevin, David, TP Friesen, and I had skied up to the face to make the third attempt in April of 1984 but it was too warm and the face was falling apart and we skied away.)

By midday on our second day we were still below the spot were Kevin, James, and I had dug our first snow cave. It started to snow heavily and Big Jim dislodged a snow mushroom from five feet above when he banged away at a piton. The mushroom, the size of microwave, fell free and knocked him out for a heartbeat. He started sliding down the slope with no anchor points on the rope between him and me, and 2,500 feet of mountain below. I was so grateful that he came too and found his ax via his wrist loop and arrested himself.

I breathed out a huge sigh of relief and said, "We have to get the fuck out of here."

That night I was doing the finishing touches on an hour and a half of hard work digging a snow cave for Jimmy and me against the rockwall (David and Jeff were dug in a separate cave seven feet away). I sliced the shovel blade across the arc of our snow roof from the outside edge of the portal and the blade hit the black rock and there was a loud *crack*! And the whole roof thumped down onto the floor of the cave like a VW Beetle dropped onto a flatbed truck from four feet.

"Holy fuck! I am so glad that didn't land on either of us, Jimmy. It would have broken our necks."

"Ya, me too. But what do we do now?"

"More digging, I guess."

The next morning we retreated through the insanity of a blizzard. Snow crowded the air and made it hard to breathe, and somewhere above us the wind raked more snow over the summit of Mount Chephren.

We could hear the avalanches coming and scream to each other to swing to the side of the gully if we were on the rope, or we would cower to the anchor if at the belay, and the avalanches would billow out from Chephren like clouds of ash exploding from a volcano. The snow would charge by, roaring like a giant wave and we would bow our heads to create a channel to breathe for the tens of seconds it took to thunder by and fall away and then we would raise our wet faces to the swirling snow. That insanity became routine for us, and our reactions became rote. We just did the same thing every time another slide thundered down.

When I got home Ward called me and said, "Man, I was really worried about you guys knowing that you were up there in that storm."

A week later Ward was in the Wildboys—a mountaineering shop that the Big Cheese had partnered into to exit his engineering career and hopefully find more time to climb.

"Peter Arbic and I are planning on trying Chephren next week," Ward said to David.

"Have you asked Barry to go with you?"

"No."

"Oh man, you must ask him. He's spent ten days of his life trying to put up that route. It is his route, man, you can't go there without at least asking him."

Ward called me and I moved heaven and earth to clear my schedule.

The dark early morning air tasted like frigid water on my teeth. The fog of exhaled breath hung in small white clouds as Peter Arbic ('PA'), Ward, and I snapped our climbing boots into touring bindings and slid from the highway toward the Mistaya River. The dark silhouette of Mount Chephren towered above us, burying us in 5,000 feet of moon shadow.

Two hours later the day had dawned and I rammed the tails of my skis into a solid drift of snow the size of a sofa. It had formed in the lee of the last huddle of pine trees. The trees were stunted and they'd been gnarled by the wind, the highest of their species claiming new habitat.

The avalanche cone beneath our couloir was massive. A small pocket glacier sat under yards and yards of spindrift-deposited snow. We ascended tight to the rockwall until it veered away. I led out into the wide-open white, nervously feeling each and every vibration in the snowpack through the toecaps of my boots. It was such a relief to get back against the rock and dig out the rack and sink an anchor in.

Ward took the lead onto gray, and then green, ice thinly draped over steep stone. He moved forcefully, shattering and dropping ice, and I thought to myself that I would be tapping my way up and climbing more delicately but also with more protection. I'd drop less ice but I'd take longer.

At Ward's anchor we began moving together with protection clipped onto the ropes between us. Occasionally we'd find rappel anchors from my retreat of two weeks earlier and it was such a juxtaposition to be kicking up the couloir in calm and quiet conditions with a beautiful blue sky overhead and no wind or avalanches.

Two thousand feet higher I tapped my ice tools into tassels and knots of ice draped like a shawl over an overhanging wall of black limestone. I found one blob of ice deep enough to take the shortest Chouinard screw. I precisely chiseled out quarter-inch edges with my front points and then I held my breath and pressed up onto them.

Above I started to dig a snow cave while PA and Ward went to fix the first of the crux pitches. Dusk was dimming our world when Pete broke a hold and plummeted. Ward wrapped the belay line tight to his chest and lunged into the rock and I heard the rat-a-tat of rocks drumming off of his helmet and the clanging of PA coming to a stop ten feet down. Everything stopped and my eyes opened wide. I was crouched in the entrance to the snow cave a hundred feet lower, then I heard Pete laughing and saw him start back up and I breathed again and got back to hacking at the snow.

The Bluet stove hummed along happy and blue-flamed and I chipped pieces of snow from the walls of the cave and stuffed them into the contoured aluminum pot.

"Do this well," I told myself. "Make sure that there is more snow in the pot before you drink. Never let the blue flame not be melting snow, or heating water. Don't waste any fuel, you may need it."

We'd overlapped our ensolite pads on the floor so that there were no cold spots and Pete and I were shoulder to shoulder with Ward's feet sardined between us. We took up the least amount of room that way, and with the doorway closed up with snow blocks save for a couple of small airholes, we'd sleep the warmest. The walls of the cave had glazed over from our body heat and the heat from the stove and grains of snow no longer sprinkled down with each movement.

It was my turn on the Walkman and I saw happiness twinkle in both Ward and Pete's eyes as I listened to the Clash. The musk of Pete's pipe filled our sanctum and I closed my eyes to "Lover's Rock" and imagined myself with a lover in a bedroom, incense smoldering. My life felt so right and fine, like I had a right to the excitement and contentedness I was feeling.

Morning came, and with it more glorious high pressure. High above the Rockies, air was converging and descending. PA, Ward, and I stepped into calm cold air that tasted crisp and a clear, clear pale morning sky, perfect for alpine climbing.

Ward threw his arm over the chockstone like he was wrapping someone in a headlock, and then his crampons grated off and I could see surprise in his blue eyes. He grunted up onto a knee and man-handled the wall until he stood in balance on top of the chockstone.

"Man, he's going for it," I whispered to Pete.

"He wants this, he's hungry for it."

He kneed and backed his way up the crux chimney to the point where he had to cross a slab like polished marble for a couple of yards left to gain the knifeblade crack that I nailed in '84. Ward leaned into a tension traverse and I remembered how it had felt like palming off of oiled glass to me and then, like me, he hooked his tool over the far edge and pulled himself over and wrestled into balance.

"I feel like I just conquered the world!" Ward yelled, and added his war cry about being born with a plastic spoon in his mouth taken from a Sex Pistols cover of "Substitute."

He started aiding up the knifeblade crack. Ten feet up a pin ripped and my hands locked down and beat the jerk of the rope. He was OK, but all of my pores had opened and I released the adrenalin in a long sigh as Ward started back up.

"Scary eh?" Pete said, his dark eyes mischievous and tinkling behind John Lennon glasses.

Ward was higher and aiding when the piton he was standing on exploded like a gunshot and he charged toward Pete and I. I howled and locked my arms and lunged into the wall trying to get as much of myself under my helmet as possible. Then I was wrenched upward and jerked to a violent stop by my anchor line with my feet three feet above the belay ledge. Shrapnel rained down and then rushed away to a hiss and I yanked my eyes up to Ward. He was thrashing to get right himself.

"Are you OK, Ward?"

"Ya, I'm OK. Fuck! Fuck! Fuck! How did I pull so many pieces?" he bellowed, his hands wrapped on to the tight belay line and his eyes looking up to the pitch.

"Can you get off of the rope?" I asked.

"Ya, ya. Fuck!"

I leaned to Pete and said, "God, I'm shaking. I think that I'm more scared than Ward."

"I don't think so," Pete replied looking up to Ward. We talked for minutes to take the edge off. Ward had fallen twenty-five feet and hammered his hip into the slab. He refused to hand over the lead and, like me three years earlier, he went back up and melted the pitons into the crack and drove himself to the belay.

Then it was my pitch and my confidence was waning like the sun that was dimming somewhere far behind Chephren. I saw myself losing control and falling, imagined my bones breaking, saw the blackness and conjured up the pain.

I lowered my eyes to the rack and got tough inside my head, "Cut the shit, Blanchard. You're hesitating. No asking Pete or Ward to take the pitch. Ward's shattered, like you were in '84. Same fall, same burn. We all only have so much to give. Do what Kevin did for you then: Grab the rack and fire. Get after it, you half-breed wannabe."

I bridged my left foot out to hook a small edge with my front points and then I pulled into the dance. For two hours I reached and strived, linking moves higher and higher up a dead-vertical offwidth, each move excavated from a curtain of snow. Finally, I stepped left onto a ledge and a bulletproof three-piton, two-nut belay.

I screamed "Jumar!" into the cold dark night. Blackness fell away for 3,300 feet from three sides of my coffee-table-sized ledge. Ice crystals danced in my headlamp and I felt like I'd been immersed in silver water and I was proud of how well I'd climbed.

"You did good, Chug," I told myself.

Ward and Pete arrived and Ward punched up the snow ledge above and anchored below a steep black chimney. It was the last pitch that we'd managed in 1984 and I told PA, "I remember it as being safe, pleasant climbing."

I rappelled to start digging a snow cave and Pete launched onto the pitch. An hour later the rope was fixed and Ward and PA arrived at the cave.

"I'd hardly call it pleasant," PA said as he narrated his hour of loose rock, spindrift, and frosted glasses to Ward and me. "I'd throw off holds and think, 'I wonder how much that hurts? I must be just beaning Ward down there.'"

"It was OK. You missed me with most of it," Ward replied.

Pete continued, "I had to lower my glasses to the bridge of my nose to see after they frosted up from the spindrift. Thank god it was dark, so I mostly just felt for the holds anyway."

Once we got our cave sealed off and warm, Ward exposed his left hip and there was dark blue bruise the size of a softball bulging from his glute.

"Does it hurt?" I asked

"With every beat of my heart, but it won't affect my climbing. I'm good."

"I hope that we can make it off tomorrow," I said.

"We climbed three hard pitches today. I think that's pretty good," Ward replied.

"Good morning, alpinist Blanchard!" PA beamed in the morning. And then we stepped out and from his highpoint of the night before and began to follow a one-foot-wide, six-inch-deep seam of ice that glowed like chrome and spoke of the hand of God. It was perfect, like the alpinism of my dreams had become my reality.

Three ropelengths up a wave in the ice bulged out to overhanging and I anchored below it. Peter vaulted up and out of sight climbing masterfully and Ward turned to me and his eyes sparkled and he smiled massively and yelled his Sex Pistols war cry.

When I jumared to Pete's anchor I could see that he was freaked and nervous. A half dozen pitons groaned under Ward's weight and Pete was leaning into the wall to take as much onto himself as possible. "These pins are the best I could do, but you need to take some of the weight too. I don't trust them."

It got dark on the next lead, which was mine. I reached high above a chockstone but my pick scratched out, and dust and gravel fell into my eyes. I was doing the splits between crampon points and my calves had turned to stone. I tried again and the pick held and I pulled higher. My forearm started to vibrate. It felt like a strand of barbed wire had been laid inside it and pulled tight. There was a frozen block above and I thrust a number three Friend behind it and it held. I yarded on it and trembled into balance in a small alcove. There was another overhang above, but I felt done in, it seemed too hard. I shouted down to Ward and Pete suggesting that I come down and we finish it in the morning.

"No! There are no options down here. You have to get up, Bubba!" PA yelled from bellow.

I focused on the beam of my headlight and climbed on, and then I was rising to my feet on the summit ridgeline of Chephren!

The night was calm and all of the stars in the universe shone like diamonds in the blackness above us. We leveled a platform in the snow 100 feet down from the top and just rolled out our pads and bags. Pete and I named the constellations that we knew, and the three of us agreed to call our route the Wild Thing.

In the morning we went back up to shake hands on the summit. We walked off of the top at 7:00 a.m. and stormed down the east ridge looking across to the north face of Howse Peak with every step and Ward said to me, "There's a line there."

Down climbing a huge diagonal glacial gully on the northeast face put us right at our skis. At 11:30 a.m. we stepped up to Pete's truck and saw that someone had broken the window and stolen some stuff, but they'd missed his wallet were he'd stuffed it way under the floor mat. Pete treated Ward and I to multiple cheesecakes and beer back in Lake Louise and it was very, very fine. We felt like kings.

Chapter 20

PERU

JAMES BLENCH, DAVE STARK, AND I guided a trip to Peru that spring with a group of Yamnuska Mountain School clients. My little brother, Steven, was floundering again and I took him along to try to help him. He was twenty-one now and even bigger—my hand-me-down mountain clothes looked tight on him. He came to the top of Ishinca with us and when I asked him if he was having any fun he cracked a big goofy grin and said, "It's fun to be on top, Bear, but it is so much work!"

When we went for the summit of Huascarán Norte, Steven stayed back in Huaraz where he made some friends and wound up hawking hamburgers from a Styrofoam cooler on the main street. He also learned how to change money on the black market off of the main street.

Our clients left and a dozen of us Canadians, including Peter Mair, Matt MacEachren, Rob Rohn, and the brothers Jim and Kevin Haberl, headed into the Quebrada Santa Cruz to attempt several different mountains. Steven came along to man our base camp and try and catch some fish.

Brothers: Steven and I on the summit
of Ishinca in the Cordillera Blanca.
Photo: James Blench

James Blench and I were on our second day on the Fowler-Watts route on Taulliraju and we were making good progress under a perfectly blue sky when we both felt a black cloak of dread settle onto our heads. There was no rational reason to go down, yet we both had a bad feeling and at 10:30 a.m. we started rappelling down to the glacier.

Back in base camp I had the first spoonful of canned ravioli to my lips when two climbers charged into our camp and said, "There's been an avalanche." Peter Mair, Matt MacEachern, and Rob Rohn had been pummeled by a collapsing sérac while climbing Quitaraju. I put the ravioli down and we packed up and headed toward the Quitaraju-Alpamayo Col.

Early the next morning we approached our friends' makeshift emergency camp. As we got in earshot of the camp I shouted out, "Anybody here order Chinese food!" and a half dozen of our friends poured out of their tents laughing for the first time since the ice avalanche at 10:20 a.m. the previous day. We learned that Rob had a badly broken leg and broken back. He was a litter case.

"I guess that explains why we came down from Taulliraju, hey, James?" I stated.

It took four days and the communal effort of twelve different people from four countries to get Rob over the col and down to the valley where a Peruvian military helicopter was able to pick him up. James, Kevin, and his brother, Jim, and I went back up to the col when the rescue was done and climbed parallel routes up the west face of Alpamayo while my brother Steven fished in the valley.

As we walked out of the Quebrada Santa Cruz I learned from my fellow guide, Dave Stark, who had run out to Huarez to organize Rob's rescue, that David Cheesmond had died on the Hummingbird Ridge of Mount Logan. Steven's brown eyes opened wide, "Oh man," he said. I saw his innocence—he had no fixed point of reference for death.

I sank to my haunches, head in hands. My brother walked over to me, and I trembled and cried, held in his enormous arms.

I quit climbing and guiding, and later, back home in Canada, I sat at my desk and wrote a letter to the Big Cheese.

Letter to a Friend, Summer, 1988

So it's true. A cornice cut loose off the Hummingbird and you're dead. I didn't think it would happen to you. You'd done so much. The crafty old fox. It's a name you gave yourself. I even use to fancy that you looked like a fox. "If Dave was an animal, he'd be a fox."

I'm bitter and sad. I know you didn't want to die climbing. I hope you had time to accept your death. Time to get beyond the terror of the event. I can feel that terror. I can raise it in me now. The pressure of the snow encasing every broken limb. The darkness like someone forcing a pillow over your face. No air to breathe, suffocating.

Maybe the fall smashed the life out of your body, quickly. I hope it was quick or that you had time enough to be calm. I just don't want to think that you died with panic in your heart.

I have regrets. I almost wish we'd chosen to be painters or musicians. Something less lethal. I don't know if five years of intense experiences was worth more than thirty years of growing friendship.

I do know we've been guilty of ignoring our mortality. We laughed off the "close ones." It's a bit of a trap. We got into it so far we lost our perspective. It always happened to someone else. Maybe they made a mistake. The mistake is forgetting that you're dancing with death. All the joy and growth we got out of it was only in us. The mountain moved and you were in the way.

The lads put you out right, Cheese. We drank. We got philosophical. I told them about the night you and I got together to do a bunch of work on our Rakaposhi Expedition but drank a case of beer instead. Jokingly, a sly glint in your eye, you told me your own philosophy that night, "Life is a pork chop. Why not? It holds together just as well as any other philosophy." We all laughed and then we told more Cheesmond stories, and we howled, and eventually we danced. I danced with my whole being, buddy. I danced for you too. Here's to you Dave. You were one of the very best I've met. You'll live in me for a long time.

Love,
Barry Blanchard

"Do you need any help?" I asked the guy who I'd been told was the boss.

"Do you have any roofing experience?"

"No, but I'm a really hard worker and I can learn."

He looked at me and bit his lip, "OK, come on up the ladder."

My roofing boss was a good guy, but cheap. He wouldn't buy a power ladder to get the heavy bundles of shingles up onto the high roofs. My partner and I would spend hours packing the bundles up the ladders on our shoulders. My mistake was to always use my right shoulder.

Tim Pochay and I got out again in August. The Yellow Edge was one of Urs Kallen and Billy Davidson's great aid lines up Yamnuska. They'd climbed it in 1974, a bold overhanging prow of limestone named after a similar feature in the Italian Dolomites. Peter Croft and Colin Zacharias had freed the route at 5.11b in January—of all months—two years before.

I got pitch four, the first 5.11 pitch, and I was splayed out in an iron cross-like position at the crux concentrating on raising my left foot, and looking to it, when I felt my right shoulder, the one I'd burdened with so many shingles over the summer, *clunk* and I heard a sound like someone tearing a drumstick off of the Thanksgiving turkey. I slashed my eyes across to it and my shoulder and deltoid were gone, a dark hollow in their place.

"Holy fuck! I just dislocated my shoulder! I'm coming off!" And I sailed clean off Yam and bounced to a stop thirty feet lower in space. My shoulder felt like a butcher knife was in it and I groaned and instinctively raised my arm over my head and it didn't hurt as much and I lowered it and the knife stabbed in again. I lifted it again and herd the *clunk* of the reduction and the pain was gone. And then I did one of the dumber things that I've done in this life and windmilled my arm aggressively through a couple of full rotations.

"Hey, Poch. My shoulder went back in and it doesn't hurt anymore. I think I can go back up and finish the pitch."

"Are you fucking insane? You just ruptured your shoulder capsule! You're coming down right fucking now!"

"Oh ya, right."

I lowered to Poch and he went about orchestrating our descent down the overhanging ground as I waited at the anchors, guarding my arm across my chest.

On our second rappel I saw our ropes sucked cello string tight over the edge and then bounce across it in a series of high tension skips. Eventually Poch yelled, "Off rappel!"

When he had hauled me through fifteen feet of air into his anchor I asked him what had happened. "I went for the giant fucking spin-o-rama through space, man."

I went to the hospital and on to a couple of months of physiotherapy for my shoulder, and a semester at the University of Alberta, in Edmonton, for my mind. I was on probation as I'd dropped out of the University of Calgary during my second semester in 1978 when I'd been put on the Dean's list, the bad one. Now I was twenty-nine and taking courses that interested me: two geography classes, the classics, philosophy, and comparative literature. I'd come to know some about the opposite sex and beer and it was interesting to see the eighteen-year-olds in the place that I had been a decade before.

During one of my sessions in the weight room I watched a guy go for his personal best bench pressing. The bar flexed under the tremendous stacks of plates on either end of it and the guy's wrists look comically small as they slowly pressed the final inches. He was groaning and his spotter was right over him shouting loads of encouragement. The guy made the lift and the bar hammered into its cradle and vibrated. The lifter limboed out from under and stood and his pecs trembled with lines of power, "All right! I hurt, therefore I am!" I smiled and laughed and wrote that one down.

By semester's end I was back on the Dean's list, but this time the good one. I continued to organize for the Rupal and Everest expeditions between my classes and the New Years saw me fit, able, and keen to climb.

"Holy crap, it's the Wild Things climbing van," Ward said, and then his blue eyes lit up and he smiled hugely and leaned forward in the passenger seat of my silver Toyota Tercel station wagon, the first new car that I'd ever owned.

"No way!" he added as he sat upright. "It must be Mark Twight! Let's stop and see."

We were driving south on the Banff-Jasper highway and the white van was emblazoned with the jagged pink logo "Wild Things" like it had been clawed into the metal. Below was "Climbing Team" and the van was parked in the Weeping Wall parking lot and two guys were shuffling around it amongst a bunch of climbing gear. I'd just seen the van pictured in an advertisement in the latest edition of *Climbing Magazine*.

Ward had met Mark in Chamonix that summer when he and PA had been climbing there. "We were at the Guide's Office looking at the weather forecast when this guy said, 'so you guys are from Banff, eh?' And it turned out to be Mark Twight and we talked to him for quite awhile. When he left I asked PA, 'How did he know we were from Banff?' and PA said, 'It's in big felt pen on the back of your pack: Ward Robinson, Banff, Alberta, Canada, dude.'"

I pulled the car around and Ward and I hopped out. "Holy shit! If it isn't Ward Robinson from Banff, Alberta, Canada!" said a guy with long Jon Bon Jovi hair wearing a pink and purple Wild Things one-piece climbing suit. It was Mark and I was excitedly shaking his hand.

"I've read 'Kiss or Kill' about forty times," I said.

"Wow that must be some kind of record," he said, and then he smiled and laughed easily.

We got introduced to his partner, Randy Rackliff, who was wearing a red and white Wild Things one piece. Randy was quiet and withdrawn, the opposite of Mark who was exuberant and engaging. We shot the shit for a long time and I ended up giving Mark my number to get out climbing while they were in the area. And he and Randy and I did get out ice climbing to Carlsberg Column.

Mark and I hit it off well, but he had a rougher start with Kevin who he met for the first time at the Wildboys climbing shop in Calgary shortly after Mark's second article on his second attempt on Nuptse, "Glitter and Despair," had been published.

"Oh, you're that Twight guy. I thought your last article really sucked, man." And not even Mark, a man rarely if ever at a loss for words, knew what to do with that so he turned and walked away.

"Bubba, I'm not going to be able to go to Nanga Parbat," Albi said. "Albi Expeditions (a guiding business that he'd started) needs my time and I just can't justify an expedition for myself right now. I'm sorry."

We would be leaving in about three months time and I knew we'd have to find someone to take Albi's place. Ward, Kevin, and I all agreed that Mark could be our man.

"I might have pissed him off, though," Wally admitted, "but it will be a good test to see if we can get beyond that. See if we can really get to know each other."

I invited Mark for dinner in a chic restaurant on the fashionable Fourth Street in Calgary.

"Would you like to come to Nanga Parbat and Everest this year?" I asked him. He grinned wide and said, "Yes, yes." Congratulating me on our decision and then he said that he'd love to come.

Our conversation shifted to some of the most important books we'd read and when I said *Motel Chronicles* by Sam Shepard he smiled and laughed and repeated "Yes, yes," again, and then he quoted the book's epigraph:

Never did far away charge so close   Cesar Vallejo

At 2:00 a.m. on March 9, 1988, Ward and I stepped from a cold street in Banff into Geoff Creighton's van. Ward took shotgun and I stretched out in the back. Geoff pushed Blue Rodeo into the cassette player and we pulled out for the four-hour drive to Mount Edith Cavell in Jasper. The north face of Cavell had never had a winter ascent and we had just two days to do it, as Geoff and I had to be back to film some ice climbing with the Canadian Broadcast Corporation on the eleventh.

We rolled into the parking lot at daybreak and clicked into skis for a long twelve-mile ski up the Cavell Road.

At a hostel close to the mountain, Ward and I waited for Geoff. He liked to train hard every day and unfortunately he'd done just that for the last two days.

"I just don't have the energy to do this," he said. "I'm going back to the van and I'll be there tomorrow when you guys come down. I promise."

The air felt Arctic and gaunt clouds clung to the face. Ward and I knew that the cold wouldn't allow long belays or bare hands and we decided to take the line of least resistance and to keep moving to keep warm. We unloaded a lot of the rack onto Geoff and continued toward the Angel ice tongue.

A beautiful sea blue emanated from the ice of the Angel, but it was deadly, as the icefall commonly calved and a half acre of glacial topography could crumble in seconds exposing blue ice that hadn't seen the light of day for at least a hundred years. Ward and I wove our way through crevasses and into troughs.

I was cramponing up a semitrailer-sized hunk of blue ice when it cracked deep and loud underfoot and at the same instant settled one centimeter. My arms shot out and everything stopped, my heart included. The blue rope slithered on and I followed it, cramponing on eggshells and peering into deep black cracks and chambers bordered by snow and gray ice. Soon we were clear of the icefall and sitting on our packs on the flats of the upper glacier. The north face of Cavell scraped skyward like the white cliffs of Dover seen from the beach.

It had already been a long day and we were tired so I dug the stove out and we brewed up and drank and ate for an hour, and then we punched steps up the lower face. Snow-covered rock commanded our attention yet we climbed unroped, both secure in the knowledge that neither of us would make a mistake. A huge ramp slanting left to right took us onto the Beckey-Chouinard-Doody route.

A large snow ledge cut across the entire face there and I worried about the avalanche hazard so we roped up. Ward began traversing left across the ledge to find a break in the overhangs above us. When the rope came tight I followed removing the gear he'd plugged into the wall and screws from the ice on the ledge. I kept the rope snug between us. One thousand feet left and still no break. Our line looked ridiculously indirect but we were moving and warm.

Ward happily ensconced in our coffin-sized snow cave on the north face of Mount Edith Cavell. Photo: Barry Blanchard

The sun set and a bitter wind began to cut the face. I probed and probed searching for three feet of snow depth to dig a cave in but there just wasn't enough. Ward balked at my suggestion of a ledge, "I have to get inside the snow, I'll freeze to death out here in my bag."

We continued into the night and a familiar feeling of desperation rose inside me as my core temperature sunk. We were losing control. Finally the spike of my ice ax did not hit ice and I dug a foot and a half down and plunged it again. It hit ice, but I thought that we could get a snow cave and I shouted to Ward. He returned and we started to dig.

We got the smallest cave I'd ever seen, about the size of a coffin. We squirmed in and I dug out the stove but it wasn't burning properly and I began to feel dozy. Ward had fallen asleep and I jolted to the realization that we were poisoning ourselves with carbon monoxide! I turned the stove off and jiggled my knee where it lay against Ward's chest.

"I think we should just go to sleep, man. This stove is going to kill us."

"No, I need water. I have to have some liquids." Ward took the stove apart and cleaned it and it fired to life full force and we ate and drank in normal consciousness. Then we turned it off, and twisted our headlamps off, and fell into unconsciousness.

The next morning we found our break at the Colorado Spur. The climbing was superb and we sprinted up sixty-degree ice and over short mixed steps. Whenever I wanted a piece of protection, it was

there. I turned the final rockband and entered a perfect couloir of rolling ice. For a moment I saw myself from a bird's-eye view and I was moving quickly and confidently in my yellow and blue suit, my tools going in with precision and purpose. I was an animal of the wall, I belonged there.

Then my reverie was shattered by Ward's bellowing, "Blanchard! You fucking lead-hog! Bring me up and let me lead some of this!"

I smiled when I passed him the rack. "What can I say, man? It was just so good, and it just kept coming."

I'd "hogged" an 800-foot block. Ward led us to the east summit. It was 10:00 a.m. and through the haze I could just make out the man-high crucifix marking the west summit. It floated in and out of my vision like a phantom, never any hard lines. We smiled and shook hands, took off the rope and started down toward the east ridge.

At one point we did a rappel and I pulled the rope down and let it pile up at my feet. Ward turned and down climbed a short wall then stood on a ledge looking back up to me. I wanted the rope out of my way and grabbed the end and took up some coils. "I'll throw this down to you Ward."

I chucked the coils just as a strong gust tore over the ridge. What happened next almost made me sick: The coils were hauled on the wind and hurled over the south face. The rope rose to life in an accelerating loop, and in a half a heartbeat the end snapped like a whip and whistled over the edge and the rope was gone. Our only rope was gone!

I wanted to yell but I had no breath. We had a thousand feet of down climbing and rappelling to go and we had no rope! I looked down to Ward's eyes and they were calm and casual under the blue hood of his down jacket. My eyes were pleading.

"Well, we don't have to carry that anymore," he smiled. And then he reassured me saying that we should be able to solo down the rest of the ridge, if he remembered right (Ward had soloed a route on the north face in the fall and descended the east ridge).

I tried to down climb to Ward five times and retreated upward each time I felt myself teetering on the edge of a fall. I was scared and considered pounding in a piton and lowering on my prussiks tied together. Ward sat patiently on his pack. I tried down climbing again and this time I found the hold that I'd been missing. My moves weren't pretty, but they worked. I made it to Ward, but I was a bit of a wreck from the adrenalin I'd just processed, and the knowledge that I'd burned a half hour of daylight.

I forced myself to peek over the south face for the rope, and the rope was hooked over a rock spike twenty feet below. I managed to recover it by rapping to the end of my tied-together prussiks, inverting at the waist, and hooking it with my ice tool.

"Nice recovery of the rope," Ward said.

My crisis had cost us an hour, but at midnight Geoff pulled us back onto the cold dark streets of Banff and he and I were up early the next morning in Canmore meeting the CBC folks at the Yamnuska Mountain School.

"Such rich and fulfilling lives we lead." I quipped.

Three days later, on March 14, Ward and I were driving north again. We had one week to climb and had wanted to try the Emperor Face on Mount Robson but concluded that it just wasn't going to fit unless we could afford, or get someone to pay, for a helicopter.

We'd looked long and hard at the north face of Howse Peak on descent from the Wild Thing the winter before and although séracs negated half of the face, a chimney system swept by them safely and a line was there, waiting for us.

On the drive Ward told me about his last shift working as a roughneck on a drilling platform. It was a job that I always thought I'd end up doing. Many of the men that my mother and aunts knew were roughnecks and I pictured myself doing what they did, but hopefully not losing all the fingers on one hand like one of those men had.

"It was -40° F and me and my partner were supposed to start our shift at midnight and we were getting ready when I asked him, 'Why are we doing this? This is just stupid in these temperatures.' He looked at me and said, 'It's gotta get done.' And that was the logic that got me through the shift, 'It's gotta get done!'"

Ward was a total lifestyle climber and he lived his climbing like Tom Waits lived his music. He'd work logging, roughnecking, or construction for four or five months then quit and climb until his money ran out. He was one of the original Squamish climbing bums driving a cab in North Vancouver, living out of his pickup truck, and climbing all over the Chief.

We'd been drinking at one of Calgary's first punk bars earlier that season and I pressed him about his lifestyle. His pale blue eyes nailed me over top of his beer glass, "I believe in what I'm doing." Hard, honest, and slightly confrontational: I loved it.

We parked at the same place as we had for the Wild Thing, but skied off toward Chephren Lake, or so we thought. The sun slowly warmed an oozing mass of cloud and we saw that we'd missed the lake and skied down the creek that drains it right back to our starting point on the Mistaya River. The mistake could have cost us an hour, maybe more, and I was pissed.

"Major fuck-up," Ward said with a laid-back West Coast fatalism. In a rage I sliced my skis through the damp air and charged back into the woods.

It was open season on anything green and in the way, a battle that I soon exhausted my rage on. A half hour later I skied onto the flat plain of the lake. Ward followed, unfazed by my tantrum. We both lost it sometimes.

The flotsam of gray cloud rose and the first part of the route was revealed like a white satin slowly being lifted from a marble sculpture. A steep rock buttress was on the right and a huge open snow slope lay to the left. The rock looked too hard and the snow too much of an avalanche threat. A faint line arced up the middle of the rock and we skied toward it hoping there was a gully.

The gully existed, and I was soon tapping my tools into emerald-green ice of grade 2 difficulty while small grains of snow sifted from the air. There was no danger, just good quality, enjoyable climbing and when I looked back to Ward he had on his big Robert Redford mouth-full-of-teeth smile and I snapped his picture for posterity.

The mountain swept us up in a gradual curve and I punched straight up. The snow soon reared to vertical and got me bridged out, wide pressing for support. It felt like Peruvian snow climbing and I appreciated the delicateness of it, and the risk of falling. It engaged me and focused my climbing and I continued into it without the rope, palming and pushing, uncovering the supportive.

Above, the angle kicked back with every step and Ward and I were soon sitting on our packs, relaxing in safety for a few minutes. Above us was a wind-sculpted edge of snow that looked like the edge of a sail blown taut. We marched up it and soon abutted into the mountain proper. We turned the first rockbands, climbing ropeless, via gullies and short traverses.

We soon roped up and I took the first lead and pounded in three pitons to protect a corner that leaned and spilled out into the abyss. When I ran out of rope we started moving together and the rope vibrated between us and I could feel Ward's enthusiasm. We were in our glory: mixed ground, full packs, climbing fast, doing what we did well.

Then a wall of black limestone kicked up in front of me and I anchored and pulled in the rope to Ward. I could see his excitement as he climbed to me grabbing gear and snatching glances above. Both of us had made ascents of this part of the ridge in summer and as Ward organized himself to lead he told me about how Sharon Wood, his partner, had thrown his camera off here in disgust when he told her he was shooting black and white prints, not slides.

Howse Peak, with the northeast ridge that Tim and I climbed in 1981 in sunlight and the north face, that Ward and I made the first ascent of over four days in March 1988, in shadow.
Photo: Barry Blanchard

"How do you give a slideshow in black and white prints?" Sharon had asked. "I guess I'm not the slideshow type," Ward replied.

"She really threw your camera off?" I asked.

"No. She dropped it here and she felt terrible about it and she bought me this new camera after the climb, which she didn't have to do, but I'm glad she did."

I told Ward about TP Frieson and I dragging ourselves back to the highway in 1981 after two extra unplanned hungry bivies and me nearly drowning in the Mistaya River. He treated me to his deep honest laugh. Ward only laughed when he thought something was funny. He was still glancing back at me and giggling as he started the pitch.

He charged onto the pitch like he did whenever he climbed in the alpine. Speed and efficiency were paramount to him and if grabbing some gear put him ahead faster, he did it. Winter alpinism was hard enough without any added concern for free climbing. "Free as can be" was his motto and he was living it up there then, front points skyhooked onto small edges, mittened hands sweeping snow from the rock to uncover handholds. I knew that he was foregoing some protection to make time.

My next lead was unique. Twenty feet up we needed to lower onto a snow ledge down and right of the ridge. Ward wanted to lower me to it, but I couldn't find any gear and the only option was to let the rope cut into the top of large cream roll of snow that clung to the ridge between him and me. I was standing on it so I lowered to my knees and bitched some before cutting the rope into the snow and sinking onto Ward's belay.

The rope sawed into the cream roll as Ward lowered me and I came up with a contingency if it broke. Both tools at the ready, I envisioned myself clawing in like a cat, then I realized that I'd be chased by a couple of tons of well bonded snow.

Once on the ledge a delicate but protectable traverse landed me at the site of our first snow cave. Ward followed the pitch by rappelling sideways from his anchor on one rope while I pulled on him with the other.

The memory of our cramped cave on Edith Cavell was still fresh in his mind and he insisted that we dig a big cave with a seven-foot-long flat floor, contoured walls, and enough headroom to sit up. We weren't done digging until 11:00 p.m. Ward believed that five hours of quality sleep was better than seven hours of cramped semiconsciousness. I knew that he'd dig all night and create a snow condo if I let him.

The sky cleared overnight. We had started out in a storm and climbed into blue sky! One fifth-class pitch and 400 feet of stiff snow yielded quickly and we stood riveted to our anchor staring into the key feature of the route, the Gash, a deep dark fissure cut into the mountain long, long ago. Snow strangled everything and our clear sky meant little. A black veil hung over the place. Humans weren't supposed to be here.

"Do you want to take the first lead?" Ward asked calmly.

I drew from his courage and replied, "It's gotta get done."

I entered the Gash and mixed-climbed to some good pitons, then higher to a huge orb of snow set into the Gash like a giant's Adam's apple. All the snow was over vertical and I had to pound feet and ax shafts into it hard to advance. The pitons were a long ways away and my body was trembling and hauling in huge lungful's of air. Gravity was trying to grab me and my fear of falling was pushing hard on my mind. I had to move and the realization of that rousted the fighter inside me and I stabbed in a solid tool and looped the rope over its shaft for protection.

I made the belay but fear started to invade my mind. I wanted to get the hell out of there, but then Ward was beside me eyeing the route above and arranging the rack. There was no reason to retreat so I stood silent and inched the rope out to him.

One hundred feet up was a vertical drape of snow that I'd never seen anything like before. Ten feet of snow three inches thick hanging like it was a white shower curtain. Behind it was a cavern with a flat floor and a fifteen-foot roof with a chimney/crack running up its edge.

My confidence was gone and Ward could see it as much as I could feel it and we agreed that it would go better if he took this pitch. He threaded his way out to the lip. Seven aid placements and then he was stuck standing in étriers and not knowing what to do. I shivered and fretted and then he said that he had a shitty horizontal pin and that he was going to move on it.

Snow sprinkled down in slow seconds and I paid out only what rope was needed. And then it all accelerated and Ward came hammering down into my field of vision like airplane wreckage. My body closed down like a steel fist on the ropes and I took the jerk and then everything stopped and I yelled, "Are you alright? What happened?"

Ward was spinning slowly on the end of the rope and he righted himself and groaned, "A frozen hold broke loose. Fuck. I'm OK."

"What do you want to do?" I asked, and I was hoping for retreat as the answer.

"I'll try it again, just lower me so I can take a minute."

The light of day faded. I stood with my fear and Ward went back up and succeeded. The shitty horizontal piton came out in his hand as he lowered back to me.

We bedded down on the ledge and the northern lights danced yellow, green, and lavender across the cold Alberta night. I told Ward about Kevin and I watching them spellbound before the Grand Central Couloir on Mount Kitchener six years earlier.

In the morning I jumared out of the cavern and into another cloudless perfect day. I aided up a snow-gagged offwidth on Friends and into the couloir above. One hundred feet up I got two wired nuts, a piton, and an RP, but I wasn't comfortable with them and I added my tools and body as backup. Ward jumared and my harness choked down onto my hips and my nerves burned, then went numb. I didn't let up until I saw him enter the couloir then the vice slackened and I massaged my throbbing pressure points. I felt good, like the more the sky opened above me the less I was under the guillotine.

We moved together out from the Gash and, incredibly, after two days of hard climbing, acres of shallow glacier planed off to our right. Above us Howse Peak scraped into the sky for another 1,500 feet. The "magic line" that we'd spotted coming down from Chephren was nothing more than a shallow crease, probably unclimbable.

"Fuck. I've had it with this," Ward said, and I couldn't believe my ears. "I think we should traverse off and get the hell out of here. I'm just not enjoying it anymore."

It was only noon and I was feeling strong. A couple hundred feet to the right another couloir was visible. I convinced Ward to come and take a look. If need be we could always retreat to here and traverse off.

An hour later Ward led a thin ice vein to an ice face where we moved together with one screw per ropelength. The mountain reared up and I followed a strip of gray ice brazed into the back of a vertical corner. I was climbing well, using my fear to hone my movement.

My pitch ended with a delicate traverse and Ward amazed me by running across it. I told him to take it easy and his eyes swept up to mine, "I'm going for it. If I fall off, I fall off."

At the belay he added, "If we keep banging away at it we're going to get up. I just hope we don't take any long falls." And then he got locked into the one really psycho pitch of the route.

He was seventy feet out when he shouted, "I can't find any protection. I can do the climbing, but nothing between you and me is going to hold fuck-all!" He stood at the threshold: Down climb and we'd be retreating because even though we wanted to do the route we won't knowingly climb onto a death pitch; or grab the next holds and become fatally committed.

He stepped over the line and took his life in his hands. Ward climbed to the very best of his ability and then he went a razor's edge beyond that. Higher up he got some gear, and then an anchor and when I climbed to him his eyes were electric and he said, "I was just fuckin' givin' 'er!"

He had his blue down jacket on and the night cold was closing in on us. I congratulated him on an amazing lead and then I tacked over to a snow mushroom that would be our home for the night.

An hour later we had a three-by-six-foot ledge leveled onto the mushroom. Dark ice slopes fell into the black all around us, and everything was tied in. Ward refused to sleep with his head and shoulders out over the drop and he thought that I was crazy to do so, but it gave us both more room. We were 5,000 feet up the face and I felt like I was sleeping on top of a weather balloon.

In the morning, I climbed up and across snow flutings interspersed with green ice. Ward tensioned right and traversed to the base of the final chimney. It was steep and choked with snow and I wedged up it for an hour clearing snow and fighting for inches.

Below, Ward was listening to the Clash and singing and dancing tied tight to his anchor. I took one last look at him and squeezed through the final foot of the chimney and rose to my feet on the back slopes of Howse Peak.

Ward and I traversed the White Pyramid that day to follow the east ridge of Mount Chephren down like we had the year before. It was long past dark when we got to the end of Chephren Lake. We were out of fuel and we had one bag of hot chocolate left. The outflow of the lake was open water and Ward and I filled our water bottles and threw handfuls of dry hot chocolate into our mouths, chased with ice cold water. We'd churned it into a slurry and swallowed it, and it was enough of a boost to get us back to the highway and our vehicle.

We'd just climbed the hardest winter route of our lives and we got it first go. Two months later we got on the plane for Pakistan and the Rupal Face of Nanga Parbat.

———————

I recently asked Wally about his katabasis—his trip to the depths— back in the mid-eighties, thirty years ago, how he'd gotten out of it.

"I finally got fucking bored with it, Blanch, and that was it, I got fucking bored with it."

The end of my idealism came in 1986 and '87. The deaths of my clients, Mary and Tom, and my dear friend and mentor, David, made me realize that I could not live up to my ideals. The world is not ideal. When I was kind to myself, which had happened too infrequently in my life, I'd say, "You're a mortal, perfection doesn't exit for you. Perfection only exists for the gods." Too often, though, I would convince myself that I wasn't good enough.

My katabasis came in the early nineties. On one of my worst nights I called Kevin, "I just can't be alone in this house tonight, Wally."

"We'll be right up, Bubba. Don't worry, man, we're on our way." Kevin and his bride, Yolande, got in their car in Calgary and drove an hour and a half to be with me in Canmore, to just be with me.

I moved out of town and sequestered myself in #6 Shady Lawn Motel, a defunct enterprise in Dead Man's Flats. One of my buddies called my minute cabin, "four sheets of plywood with a roof."

"Mr. Blanchard, why didn't you file your taxes last year?" The woman with Revenue Canada asked me over the phone. What do you say about a black year? A year of living in your darkness?

"Well, to be quite honest, when I got up every morning I didn't know if I would be going to bed at night so taxes seemed pretty damn far down the list." There was absolute silence over the phone line, thirty seconds of it.

"And I was busy, really busy." I added.

"Busy is good. Yes, busy is good."

Climbing kept me moving upward, going toward the light. I climbed almost every day. Now I see my young daughters growing toward the sun each and every day. The divine beauty of that is a miracle.

When I asked my mother what was good in our family she said, "We always treat everyone as human beings." And then she took me into her arms and hugged me and kissed me on the forehead. I heard an ancestral voice in her words..."human beings."

A dark lake of sadness underlies human life and we skate on thin ice. Most of us break through at some point and it is solely human hands that bring us back to the surface. Hopefully we bring truth back with us, and share it.

I couldn't answer Kevin when he asked, "Why are we here?" in a dank basement thirty years ago. I can now, and I know that he knows too, it is for love. Love is the reason we exist.

Do we have the resolution to do this?
if not, are there higher resolution images that
we could use for detail shots?

ALPHABET BLOCKS

Also known as ABC/123 Blocks. Exceptionally loose walls of rock are often said to resemble vertically stacked alphabet blocks, a bookcase, or vertical kitty litter.

ARÊTE

A thin, almost knifeblade-like ridge or rock created by two glaciers eroding parallel U-bottomed valleys. The word is applied to all like structures in the mountains whether they are composed of ice, snow, or rock, or various combinations of the three.

BERGSCHRUND

German for "mountain cleft" it is the standing crevasse that separates flowing glacial ice from the stationary rock, ice, or snow of the mountain above. Often difficult and delicate to climb over, climbers shorten the name to just 'schrund.

BREAKOVER

The point at which the mountain changes from vertical to less than vertical.

CLIMBING GRADES

Globally there is a plethora of scales to grade the technical difficulty (how hard it is to advance your body upwards) on rock, ice, and snow; as well as grades that express the seriousness of the climb. Some scales combine both the technical grade and the seriousness grade.

In the pages of this book, reference is made to the Yosemite Decimal System (YDS) to grade the technical difficulty of rock climbs from the very novice, 5.1, to the intermediate, 5.5–5.8, and then to the expert, 5.9. Originally 5.9 was the ceiling of difficulty but rock climbers just kept getting better and better and 5.10 was added along with subgrades of a-d (note that the difference between 5.10b and 5.10c is a full grade and equivalent to the difference between 5.6 and 5.7). When I started rock climbing in the mid 1970s, 5.12 was the hardest people could climb, and there were precious few who could. With climbers ever improving their skills, a precious few are now knocking on the door of 5.16a.

The extended YDS included six classes of climbing from walking on even ground, class 1, to scrambling up exposed ridges without a rope, class 3, to tying-in to the rope and using it to safeguard a fall while both climbers move together, either with the mountain's features, or running pieces of protection, class 4. Class 5 climbing is technical climbing where only one of the climbers moves at a time and is safeguarded via a belay from the other climber.

Class 5 is where the technical grades of 5.1 to near 5.16a exist. Class 6 is direct aid climbing where the climber uses the support of climbing equipment to advance, as opposed to just his hands and feet as in class 5.

Direct aid climbing grades are abbreviated to A0 through to A5, with A1 being simple and secure aid (A0 being were pitons are used as hand or foot holds) and A5 representing a number of placements that will just support body weight, if you jump on them they will rip out and your subsequent "zipper" fall (because of the unzipping of a number of placements) will be at least seventy feet in length.

The YDS grade for seriousness and length of a route is expressed by the Roman numerals I–VII, with grade I being a climb that takes an intermediately skilled team one to two hours to complete. A grade IV would take the same team a day and a grade VII would take an expert team a week or more.

The Union Internationale des Associations d'Alpinisme (UIAA) grade system for seriousness has its origins in the rock difficulty grades of VII (easiest) to I (hardest) developed by the Austrian mountaineer Fritz Benesch in 1894. The great German alpinist Willo Welzenbach inverted the scale and applied it to alpine routes with grade V being the hardest. The UIAA added grade VI when it adopted the scale in 1947. Reinhold Messner's manifesto, *The Seventh Grade*, argued the scale into open-endedness on its publication in 1974.

The water-ice grading system applies to waterfall ice climbs and is represented with a commitment grade, a Roman numeral from I to VII that mirror the seriousness grades of the YDS system but take into account the winter threats of cold and avalanche. A grade VII will take days and have a fifty-fifty chance of getting the chop (killed). The technical grade on waterfalls is open-ended, starting at WI 1, which is frozen lakes or creek beds. WI 4 has up to eighty feet of vertical ice. WI 7 is a full ropelength of vertical ice that is very thin or a long overhanging technical column of dubious adhesion (a very physically and emotionally demanding pitch).

Mixed climbing grades are expressed by the M grade and have come into use with the popularity of modern mixed climbing, which can largely be viewed as the winter equivalent of sport climbing. Instead of chalked-up hands and rock shoes, a winter climber uses ice tools and crampons to cling to combinations of rock, ice, and occasionally snow. M grades are a technical grade and have been compared to similar physical experiences on the YDS. M4 feels like 5.8, M9 feels like 5.12, M12 feels like 5.13+.

CHOCKSTONE

A rock stuck in a crack. The rock may be as small as a jawbreaker and offer protection, if you can get a sling around it, or it could be as big as a house and create an overhanging obstacle to upward progress.

ÉTRIERS

Short rope or sling ladders to stand in, and advance, while aid climbing. In North America they have been commonly constructed, or tied, out of webbing. In Europe it was more the custom to incorporate metal or plastic rungs and tie them in sequence with small-diameter rope.

FRIENDS

The first mass-marketed universal spring-loaded camming device, debuted in 1978. Friends changed the climbing game because once difficult-to-protect, sustained crack climbs with parallel sides could now be protected quickly and securely.

HAND-RAIL

The act of going sideways with your hands wrapped over an edge and your feet frictioned against a rockwall. It also refers to the practice of staying within sight of a mountain feature to steer you in a direction of travel when on a glacier during a whiteout.

HEXCENTRICS, HEXES

An eccentric hexagon constructed from extruded aluminum. Hexes where invented and patented by Yvon Chouinard and Tom Frost in 1976 and they were an innovation on the six-sided engineering nuts that climbers had been inserting into cracks to gain protection. The Hexcentric had the ability to fit into three different sizes of cracks with the smaller two dimensions also exerting a camming force on the crack.

ICE AX

The mountaineer's principal tool. Present-day models range from fifteen to thirty-five inches in length and always have a pick and an adze comprising their head (as opposed to an ice hammer which has a hammer head and pick).

JUMARS, JUGS

The first marketed versions of a handled eccentric cam ascender, or "ascender." Jumars debuted in 1958 and where soon incorporated into the developing big-wall techniques in Yosemite Valley. Spring-loaded cams clamp onto climbing rope and allow the climber to ascend ropes, including free-hanging ones, via the device's handgrips.

KNIFEBLADE PITON, KNIFEBLADE

Flat-bladed spikes driven into rock cracks that vary from one to three inches in length by about three-quarters of an inch wide.

LONG DONG

The longest of the Lost Arrow pitons (rock spikes). The Long Dong had a six-inch blade that was notched at its end so that it could be used as an extraction tool.

NÉVÉ

Granular snow that has been thawed, then refrozen. In time it will gain density and become firm snow and, eventually, glacial ice (if it has accumulated on top of a glacier).

NUTS

From engineering nuts, any metal wedge, hex, or passive cam that is placed in a crack for anchorage or protection.

OFFWIDTH

A crack that is too wide to jam with the sides of your fist, yet too narrow to squeeze your body into. Offwidths are notoriously difficult to climb and often involve wrestling to insert your knee, shoulder, and elbow, all on one side of the body.

PITONS

Blades, angles, and Z profiles of metal hammered into cracks in rock to gain anchorage and protection via a carabiner clipped into the piton's eye. Normal lengths of pitons range from one to four inches with widths being one half to one inch. Also referred to as pins or pegs.

PRO

Short for "protection." Any piece of equipment inserted, hammered, screwed, or threaded into the mountain to anchor the climber. Friends, nuts, wedges, cams, ice screws, pitons, threads, chickenheads, spikes, and trees are all examples of protection.

PRUSIK, PRUSIKING, PRUSIKED

A prusik is a friction hitch that is tied onto a climbing rope. Two prusiks can be used to ascend the rope with inchworm-like movement, the climber is said to be *prusiking* or to have *prusiked* the rope. Named for the Austrian mountaineer, Karl Prusik, the alleged inventor, 1931.

PIN

A piton.

RP

Small climbing stoppers made from brass with the attachment cable soldered into the brass with silver, a manufacturing technique developed by the East German immigrant to Australia, Roland Pauligk. RPs are able to fit into cracks smaller than previous stoppers and give more security than like sized aluminum alloy stoppers. Both traditional free and aid climbers are able to climb harder on RPs.

ROCK HAMMER

A hammer specifically designed to hammer pitons into cracks. Rock hammers often have a blunt pick opposite to the hammer to help extract pitons and nuts.

SALOPETTES

Bibbed trousers with shoulder straps similar to overalls but usually made of shell material, sometimes insulated, meant to be worn as an outer layer. Salopettes can also be made out of insulation fabrics alone, or integrated with shell fabrics. Originally referred to French skiwear from the seventies.

SERÁCS

Ice cliffs that collapse catastrophically where a glacier cannot maintain its integrity while flowing over a steep drop on the underlying mountainside. Sáracs also form as isolated columns from the crosshatching of crevasses where a glacier is under tension in several directions.

STOPPERS

Wedge-shaped nuts placed into a constriction in a rock crack for protection. Also called "wedges."

TRIFFIDS

The mobile, human-killing, extraterrestrial plants that were the villains in John Wyndham's 1951 novel *The Day of the Triffids.*

TOQUE, TOQUES

A Canadian term of Métis origin for a knitted winter wool hat. Common in Canada to say that someone has "torched his toque" if they've lost their marbles through substance abuse.

WARTHOG

An ice piton with a spiral pattern of lugs, or warts, to facilitate more holding power when driven into the ice. Warthogs fractured tremendous amounts of ice and have come to be used in frozen turf and mud-filled frozen rock cracks rather than ice.

WEDGES

See stoppers.

ACKNOWLEDGMENTS

My ancestors hunted buffalo on horseback, and before there were horses they ran the great beasts into pounds. I feel the pride of my forebears in my blood, have always seen it in my mother's deep brown eyes. I am so proud to be her son, to share our bloodline.

I was called to mountain climbing and much of that voice came to me through reading the words of Heinrich Harrer, Walter Bonatti, Lionel Terray, Gaston Rebuffat, Giusto Gervasutti, Reinhold Messner, Fosco Maraini, Tom Patey, Warren Harding, Yvon Chouinard, and James Salter. May their words stay in print, and may other young people find them.

Reading about mountain climbing got me interested in reading, period. I often joke that if it wasn't for books and magazine articles about climbing, I'd be illiterate. The writers who sit in my literary pantheon are: Ernest Hemingway, John Irving, Paul Bowles, Sam Shepard, Cormac McCarthy, Charles Bukowski, César Vallejo, Jalād ad-Dīn Rūmī, and Bruce Springsteen (unarguably, in my mind, a poet). I have faith that their words will stay in print, or in whatever medium comes next.

My many thanks to Andy Arts, my brother-from-another-mother, who couldn't wait to get the next chapter of my manuscript to read and encourage me by telling me exactly what he thought, no one can keep an Andy-sized heart under raps. Equally as many thanks to Kat Wiebe, Andy's wife, who's finely tuned writer's insights made this a better book. And to Franki Schafrik who read much of the manuscript and laid a bunch of feedback on me in her saucy stand-up style.

I am very thankful for everyone at Patagonia Books, and Patagonia, for creating *The Calling*. John Dutton, my editor, got me a contract and an advance and I spent all the money so I had to write the book, yet above and beyond that he had the commitment to kick me in the ass when my commitment faltered. Thanks John, as much for that as for your fine editing. Jane Sievert has sifted through my photos since I started as a "Key Climber" with Patagonia in 1993, and she did so here along with the kind hand of Sus Corez (love you two, full heart). Haruna Madono came on board in the eleventh hour to design *The Calling*: mighty fine Haruna, mighty fine. Karla Olson steers the good ship *Book* at Patagonia and I thank her for her steady hand. Malinda and Yvon Chouinard: where did the last 21 years go? My eternal gratitude for a particularly fine ride.

My spirit swells when I think about John Lauchlin, each and every one of us needs heroes and John has endured as one of mine. Much of that longevity is due to his early death and I would far rather have come to know him as John, the man.

At the time that I climbed most of the routes in this book I wanted to succeed on them and create new lines. Paint masterpieces, if you will. Poetically, some of my greatest lines are melting away as they all will with the passage of time. All mountains will erode to dirt, sand, and dust. I have come to realize that what really matters—and mattered then—is the bonds that I formed with my partners. They are some of the strongest of my adult life, equal to the spousal bonds that I've been blessed with. To the men that I've had the pleasure to climb with:

Kevin Doyle, who Gilles Claret-Tournier long ago labeled "Zee Master," and whom the gods touched at birth with an innate sense of balance and body position that would take me three hundred days of imitating to learn. Wally also got a prize-fighter's heart and an ardent will that drove us to the top of many mountains. I love the guy, and he knows it. We're still brothers. May we make it through the challenges of our man's hearts to get back to that day in Chamonix when we met and bear hugged each other and our futures were an open plain and our hearts were as light as feathers. I want us both to go out with hearts as light as feathers: boy's hearts.

David Cheesmond, "le Grand Fromage," I learned so much about the big picture of alpinism, and life, from David's kind and engaged way of being. I wish he'd been able to out fox death on Mount Logan. I didn't know myself well enough to tell him that I loved him back then, but I do now, "I love you Cheese." I cherish seeing his daughter because I see David's face in hers. Not a week goes by that I don't think of David, in the mountains, he lives on in me.

Ward Robinson, our spirits recognized each other instantly. It took our beings awhile to catch up. Ward is the toughest guy I've known in the mountains. As hard as nails. I still marvel at how he paired his life down to climbing, "Let's just fucking go climbing already."

Mark Twight, if I'd proposed slicing our palms open to become blood brothers, Mark would have done it. He rocked my world with punk music and the discipline to practice what he heard in the music: to use alpinism as a crucible for creating, and recreating, yourself. He read my writing at a time when his writing was changing climbing and he nailed some of what has become my voice. I can talk to Mark about anything from the black depths of my being, to the love that I have for my daughters (he is one of the few people I know who is not a parent, yet gets that).

And to the other men in this book, Ron Humble and Stewart Buroker (both taken too young and too soon), Phil Conway, Bill Stark, Tim Friesen, Gregg Cronn, Steve Langley, Albi Sole, Jeff Marshall, James Blench, Chris Miller, Jim Elzinga, Carl Tobin, George Lowe, Tim Pochay, and Peter Arbic, it has been an honor to tie in with you lads. Cheers!

Lastly to the mountains, they all point up into the sky and lift us up physically, intellectually, emotionally, and spiritually. Climbing mountains is good for the soul.

Climb on,
Barry Blanchard